A LEGAL HISTORY FOR AUSTRALIA

This is a contemporary legal history book for Australian law students, written in an engaging style and rich with learning features and illustrations. The writers are a unique combination of talents, bringing together their fields of research and teaching in Australian history, British constitutional history and modern Australian law.

The first part provides the social and political contexts for legal history in medieval and early modern England and America, explaining the English law which came to Australia in 1788. This includes:

- the origins of the common law;
- the growth of the legal profession;
- the making of the Magna Carta;
- the English Civil Wars;
- the Bill of Rights;
- the American War of Independence.

The second part examines the development of the law in Australia to the present day, including:

- the English criminal justice system and convict transportation;
- the role of the Privy Council in the nineteenth century;
- Indigenous Australia in the colonial period;
- the federation movement;
- constitutional independence;
- the 1967 Australian referendum and the land rights movement.

The comprehensive coverage of several centuries is balanced by a dynamic writing style and tools to guide the student through each chapter including learning outcomes, chapter outlines and discussion points.

The historical analysis is brought to life by the use of primary documentary evidence such as charters, statutes, medieval source books and Coke's reports, and a series of historical cameos – focused studies of notable people and issues from King Edward I and Edward Coke to Henry Parkes and Eddie Mabo – and constitutional detours addressing topics such as the separation of powers, judicial review and federalism.

A Legal History for Australia is an engaging textbook, cogently written and imaginatively resourced.

A Legal History for Australia

Sarah McKibbin
Libby Connors
and
Marcus Harmes

•HART•
OXFORD • LONDON • NEW YORK • NEW DELHI • SYDNEY

HART PUBLISHING

Bloomsbury Publishing Plc

Kemp House, Chawley Park, Cumnor Hill, Oxford, OX2 9PH, UK

1385 Broadway, New York, NY 10018, USA

29 Earlsfort Terrace, Dublin 2, Ireland

First published in Great Britain 2021

A catalogue record for this book is available from the British Library.

Library of Congress Cataloging-in-Publication data

Names: McKibbin, Sarah, author. | Connors, Libby, 1960- author. | Harmes, Marcus K., author.

Title: A legal history for Australia / Sarah McKibbin, Libby Connors and Marcus Harmes.

Description: Gordonsville : Hart Publishing, an imprint of Bloomsbury Publishing, 2021. | Includes bibliographical references and index.

Identifiers: LCCN 2021024039 (print) | LCCN 2021024040 (ebook) | ISBN 9781509939572 (paperback) | ISBN 9781509939596 (pdf) | ISBN 9781509939589 (Epub)

Subjects: LCSH: Law—Australia—History.

Classification: LCC KU120 .M35 2021 (print) | LCC KU120 (ebook) | DDC 349.94—dc23

LC record available at https://lccn.loc.gov/2021024039

LC ebook record available at https://lccn.loc.gov/2021024040

ISBN: PB: 978-1-50993-957-2
ePDF: 978-1-50993-959-6
ePub: 978-1-50993-958-9

Typeset by Compuscript Ltd, Shannon
Printed and bound in Great Britain by CPI Group (UK) Ltd, Croydon CR0 4YY

MIX
Paper from responsible sources
FSC® C013604

To find out more about our authors and books visit www.hartpublishing.co.uk. Here you will find extracts, author information, details of forthcoming events and the option to sign up for our newsletters.

FOREWORD

THE HON. MICHAEL KIRBY AC CMG*

Decline and Fall

When I began the study of law, undertaking a course in legal history was compulsory in every Australian law school. For me, it began on the first day, in the first week, of my arrival at the Sydney Law School in 1958.

Our lecturer was Dr CH Currey. He read from cyclostyled notes that were provided to us by the faculty office. He had his merits. However, enlivening his lectures with relevance, especially injecting local and recent stories, was not amongst them. Most of his lectures were about the slow emergence of the English common law. There were few lectures on Australia's own legal history. I was soon made to understand that we, in the South Pacific, were a branch office of an imperial legal system whose headquarters were at Westminster. There were lectures by WV Windeyer[1] that offered a few scattered insights into Australian legal history. However, it was not until Alex Castles published his introduction to Australian legal history in 1971 that a complete text for that topic became available.[2]

Given this inauspicious introduction to the subject, probably replicated in most of the other law schools at the time, it is little wonder that legal history largely faded away. A huge flowering of law schools emerged in Australia after the 1970s. However, comparatively few evidenced a specific interest in legal history. The legal profession did not clamour for courses on the topic. The *Priestley Eleven* 'core topics' quietly deleted legal history from the list. Students did not protest. Few other voices were raised to contest this trend.[3] Indifference to legal history entered the soul of Australian lawyers.

I lamented and criticised this development.[4] However, the attrition merely gathered further steam. When legal academics were tackled about the unwisdom of this trend, they ticked off the usual excuses: legal history was taught, they said, only where necessary, and then in explaining particular subjects of law; the shift from common law to statutory sources of law made history less important than it had been; law schools were now money-making hubs for universities mainly keen to attract full fee-paying foreign students whose interests lay elsewhere; and there were already too many subjects in the law curriculum. Even if there

* Justice of the High Court of Australia (1996–2009).

[1] WJV Windeyer, *Lectures in Legal History*, LawBook Co; BM Debelle (ed) *Victor Windeyer's Legacy: Legal and Military Papers*, Federation Press, Sydney, 2019.

[2] AC Castles, *An Introduction to Australian Legal History,* LawBook Co, Sydney, 1971. See also JM Bennett and AC Castles *Course Book of Australian Legal History*, Lawbook Co, Sydney, 1979.

[3] W Prest, 'Legal History in Australian Law Schools' (2006) 27 *Adelaide L Rev* 267.

[4] MD Kirby, 'Is Legal History Now Ancient History' (2009) 83 ALJ 31.

were interest, academics able to teach this specialty were thin on the ground and lacked an effective community to lobby for revival.

A few Australian law schools have continued to offer legal history to their students, usually as an elective. What was missing was a good business case for the teaching of legal history as such; a growing body of scholars with an interest in that direction; and a new textbook that could help to show that the subject was interesting, important, relevant and useful. Without such a text that demonstrated the centrality of legal history for a modern law school the prospects of revival were poor. So this is where *A Legal History for Australia* comes in.

A Plan for Legal History

There is no point repeating the previous arguments as to why the legal history discipline should be taught. In any case, I would not advocate a return to past techniques. The hard-nosed university administrators and law deans, in competition for students once the current pandemic has receded, are unlikely to be convinced by such arguments. What can be offered now to make legal history relevant to the practical life of the law? What arguments can be marshalled to support the bid to turn the corner and restore the teaching of legal history by a new approach? This book affords ample evidence that a strong case exists for generic instruction in legal history in Australian law schools:

- For both good and bad, our legal history is joined at the hip with the constitutional and legal stories of the British Isles, of the Empire and Commonwealth of Nations, and the United States of America. This book charts some of the most important chapters in the overall story. Without getting into excessive particularities, this new outline of the story of our legal history is provided, specially tailored to Australian needs. Unless Australian lawyers have a good hold on the main outline of English, imperial and American legal history, they will not readily see the way that any particular legal category or constitutional or statutory text, fits into the large mosaic of Australia's history. Learning masses of legal rules, in all their particularity, will inevitably recede in the minds of law students and lawyers, unless they can anchor those rules in their historical context. Finding and applying legal rules necessitates an appreciation of their context. For the tasks of statutory and constitutional interpretation, so important to legal practice today, context is always critical. A young lawyer deprived of a background briefing on the contours of legal history will be like a surgeon who suffers from cataracts. They will see the immediate text in a blur. But they run the risk of failing to appreciate its context and purpose that add precision and sharpness to their understanding.
- Throughout this text, the reader will be reminded of the way in which history has helped to mould legal outcomes and contributed to developments that are the mark of human progress. For example, we can understand the blight of homosexual and other sexual offences when we know something of how and why they came into our legal system. Legal history teaches us to be questioners about the law. The bullying of minorities in the past, and the story of the achievement of reforms in our legal history represent an encouragement for the ongoing questioning of the present law that is the lawyer's duty. The 'Me Too' movement today, is simply one of the latest examples of victims, and their supporters, standing up against injustice and oppression. Sometimes (but not always)

knowledge of legal history will afford encouragement and inspiration. At the very least it will often provide an important tool that will remind the contemporary lawyer of occasions when desirable outcomes were reached; and occasions when the 'system' failed the cause of justice.

- The many instances in this book of struggles against racial bias in our legal history, from *Somerset's* case against slavery through the early Australia denial of land rights to our First Nations People told in *Mabo*,[5] certainly helps to alert lawyers to the ongoing struggle for justice. This was the background to the High Court's decision in *Love v The Commonwealth*.[6] The 'Black Lives Matter' movement in the United States requires knowledge of the long history of other racial injustices. However, this is also important for the special role of the lawyer in contemporary Australia. The *Mabo* and *Love* decisions, that are recounted here, would not have been made, or even possibly argued, without a basic knowledge of the features of racism in our own legal journey. Those who can put the instant case into a proper historical context will be better able, as judges, lawyers, administrators or otherwise to interpret and apply the law so as to point it in the right direction.
- Reading this book, and understanding legal history, teaches lawyers and citizens to view the current state of the law as a project in the course of constant evolution. Every chapter demonstrates how the law continues to advance and rarely expresses a final rule: correct and complete for all time. The important constitutional decision of the High Court of Australia in the *Communist Party case*, one of the greatest and wisest decisions of the Court, saw Justice Dixon invoking the lessons of legal history. He warned: 'History, and not only ancient history, shows that in countries where democratic institutions have been unconstitutionally superseded, it has been done not seldom by those holding the executive power. Forms of government may need protection from dangers likely to arise from within the institutions to be protected.'[7] Such knowledge is important in every branch of the law. But it is crucial in public law where liberty is at stake. And where key features of our constitution are at risk, as in the accurate application of the appropriations power[8] or the limits upon the power to make laws.[9]
- As the many stories told in this book illustrate, legal history is also a story about people and their encounters with the law. It should not be a dull chronicle of ancient happenings of little contemporary relevance. One of the special features of this new venture into legal history is the way key actors are introduced. Some are judges. Some are parliamentarians. Some are prisoners. Some are First Nations People who have challenged long-standing rules, like Eddie Mabo, Faith Bandler and advocates like Ron Castan who brought the *Mabo* challenge, when most other lawyers at the time, would have written it off as doomed to fail. This text personifies its lessons by identifying those who have played important roles on our legal story, from the judges who declared that women were not 'persons' to Sir Henry Parkes, the famous Australian colonial Premier, uxorious

[5] *Mabo v Queensland [No 2]* (1992) 175 CLR 1.
[6] (2020) 94 ALJR 198.
[7] *Australian Communist Party v The Commonwealth* (1951) 83 CLR 1 at 193.
[8] *Combet v The Commonwealth* (2005) 224 CLR 494; *Pape v The Commonwealth* (2009) 238 CLR 1; *Williams v The Commonwealth* (2012) 248 CLR 156.
[9] *White v Director of Military Prosecutions* (2007) 231 CLR 570; *Thomas v Mowbray* (2008) 233 CLR 307 at 442 [386]. *R v Private Cowen* (2020) 94 ALJR 849 at 876 [117], per Nettle J.

and thrice married, who still found time to dream of federation whilst looking after 17 children, three of them born 'out of wedlock'. Proving that even politicians are sometimes human.

History will also teach that the future of the legal discipline will increasingly be written against the background of international law. The reconciliation of the time-honoured and sometimes dishonoured history of our legal tradition with the growing body of international private law and the increasing relevance of international human rights law to our law should be known by every lawyer today.[10] This is not heresy. It is part of the reality of the legal discipline, which now operates in the world of the internet, cell phones, climate change, nuclear proliferation, refugees, terrorism and global pandemics such as COVID-19.

Lawyers are, or should be, more than mere technicians familiar with a jumble of complex rules crowding their brains. They must have a concept of the practical world in which the law operates and fits together. But also of the noble aspirations of justice, human rights, the rule of law and peace and security that lie at its heart's core. Legal history helps the lawyer of today to escape the mistakes of the past by appreciating the journey that has been taken, to which contemporary lawyers must add their skills and experience.

Great Expectations

Most of those who study law do not become judges. Many do not become advocates. Some do not become solicitors, attorneys or proctors. A number go off into public administration. Still more enter business, the prosecution service, publication and education. Doubtless a few grow wine. A handful go to prison. Courses in law and legal studies need to cater for the variety of occupational groups now attracted to the study of law. It would be a scandal to let them loose on society without a general knowledge of the history of how their discipline emerged and became one of the foundations of the freedoms and governance of the English-speaking nations across the world.

I congratulate those who conceived A *Legal History for Australia*. I hope that it will encourage the journey back to a stronger awareness of our legal history; because the present and the future do not exist disjoined from the past. Let the words ring out to judges, scholars, lawyers and students alike. The study of legal history is fruitful, fascinating and fun.

I congratulate Dr Sarah McKibbin, Associate Professor Marcus Harmes and Dr Libby Connors for writing this book. I thank Dean Reid Mortensen for his support for the course on Legal History at the University of Southern Queensland. I applaud USQ for its initiatives, including the organisation of conferences and discussions of relevant topics. Leading judges, scholars and lawyers throughout the Australia and beyond are watching these initiatives with admiration and great expectations. Truly, they are historic.

Michael Kirby
Sydney,
1 October 2021

[10] *Al-Kateb v Godwin* (2004) 219 CLR 562 at 589 [62] per McHugh J; at 626 [184], per Kirby J (diss).

TABLE OF CONTENTS

ABBREVIATIONS

AG	Attorney General
CJ	Chief Justice
CJCB	Chief Justice Common Bench
CJCP	Chief Justice Common Pleas
CJKB	Chief Justice King's Bench
J	Justice
JKB	Justice of the King's Bench
KB	King's Bench
KC	King's Counsel
LANSW	Legislative Assembly of New South Wales
LAQ	Legislative Assembly of Queensland
LASA	Legislative Assembly of South Australia
LAT	Legislative Assembly of Tasmania
LAV	Legislative Assembly of Victoria
LAWA	Legislative Assembly of Western Australia
LC	Lord Chancellor
LCNSW	Legislative Council of New South Wales
LCQ	Legislative Council of Queensland
LCSA	Legislative Council of South Australia
LCT	Legislative Council of Tasmania
LCV	Legislative Council of Victoria
LCWA	Legislative Council of Western Australia
MR	Master of the Rolls
QC	Queen's Counsel
SG	Solicitor General
SL	Serjeant at Law

CALENDAR

The early chapters in this book cover content before the passing of the *Calendar (New Style) Act 1750* (24 Geo II c 23), which changed the Julian to the Gregorian calendar. Traditionally the new year began on the Feast of the Annunciation or 'Lady Day' (25 March) not on 1 January. For example, the execution of King Charles I is given as 30 January 1649, but the year was still 1648 as reckoned at the time. In Scotland, where the new year started 1 January, it was 30 January 1649.

LIST OF ENGLISH AND BRITISH MONARCHS

Saxon Kings of Wessex and England (including Danish Kings of England)

Egbert (827–839)
Æthelwulf (839–856)
Æthelbald (856–860)
Æthelbert (860–866)
Æthelred I (866–871)
Alfred the Great (871–899)
Edward the Elder (899–924)
Æthelstan (924–939)
Edmund (939–946)
Eadred (946–955)
Eadwig (955–959)
Edgar (959–975)
Edward the Martyr (975–978)
Æthelred II the Unready (978–1013)
Sweyn Forkbeard (1013–1014)
Æthelred II the Unready (1014–1016)
Edmund II Ironside (1016–1016)
Cnut the Great (1016–1035)
Harold I Harefoot (1035–1040)
Harthacnut (1040–1042)
Edward the Confessor (1042–1066)
Harold II (1066–1066)

Norman

William I (1066–1087)
William II (1087–1100)
Henry I (1100 1135)
Stephen (1135–1154)

Plantagenet

Henry II (1154–1189)
Richard I (1189–1199)
John (1199–1216)
Henry III (1216–1272)
Edward I (1272–1307)
Edward II (1307–1327)
Edward III (1327–1377)
Richard III (1377–1399)
Henry IV (1399–1413) (Lancaster)
Henry V (1413–1422) (Lancaster)
Henry VI (1422–1461) (Lancaster)
Edward IV (1461–1470) (York)
Henry VI (Restored) (1470–1471) (Lancaster)
Edward IV (Restored) (1471–1483) (York)
Edward V (1483–1483) (York)
Richard III (1483–1485) (York)

Tudor

Henry VII (1485–1509)
Henry VIII (1509–1547)
Edward VI (1547–1553)
Jane Grey (1553–1553)
Mary I (1553–1558)[1]
Elizabeth I (1558–1603)

Stuart

James I and VI of Scotland (1603 1625)
Charles I (1625–1649)

[1] Married to Philip II of Spain, who is therefore sometimes identified as a monarch with Mary I in the regnal years of statutes.

Commonwealth

Oliver Cromwell, Lord Protector (1653–1658)
Richard Cromwell, Lord Protector (1658–1659)

Stuart (restored)

Charles II (1660–1685)[2]
James II and VII of Scotland (1685–1688)
Mary II (1689–1694) and William III (1689–1702)
Anne (1702–1714)[3]

Hanover

George I (1714–1727)
George II (1727–1760)
George III (1760–1820)[4]
George IV (1820–1830)
William IV (1830–1837)
Victoria (1837–1901)

Saxe-Coburg-Gotha and Windsor

Edward VII (1901–1910)
George V (1910–1936)[5]
Edward VIII (1936–1936)
George VI (1936–1952)
Elizabeth II (1952–)

[2] King Charles II's regnal years were reckoned from the death of his father, Charles I.

[3] United Kingdom of Great Britain formed on union of England and Scotland, 1707.

[4] United Kingdom of Great Britain and Ireland formed on union of the United Kingdom of Great Britain and the Kingdom of Ireland in 1801.

[5] Royal House renamed Windsor in 1917. Kingdom renamed United Kingdom of Great Britain and Northern Ireland after partition of Ireland and the creation of the Irish Free State in 1922.

ABBREVIATIONS FOR MONARCHS' NAMES

Monarch's name	Abbreviation	Monarch's name	Abbreviation
Charles	Car or Chas	**William and Mary**	Wm & M or Wm & Mar
Henry	Hen	**George**	Geo
Stephen	Steph	**Richard**	Ric
Edward	Edw	**Victoria**	Vic or Vict
James	Jac	**John**	John
William	Will or Wm	**Anne**	Anne
Elizabeth	Eliz	**Jane**	Jane
Philip and Mary	P & M or Ph & M	**Mary**	Mary

REGNAL YEARS OF ENGLISH MONARCHS

While the regnal year system formally stopped on 1 January 1963, the citation of regnal years is still important for English statutes enacted before that date. Regnal years coincide with the monarch's day of accession to the throne and accession eve.[1]

The citation format for pre-1963 English statutes is **Year(s) of reign | Monarch's Name | Regnal Number of Monarch (in Roman numerals)**. Death, abdication or deposition meant the untimely end of a regnal year. One example of deposition is the period known as the 'Interregnum'. Between 1649 and 1660, the English monarchy was abolished. The interregnum commenced with Charles I's beheading on 30 January 1649 and concluded with the return of his son Charles II to London on 29 May 1660. With time, the old and unique system of citation became confusing. If a parliamentary session extended over two regnal years, the citation might have appeared as '8 & 9 Geo 6, c 4'. If there were multiple sessions (abbr 'sess') for one regnal year, a session number would have to be included after the year of reign, the monarch's name, and regnal number, eg '1 Wm & M sess 2'. The parliamentary session might overlap between one sovereign and their successor. In 1837, the parliamentary session spanned the seventh regnal year of William IV and the first regnal year of Victoria, ie '7 Wm 4 & 1 Vict'. The *Acts of Parliament Numbering and Citation Act 1962*, 10 & 11 Eliz 2, c 34 abolished the regnal year system.

The new citation format (post-1963) for English statutes is: **Title of Act | Year | Chapter Number**.

[1] Until the 13th century, the legal year began on 25 December. The legal year commenced on 25 March from the 14th century until 1 January 1751. Official records, on the other hand, followed the calendar system beginning from 1 January each year. If an Act passed on 15 January 1725, it would be dated 15 January 1724 since the 1725 law year has not yet commenced.

AGLC CITATION OF PRE-1963 ENGLISH STATUTES[1]

Title and Year	Regnal Year	Chapter	Pinpoint
Slavery Abolition Act 1833,	3 & 4 Will IV,	c 73	, s 25
Statute of Uses 1535,	27 Hen VIII,	c 10	

[1] See *Australian Guide to Legal Citation*, 4th edn (Melbourne University Law Review Association Inc in collaboration with Melbourne Journal of International Law Inc, 2018) rule 23.2.

COMPANION WEBSITE

This textbook is accompanied by a companion website. Whenever you see this symbol, it directs you to additional resources on the website, including links to complete legislation, lectures on people and topics, and additional cameos and detours.

A Legal History for Australia

Companion Website

www.bloomsburyonlineresources.com/a-legal-history-for-australia

TABLE OF CASES

TABLE OF LEGISLATION

Introduction

The Australian jurist the Hon Michael Kirby has remarked that 'to be a lawyer in Australia is, in a sense, to be a legal historian'.[1] His statement may please some, surprise others, and pose a challenge for a crowded undergraduate law curriculum, where it is difficult to devise an introduction to legal history that is capable of inspiring and enthusing but introduces complex questions of legal theory, fundamental legal institutions and principles and ethical understanding of the breadth of problems caused by political and legal marginalisation. Many universities opt for a law in context or legal foundations approach with varying success. Fortunately, faculty research seminars brought the three of us together – two historians and a law academic – with overlapping interests in legal history as well as law's formative role in British and Australian history and society.

Those of us engaged in legal history research knew what a vibrant field it had become. Historians inspired by the paradigm-shifting work of EP Thompson, Douglas Hay and Peter Linebaugh nearly half a century ago had continued to sift legal records to tell the stories of those who had once seemed historically invisible. Courtrooms, especially those of the lower courts, were peopled by women and workers and non-whites. Both French and British historians had successfully used legal records to bring the past to life in thirteenth century France and seventeenth century England.[2] Legal history was no longer Whig history; instead, it has highlighted processes of marginalisation, of voices struggling to be heard, and of courtrooms as contests of power. In addition, legal history's traditional strengths, including the scrupulous editorial work of the Selden Society, meant that miles and miles of medieval and early modern legal records became available, illuminating the work of the courts and sometimes the personalities of long dead judges and lawyers.

We were aware too of the great research being done across the common law world through involvement with the Australian and New Zealand Law and History Society and 'sister' conferences such as the 2018 Legal History and Empires hosted by the University of the West Indies and the 2012 Legal Histories of the British Empire hosted by the National University of Singapore. Transnational perspectives have enlivened Australian legal history scholarship with greater awareness of the impact of North American experiences on early colonial decision-makers. Accepted histories of how Australia's First Nations were viewed by English law continue to be revised and problematised.[3] The field of legal history is not a dull story of constitutional 'progress', but one enlivened by the ways men and women across generations dared to shape and re-shape political and legal power.

These are compelling stories. Rather than attempting to teach first year students theoretical perspectives on law, they instead discover situations where the exercise of law was

[1] Michael Kirby, 'Living with Legal History in the Courts' (2003) 7(1) *Australian Journal of Legal History* 17.

[2] Emmanuel Le Roy Ladurie, *Montaillou: Cathars and Catholics in a French Village, 1294–1324* (London, Penguin, 1980); Margaret Spufford, *Contrasting Communities: English Villagers in the Sixteenth and Seventeenth Centuries* (Cambridge, Cambridge University Press, 1974).

[3] Lauren Benton and Lisa Ford, *Rage for Order* (Harvard, Harvard University Press, 2016); Lisa Ford, *Settler Sovereignty: Jurisdiction and Indigenous People in America and Australia, 1788–1836* (Harvard, Harvard University Press, 2010).

about class, gender and racial repression, when and how actions and institutions came into existence, to see where the legal past powerfully impinges on the legal present, but they also learn of historical episodes where rights are finally gained.

We wanted the course to be empowering for them as individuals – that they would finish the course with a better understanding of why they have assumed that they have 'rights' and where this notion has come from. Equally, we wanted them to understand that such 'rights' are historically-bound and that the law is not fixed but is dependent on the experiences of past generations – the significance of which they need to understand – and that it will continue to be shaped by their generation. Equally, they should understand that the law and the legal system did not just drop out of the sky fully formed but is a product shaped by centuries.

It is not a simple teleology. Legal practitioners need to understand how and why one era impacts the next, so this book covers the Anglo-Saxons to the Glorious Revolution before this linear development is challenged by the constitutional thinking of the American revolutionaries. We return to important developments in eighteenth and nineteenth century England, but they are in turn disrupted by the extraordinary notion that residents of a penal colony also had rights, and how speedily the Australian colonies found the common law in this new environment had to move in new directions. While Englishmen gained access to parliaments and law-making with surprising speed in the circumstances of their new environment, they wielded their power with savage disregard for the First Nation peoples they displaced and their Pacific neighbours whom they sought to bind in new forms of cheap, unfree labour. These are big events within colonial and twentieth century legal history and again the chronology diverges to explore them effectively. It says much about how full school and university curricula are – that in the classroom these topics are met with stunned responses. 'How could we not know this!' and 'Why weren't we taught this?' seem to be balanced by the appreciation of Aboriginal, Torres Strait Islander, South Sea Islander and Pacific Island nation students; the failure to enforce by various legislatures and the enactment of repressive legislation are laid bare and critically analysed. The development of law as an institution that refuses to accept the exercise of arbitrary power is a great historic achievement, but one which must always be weighed against its power to oppress those members of society who are excluded from law-making.

In the Australian university lecture theatre, we had just 12 weeks to cover this ground. Our goal was to move students towards a critical understanding of law not through sociology or through abstract thinking but through concrete historic events. In our view, the conciseness of this material is an advantage over many other works of legal history, yet in the process the development of English law and legal study, legal professional identities, core doctrines and the colonisation of Australia are covered. The symbolic but also the actual importance of the legal past is conveyed in a way which should not overwhelm. Equally, the law is demystified as a dynamic, changing and shifting entity, shaped by its historical context, and not just a collection of rules.

Using this Text

This text does not depend on having an entire course or subject devoted to legal history. While the chapters respond to each other and proceed mostly chronologically, there are different options for use.

The accompanying website gives space for additional resources, links and teaching aids, organised on a chapter-by-chapter basis.

The content in each chapter contains pedagogical features that support learning, which includes:

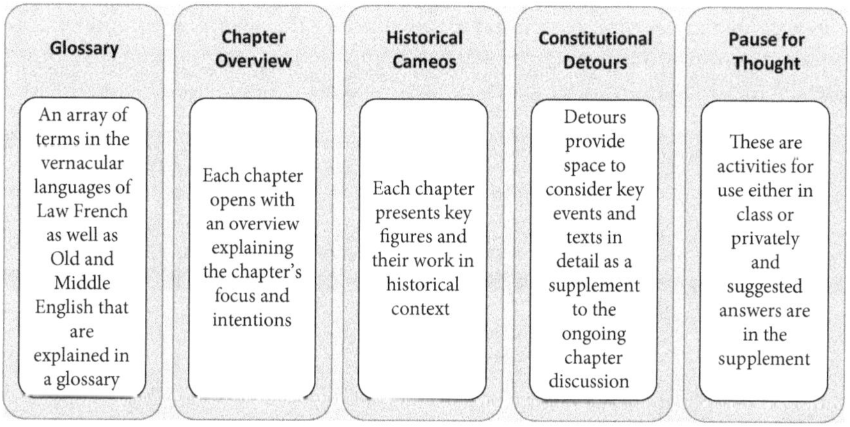

Introduction for Students

A first question many students have is why you would study or even need legal history as part of a law degree and as part of future training to be a legal professional. Here are some answers.

First, law itself is inherently historic. This work introduces Australia's common law traditions and common law is always looking backwards. A judge will find in the common law a precedent to guide her or his decision-making. Textual and documentary evidence is essential and legal decisions must be intellectually defensible. None of that is possible with novelty but rests upon historic continuities. At the time of writing, issues of vast constitutional significance are being debated in the British parliament and courts about 'Brexit', issues that will shape British law and society for generations to come. But in looking to the future, the courts also look backwards. The President of the UK Supreme Court ruled on the prorogation of parliament by referring to legislation from the fourteenth century and the cases from the seventeenth and eighteenth centuries.[4] One of these was the *Case of Proclamations*, which will be covered in a later chapter. The law's past is just as important in Australia. For example, thirteenth century law remains in force in the state of Queensland.

So, very practical reasons abound for why practising lawyers need a grounding in history. The Australian legal system has been formally received from England and a legal heritage from the medieval period, including forms and theories, underpins modern practice as well as professional identity. Its reception also pinpoints colonial complexity. Its historical oppression of Indigenous Australians and their challenges to its authority

[4] *R (Miller) v The Prime Minister* and *Cherry v Advocate General for Scotland* [2019] UKSC 41.

is one of the themes this work explores in detail that a culturally competent lawyer must understand.

Second, there are benefits in studying a complementary discipline like history. Historical skills are those required for successful advocacy. Retired UK Supreme Court judge, Lord Sumption (who is also a renowned historian of Medieval England) urges law students to study history and argues that, 'A command of reasoning skills, an ability to understand and use evidence, and broad literary culture are all tremendously valuable to any advocate.'[5]

Michael Kirby makes similar points, suggesting that:

> Law is not itself history. But it can often not be fully understood without appreciating its rules in context, whether those rules are stated in statutory form or expressed in judicial opinions. One of the great changes in the past 30 years of judicial decisions, in Australia as in Britain and elsewhere, has been an appreciation of the importance of context to an understanding of the commands of the law, whether parliamentary, bureaucratic or judicial. So history is a vital ingredient for the legal context, whether the law in question is expressed in the Constitution, in statutory texts or in the decisions of the judges.[6]

Third, legal history is disruptive. Far from a settled past or a series of stable 'facts', legal history reveals ongoing shifts in meaning and emphasis. The legal historian, Sir John Baker sums up this point with the useful observation that 'legal history is the study of legal change. Unless we regard law as nothing than a bundle of randomly changing rules, its history must be an essential dimension of its study'.[7] Much of the contemporary Australian university law curricular is determined and even limited by the 'Priestley 11', a series of subjects deemed essential to the practising lawyer. They do however run the risk of making the law seem like this bundle of rules. This study of legal history fills in context, explains why and how change occurs, why doctrines, theories and processes have assumed the forms they have, and casts light on the operation of the modern law by understanding its foundation. Teaching law in its historical contexts and as the product of dynamic historical changes resonates with the increasing realisation that teaching law in isolation from cultural and social dynamics is undesirable and limiting.[8]

There is a similar point to be made from the bracketed list below. None of these lists are definitive and are not intended to be exhaustive in any of the three categories, but they are intended to show different aspects not of legal history but the legal present. In the first block are doctrines, theories, forms, practices and institutions that in some cases are more than a thousand years old but still lively and important aspects of the current Australian legal system. For example, for there to be a general election the Governor General has to issue a writ. What are termed in the list the 'survivors' are not historical curiosities or archaisms, but potently alive parts of the modern legal system. For example, in Australia there has been a series of highly important Royal Commissions: from the Commission into

[5] 'The Best Lawyers are not Law Graduates, Claims Judge' *The Telegraph* (London, 8 July 2012), available at www.telegraph.co.uk/news/uknews/law-and-order/9384619/The-best-lawyers-are-not-law-graduates-claims-judge.html.

[6] Michael Kirby, 'Teaching Legal History in Australia: Decline and Fall' (2009) 12(1) *Australian Journal of Legal History* 17.

[7] Sir John Baker, 'Why the History of English Law has not been Finished' (2000) 59(1) *CLJ* 63.

[8] David W Raack, 'Some Reflections on the Role of Legal History in Legal Education' (1988) 26(893) *Duquesne Law Review* 902.

Aboriginal Deaths in Custody in 1989 to more recent commissions into the banking sector, aged care, unions and sexual abuse in institutions. These commissions have some literally awe-inspiring powers to look into the most privileged documents. These powers come from the Letters Patent issued by the Crown.

The block of 'recently defunct' is so-called because the legal profession and legal system both move slowly and changes a century or so ago can still be considered quite recent, especially for the legal system in England and Wales. Very defunct are those aspects of the administration of justice that faded from use or were actively and deliberately discontinued more than a century ago. But even they continue to matter. Although the accused are no longer subject to an ordeal to determine the truth of what they say, proofs are nonetheless still required as are ways to determine both the facts and the law.

Figure 0.1 Aspects of Legal History

Survivors from history

- Writ
- Moot
- Letters Patent
- Commissions
- Terms of art
- Courts of record
- Privy Council
- Exchequer
- Trial by jury
- Oath taking
- Coroner and inquest
- Sheriff
- Rules of evidence
- Fee simple
- Habeas corpus

The 'recently'* defunct

- Serjeants
- Assizes
- Doctors' Commons
- *A century or so ago or less

The *very* defunct

- Trial by ordeal
- Public execution
- Monarch presiding in person
- Justiciar

The Language of the Law: Then and Now

On first encountering legal history, students can be disconcerted by the use of what are apparently archaic words from dead languages. Pick up any standard legal dictionary, turn to a page at random, and it is notable how many words and phrases are written in (or derived from) Latin or a peculiar language called Law French. These languages may be obsolete;

however, these words remain in use because there is no better way to state what they represent. From Latin, the notion of *habeas corpus* remains widely used, not just as a piece of legal jargon but words that encapsulate a key birthright not to be detained without trial for an undue period of time. Is this Latin obsolete? Try telling that to inmates of Guantanamo Bay, who used writs of *habeas corpus* to protest their imprisonment during the War on Terror.

As for Law French, many words lawyers still use are from this language, because it was the language used by lawyers in court and in their reports for centuries, even though they spoke English in other contexts.

Figure 0.2 Surviving Law French Terms

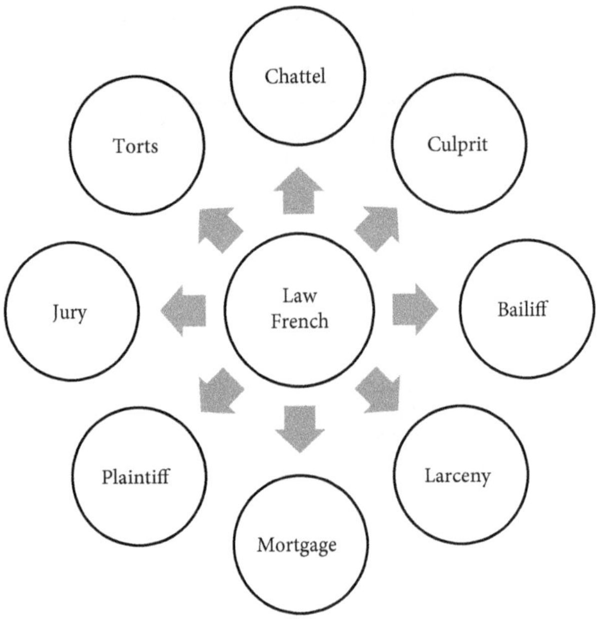

One final point is that to access these records of legal history would require the command of many languages. Chief among them is medieval Latin, together with Law French, Old English (for the Anglo-Saxon law codes) and various dialects of medieval English. But that is not to say that all people in the Middle Ages spoke all these languages, and legal proceedings could seem remote, intimidating and alien because they were happening in either another language (including the language of a foreign conqueror), or in a version of one's own language that was excessively technical and formal.

That is still an issue for the administration of justice in modern Australia, not just a historical circumstance safely relegated to the past. In 2015, the Chief Justice of Western Australia, Wayne Martin, suggested that 'if the accused person does not understand the language in which the case is being conducted, then the process is invalid, it's ineffective and it's a nullity',[9] which is a sharp reminder that the language of the law is a major factor in how

[9] Courtney Bembridge, 'WA Chief Justice Wayne Martin Fears Language Barriers Putting Innocent People Behind Bars' *ABC News* (27 September 2015), available at www.abc.net.au/news/2015-09-27/language-barriers-putting-innocent-people-in-jail,-judge-fears/6803004.

it is accessed and understood and that even the modern legal system is speaking a highly formal and technical language that many will not understand. The context for Martin CJ's comments was the trial of an Indigenous man who had not been provided with an interpreter. The case raises important points about the alienation of Indigenous Australians from the Australian legal system that will unfold in this textbook.

The Structure of this Book

This textbook leads through key developments in Australian legal history, roughly divided geographically between England and Australia. Chapters one to four and six carry forward the development of English common law from the Norman Conquest of Anglo-Saxon England in 1066 to the late-nineteenth century. Consideration is given to the American Revolution in chapter five. Chapters seven to 12 consider the reception of English law in Australia including its complex relationship with Indigenous Australians.

Front matter provides abbreviations of commonly used words and terms, a regnal list (the names and dates of the reigns for English kings and queens) and the use of monarchs' names in law, dating conventions for pre-modern England, and information on citing pre-1963 English statutes, respectively.

The first chapter now turns to medieval England, to the Norman Conquest of Anglo-Saxon England, and the emergence of English common law.

1

The Origins of the Common Law

Introduction

Medieval English law was the product of a different world and, in many respects, is remote and even terrifying. The opinions and precedents of medieval law survive in miles and miles of written texts that only specialists can decipher and translate. The people who were agents of and participants in the legal system can be hard to discern as individual personalities. Even so, from time to time, human personalities shine through in fascinating ways. Later in this chapter, attention will be focused on Edward I, one of the greatest rulers of his time. Yet however important he was, when a laundress complained directly to him that a man had raped her, but she had not yet received justice in her plea, Edward intervened swiftly and decisively. He wrote to the Earl of Cornwall, whom he had left in charge in England while fighting foreign wars, ordering restitution.[1] Edward's action is part of his direct involvement in English law, which mirrored other medieval monarchs whose involvement in the law was not ceremonial but actual.

Medieval law can seem remote because of its language and horrifying medieval punishments, but looking beyond that reveals a sophisticated system in operation and the personalities involved come into view. It is not static; Sir John Baker's reminder quoted in the Introduction that legal history is the history of change rings true for medieval law.[2] Many centuries of legal activity, developing actions, emerging and maturing legal doctrines and some of the greatest minds among the judges cannot be simply compacted to a simplified notion of 'medieval' law as something consistent and remote. The actions and doctrines as well as the personalities of medieval English law live on into the present.

This chapter offers a broad overview of the origins of the common law in England, with a focus on property law. Today, the common law exists in countries across the world that were once parts of the British Empire (such as Australia) or which began in the British Empire (such as the United States). There are, nevertheless, former parts of the British Empire that have not 'received' the common law – Quebec in Canada maintained French civil law; South Africa and Sri Lanka have Roman-Dutch legal systems inherited from The Netherlands (which held them as colonies before the British) in a hybrid with aspects of English law. The legal history covered in this text is also primarily English, not British. Scotland to this day has a different jurisprudence as the basis of its legal system, which has far more in common with European civil law codes derived from Roman law than English law.

[1] Michael Prestwich, *The Three Edwards: War and State in England, 1272–1377* (London, Routledge, 1980) 22.
[2] Sir John Baker, 'Why the History of English Law has not been Finished' (2000) 59 *CLJ* 62, 63.

This chapter charts the emergence of legal decisions based on precedent and legal actions based on writs from the Norman Conquest of 1066 onwards. Yet, consideration should be given to what came before the common law took hold. On that score, law and governance in Anglo-Saxon society opens this chapter, followed closely by the changes of the Norman Conquest. Feudalism, the Magna Carta, and the centralisation of royal justice are introduced as landmarks in thirteenth century law. The present though is never far away, and the chapter broadens to include the *Mabo* case, one of the most significant moments in Australian legal history, which will be considered here in relation to land tenure stretching from the Norman Conquest to the present era.

Learning Resources

The content in this chapter is supported by:

Glossary	Chapter Overview	Historical Cameos	Constitutional Detours	Pause for Thought
Latin, Law French and Middle English terms are defined	The chapter begins with an overview explaining its intentions and focus	Henry II Edward I	The Magna Carta	Modern Significance of the Magna Carta

Chapter Overview

Place	Time Period	Dates	Key Figures	Key Institutions and Officers	Key Terms
• Kingdom of England • Dukedom of Normandy	• Medieval (or the Middle Ages)	• 10th–13th centuries	• William I • Henry II • John • Edward I • Richard fitzNeal • Eddie Mabo	• Curia Regis • Exchequer • Chancery • Justiciar • Witenagemot • Magna Carta	• Folkright • Norman Conquest • Seigniorial lordship • Feudalism and land tenure • Assizes • Eyres • *Mabo v Queensland (No 2)*

Learning Outcomes

At the end of this chapter, readers should understand:

- The impact of the Norman Conquest on English law.
- The historical importance of Henry II and Edward I in the development of common law.
- The symbolic and actual importance of the Magna Carta in modern Australian law.
- Feudal land tenure and its continued application in modern Australian law including in the context of Indigenous land rights and native title.

The Sources for Medieval Legal History

Seeking the origins of the common law means first asking what evidence survives from the past to reconstruct the legal processes, doctrines and people involved. Vast but incomplete records survive for medieval law. As a result, some important preliminary questions for any student of legal history are:

- Where do the documentary records for this subject matter come from?
- Where and how have they survived?
- How should they be interpreted, and how can they be interpreted?

Major gaps exist and knowledge of the history of medieval law is partial and far from systematic.[3] These documents are not dead letters but lively and living sources of information that, in some cases, still have functional value. The sources bring to life a range of important aspects of legal history. Among them are laws – statutes and law codes – themselves. However, the personalities and priorities of the people who wrote, enacted, or were subject to the law are also recoverable. Sometimes the personalities of the clerks and lawyers stand out. In a case from the memorandum rolls of the Exchequer of Pleas, a clerk has drawn two barrels pouring out their content into a goblet, perhaps daydreaming as plea of trespass involving a wine broker was taking place![4] It is not possible to cover every surviving source for English law in this period; however, it is worthwhile having familiarity with some of the major sources of evidence.

Documentary Evidence

Documentary evidence are the working papers of the legal system as well as the public documents that announced legal circumstances (such as charters). Part of that process was the increasing attention paid to the keeping of centralised records by those in proximity to

[3] Geoffrey Elton, *England 1200–1640: The Sources of History* (Cambridge, Cambridge University Press, 1969) 173.

[4] Hilary Jenkinson and Beryl ER Fermoy, *Select Cases in the Exchequer of Pleas* (London, Selden Society, 1932) 103.

the monarch who administered justice – initially in person. The content of writs, the names of judges and other information about the workings of the court are here. Among these papers are:

- The pipe rolls are so called because they literally look like pipes. They are in fact layer after layer (each layer is called a membrane) of animal hides – a full sheep hide – on which financial information was 'engrossed'.
- The *Curia Regis* rolls like the pipe rolls were documents recording the activities of royal justice.
- The plea rolls are the records written on parchment of writs and court proceedings and judicial proceedings, written by clerks in terse, brisk Latin.[5]
- The Year Books are in Law French and are a lively source for the interlocutory proceedings in the Court of Common Pleas.[6] The legal profession truly comes to life. There are occasions where judges made dirty jokes that nineteenth century editors were loath to translate. Many witty comments made from the bench by John of Mettingham CJCP (died 1301) and William de Bereford CJCP (died 1326) were written down in the Year Books by people who clearly having fun listening to them. The Year Books record the judges and the many other people involved who are part of legal history. They are lively as students who were present in court watching the live proceedings unfolding most likely wrote them. They are also the forerunner to the formal reports (see chapter two). Law French is the archaic language spoken in the English law courts.[7] Many of the terms used throughout this text, including jury, tort and attorney, are modern survivors of Law French. The Year Books are important sources for understanding the intersections between common law and civil law, and they often record judges, including Bereford, quoting Latin maxims from so-called 'written law' (civil or canon law) and showing the extent of common lawyers' awareness of the rules of civil law.[8]

Treatises

The workings of the law and the reputation of the legal system were of great interest to the practitioners of the law in medieval England. Some wrote extensive theoretical or historical works about it in which they described the operations and personnel of the legal system. Major works include:

- Richard FitzNeal (died 1198) wrote *Dialogus de Saccario* (Dialogues of the Exchequer) in which he describes the officers, functions and working methods of the Court of the Exchequer, which was both a court and a Crown auditing office.

[5] Donald W Sutherland, *Quo Warranto Proceedings in the Reign of Edward I 1278–1294* (Clarendon Press, 1963) 31.

[6] George Garnett, 'Sir Edward Coke's Resurrection of Magna Carta' in Lawrence Goldman (ed), *Magna Carta: History, Context and Influence* (London, Institute of Historical Research, 2019) 52.

[7] John Pocock, *The Ancient Constitution and the Feudal Law: A Study of English Historical Thought in the Seventeenth Century – a Reissue with a Retrospect* (Cambridge, Cambridge University Press, 1987) 34.

[8] David J Seipp, 'The Reception of Canon Law and Civil Law in the Common Law Courts before 1600' (1993) 13 *Oxford Journal of Legal Studies* 390.

- Sir Ranulf de Glanvill (or Glanville) CJ (died 1190) is the attributed author of *De Legibus et Consuetudinibus Angliae* (On the Laws and Customs of England).
- Henry de Bracton JKB (died 1268) is also the traditionally accepted author of a treatise with the same title as Glanvill's. Both are important early records of royal justice and the workings and traditions of the royal courts. Whoever wrote it, the author was aware of both Roman law but also used the rolls generated by the courts.[9]
- Sir John Fortescue CJKB (died about 1477) wrote two major treatises, *In Praise of the Laws of England* and *The Governance of England*. Both tend to idealise and, certainly, valourise the common law. Nevertheless, his work contains much valuable information on the workings of the legal system. Links to their works are available on the website.

Educational

Common law lawyers did not study at either of the universities (Oxford and Cambridge) until many centuries after the Middle Ages but they did receive a legal education. Works survive on what and how they learned and the daily workings of the Inns of Court where they lived and learned. For example:

- The **Black Books of Lincoln's Inn** are the membership registers of this Inn of Court. The data is a significant source for observing the growth of the legal profession as the numbers of members of the Inn increase over decades and centuries.
- Statute books were a form of legal literature containing the body of statutes.

To bring the legal past to light and life is a huge undertaking. The writing is often cramped and the medieval clerks were not always good record-keepers as the membranes did not always get stitched together straight away, causing confusion for later archivists and editors.[10] The legal historian Maitland referred to the 'tons of unprinted plea rolls' that confront the editor, the historian and the student.[11] John Baker offers the mind-blowing reminder that over a million sheep died and gave their skins to produce the English legal record, which includes 'thousands of miles of abbreviated Latin'.[12] However, these records also show that medieval judges and others involved in legal processes valued accuracy. For instance, Edward I, whose active interest in law is explored later in the chapter,

> sent word to Guncelin of Badlesmere, his justice of Chester, and to Ralph of Hengham thus: because the same lord king has learned from the account of trustworthy men that there was an obvious error in the record and process of the assize of last presentment … and there would be greater error in the same unless the same record and process were fully examined before the lord king and his council and wiser provision made how in such a case and similar cases ought to proceed in future …[13]

[9] Frederic Maitland, 'Materials for English Legal History II' (1889) 4 *Political Science Quarterly* 635.
[10] Roy Hunnisett, 'What is a Plea Roll' (1988) 9 *Journal of the Society of Archivists* 111.
[11] FW Maitland, *Why the History of English Law is Not Written* (London, CJ Clay & Sons, 1888).
[12] Baker (n 2) 62, 70.
[13] Coram Rege Roll, no 37 (Easter 1278) m 29d in George Sayles, *Select Cases in the Court of King's Bench under Edward I Volume I* (London, Selden Society, 1936) 42–43.

The judge had to send the records under seal to Edward I for his perusal. That was not the only occasion where Edward demanded records were sent to him in order to check them.[14]

A modern lawyer may gain skills and insights from these sources. One is that there is a legal memory. The plea rolls in particular are largely complete from the late twelfth century until the keeping of rolls lasted into the nineteenth century. Not all legal sources agree with each other and suggest how the clerks and other officials of different courts perceived processes differently from each other. That awareness leads, courtesy of Sir John Baker, to the very modern insight that a modern practising lawyer needs to have more than book learning and must have the skill to 'assess the likelihood of success in alternative situations'.[15] Baker continues that it is

> more a matter of how a tribunal can be persuaded of the facts as the party sees them, and how it can be persuaded to see those facts in a warm light which does not relegate the party's best point of view to the shadows.[16]

Now that is suggestive of cunning and skill and, arguably, the technicalities of the Priestley 11 (technically specific subject areas every student must study to be admitted as a lawyer) may not convey this. History reveals how practising lawyers negotiated their way through complex situations, using precedent while innovating. This history sketches both the technical and the functional.[17]

Law and Governance in Pre-Conquest England

What is pre-Conquest England? This text will refer to particular periods or phases of English history that historians traditionally organise around regnal periods (named after a particular monarch or royal house such as 'Victorian England' or 'the Tudor period') or else after a major event (for example, 'the Interregnum' is the time period between the execution of King Charles I in 1649 and the restoration of the monarchy in 1660).

The first such period for study is pre-Conquest England, meaning the centuries before the invasion of England by William, Duke of Normandy in 1066. The Anglo-Saxon monarchies have left written evidence of their **laws**, and some of the earliest vernacular[18] documents from the seventh century are law codes.[19] A tradition of dispute resolution flourished in England before the Norman Conquest in 1066. Custom or 'folkright' (sometimes also called 'Folklaw') was at the heart of Anglo-Saxon law. Folkright varied between communities: disputes were resolved and wrongdoing punished locally according to regional or village customs.

No clear division between civil and criminal matters existed in Anglo-Saxon times. This seems remarkable but custom was the basis of Anglo-Saxon society. That necessarily meant

[14] Coram Rege Roll, no 75 (Easter 1283) m 16 in *ibid* 116.

[15] Baker (n 2) 69.

[16] *Ibid.*

[17] See Chris Phillips, 'Medieval Source Material on the Internet: Common Law Records' (*Medieval Genealogy*), available at medievalgenealogy.org.uk/sources/law.shtml.

[18] That is to say, they are not in Latin.

[19] Susan Kelly, 'Anglo-Saxon Lay Society' in Roy Liuzza (ed), *Old English Literature: Critical Essays* (New Haven, Yale University Press, 2002) 41.

that it was local and often based on memory. Free men (aged over 12) possessed certain law enforcement responsibilities. If a free man witnessed a crime, he was obliged to raise the 'hue and cry' to attract the attention of free men in his tithing or hundred. Other free men would join him to pursue and capture the offender. Likewise, sheriffs at shire-level could summon a 'posse' of free men to capture offenders or otherwise to enforce the law.

The system of *wer*, *bot* and *wite* was a prominent feature of Anglo-Saxon law enforcement. Written laws or *dooms* issued by Anglo-Saxon kings fixed monetary compensation for physical loss, for damage suffered and for rights violated. *Bot* was payable to victims of crime depending on the severity of injury suffered. The amount of compensation payable in the event of death or for a fine (*wite*) depended on the victim's status in the community (*wer*). *Wite* was payable to the king or the community.

While this environment was not conducive to centralised justice – which would emerge much later in post-Conquest England – the Anglo-Saxons left an indelible mark on the law. Sheriffs (short for shire reeve, a court officer), writs (document used to commence legal action) and the king's peace are all products of Anglo-Saxon innovation. The Norman Conquest retained these and the writ served Norman kings as the means to carry their orders throughout their kingdom.[20]

The organisation of government in Anglo-Saxon England deserves special mention, not least because of how radically judicial administration changed in the centuries following the Norman Conquest. By the tenth century, Anglo-Saxon England was organised into counties or shires. Shires divided into hundreds – an administrative division of land still preserved in South Australia. Tithings, made up of ten families, were subdivisions of hundreds.

Earldorman (Old English): a leading man in a district. Until recently, city councillors were called the aldermen, a related term

At all levels, shire, hundred and tithing, assemblies were convened to resolve judicial, administrative and legislative business. Folkright was dispensed at these assemblies. Inhabitants of hundreds and tithings were responsible for maintaining legal order whereas the sheriff at shire-level was entrusted with keeping the king's peace in the shire. Aside from these assemblies, lords' courts existed emanating from 'seigniorial' authority, ie the authority of the lord because of his status. Lords had jurisdiction to manage the behaviour of their men and over some land transactions.

The **earldorman** tried thieves and adjudicated feuds. Administrative details were given to deputies – the gerefa or king's reeve. A key official in Anglo-Saxon justice was the shire reeve, which contracts to the sheriff. The sheriff remains a lynchpin of the Australian legal system. The sheriff and the writ are two notable survivors into the modern day of the Anglo-Saxon legal system.

Justice before Anglo-Saxon kings and their wise men ('witan') was only typically allowed for persons if they had previously approached their shire or hundred assembly. The **witenagemot** comprised the great men of the kingdom. This was an occasion, not an institution. It was not based on feudal obligation. The witans were there because of status; indeed, they could overthrow a king. By contrast, those who administered

Witenagemot (Old English): an Anglo-Saxon king's council or parliament

[20] Doris M Stenton, *English Justice between the Norman Conquest and the Great Charter, 1066–1215* (London, George Allen and Unwin, 1965) 17.

justice after the Norman Conquest were members of a feudal household. Soon we will consider the machinery of justice that the Normans created in England that emerged out of this tight-knit household.

Impact of the Norman Conquest

After the Anglo-Saxon monarch Edward the Confessor died in January 1066, Harold II succeeded to the throne as the last Anglo-Saxon king of England. In September 1066, Harold and his army had repelled an invasion of Norwegian Vikings at the Battle of Stamford Bridge near York in northern England. Harold then marched his army some 260 miles south to Sussex to confront the invading forces of William, the Duke of Normandy. On 14 October 1066, William defeated Harold at Hastings in southeast England. On Christmas Day 1066, William was crowned King of England in Westminster Abbey. He gradually took control of the whole of England, often by fire and sword.

William's accession wrought no immediate change to the Anglo-Saxon legal order. One of William's first acts was to declare that old Anglo-Saxon law would continue. The hundred and county system was maintained though, in time, manorial courts assumed higher standing. What brought significant change was the superimposition of Norman traditions on the existing Anglo-Saxon legal order. These changes included a new system of landholding (feudalism) and another mode of trial (trial by battle or trial by ordeal), which was originally reserved for Norman nobles loyal to William. England became feudal by William I leasing land to lords in return for 5,000 mounted knights. In turn, the lords leased to subtenants in return for knight service. Like in Normandy, rights ultimately reserved to William. This tenure was the fee (*feod*, *feud*, *fief*) and feudal dues were incidents of tenure. The land could escheat (return) back to the crown if, for example, there was a failure in the hereditary line to produce an heir.

One further change is that England started to look different after the Norman Conquest. William and his successors asserted their rule visually by building castles throughout their conquered territory. One of these is the Tower of London. Another surviving Norman structure is Westminster Hall, built by William II (also known as William Rufus). This vast structure, now part of the Houses of Parliament, is of central importance to English legal history as it was the home of the courts of King's Bench and Common Pleas until the nineteenth century. It is where many of the lawyers and judges discussed in this text will have worked (and have struggled to be heard).

Feudalism

In 1066, William I acquired all land in England by conquest. He stripped land from most Anglo-Saxon nobles and rewarded loyal Norman nobles with it. Gradually, Normans replaced many Anglo-Saxon bishops. The introduction of feudal tenure by the Normans drastically altered landholding in England.

Feudalism is a hierarchical system of landholding and inheritance, as well as obligations of military service. During a coronation, lords took an oath of fealty to the king. All superiors committed to the protection of their subordinates.[21] This system came to England from the Dukedom of Normandy across the English Channel. It was not distinctive to Normandy but appeared across Europe, including in the acts of commendation between lords and vassals in the Frankish kingdoms.[22] The term of art, 'feudalism', is actually an eighteenth-century abstraction. In many history textbooks it is schematically represented by a pyramid, with the king at the apex and descending layers in a hierarchy. That, however, is too simple. As royal and centralised legal institutions matured in England, the king's courts and justices actually disrupted the feudal relationships between lords and tenants. These relations are where we see feudal land ownership in action. William the Conqueror was himself the feudal vassal of the King of France. Charles the Simple had granted Normandy to William's ancestor Rollo (a Viking) in the Treaty of Saint-Clair-sur-Epte (911 AD).[23]

To stay in the Dukedom of Normandy for a moment, the feudal institutions there functioned as follows:

1. Dukes of Normandy granted fiefs (land, estates) to aristocratic men without parage (in other words, without splitting among younger sons).
2. Vassals swore *fidelitas* and performed *homagium* (possibly to more than one lord). They swore their loyalty to the lord, and sealed the feudal relationship with a kiss.
3. The estate or fief (*feodum*) that the lords acquired from the Duke was typically land with workers, buildings and 'judicial prerequisites' of holding a seigniorial court. They were now obliged or in a state of vassalage to the Duke but this did not constitute ownership but rather possession with feudal obligations and eventually heritable tenure (Lyons). Reciprocity was at the core of feudalism; perfidy was failure to carry out feudal obligations.

Seisin (Old and Middle English): freehold possession of land

The tenant's right to have possession (***seisin***) of land of an overlord depended on an oath of allegiance or loyalty and a promise to provide services ('incidents of tenure'). These incidents of tenure included:

- Knight service, providing the king with a fixed number of knights for 40 days every year.
- Socage or scutage, initially with different forms, socage eventually just involved the payment of money as rent.
- Serjeanty, providing personal service to the monarch or great lords, for example serving as the king's chamberlain or butler, guarding the Scottish border, or providing services such as foot soldiers or goods such as arrows.
- Frankalmoigne, spiritual tenure paid by members of religious orders to pray for the grantor's soul.

The king ultimately owned all land in England. Everyone was his tenant or vassal. Swearing homage was a religious ceremony. In terms of obligation, the king sat at the top of the feudal

[21] Judith Richards, 'English Allegiance in a British Context: Political Problems and Legal Resolutions' (2001) 18 *Parergon* 103, 107.

[22] Ralph Davis, *A History of Medieval Europe from Constantine to Saint Louis* (London, Longmans, 1957) 123.

[23] *Ibid* 166.

pyramid followed by lords in the middle and sub-tenants at the bottom. However, this picture is complicated by the fact that one king could in fact be the vassal of another. After the conquest, William was King of England *and* the Duke of Normandy; he therefore paid homage to the King of France.[24]

As lord paramount, the king granted tenure to lords. Tenure was not equivalent to ownership, however; it simply amounted to a right to possession (*seisin*) of land so long as the incidents of tenure were honoured. The tenant held 'an estate' in the land, and not the land itself.

Tenants-in-chief were lords who held land granted directly from the king. These lords could divide their land into smaller portions, granting tenure to *mesne* (pronounced 'meen') lords, who could then further sub-divide the land. This series of subordinate tenures – or the process of subinfeudation – could go on. The centre of feudalism – the law relating to landholding – was the constitutional law of the Middle Ages. Feudalism was therefore primarily about land and the laws and legal actions to preserve or acquire land. As a result, the legal history that feudalism presents to us in Europe and in England relates to owning land or having certain rights to land.

Australia still has a feudal system of landholding. The Crown is sole owner of all land, and all that others hold is an estate in land. This is now complicated in Australia by the recognition of native title (see chapter 12). Australian law now recognises that the Crown shares tenure with First Nations, as was the practice in other British colonies such as Canada. For the most part, however, landholding in Australia is still feudal. Those who 'buy land' normally purchase an estate 'in fee simple' – or 'a freehold estate'. In Queensland for example, the tenure under which an estate in land is held is still 'common socage … without any incident of tenure for the benefit of the Crown'.[25] That means the owner pays no rents to the Crown to hold the estate.

Centralisation of Royal Justice

Norman kings were adept at administration. These kings were frequently absent from England as they had significant land holdings across the Channel to manage. To lessen the impact of these absences, early English kings developed a practice of sending judges throughout the English countryside to hear and settle disputes, instead of requiring subjects to travel to the king's court (*curia regis*) to have a matter settled. Having to approach the king in person could be challenging especially if, as for most of the reign of Richard I (1189–1199), the king was crusading. In a moment there will be a cameo of Henry II, but we will first consider Henry I (1100–1135), a younger son of William the Conqueror. The evidence relating to civil and criminal law in his reign is extensive, including the role of his itinerant justices in trying indicted people. It is a subject of historical debate whether developments in the role of itinerant justices and their growing influence over the justiciar took place in Henry I's reign or Henry II's. What is clear however is the growing range and sophistication of the Norman machinery of justice. Both itinerant justices and local justiciars had the

[24] Christopher Brooke, *From Alfred to Henry III: 871–1272* (New York, Norton, 1961) 99.
[25] *Property Law Act 1974* (Qld) s 20.

right of hear cases ***omnia placita regis***. Legal activity covered both criminal and civil spheres, and local justiciars heard pleas of the crown. Like the witan in Anglo-Saxon times, the *curia regis* comprised trusted advisors to the king. These early kings also appointed justiciars to act on their behalf while they were out of the kingdom and perform roles such as witnessing charters.[26] There is an important insight to the role from an early surviving writ issued sometime between 1123 and 1126, in which the justiciar Roger of Salisbury had the writ issued and referred to himself in these terms: 'Rogerius episcopus Saresb. Sub domino nostro rege Henrico regni Anglie procurator'. In other words, he proclaims that he is the bishop of Salisbury (Saresburiensis) and the procurator (king's deputy) in England serving under King Henry.[27]

***Omnia placita regis* (Latin):** hearing all kinds of pleas

Historical Cameo

Henry II

The centralisation of royal justice was a particular concern for the first Angevin king, **Henry II** (1154–89). Henry is regarded as the father of the common law, but such titles can simplify. His justiciar Ranulf de Glanvill and his bench of judges were intrinsic to the operation of the law in Henry's reign and his father, Henry I, deserved credit as a legal innovator. Nonetheless, Henry is a notably significant figure who has left behind a clear impression of his assertive personality and the range and extent of his power. He was the greatest landholder in Europe. Through inheritance, marriage and conquest he governed England, much of Ireland and Wales, and all of the western duchies and counties of France. Owing to his frequent absences from England, Henry II had to delegate administration in England to others. It is through this delegation that the common law started to emerge. Appointed judges, who travelled around England on circuit to hear disputes, developed a bank of principles applying to like cases ('precedent'). Glanvill, or whomever wrote the treatise attributed to him, valourised Henry and his judges, discussed legal changes and developments during the reign, and noted the importance of having the laws written down.

Henry II's contributions to the law included:

- General eyres – Itinerant justices (with extensive jurisdiction over civil, criminal and administrative matters) were sent to counties and boroughs at semi-regular intervals. Routine activities came to a standstill as justices 'in eyre' audited the conduct of local government and their books. General eyres also dealt with administrative and judicial business arising between eyres. General eyres caused such upheaval (and sometimes sheer terror) that they became less regular and prompted the establishment of central courts.

[26] Emile M Amt, 'Richard de Lucy, Henry II's Justiciar' (1988) 9 *Medieval Prosopography* 61, 64.
[27] Doris Stenton, 'Roger of Salisbury, Regni Angliae Procurator' (1924) 39(153) *English Historical Review* 79, 79.

- New courts – During Henry II's reign, the Court of Common Pleas (the Bench) was established (and later gained statutory basis from the Magna Carta) and comprised five judges in Westminster Hall.
- The jury – A new method of proof, trial by jury, was introduced in the first clause of the *Assize of Clarendon* (1166). The 'grand assize' was available in royal courts. It enabled litigants to have a trial by jury of 12 men chosen by four knights. Other modes of proof – trial by battle and ordeals – lost appeal over time. Defendants in criminal trials could be pressured into choosing trial by jury rather than by battle. If a defendant refused, they could be imprisoned and tortured by being crushed under heavy stones (*peine forte et dure*).
- Returnable writs – Common law writs that came to assume a standardised form and, being returnable, became a record of when an issue or dispute was settled.
- Defining ecclesiastical and common law matters – Henry II issued the *Constitutions of Clarendon* in 1164. Under Article 3, a cleric convicted of a criminal offence in the Church courts was to be sent to the temporal (royal) courts for sentencing. The Archbishop of Canterbury (and former Lord Chancellor) Thomas Becket, resisted these changes. In 1170, supporters of Henry II murdered Becket in Canterbury Cathedral, causing a European-wide scandal and Becket became a saint in 1173. This shocking event encouraged a moderation of Article 3: clerics charged with serious offences were tried in Church courts (receiving the 'benefit of clergy'); less serious offences could be handled in temporal courts.

Juries

Trial by jury is a cornerstone of Australian, British and American justice, whereby a randomly assembled panel hear the facts of the case and reach a verdict. These people comprise a petty jury and receive information rather than being self-informing or being the source of information. A grand jury by contrast is self-informing.

The jury now commonly encountered in a modern trial is the product of evolution. A medieval jury was part of what the legal historian Theodore Plucknett calls a 'definite system of inquisitions as part of the machinery of criminal justice'.[28] The Domesday Book, a massive record of the revenues of the entire kingdom, completed in 1086, was the result of inquisitions. These were carried out by commissioners moving throughout the hundreds, calling on local juries to provide responses to questions such as 'What is the name of your manor? Who held it under King Edward? Who holds it now? How many hides does it contain? How many ploughs are there on the demesne?'[29] The Domesday Book remained authoritative for centuries afterwards. Sir Edward Coke, whose long career and extensive writings later

[28] Theodore Plucknett, *A Concise History of the Common Law* (Union, New Jersey, The Lawbook Exchange, 2001) 112.

[29] Henry Davis, *England under the Normans and Angevins* (London, Methuen and Co, 1905) 44.

chapters will discuss, quoted from it in the seventeenth century.[30] Medieval judges turned to it looking for answers about who owned what.[31]

That same principle of inquisition was followed by Henry II's Assize of Clarendon a century later in 1166 (named after the royal palace of Clarendon). This instructed that

> inquiry shall be made in every county and in every hundred by the twelve most lawful men of the hundred and by the four most lawful men of every vill, upon oath that they shall speak the truth, whether in their hundred or vill there be any man who is accused or believed to be a robber, murderer, thief, or a receiver of robbers, murderers or thieves.[32]

This jury was the presentment jury and the boundary between the witness and the juror was blurred; juror means a person who has sworn to say something.[33] But note there is also an evaluative process here, as the jurors needed to decide about a person being 'notorious' or not before they, the jurors, said anything before the justices.[34]

The Assizes of Clarendon elaborated on the procedures that then followed, including the sheriffs bringing any such accused people before the King's judges. Later, in 1170, Henry ordered an inquest investigating conduct of the sheriffs.[35] The juries therefore are not like a modern jury: they provide information actively, rather than passively soak it up. The medieval machinery of justice required modes of proof to turn accusations from the vills and hundreds into verdicts based on proofs. Ordeal and compurgation, both supernatural processes, brought God directly into the process. Undergoing ordeal by risking injury or death, an outcome averted by God for the innocent, could include taking hold of red-hot metals or being held underwater. Compurgation involved the accused swearing innocence with the support of 12 compurgators or oath helpers.

Instruments of Justice

William I and his Norman and Angevin successors were both kings of England and dukes of Normandy. Their attention and energies were divided either side of the English Channel. Years of their reigns were spent abroad. Many Norman and Angevin kings and their wives died and were buried in Normandy. Because of their prolonged absences, offices and institutions developed out of the *curia regis* to ensure continuity of government and justice. When William the Conqueror returned to Normandy in 1067, one of his noblemen, William FitzOsbern, became the regent and may have taken on legal functions including issuing writs.

[30] Edward Coke, *The Third Part of the Institutes of the Laws of England: Concerning High Treason, and Other Pleas of the Crown and Criminal Causes* (Lawbook Exchange, 2002) 205.

[31] Samuel Stoljar and Leslie Downer (eds), *Year Books of Edward II Michaelmass 1320* (London, Selden Society, 1988) 45.

[32] Quoted in Plucknett (n 28) 112–13.

[33] John H Langbein, Renee Lettow Lerner and Bruce P Smith, *History of the Common Law: The Development of the Anglo-American Legal Institutions* (New York, Wolters Kluwer, 2009) 41.

[34] *Ibid* 40–43.

[35] Frederick Pollock and Frederic William Maitland, *The History of English Law before the Time of Edward I*, vol 1 (Clark, New Jersey, The Lawbook Exchange, 2013) 137–38.

Kings would supervise royal justice through officials. Chief among these was the office of the justiciar. While the office no longer exists, it was of first importance in Anglo-Norman England. Being dukes of Normandy too, the kings of England could be absent from England and therefore needed someone to govern in their place.[36] On several occasions Henry I delegated rule to his wife Matilda, but increasingly Norman kings relied on their officials.[37] The Normans ruled elsewhere in medieval Europe where the legal and administrative machinery emulated English examples. In the Norman kingdom of Sicily, there were justiciars who were, like their English counterparts, busy legal officials.[38]

William Rufus, William the Conqueror's successor, appointed low-born clerics beginning with Roger of Salisbury, a priest, who was also bishop of Salisbury and chancellor. Roger was not actually called the justiciar but served as such and was also the first of a dynasty, being followed by Nigel of Ely and Richard FitzNeal.[39]

Where there are officials, there will be official records and serious record keeping begins from 1170s in the form of the memoranda rolls. These records show the work of a regular office and not just the king's will.[40] The justiciar directed the itinerant justices, as well as being chief of the Exchequer and the justiciar himself could be sent anywhere in the kingdom.

Justice therefore transmitted throughout the kingdom. In 1179, a great general Eyre was held, involving 21 judges and four circuits, hearing complaints of the people. The judges of the Eyre held extensive powers. The judges with their entourage would arrive in a town and call for anyone with a complaint to present a bill. That is an important procedural difference from commencing with a writ. The barrister and historian William Craddock Bolland envisages the outcome in vivid terms, with the judges 'bound by none of the shackles which bound them when trying a case commenced in the ordinary way by writ', instead they had the freedom to directly interrogate the witnesses in order to find out 'the exact truth of the matter'.[41]

Along with the office of justiciar, institutions (what we could now call government departments) emerged. The Exchequer, named after a chequered cloth, was originally a treasure chamber with a chest in it. Edward the Confessor kept a chest in his bedroom to keep it safe from thieves. To the Exchequer sheriffs came to render accounts twice a year. The Exchequer was not itinerant with the King. It was stable and kept records such as the pipe rolls recording fines.[42] The Exchequer was a Norman institution and

[36] Davis (n 29) 44.

[37] Francis West, *The Justiciarship in England 1066–1232* (Cambridge, Cambridge University Press, 1966) 14.

[38] Ernst Kantorowicz, *Frederick the Second 1194–1250* (translated by EO Lorimer) (New York, Frederick Ungar Publishing, 1957) 274.

[39] West (n 37) 16, 24.

[40] Alan Harding, *The Law Courts of Medieval England* (London, George Allen and Unwin, 1973) 74.

[41] William Craddock Bolland, *The Year Books: Lectures Delivered in the University of London at the Request of the Faculty of Laws* (Cambridge, Cambridge University Press, 1921) 56–57; William Craddock Bolland, *The General Eyre: Lectures Delivered in the University of London at the Request of the Faculty of Laws* (Cambridge, Cambridge University Press, 1921) 86.

[42] JL Bolton, *Money in the Medieval English Economy: 973–1489* (Manchester, Manchester University Press, 2012) 32.

there were exchequers in Normandy and in Sicily, where Normans also ruled. In this department, the seneschal, chamberlain, marshal, treasurer and clerks sat in judgment to determine.[43] The earliest pipe rolls date from 1130, but they show that procedure in the department was already well developed and sophisticated. Its procedures endured for centuries, including keeping records on notched wooden tallies even after paper and ink became widely used everywhere else. Royal officials provided annual record of the king's finances. The chamber acted as a court of revenue with the king as plaintiff (although not present in person).

In this chamber was an oak table covered in a chequered cloth, which gave it the appearance of a chessboard. Around the table sat officials and servants. One was the human calculator. There was the treasurer, a scribe keeping the roll, and a scribe taking the antigraph (or copy), writing on sheepskins. On the table were the tallies issued as receipts (as they were until the nineteenth century). What ensued was a legal process, following up on a writ that had authorised expenditure on behalf of the Crown. The chequers on the table showed the sums of money demanded and received. Sheriffs, summoned by writ, came to the Exchequer to account for royal revenues.

The doctrines, processes and structures of Norman law emerged in a framework influenced at all points by religion. Richard FitzNeal's ***Dialogus de Scaccario*** (written in about 1180) describes the functions of the Exchequer in a way that combines an account of the routine functions and activities of this department with highly charged mystical meaning. FitzNeal was a priest and royal servant. In this work, the royal authority of the English Government merged with the divine. The auditing done on Earth is akin to the judgment of souls that take place in heaven. FitzNeal said:

> And not alone in these things that thou cost? mention, but in the whole description of the exchequer there are hiding places, as it were, of holy truths. For the diversity of officials, the authority of the judicial power, the impression of the royal image, the sending out of summonses, the writing of the rolls, the account of land rents, the exaction of debts, the condemnation or absolution of the accused, are a symbol of the strict examination that will be made when the books of all shall be opened and the gates closed.[44]

Note the detail here of what the Exchequer officials did, such as sending out writs and use of the king's seal (his image) as a symbol of authority. Then the tone becomes more eschatological, or concerned with divine judgment, when he compared the auditing in the Exchequer with how God will examine people's souls, and the wording alludes to texts from the Bible. A core aspect of this religion was judgment. Above the portals of churches and inside in wall paintings, medieval people saw depictions of God and Jesus Christ judging and weighing souls. At an institutional level, the links between the Church and the law were tight. Bishops and archbishops often held the office of Lord Chancellor, the highest legal office in the kingdom. Laws enunciated in the Bible, especially in *Deuteronomy*, provided instruction on the obedience that was expected to kings. FitzNeal was a priest and his contextual

[43] Charles Homer Haskins, *Norman Institutions* (New Haven, Harvard University Press, 1918) 89.
[44] Ernest F Henderson, *Select Historical Documents of the Middle Ages* (London, George Bell and Sons, 1896).

society was Christian. However, there were also Jewries, or Jewish communities, in medieval English cities. Jewish people were intrinsic to English finance as lenders, and English kings maintained a separate department, the Exchequer of the Jews, for their financial affairs and 'squeezed' profits out of them.[45]

The next department is the Chancery, named after the *cancelli* or the screen behind which sat royal secretaries. In this period, many royal officials were priests, as this body was literate and from its earliest periods, English justice required record-keeping. Many chancellors were also bishops and the royal chapel was a scriptorium, or a place where writing took place. The output of the chancery was the writ (breve) and the charter and the function of the chancery as a secretariat emerges staffed by clerical (and therefore literate) members of the royal household. The head of the secretariat held the Great Seal and the chancellor ranked beneath the justiciar.

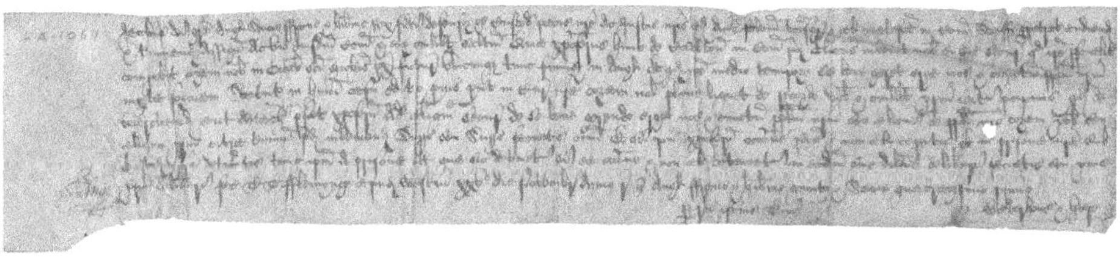

Figure 1.1 An example of a writ obtained from the Chancery

Writ addressed to the justices of Staffordshire (25 November 1607). Call #: L.a.1064.

Experiences of Justice

In the list of early Norman kings, the standout name is Henry II who protected royal law, raised revenue and administered his justice through his departments and courts of Exchequer, Common Pleas, and Chancery. Plucknett regards Henry II's reign as an era of expansion of itinerant justices, more widespread use of jury, and developments such as the coming Assize of Clarendon.[46] Henry II heard cases in person, expanded powers of permanent departments, created 'a concurrent royal jurisdiction in ordinary cases involving particular types of claims – and they were fairly numerous – which had a direct bearing upon peace' and oversaw a development in his reign in presentment or indictment, or public communal accusation. In short, he placed justice at the disposal of anyone who could bring their case.[47]

[45] John Clapham, *A Concise Economic History of Britain from the Earliest Times to 1750* (Cambridge, Cambridge University Press, 1963) 139.

[46] Plucknett (n 28) 16.

[47] Harold J Berman, *Law and Revolution, the Formation of the Western Legal Tradition* (New Haven, Harvard University Press, 2009) 451.

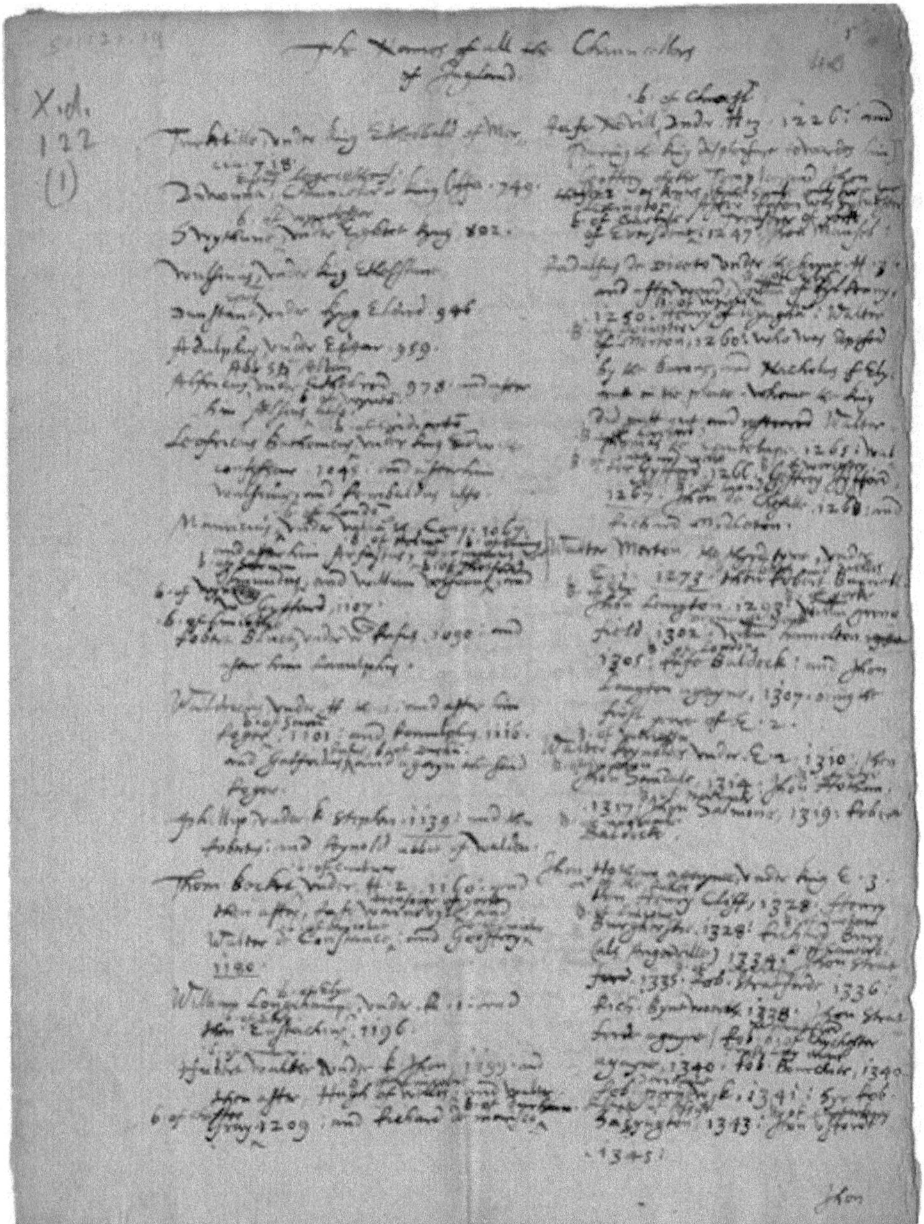

The Names of all the Chancellors of England

Figure 1.2 A List of Early Lord Chancellors

W Lambarde, Miscellaneous legal notes of William Lambarde (ca. 1577–1587). Call #: X.d.122 (1).

To facilitate their appropriate use, exemplar writs circulated. These writs became the basis of Glanville. There is much here that can be recognised in the current legal system, and helps comprehend the current Australian legal system, despite its remoteness from twelfth century England. In the legal archives from Henry II's reign, there are ample records of plaintiffs, defendants, covenants and malfeasance, meaning wrongful act rather than a failure to keep one's word.[48] In short, the working papers contain processes that are familiar today such as plaintiffs, claimants and defendants.

They can be best understood as the logic of the feudal system with its series of interlocking relationships – a vassal was the lord's, but the lord was the vassal's. The king's courts provided opportunities to confound a lord's actions by going to a court above the lord's own court including through actions such as *novel disseisin*, where the lord was defendant in actions if a tenant felt they had been unjustly and recently deprived of their land.[49] The king's court could find that the lord's court had acted wrongly, such as it should have distrained (fined) with chattels and not gone straight to taking land.[50] Or the king's court could find that the lord's actions should have been limited, for example they should not have distrained if there are infants to care for or the father is away.[51]

If all that sounds rather involved, note the king's courts could enforce a clear sense of appropriate obligations whereby:[52]

Figure 1.3 Legal Steps at King's Court

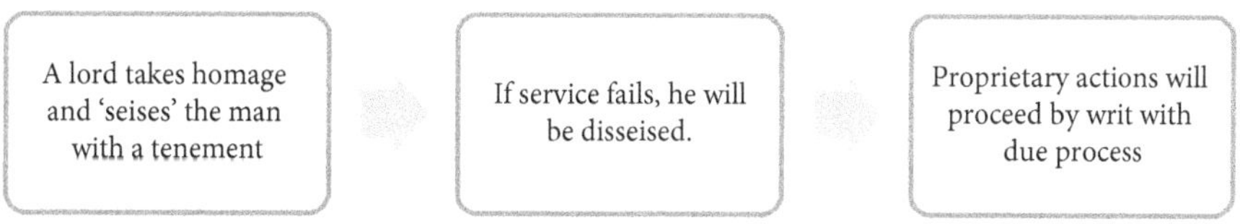

The notion of a legal action by due process is not new.

A king could not do everything. During and after the reign of Henry II, the machinery of justice was getting larger and more sophisticated. The eyre (from the Latin *iter* from which 'itinerary' developed) had a precursor in the journeys made by royal officials to compile the **Domesday Book** in 1086. Eyres were a source of royal revenue. They were not the only place to seek justice; cases could go from eyre to the specialist court of the Exchequer.[53]

Domesday Book (Old English): a record of the land and property in the entire kingdom of England, from *doom* or judgment

The Court of Common Pleas was founded in 1178 during the reign of Henry II. In 1215, Magna Carta (see below) demanded that common pleas sit at 'some place certain'. This was Westminster Hall. The Court of King's Bench was another court to have emerged during Henry II's reign. It concerned cases involving the royal person. This court derives from *coram rege* – in the presence of the king – in the ***curia regis***.

Curia regis **(Latin):** the council formed around the king

[48] Sir John Baker, *An Introduction to English Legal History*, 4th edn (London, LexisNexis Butterworths, 2002) 329.
[49] Stroud Milsom, *The Legal Framework of English Feudalism* (Cambridge, Cambridge University Press, 1976) 13.
[50] *Ibid* 14.
[51] *Ibid.*
[52] *Ibid* 39.
[53] Harding (n 40) 74.

That meant litigants had to follow an itinerant king. While Magna Carta laid down that common pleas should not follow the king but be in a certain place, Ralph Turner points out that did not mean there was a clear-cut division between the common pleas being civil cases and criminal cases being heard in the King's Bench.[54] Magna Carta also stipulated that two royal justices and four knights were to hold Assizes four times a year.

When they ascended the throne, Henry I, Henry II and John issued charters against evil customs and promising reform. Using a charter to promise reform and articulate certain standards was not anything new. John, who was King of England from 1199 until his death in 1216, is now synonymous with another charter: the Great Charter or the Magna Carta. This Great Charter emerged after many troubled years of John's rule including conflict with the papacy and unsuccessful military campaigns.[55] The draft terms of the Articles of the Barons – forceful statements about the Church and the kingdom – provided the basis for Magna Carta.

Constitutional Detour

The Magna Carta

Magna Carta (Latin for 'Great Charter') is an important document in English constitutional history and the constitutional law of all common law countries. The first Magna Carta formally issued on 19 June 1215 contained 63 clauses which, among other things:

- Declared that the royal court should be held at a fixed place (cl 17), which is the basis of the Court of Common Pleas.
- Prevented a person from being imprisoned 'except by the lawful judgment of his peers and/or by the law of the land' (cl 39).
- Asserted that justice would not be sold, or delayed, or denied (cl 40).
- Declared that 'only men that know the law of the realm' will be appointed as judges, constables and sheriffs (cl 45).

As Magna Carta was a Charter by which the king had agreed, or rather was forced, to limit his power in these ways, it is taken as acknowledgment that no person, not even the king, is above the law. On 15 June 1215, the barons forced King John to sign the penultimate draft of Magna Carta, the Articles of the Barons, at Runnymede close to the Thames. Magna Carta was formally issued on 19 June. John promised to uphold the demands within Magna Carta, but he did not. John was a deeply unpopular king. The barons rebelled against John's system of heavy taxation used to fund futile military campaigns. John's predecessor, his brother Richard I ('The Lionheart'), had done the same. The difference was that John stayed in England while Richard I spent most of his reign crusading or on the continent.

[54] Ralph Turner, 'The Origins of Common Pleas and King's Bench' (1977) 21 *American Journal of Legal History* 238, 251.

[55] Walter Ullmann, *A History of Political Thought: The Middle Ages* (Harmondsworth, Penguin Books, 1965) 151.

Magna Carta was not actually a singular or stable document. Indeed, the first Magna Carta was not a success. Within three months of its issue, the charter was annulled by Pope Innocent III at John's request. John's death in October 1216 – perhaps from eating a 'surfeit of peaches' – was not the end of the matter. In November, the guardians of Henry III, John's nine-year-old son, reissued Magna Carta. It was reissued for a second time in 1217 and a third time in 1225.

Later generations of lawyers considered the 1225 issue to be the definitive one. Magna Carta was first placed on the English statute books in 1297 during Edward I's reign. There are textual differences between these different incarnations. Nor was the Magna Carta a stand-alone item as the Charter of the Forest issued in 1217, at times called the 'Great Charter', contained clauses on the administration of royal forests once contained in the Magna Carta.

Pause for Thought

Modern Significance of the Magna Carta

The Magna Carta's 800th birthday was widely celebrated in 2015.

Why do you think Magna Carta has assumed such mythic status? Conduct research from relevant print and academic sources including the great quantity of speeches and commemorations made in 2015.

Questions to Consider

Read David Clark, 'The Icon of Liberty: The Status and Role of Magna Carta in Australian and New Zealand Law' (2000) 24 *Melbourne University Law Review* 866, and answer the following questions:

1. What reasons does Clark give for the frequent use of Magna Carta in Australian and New Zealand courts?
2. Do you agree with Clark that today Magna Carta has 'chiefly "sentimental value"', rather than practical use, for litigants and judges? Why or why not?

Further commentaries on the Magna Carta are available on the website.

In the Wake of Magna Carta

Thirteenth Century Law

The Magna Carta stands at the beginning of a century of astounding legal achievement, much of it associated with Edward I and brilliant legal minds of the time including Ralph Hengham CJCP. Edward I took direct and decisive intervention in the administration of justice. That included imposing ethical standards and dismissing judges from the King's

Bench and Common Pleas who did not meet these standards. One of the dismissed judges, Hengham, was compelled to pay a major fine. From the reign of Henry II, many of the judges were laymen. In Edward I's reign, a recognisably professional body of men formed the nucleus of judicial appointments with the judiciary taken from the ranks of serjeants (see chapter two).[56]

Historical Cameo

King Edward I

King Edward I (reigned 1272–1307), known for subduing Wales and Scotland, was a superb administrator. He brought remarkable order and stability to the Government and legal structures of England. Modern audiences may be familiar with Edward I as the antagonist in Mel Gibson's 1995 film *Braveheart*. As with other kings who were constantly engaged in war, Edward needed to raise money by taxation. If the king wanted money over and above what he could get through the incidents of tenure, cl 14 of Magna Carta required him to summon the archbishops, bishops, abbots, earls, greater barons and those who held land directly from the Crown. These formed different councils and 'parliaments' – forums for speaking. To raise money, Edward summoned parliaments regularly. In 1295, in addition to the prelates (archbishops, bishops and abbots) and magnates (earls and barons), Edward summoned two knights from every shire and two representatives from every borough. This 'Model Parliament' comprised the prelates, magnates and commoners (knights and burgesses). By the mid-1300s, these groups had formed two 'Houses' of Parliament comprising three estates – the House of Lords (the estates of prelates [or bishops and senior abbots] and magnates) and the estate of the burgesses who sat in the House of Commons.

Edward used Parliament for law reform – the first use of statute in a significant way to change the common law and customs of the realm. These statutes all relate to landholding. Remember, the law of landholding determined how the kingdom was governed. They include:

- The *First Statute of Westminster 1275* (Eng)[57] which (in a section now replaced) defined 'time immemorial' as 6 July 1189 – the beginning of Richard I Lionheart's reign. If land had been held in possession since 'time immemorial' there was no need to prove the original grant of title to it. It reads in part: 'That the Will of the Giver, according to the Form in the Deed of Gift manifestly expressed, shall be from henceforth observed; so that they to whom the Land was given under such Condition, shall have no Power to aliene the Land so given, but that it shall remain unto the Issue of them to whom it was given after their Death, or [shall revert] unto the Giver or his Heirs, if Issue fail.'

[56] See ch two of this volume.
[57] 3 Edw 1, c 5.

- The *Statute of Mortmain 1279* (Eng) and the *Statute of Mortmain 1290* (Eng) (now repealed) prohibited donations of land to the church (with church ownership likened to a 'dead hand' or mortmain). Once land was held by the church, it would escape feudal tenures (like knight service or socage) and levies of tax. These statutes were effectively designed to maintain the kingdom's revenue and the resources available to the king for government and warfare.
- The *Second Statute of Westminster 1285* (Eng), also known as *De Donis Conditionalibus*. This provided that if an estate in land had been granted to a man and his heirs (this was called a 'fee tail' or an entailed estate), the current holder of the estate could not sell it and it had to pass to any male heir.
- *Quia Emptores 1290* (Eng), which addressed 'subinfeudation'. The statute prohibited landholders from creating new feudal obligations when passing land to another, and required anyone who wanted to pass land to another to do so by 'substitution', meaning by selling it. So, before *Quia Emptores*, the original landholder would (by subinfeudation) receive an 'incident of tenure' such as knight service or serjeanty when passing land to another. After *Quia Emptores*, he would (by substitution) get money for it either by selling the land or leasing it for rent. *Quia Emptores* is therefore seen as contributing to the decline of feudalism.

Edward's personal intervention in a rape plea was noted at the beginning of this chapter; it is not alone in showing his direct involvement with the law. Most drastic was his purge of his ministers and judges following an inquiry into their misdeeds. Many judges were fined. One of his officials, the escheator Henry de Bray, was so desperate to evade the king's justice that he tried to kill himself twice, first by trying to drown himself and then by trying to bash out his brains against a stone wall!

From the Middle Ages to *Mabo*

The Magna Carta resounds through legal history around the world. In the thirteenth, fourteenth and fifteenth centuries large bodies of jurisprudential readings and interpretations on and of the Charter appeared. Its clauses were the staple of the teaching in the Inns of Court. The Charter was of exceptional importance during constitutional conflicts in the seventeenth century. King Charles I tried to dampen down an angry parliament by promising to reconfirm the Magna Carta and its clauses.[58] Sir Edward Coke – discussed throughout this text – used the Charter as a means to enshrine *habeas corpus*.

Parts of this extraordinary document remain law in Australia. It has withstood attempts to remove it entirely from the British statute books – and its 800th anniversary in 2015 was the subject of global celebrations. In terms of relevance, if not practical utility, it remains a supercharged and compelling aspect of the legal past and the legal present. Magna Carta, on the English statute book as *Magna Carta 1297*[59] is substantive law in some parts of Australia

[58] See ch three of this volume.
[59] 25 Edw 1, c 29.

and received law in New South Wales,[60] Victoria,[61] the Australian Capital Territory,[62] and **Queensland**.[63] So too are other major historic Acts including those shown in Fig 1.4:

Figure 1.4 Historic Acts Part of Australian State and Federal Law

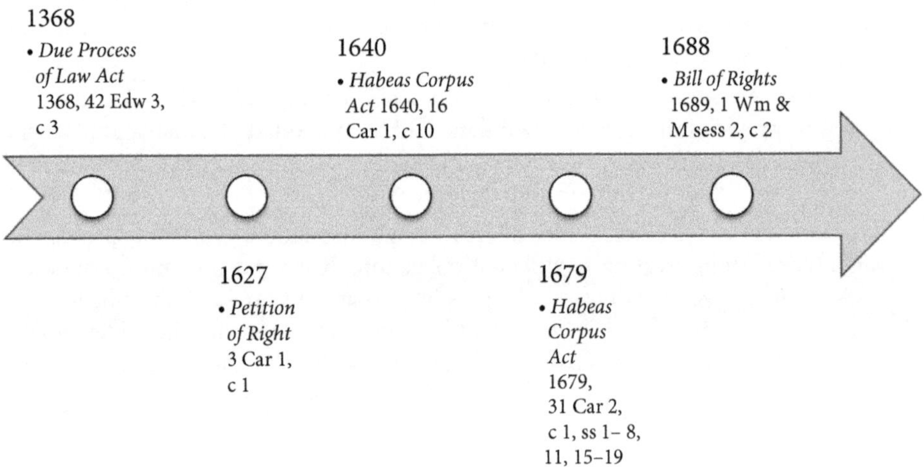

These ancient enactments are still necessary. They comprise the foundations of what are now considered the 'birthright' to a fair trial by due process. In some cases, their importance is far more than symbolic. The *Bill of Rights*, for example, governs the terms upon which the armed forces serve and members of parliament enjoy parliamentary privileges.

A copy of the Magna Carta from 1297 is permanently on display in Parliament House in Canberra. It is undoubtedly the most important medieval document in the southern hemisphere. In Australia, the Indigenous poet Oodgeroo Noonuccal wrote 'the Aboriginal Charter of Rights' in 1962 to articulate the political and social needs of Indigenous Australians. Once more, the idea of a 'charter' is employed to embrace these key rights.

The legal fiction of *terra nullius*, land without a master or an owner, appears through Australian legal history as a means for the settlement of Australia in the eighteenth century. The notion of masterless land is not distinctive to Australia. Borderlands or marches between kingdoms were considered *terra nullius*, including the marches between England and Wales. The intersections among these are sites of important development in international law.[64] Edward Koike (Eddie) Mabo is justifiably one of the most important figures in Australian legal history. His place in Australian legal history intersects with medieval

[60] *Imperial Acts Application Act 1969* (NSW).
[61] *Imperial Acts Application Act 1980* (Vic).
[62] *Legislation Act 2001* (ACT) s 17(2).
[63] *Imperial Acts Application Act 1984* (Qld) sch 1. See also Steven Rares, 'Why Magna Carta Still Matters' (*Judicial Conference of Australia Colloquium*, 9 October 2015), available at www.fedcourt.gov.au/digital-law-library/judges-speeches/justice-rares/rares-j-20151009#_ftn5.
[64] Sybil M Jack, 'The "Debatable Lands", Terra Nullius, and Natural Law in the Sixteenth Century' (2004) 41 *Northern History* 289, 293.

English law on land tenure. His long campaigns relating to the claim to land in the Torres Strait are discussed in chapter 12, but this history belongs aside medieval English law. Landmark native title cases heard in the High Court, such as *Mabo v Queensland (No 2)*[65] and *Wik Peoples v Queensland*,[66] cannot be understood without an understanding of feudal land tenure transmitted from medieval England to colonial Australia. The academic literature on native title resounds with references to feudalism, fee simple, and seisin as explanations of crown ownership. Literature even notes that Mabo prompted the re-emergence of feudalism in Australian law.[67] Fee simple is essential to understanding the circumstances in which native title is or is not extinguished. Core aspects of medieval land law frame the lengthy ruling by the High Court judges, from escheat to allodial title, and the ruling famously to a

> basic doctrine of the land law is the doctrine of tenure, to which Stephen CJ referred in *Attorney-General v Brown*,[68] and it is a doctrine which could not be overturned without fracturing the skeleton which gives our land law its shape and consistency. It is derived from feudal origins.[69]

Conclusion

This chapter has examined the emergence of common law doctrines and legal machinery before and after the Norman Conquest. Throughout, the intersection between past and present has been apparent, including the importance of understanding feudal land tenure law as background to native title in Australian law and the continuing importance, both actual and symbolic, of the Magna Carta. Major personalities, the impact of kings, the government officials and departments and the historical backgrounds that explain the experiences of justice have all featured. In the next chapter, much focus will be on and at Westminster Hall and the judges, serjeants, benchers, students and clerks working there. The actions they initiated, the laws they upheld and the education they received will all receive attention.

[65] (1992) 175 CLR 1.

[66] (1996) 187 CLR 1.

[67] Michael Stuckey, 'Feudalism and Australian Land Law: A Shadowy, Ghostlike Survival' (1994) 13 *University of Tasmania Law Review* 102; Samantha Hepburn, 'Feudal Tenure and Native Title: Revising an Enduring Fiction' (2005) 27 *Sydney Law Review* 49, 51.

[68] [1847] 1 Legge 312.

[69] *Mabo* (n 65) 47.

2

The Intellectual Life of the Law and Lawyers from the Middle Ages to Edward Coke

Introduction

This chapter examines institutional and intellectual developments in the English legal system: the jurisdiction of royal courts, membership of the legal profession, legal education, and the evolution of law reporting from the medieval period into the Tudor era (1485–1603). From time to time, the chapter breaks its historical chronology because study of the emergence of a recognisable legal profession does beg the question of women's involvement. The special topic of women and the law is therefore included in this chapter. Once excluded from legal practice by virtue of sex, women now comprise more than half of the legal profession in Australia. Considering this more modern development against the historical contours of the education of the legal profession and the profession's sense of self-identity is a stimulating and thought-provoking way to understand this history. The focus on institutions does not obscure the vivid personalities of the medieval people making legal history. Judges such as Sir William Bereford (d 1326) and Sir Edward Coke (1552–1634), steeped in the law, made shrewd judgments showing their organic intersection with actions and rules. Where chapter one focused on property law, much of this discussion sits in the domain of the history of contract law. It will also introduce crime and tort.

Learning Resources

The content in this chapter is supported by:

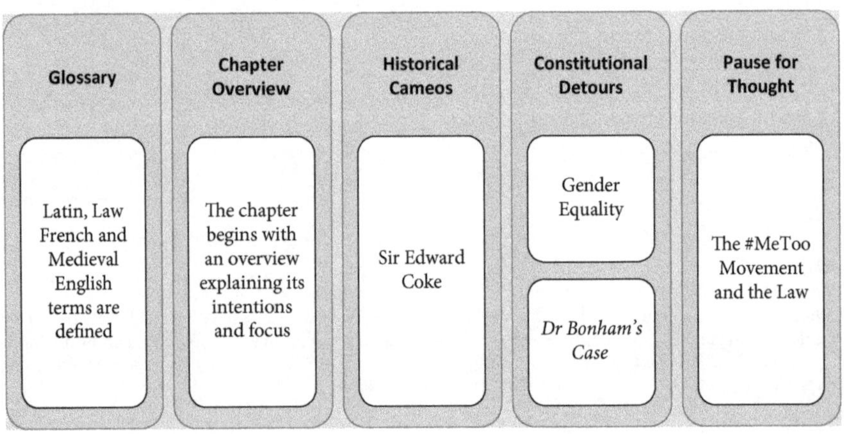

Chapter Overview

Place	Time Period	Dates
• Kingdom of England	• Late Medieval • Tudor and Stuart dynasties	• 14th–17th centuries

Key Figures	Key Institutions	Key Terms and Cases
• Edward I • Ralph Hengham • Sir William Bereford • Sir William Shareshull • James VI and I • Sir Edward Coke	• Inns of Court • King's Bench • Common Pleas • Court of Exchequer Chamber	• Tort • Crime • *Humber Ferry Case* • Trespass and trespass on the case • Assumpsit • *Dr Bonham's Case* • *Slade's Case*

Learning Outcomes

At the end of this chapter, readers should understand:

- The common law courts as the sites of activity for the legal profession and the forms of actions used in them, particularly trespass, trespass on the case and assumpsit.
- The interaction between court of equity or conscience and the common law courts.
- The nature of medieval and early modern legal education at the Inns of Court and the two universities.
- The growth of the legal profession, including its ranks and education.
- Historical influences on the participation of women in the law.
- Artificial reason as a way that legal expertise and professional identity was conceptualised and turned into a rhetorical argument.
- Precedent, law reporting and judicial review.

The Crown and the Courts

Developments of legal mechanisms and infrastructure took place over multiple centuries after the Norman Conquest (1066). The machinery of justice emerges, including the courts, writs, oaths and juries. Local courts included the manorial, the local and church courts (notably the Archdeacons' Courts, discussed in chapter three). The intersection of central and regional emerged through the sheriff; the writs were sent to him and his staff of clerks, retainers and receivers.[1] The royal or central courts included the King's Bench, the Common Pleas, and the Exchequer. No court of appeal existed. However, the Court of Exchequer Chamber (not to be confused with the Exchequer) could review decisions, doing so in major cases such as *Shelley's Case*[2] and *Sutton's Hospital Case*.[3] *Sutton's Hospital Case* required referral to all 12 common law judges. The Court of Exchequer Chamber had medieval origins and a firm statutory basis from 1585 onwards.[4] Earlier, complex cases may have gone up to the king and his council, or the case might simply have ended with all parties dismissed.[5]

To his subjects, the king was the fountain of justice, and kings did intervene in the administration of justice. Chapter one studied Henry II, who energetically intervened in the law. Later, the so-called 'English Justinian', Edward I (r 1272–1307), took an active interest in the law. Edward had a strong chief justice, Ralph Hengham (1235–1311), yet still purged his own judiciary for corruption during a large-scale review of his officers of state, including Hengham. Hengham was far from being the only justice with complaints against him.[6] In 1341, Edward III had his own judicial purge, including Sir Richard de Willoughby CJKB.[7]

The courts of medieval England encountered in chapter one included both itinerant and settled courts. The itinerant eyres heard business on commission of *omnia placita*, including cases relating to crime, the royal finances, robbery, murder, or sheriffs' illegally obtained profits.[8] There are records from 1130 of the eyres in operation.[9] The number of eyres increased in 1176 with the Assize of Northampton ordering the creation of six circuits issuing.[10] Three judges itinerated on each circuit, prompting a 'flurry of judicial activity'.[11]

The eyres brought the king's justice into the counties and shires. They frightened people as judges appeared in their midst with the book of death.[12] When the eyre's personnel arrived, they would send a writ of summons to the reeve and four men from every village in the district, 12 burgesses from every town, the free tenants, and the senior clergy.[13] They also collected significant profits.[14] Many English kings were warriors and waged war against

[1] Ernest Jacob, *The Fifteenth Century 1399–1485* (Oxford, Oxford University Press, 1993) 451.

[2] *Wolfe v Shelley* (1581) 1 Co Rep 93b, 76 ER 206 (CP).

[3] (1612) 10 Co Rep 23a, 77 ER 960.

[4] 27 Eliz 1, c 8.

[5] Donald W Sutherland, *Quo Warranto Proceedings in the Reign of Edward I 1278–1294* (Oxford, Clarendon Press, 1963) 180.

[6] Paul Brand, 'Ethical Standards for Royal Justices in England, c 1175–1307' (2001) 8(2) *University of Chicago Law School Roundtable* 239, 252.

[7] David Crook, 'The Disgrace of Sir Richard de Willoughby, Chief Justice of King's Bench' (2004) 48 *Nottingham Medieval Studies* 15.

[8] Bruce Lyon, *A Legal and Constitutional History of England* (New York, WW Norton, 1980) 445.

[9] Doris M Stenton, *English Justice Between the Norman Conquest and the Great Charter 1066–1215* (London, George Allen and Unwin, 1965) 65.

[10] Joseph Biancalana, 'For Want of Justice: Legal Reforms of Henry II' (1988) 88 *Columbia Law Review* 433, 484.

[11] J Enoch Powell and Keith Wallis, *The House of Lords in the Middle Ages: A History of the House of Lords to 1540* (London, Weidenfeld and Nicolson, 1968) 86; Robert Bartlett, *Trial of Fire and Water: The Medieval Judicial Ordeal* (Brattleboro, Vermont, Echo Point Books and Media, 1986) 67.

[12] Theodore Plucknett, *A Concise History of the Common Law* (Union, New Jersey, The Lawbook Exchange, 2001) 145.

[13] Paul Brand, *Kings, Barons and Justices: The Making and Enforcement of Legislation in Thirteenth-Century England* (Cambridge, Cambridge University Press, 2003) 91.

[14] Frederick Pollock and Frederic William Maitland, *The History of English Law before the Time of Edward I* (Clark, New Jersey, Lawbook Exchange, 2013) vol 1, 147.

multiple domestic and foreign enemies. The administration of justice, for example, assisted Edward I to recoup the cost of wars by amercing (or fining) hundreds or counties.[15] Edward I embarked on large scale and ambitious judicial activity, including sending eyres on northern and southern circuits from 1278 onwards, implementing articles of inquiry into the King's rights and franchises.[16]

The eyres were not the totality of available justice. The petty assizes meant routine criminal cases did not have to go to the central courts.[17] Commissions included the assizes of novel disseisin, mort d'ancestor and darrein presentment, which would concern cases related to possession and title of land or, in the case of darrein presentment, a Church benefice. Novel (as in recent) disseisin meant trying title to land,[18] as in possessory actions.[19] Commissions of trailbaston commenced in 1305 with the commissioners on circuit empowered to hold assizes.[20] Trailbaston itself referred to a type of outlawry by bands of armed men in the countryside.[21] The eyres were part of a wider legal fabric concerned with maintaining or in some instances restoring law and order throughout the kingdom in the earlier fourteenth century.[22] These commissions return attention to the reign of Henry II and the development of land law writs during his reign. These writs, and the legal actions that ensued because of them, were not necessarily anti-feudal (as in the king disrupting the legal relationship between lords and their vassals) but they did regulate seigniorial relationships.

Eventually other actions became triable before the assizes, so parties did not have to make the trip to Westminster Hall.[23] A case could be at Westminster unless (the Latin term for that opportunity is *nisi prius*) it was before the date the assizes would arrive.[24] A machinery of justice emerged and settled, involving jurors and judges. The Quarter Sessions could not try a person accused of a felony but *presentments* at the Quarter Sessions could enable investigation. From presentment, a person could be indicted at the assizes. When the judges of the assizes arrived in town, a Grand Jury took an oath to tell the truth ('*jeo verite dirrai*') and looked at each presentment, to make one of two declarations: the grand jurors could declare themselves '*ignoramus*' (meaning 'we do not know' in Latin), or else they could decide it was a true bill, and then the presentment became an indictment.[25] Another change was that the Grand Jury gave way to the petty jury. The petty jurors may have needed good memories and lots of stamina as the court would try multiple people one after another, and

[15] Plucknett (n 12) 145.

[16] Sutherland (n 5) 28.

[17] Sir John Baker, *An Introduction to English Legal History*, 4th edn (London, LexisNexis Butterworths, 2002) 20.

[18] Morris S Arnold, 'Law and Fact in the Medieval Jury Trial: Out of Sight, Out of Mind' (1974) 18(4) *American Journal of Legal History* 268; Baker (n 17) 233.

[19] David J Seipp, 'Bracton, the Year Books, and the "Transformation of Elementary Legal Ideas" in the Early Common Law' (1989) 7(1) *Law and History Review* 181.

[20] Ralph Bernard Pugh, *Wiltshire Gaol Delivery and Trailbaston Trials, 1275–1306* (Wiltshire Record Society, 1978) 6; Edward Coke, *The Fourth Part of the Institutes of the Laws of England: Concerning the Jurisdiction of Courts* (London, E and R Brooke, 1797) 185.

[21] Luke Owen Pike, *A History of Crime in England: Illustrating the Changes of the Laws in the Progress of Civilisation*, vol 1 (London, Smith, Elder & Company, 1873) 222; Colin Platt, *Medieval England: A Social History and Archaeology from the Conquest to AD 1600* (London, Routledge and Kegan Paul, 1978) 109.

[22] Helen M Cam, 'The General Eyres of 1329–30' (1924) 39(154) *The English Historical Review* 241, 243–44.

[23] Lyon (n 8) 446.

[24] Sir John Baker, *A History of English Assizes 1558–1714* (Cambridge, Cambridge University Press, 1972) 140.

[25] Baker (n 17) 505; Paul Brand, 'Judges and Juries in Civil Litigation in Later Medieval England: The Millon Thesis Reconsidered' (2016) 37(1) *The Journal of Legal History* 1, 9.

the jurors then retired to consider verdicts for all of them.[26] Judges may also have loaded jurors into a wagon and carried them about the countryside!

The King's Judges

After the jurors gave a verdict, the judge would sentence the person. There were 12 common law judges, four a piece for King's Bench, Common Pleas and Exchequer. This professional tier was not static in character or identity. The nature and background of the judicial personnel changed over time, especially as men who were clerks in holy orders gradually ceased to sit as judges. The earliest justiciars came from the ranks of bishops and abbots, including Roger of Salisbury (d 1139), the Bishop of Salisbury.[27] The reign of Henry II is important for the increasing use of professionalised officials who were themselves keeping or causing to have kept written records. Henry II's sons, Richard I and John, maintained a group of about 90 judges in Westminster or as itinerant justices.[28]

By about 1194, records indicate a consistent group of men sitting as judges, not as financial officials, and their presence and demarcated legal role separate from financial functions indicate the different branches of the King's government were separating into coherent bodies. The intersection between the judiciary and the episcopate (the bishops) begins to separate as well. The Lateran Council of 1279 – a council of the Western Church presided over by the pope – mandated that clergy should not sit as judges unless the issues concerned religion, and Church authorities remained uneasy at clerical involvement in the law as priests should not shed blood, even indirectly by passing sentence.

This professional class of judges had relationships to king and patrons, sometimes in unexpected ways. For example, Richard of Herriard (d 1208) paid the royal prostitutes.[29] Judges became intrinsic to the governance of medieval England. As an example, the career of Sir William Bereford (d 1326) included being a justice of the eyres, the Chief Justice of Common Pleas but also being of service to parliament, a member of legal and political commissions, and a member of a panel of negotiators with the Scottish kingdom.[30]

Judges could act as legal consultants and organisations such as monasteries found it a good strategy to have a judge as a consultant. Gilbert of Rothbury (c 1260–1321) was patronised by religious houses to protect their interests.[31] It was noted earlier that Edward I purged his Chief Justice, Sir Ralph Hengham CJKB, for corruption. Hengham's career, which traversed both professional esteem and disgrace, is instructive for showing the fine line judges walked between corruption and normal practice. Hengham's practice of seeking fees survives on record, showing him speaking in terms reminiscent of a supermodel

[26] Alan MacFarlane, *Witchcraft in Tudor and Stuart England: A Regional and Comparative Study* (London, Routledge, 1999) 23–24.

[27] John Gillingham, 'The Historian as Judge: William of Newburgh and Hubert Walter' (2004) 119(484) *English Historical Review* 1276.

[28] Ralph V Turner, 'Simon of Pattishall, Pioneer Professional Judge' (1977) 9(2) *Albion: A Quarterly Journal Concerned with British Studies* 115.

[29] Ralph V Turner, 'The Judges of King John: Their Background and Training' (1976) 51(3) *Speculum* 460.

[30] William Craddock Bolland, *Chief Justice Sir William Bereford: A Lecture Delivered in the University of London at the Request of the Faculty of Laws* (Cambridge, Cambridge University Press, 1924) 6.

[31] Ryan Rowberry, '*The Social Status, Education, and Benefices of Gilbert Rothbury, a Clerical Common Law Justice (1295–1321)*' (2015) 15(453) *Monumenta Iuris Canonici* 14.

who would not get out of bed for less than $10,000 a day. Hengham checked how much his fee for legal service would be and, finding the amount paltry, he said he would not even be bothered getting up and leaving his house for such a small amount.[32]

Hengham was not alone in having a handful of bribes.[33] In 1350 William de Thorpe CJKB (d 1361) was accused of receiving gifts.[34] There is also a lurid religious vision of the judge Osbert fitz Hervey (d 1206) being in hell and being forced to eat burning coins while a wheel was run down his back until he vomited the coins up again.[35] However, judges were also mindful of their dignity. On its journeys around England, the King's Bench had visited Ipswich (a town in Suffolk) in 1344. After the judges left, disturbing rumours reached them that local 'evildoers' had publicly mocked the judges, holding a kind of folk court and naming the judges (among them William of Shareshill and William of Notton) to appear before their 'court' and pay large fines. Neither the King nor his judges were amused, describing it as '*in contemptum domini regis et in derisionem prefatorum iusticiariorum et ministrorum domini regis ei deseruiencium*', or in contempt of the King and the judges and ministers serving him. Retribution was swift against the town bailiffs who had failed to keep order.[36]

Although the line blurred between the acceptable and the disgraceful, the medieval judiciary also shows there was a career trajectory for ambitious lawyers. The pleaders in the Year Books appear in later volumes as judges, indicating their professional advance. By the fourteenth century, judges came from the ranks of the serjeants (of whom more below).[37] Judges' clerks could become judges in time having gained professional experience. Judges recognised their own professional expertise and their role in shaping law. One of the most emphatic statements of this self-identity comes from Hengham, who once interrupted an advocate to bellow 'do not gloss the statute, we understand it better than you do, for we made it'.[38] Judges also gained social status, externally signified by them receiving a knighthood and their robes, provided as perquisites ('perks').[39] When they died, substantial tombs and tomb brasses memorialised their names, appearance and garb.[40]

The personalities of medieval judges stand out in the records, especially in the Year Books, including when they disagreed with each other. In 1313, in Common Pleas, Justices Scrope and Bereford came to different interpretations of the *Statute of Marlborough 1267*[41] in an embezzlement case. The account records them splitting legal hairs on the exact wording of the statute as to whether the defendant simply needed to own land in general or own a specific amount of land to be exempt from arrest.[42] The Year Books show Bereford and other

[32] George Sayles, 'Medieval Judges as Legal Consultants,' (1940) 56(2) *Law Quarterly Review* 247, 250.

[33] Ralph V Turner, 'The Reputation of Royal Judges under the Angevin Kings' (1979) 11(4) *Albion: A Quarterly Journal Concerned with British Studies* 304.

[34] Bertha Haven Putnam, 'Chief Justice Shareshull and the Economic and Legal Codes of 1351–1352' (1944) 5(2) *University of Toronto Law Journal* 251, 252.

[35] Turner (n 33) 306.

[36] George Sayles (ed), *Select Cases in the Court of King's Bench under Edward III* (London, Selden Society 1965) vol 6, 37.

[37] Turner (n 29) 458.

[38] Theodore FT Plucknett, *Statutes and Their Interpretation in the First Half of the Fourteenth Century* (Cambridge, Cambridge University Press, 2013) 95.

[39] Frederick Bernays Wiener, 'Tracing the Origins of the Court of King's Bench' (1973) 59(7) *American Bar Association Journal* 756.

[40] Sir John Baker, 'A History of English Judges' Robes' (1978) 12(1) *Costume* 27.

[41] 52 Hen 3.

[42] William Craddock Bolland, *Year Books of 7 Edward II (1313–1314)* (London, Selden Society, 1922) 9; Thomas Lund, *The Creation of the Common Law: The Medieval Year Books Deciphered* (Clark, New Jersey, Talbot Publishing, 2015) 38.

judges as lively and involved participants in making the law and issuing sharp demands to the participants.[43] In *Ferlington v Fleming*, Bereford sharply told the participants to go outside, get their story straight, and not to come back until they had.[44] In *Shrewsbury v Shrewsbury*, he tersely demanded answers in a case brought with a writ of nuisance.[45]

The Year Books preserve the technically astute points judges introduced to their courts, including directly disagreeing with the litigants. They were willing to innovate and did not necessarily view law as merely declarative or giving voice to what already existed.[46] In a case about land, Bereford heard arguments about rent, but did not like what he heard and told the court '*Noun pas par mesme la reson mesqe eide dust estre grante, mes respoundez outre*', therefore not only laying down the law but demanding a further response.[47] Throughout the Year Books, judges like Bereford appear to be demanding variously that people speak up, be quiet, get their thoughts in order and work out what they want to plea, issuing these demands in sharp retorts. Some of his comments, even without full context, give a flavour of how his personality and sharpness drove the action in his court: 'There are various ways of pleading, either as patron or as prebendary; and therefore, tell us how you plead, either as patron or prebendary', 'Did he not say to you that the tenements are out of your fee … therefore answer'.[48] The judges, Bereford included, were also masters of procedure and could advise plaintiffs and defendants, suggest actions, and decide when an action was inappropriate; whether to use a writ of covenant, a writ of mesne, whether a person's age was a factor, who could or could not come into court, and more. These were all issues judges like Bereford could decide in an instant based on their living, breathing knowledge of the law. As he said of one highly involved technicality, whether a woman could 'deraign the acquittance', Bereford found his experience provided the answer was to use a writ of mesne, for 'we have seen that here half a score of times'.[49] Again, even without context, Bereford's sharp mind stands forth clearly in the comments recorded in the Year Books:

> In such a case you will not obtain a writ of execution without alleging the right to present, for the fine was levied upon a writ of warantia cartae, and it supposes that the person to whom the right is confessed is seised.[50]

Forms of Action and Types of Court

The original writ returnable before courts and judges defined the course of the common law. At first, the original writ was an official document under the King's seal issued out of the Chancery, presided over by the Lord Chancellor. To commence action in the royal courts,

[43] William D Riter, 'Westminster Hall: A Retrospect,' (1913) 47(4) *American Law Review* 544.

[44] George Turner, *Year Books of Edward II, 4 Edward II* (London, Selden Society, 1914) vol 6, 86.

[45] *Ibid* 93. Morris S Arnold, 'Statutes as Judgments: The Natural Law Theory of Parliamentary Activity in Medieval England' (1977) 126(2) *University of Pennsylvania Law Review* 333–34.

[46] See following sections on forms of action.

[47] Samuel Stoljar and Leslie Downer (eds), *Year Books of Edward II Michaelmas 1320* (London, Selden Society, 1988) 70.

[48] *Ibid* 58.

[49] Turner (n 44) 102.

[50] Frederic William Maitland (ed), *Year Books of 1 and 2 Edward II (1307–1308 and 1308–1309)* (London, Selden Society, 1903) 8.

a complainant paid for a writ from the Chancery. The writ commanded the local sheriff to summon the defendant to appear before the King's justices to answer the plaintiff's claim.

The number of writs issued enlarged throughout the twelfth and thirteenth centuries to such a degree that the Provisions of Oxford 1258 limited Chancery's ability to issue new writs. The original writs were kept in a collection compiled by Chancery clerks: the Register of Writs. By the sixteenth century, there were 321 folios or pages of original writs in the Register, which was an organic document, growing as the common law evolved. Medieval law students learnt the original writs by rote; choosing a writ to govern a claim could be fraught with danger. Royal justice was available to plaintiffs only if the claim was actionable in the common law courts. Either an existing writ described the plaintiff's claim, or the plaintiff had managed to convince Chancery to create a new writ. The original writ governed the procedures and methods of trial for the litigation. If the plaintiff chose the wrong writ, the whole matter could be thrown out of court.

Jurisdiction of the Royal Courts

Royal justice was initially 'exceptional'. Before common law courts gained dominance over local courts, litigants had an ordinary 'right' to be heard in ordinary courts: the local courts and at the itinerant eyres. Local courts included county, hundred, seigniorial, manorial and borough courts. Seigniorial and manorial courts had jurisdiction over defendants who were their tenants or vassals.

Actions in ordinary courts commenced by simple complaint. The plaintiff – the person who brought the action – had to give **'security'** before the defendant – the person against whom the action was brought – could be summoned by the court. That means that the plaintiff had to lodge money in court (like a bond) to ensure that, if the plaintiff lost, there would be money to pay the costs the defendant wrongly suffered by having to appear in court. We see a reflection of this practice in court rules today.

The pattern for commencing an action in court started with the plaintiff stating his claim and the defendant denying each allegation one after the other. Following the denial, the issue was decided by the method of proof chosen. Three methods of proof were:

1. Wager of battle: trial by combat.
2. Compurgation: taking oaths and having witnesses take oaths.
3. Ordeal: a procedure believed to show the judgment of God. It was less often used in England and disappeared in the early 1200s, especially following objections at the Lateran Council of 1215. Before then, ordeal by water might be used for various crimes including theft or murder. This involved throwing the accused in a river; if he sank, he was innocent. Alternatively, the accused would plunge his hand into a cauldron of hot water or hold a hot iron. The extent to which the injuries healed would be monitored.

Two features distinguished royal justice in common law courts from local courts. First, access to royal justice was possible for certain types of claims at a fee. Second, a new method of trial – the recognition or trial by jury – proved popular among litigants. A sheriff would summon people from the locality in which the dispute arose to give an answer to the action. The original writs were returnable before three courts administering royal justice: Court of Common Pleas, King's Bench and the Exchequer.

Figure 2.1 Common Law Courts' Jurisdictions and Personnel

	King's Bench	**Common Pleas**	**Exchequer**
Jurisdiction	• All crimes • Challenges to decisions of inferior courts • Civil actions against the king	Litigation involving land, and civil actions between subjects (the action does not involve the king)	Recovery of tax, and actions involving taxation officials
Personnel	Chief Justice supported by several puisne (pronounced 'puny') justices	Chief Justice supported by several puisne justices	Chief Baron and Barons

The Court of King's Bench meant the bench from which the King had once sat to dispense justice. As late as the reign of Richard III (1483–85), kings still sat on the King's Bench in person.[51] Whether physically present or not, the law presumed the King's legal presence on the King's Bench.[52] Its business centred on crime and the writ of trespass (more below), both of which generated little revenue. By 1420, the King's Bench had its permanent seat in Westminster Hall.[53] The courts were public and noisy. The Court of King's Bench, Court of Chancery and Court of Common Pleas were together; the Exchequer was nearby and there were even shops.[54] As legal historian John Baker described,

> Each court occupied a space marked out by a wooden bar at which counsel stood, and in the centre was a massive oak table covered with green cloth at which court officials sat and spread their records .... Until the 18th century there were no seats for counsel, nor any walls to divide courts from open thoroughfare; each court was scarcely out of earshot of the others, and speakers had to compete with the noise.[55]

People inside the Court would have heard the regular chimes of a bell in the clock tower outside – the medieval precursor of the Victorian clock tower housing the famous Big Ben – and noticed the time passing as the arguments ensued. The legal year was measured out by four law terms, Michaelmas, Hilary, Easter and Trinity. When Trinity term ended, and before the next Michaelmas, the commissions of assize set out.[56] The legal term was also measured by various saints' days and feast days. Year Books and records note the date and the passage of time as people must be in court by the 'quindene of Easter', 'the octaves of Michaelmas', 'Quinzaine of Trinity', and so forth.[57]

An active chief justice can still shape the character and impact of their court, as was the case with chief justices of the Middle Ages. Sir William Shareshull CJKB (1290–1370)

[51] Turner (n 44) xviii.

[52] Sir John Baker, *The Reinvention of Magna Carta* (Cambridge, Cambridge University Press, 2017) 167.

[53] Wiener (n 39) 757.

[54] Anthony Musson, 'Legal Landmarks: The Architecture of Justice in Late Medieval England' (2006) *Australia and New Zealand Law & History* 4.

[55] Baker (n 17).

[56] Robert C Palmer, 'County Year Book Reports: The Professional Lawyer in the Medieval County Court' (1976) 91(361) *English Historical Review* 776.

[57] Anthony Emery, *Greater Medieval Houses of England and Wales, 1300–1500: Volume 3, Southern England* (Cambridge, Cambridge University Press, 2006) 255; Susanne Jenks, 'Bill Litigation and the Observance of Sundays and Major Festivals in the Court of King's Bench in the Fifteenth Century' (2004) 22(3) *Law and History Review* 619.

presided over the bench as the eyres were slowly dying out. The King's Bench sat at more frequent intervals than the seven-year intervals between eyres. Shareshull made the King's Bench an important site for definitions for crimes and felonies.[58]

The King's Bench sat at Westminster Hall and travelled itinerantly. When the King's Bench arrived in a town, the lower courts ceased operating; they received a general writ and obeyed its order to send their own papers up to the King's Bench.[59] While criminal cases could be initiated before itinerant justices, the arrival of the King's Bench made it the Court of First Instance.[60] The King's Bench could be a deterrent to local disorder[61] and, like the eyres, it frightened people. The King's Bench also supervised challenges to decisions of inferior courts. For example, the King's Bench could override decisions of the Court of Common Pleas. The King's Bench had jurisdiction over lower courts when the correctness of decision was in doubt, a jurisdiction driven by a writ of error. The writs of ***mandamus*** or ***certiorari*** removed cases into the King's Bench for this purpose. Processes existed for when people resisted legal proceedings and bailiffs would follow up on and enforce royal orders.[62]

> Writ of *certiorari* (Latin): prerogative writ for a higher court to review the decision of a lower court

> Writ of *mandamus* (Latin): prerogative writ ordering a case from a lower court to a higher court

Until the King's Bench took over some of its business, the Court of Common Pleas was the busiest common law court due to its exclusive jurisdiction over land and debt. The Court heard pleas between ordinary subjects. The Court of Common Pleas' high volume of land and debt actions generated revenue when judges did not receive a salary. That reality – the amount of money going into the judges' pockets – drove the creative and determined use of a **legal fiction** that enabled the King's Bench to take over business from the Court of Common Pleas by introducing novel plaintiff-friendly procedures: the bill and the Bill of Middlesex.

> Legal fiction: allows a court to achieve an outcome

The bill removed the need for a writ that was still required in the Court of Common Pleas. A plaintiff no longer had to bother with the purchase of an expensive writ from Chancery. The second procedure, the Bill of Middlesex, had the plaintiff alleging that a fictitious trespass had occurred in the County of Middlesex – the area around the cities of Westminster and London. This meant that the King's Bench could arrest or bail the defendant because the King's Bench sat at Westminster. Middlesex too was the location of the King's Bench prison, the Marshalsea.[63] The sheriff of Middlesex was able to order the defendant's arrest and subsequent imprisonment in the Marshalsea.

If the court could not find the defendant, other procedures were put in motion to arrest the defendant and put him into the custody of the marshal. The plaintiff would respond that

[58] Bertha Haven Putnam, *The Place in Legal History of Sir William Shareshull: Chief Justice of the King's Bench 1350–1361* (Cambridge, Cambridge University Press, 2013) 111.

[59] Putnam (n 34) 268.

[60] Lyon (n 8) 443.

[61] Putnam (n 34) 269.

[62] Such as *R v Richard de Panes* KB 27/255, Rex m 15 (Coram Rege Roll, Hilary 1324 in Morris S Arnold, *Select Cases of Trespass from the King's Courts 1307–1399* (London, Selden Society, 1985) 63.

[63] Liron Shmilovits, 'Deus ex Machina: Legal Fictions in Private Law' (DPhil Thesis, University of Cambridge, 2019) 27.

the defendant was 'lurking and roaming about' in his home county; the lurking comes from the Latin name of the writ, *latitat*. The sheriff of that county would arrest the defendant. With the defendant in the Marshalsea, the plaintiff would abandon the fictional trespass and plead the actual cause of action.

The Court of Exchequer was the third common law court. It heard matters for the recovery of tax and actions involving taxation officials and placed the recovery of the King's debts before all others.[64] The Chief Baron and Barons were the personnel of Exchequer. The Court was originally housed in a special room at the Palace of Westminster which contained a table with chequer marking on it (hence 'exchequer') but later found itself adjacent to Westminster Hall. The Court of Exchequer had its own legal fiction to expand its caseload. Technically, the Exchequer heard cases involving the King's revenues. The writ of *quo minus* allowed a commoner to plead that part of his case involved the King. The claim was a legal fiction, but it allowed the Exchequer to hear the case.[65]

Why were there two principal common law courts, Common Pleas and King's Bench? Cases in the King's Bench were those involving the King's interests, based on the Court's connection with the royal council, with which it originally shared staff. The major actions were debt actions so what therefore happened in court in a case of debt? If the plaintiff possessed a written deed, the plaintiff (creditor) would likely prevail. If the plaintiff did not have such a deed, the action could be settled by wager of law involving oath helpers (the compurgators), who would likely endorse the blank denial by the defendant.[66] In the King's Bench, there was another option: actions for trespass involved trial by jury, a distinction explored next.

Being in a Medieval Court

These noisy, busy courts contained ordinary human beings, including plaintiffs who felt wronged and defendants called to defend themselves. To come into the King's Bench and Common Pleas normally required a writ from the Chancery, although judges in the King's Bench sometimes argued that a plaintiff did not need a writ for their court.[67] The writ characterised the wrong that they claimed had taken place.[68] The plea rolls and Year Books reveal an astonishing vista of the lives and concerns of the ordinary people of medieval England. A diversity of people and cases came before the judges. Some were simply weird, such as in the King's Bench in 1371 where a sorcerer had a dismembered head in a bag that he used for necromancy. According to the record,

> he says that the said head was the head of a Saracen and that he bought the head in Toledo, a certain city in Spain, in order to shut a spirit up in it so that the said spirit would answer questions, and that the book had to do only with experiments, and he had so far done nothing with the head.[69]

[64] Sybil M Jack, 'In Search of the Custom of the Exchequer' (1993) 11(2) *Parergon* 91.

[65] Harold Wurzel, 'The Origin and Development of Quo Minus' (1939) 49(1) *Yale Law Journal* 39.

[66] Daniel Klerman, 'Jurisdictional Competition and the Evolution of the Common Law' (2007) 74(4) *University of Chicago Law Review* 1191.

[67] Fredrick Maitland and George Turner (eds), *Year Books of 3 and 4 Edward II (1310)* (London, Selden Society 1907) 115.

[68] Thomas A Lund, 'Activist Judges of the Early Fourteenth Century' [2008] 2 *Utah Law Review* 471, 473.

[69] Sayles (n 36) 162–63.

The Court ordered that the head be disposed of.

The records of the central courts show different layers of society interacting with each other in lively and timeless ways. In 1308, a bailiff brought a writ of trespass against his master. It was possible for the man of lower status to bring this action in royal court, and force his master (or, in this case, a man the bailiff claimed was his former master) to defend himself. Actual personalities reveal themselves including the character of the judges. Bereford, the judge hearing the case between Simon of Paris (the bailiff) and Sir Robert Tony, made a dirty joke about a man in a brothel after hearing the arguments of both sides![70] That was not an isolated occasion. Bereford's predecessor John of Mettingham CJCB once used the following analogy in a case in 1296: 'You are like the young lady who took money to be fucked and later repented and said to the young man who had fucked her "dear sweet young man, take your money back and unfuck me because I repent"'. Bereford made a similar sort of comment, 'As the maiden said to the varlet that asked her were she a maid "Make trial! Make trial!"'.[71] Why speak in this way? The judge's analogies helped to explain the law and their decisions in the language of everyday life. They are not far removed from television judge Judy Scheindlin's legal logic: 'you ate the steak, you pay for the stake'.

There will have been a writ to initiate proceedings for hearing in a competent court. What happened next? The plaintiff may have wished to try for an action that avoided wager of law (compurgation). With that thought in mind, this section of the chapter will examine the possible actions, especially to recover damages.[72] It is important to note that actions to recover damages had not always existed; early plea rolls show compromises worked out rather than mobilising a specific action. Over centuries, actions developed in ways that marked a distinction between real actions and personal actions: real meaning the recovery of land, and personal meaning personal property or monetary damages.

Some of the personal common law actions that emerged during the Middle Ages included assumpsit, trover, trespass, covenant, debt and replevin. A plaintiff pursued an ***assumpsit*** to recover damages. Trover and trespass sit in tort law, not contract. Covenant and debt are actions pursued by a plaintiff wishing to recover an agreed sum.[73] For the action to be a covenant, the fixed sum needed to be under a seal.[74] Replevin, rather than seeking to recover monetary damages, recovers tangible property.[75] Trover will be encountered again in chapter four's discussion of slavery, as human slaves were deemed property.

Real actions included ejectment, summary proceedings to recover possession of lands, trespass on lands, nuisance, waste and foreclosures of mortgages. Finally, there are statutory remedies including contempt, *habeas corpus*, *quo warranto* (meaning 'by what warrant'), and *mandamus*. Much, but not all, of this terminology is still recognisable to a modern lawyer either in original form or a modern adaptation.

[70] Maitland (n 50) 11. A modern gloss is provided in Lund (n 42) 17.

[71] We owe this reference to Dr Paul Brand.

[72] George E Woodbine, 'The Origins of the Action of Trespass' (1924) 33(8) *Yale Law Journal* 802.

[73] Morris S Arnold, 'Fourteenth-Century Promises' (1976) 35(2) *Cambridge Law Journal* 322.

[74] David J Ibbetson, 'Words and Deeds: The Action of Covenant in the Reign of Edward I' (1986) 4(1) *Law and History Review* 79–80.

[75] Brand (n 13) 94, 98.

Trespass: The Versatile Action

Out of the long lists of actions above, two merit detailed discussion. The first is trespass; the word trespass coming from 'transgressio'. A plaintiff used a writ of trespass to claim someone had committed a positive wrong.[76] Specifically, the accusation against the defendant was of having broken the King's peace.[77] The writ of trespass then shaped what transpired. A law student will learn a tort is where one party has wronged or injured another party and then seeks civil damages; the law therefore can provide a remedy or restitution. A crime means the accused faces public prosecution. A crime has further meaning and elaboration with consideration of the criminal intent underpinning the criminal act, a notion known as the ***mens rea***.[78] An indictment and appeal of felony remedied a crime, and torts by bringing a writ of trespass.[79] Trespass and trespass on the case were torts arising from medieval English law. From where did they emerge?

> *Mens rea* (Latin): literally, the guilty mind

Earlier forms of action were covenant, debt, detinue, and account, originally limited to the jurisdictions of the smaller scale county courts.[80] Covenant, or its inherent limitations, shows how the actions expanded and stretched. An action of covenant was limited:[81] the plaintiff had to show something should have been performed as evidenced by a written deed. If there was no written deed, the defendant could use oath helpers (the compurgators) to swear the defendant had not agreed to have performed any undertaking. If covenant could not give a remedy, how else could the plaintiff obtain a remedy when someone had failed to do something and had, in addition, caused injury? Trespass was an option, but it required force of arms. To have a judge hear the case, the plaintiff traditionally needed to prove that the trespass had involved a force of arms.[82]

In the mid-fourteenth century, a type of trespass emerged in the Year Books and plea rolls that did not require force of arms or breach of peace: trespass on the case. In 1304, William Bereford heard a case in which the plaintiff brought a writ of trespass, claiming he had been beaten and wounded, a claim the defendants denied. The jury accepted the plaintiff had been imprisoned but not beaten up. Bereford ruled that 'he [the plaintiff] should recover his damages &c and that they [the defendants] should be taken'.[83] In other words, Bereford threatened to imprison the defendants unless they paid their fine, and had allowed the writ of trespass, even though violence had not been proven.[84] Yet in 1313, Bereford insisted that 'naught can be against the peace unless it be done by force' or, in plain English, 'the threat of violence is the reason the trespass writ allows the imprisonment of a defendant'.[85]

[76] Louis A Knafla, 'Conscience in the English Common Law Tradition' (1976) 26(1) *University of Toronto Law Journal* 1–16.
[77] Plucknett (n 12) 366.
[78] Baker (n 17) 523.
[79] David J Seipp, 'The Distinction between Crime and Tort in the Early Common Law' (1996) 76(1&2) *Boston University Law Review* 59.
[80] James Ames, 'Parol Contracts Prior to Assumpsit' (1894) 89 *Harvard Law Review* 258; Theodore FT Plucknett, 'New Light on the Old County Court' (1929) 42(5) *Harvard Law Review* 646.
[81] Knafla (n 76) 14.
[82] Putnam (n 34) 267.
[83] Alfred Horwood, *Year Books of the Reign of King Edward the First xxxii–xxxiii Part 4* (Rolls Series, London, Longmans, Green, Reader, and Dyker, 1864) 258.
[84] See Lund's gloss in *The Creation of the Common Law* (n 42) 32.
[85] Bolland (n 42) 14; Lund (n 42) 33.

The gradual, if not consistent, relaxing of the rule of proving force of arms is a procedural change. By the fourteenth century, courts admitted actions of trespass where there was no allegation of force and arms and thereby enlarged royal jurisdiction.[86] These developments point towards modern notions of negligence. Trespass on the case was a new type of liability. The key change is that the writ of trespass, originally, did not extend a liability to protect people and their property. Trespass on the case therefore is for protection where people had negligently carried out their promise or had done it badly.

> *Assumpsit* (Latin): he has undertaken

By the fifteenth century, writs started including the words *Assumpsit super se* indicating the claim that someone had undertaken to do something.[87] *Assumpsit* is a new action not involving breach of peace; the plaintiff seeks redress where something had *not* happened. *Assumpsit* covers nonfeasance (not doing something); misfeasance (an inappropriate action), and implied promise.[88] These developments are in contract law and, in particular, breach of contract. In the action of assumpsit, a common law court could give the plaintiff recovery of damages.

The *Humber Ferry Case*

The King's Bench decision of *Bukton v Tounesende* (the *Humber Ferry Case*) in 1348 is a landmark case in the development of modern contract law. According to Baker, the *Humber Ferry Case* is momentous because here the King's Bench first imposed liability in trespass on a defendant who had promised to do something and had done so negligently.[89]

The plaintiff, John of Bukton, entrusted his mare to the defendant ferryman, Nicholas atte Townsend, to take it across the River Humber – a large estuary in the north of England. The plaintiff alleged that the defendant ferryman overloaded his ferry: 'Nicholas loaded that boat against John's wishes in such a way that he lost the aforesaid mare through Nicholas's lack of care'.[90] Modern accounts often state that the plaintiff's mare drowned in the Humber; all we know for sure is that the animal somehow died.[91]

The King's Bench was sitting at York in the north of England. There was no obvious reason for the King's Bench to have heard *Bukton v Tounsende* but, significantly, it did. Why does that matter? To get the case heard in the King's Bench it was normally necessary to show the breach of peace (*vi et armis* or force of arms). Thus, in a representative 1345 case, it was alleged that the defendant had '*apud Westmonasterium in presencia iusticiariorum vi et armis, scilicet gladiis, bokelariis, cultellis et bodekyno*', or had with force of arms namely 'swords, bucklers, knives and bodkin' committed assault in Westminster while the judges were present.[92]

[86] Baker (n 17) 329, 330.
[87] Plucknett (n 12) 374; Baker (n 17) 330.
[88] David Ibbetson, 'Revolutions in Private Law?' in Sarah Worthington, Andrew Robertson and Graham Virgo (eds), *Revolution and Evolution in Private Law* (London, Bloomsbury, 2018) 28.
[89] Baker (n 17) 351.
[90] Sayles (n 36) 66.
[91] Robert C Palmer, *English Law in the Age of the Black Death, 1348–1381: A Transformation of Governance and Law* (Chapel Hill, North Carolina, University of North Carolina Press, 2001) 174.
[92] (1345) KB Trin Edw III, fo 341, m 77; Sayles (n 36), 40.

There was no force of arms in the mare's death. The normal action would have been covenant; however, that was not available in the King's Bench and only applied to non-performance of an agreement evidenced by a written deed. Indeed, the ferryman's counsel argued that the case should have been brought in covenant. That could have killed the case: there was no covenant.[93] However, the Court accepted the act of overloading and causing the mare's death was a trespass.[94]

Humber opened the way for a constellation of subsequent cases in trespass on the case. In 1364 an action of *assumpsit* by John and Mariot Broadmeadow against Roger Rushenden concerned how 'the left arm and hand of the same Mariot were accidentally injured and the same Roger faithfully promised … he would restore the aforesaid arm and hand to health'.[95] In 1370, a blacksmith lamed a horse when applying a horseshoe. In 1374, a surgeon undertook to heal a woman's hand but instead maimed it through subsequent infection.[96] A year later, a barber disfigured a man's face using a blunt razor, despite having promised to use a good, clean razor. Where a defendant had promised to do something and had done so negligently, the plaintiff could now succeed with a writ of trespass on the case. These are cases involving a defendant undertaking to do something, causing damage to people or their property and being sued by the plaintiff with a writ of trespass. As in the *Humber Ferry Case*, the plaintiffs' cases involve contracts but do not involve breaches of the King's peace. The cases possess particular significance as actions were allowed, despite there being no force of arms, showing a development in procedure.

The lawyers and judges discussed in this section were educated professionals, regulated, self-conscious of status, and bound together by an awareness of educational and professional activity. The next section therefore turns attention to the educational and professional history of the legal profession we have so far seen active in the courts.

The Legal Profession and its Education

There are two kinds of lawyers in Queensland and New South Wales: barristers (who concentrate on advocacy) and solicitors (who can do any legal work – advocacy, litigation, transactions, wills and estates, legal advice). This 'divided profession' is inherited from England. To understand this circumstance, we must look at the evolution of the legal profession and the gradual development – the decline and then the flourishing – of legal education.

During the reign of Henry II (1154–89), litigants represented themselves, but on occasion friends and family appeared as their representatives and wives could represent husbands.[97] Men were making a living practising in the *Curia Regis* or King's Court as early

[93] Baker (n 17) 330.

[94] *Ibid* 351.

[95] KB 27/414, m 37d (Coram Rege Roll, Easter 1364) in Morris S Arnold, *Select Cases of Trespass from the King's Courts 1307–1399* (London, Selden Society, 1987) vol 2, 422; Arnold (n 73) 329.

[96] *Stratton v Swanlond* (1374) in Sir John Baker and Stroud Milsom, *Sources of English Legal History: Private Law to 1750* (Oxford, Oxford University Press, 2010) 360.

[97] Anton-Hermann Chroust, 'Legal Profession during the Middle Ages: The Emergence of the English Lawyer Prior to 1400' (1956) 31(4) *Notre Dame Lawyer*, 570

as 1210. Two categories of practitioners began to act as agents for litigants, although there is no certainty that they could be called professional lawyers.[98] First, there were pleaders or advocates who stood beside a litigant and spoke on his behalf. Second, there were procurators, or attorneys and *essoiners*, who stood in the litigant's shoes as an agent. The procurators could make binding decisions on the litigant's behalf.

Attorneys only appeared if a litigant had a good excuse (an *essoin*) for his non-attendance. Later, we find attorneys beginning to act as agents for litigants. Then, in the late thirteenth to early fourteenth centuries, a splitting of the profession takes place: attorneys prepared for court, while 'counters' (or *narratores*) presented in court. The oral work of *narratores* was to recite litigants' formal statements. From the ranks of the counters, courtroom advocates – serjeants-at-law, barristers-at-law, and advocates – emerged who had 'right of audience' in the courts.

Serjeants-at-law were the most important class of lawyers to practise in England. Fewer than 1,000 men became serjeants-at-law in its 700-year history. In the early fourteenth century, the advocates in Common Pleas were organised into a guild: the order of serjeants-at-law.[99] Though the Chancellor chose serjeants on advice, judges of the Court of Common Pleas really controlled entry, and they would admit no more than eight barristers (always a bencher, meaning a senior member of the one of the Inns of Court) to the order every few years in a 'call'.[100] At that point, the barrister would have to leave his Inn of Court and take up membership of Serjeant's Inn.[101] This guild's name was 'the order of the coif' after the serjeants' distinctive headdress, a skullcap tied under the chin. The serjeants would have looked magnificent for, in addition to the coif, they wore brightly coloured robes and a furry cloak. They would have been prominent standing by the pillars in the nave of St Paul's Cathedral to interact with their clients and writing their notes on paper balanced on their knee.[102]

The serjeants received a salary from the King and therefore undertook legal work for the Crown. As a group, they were mainly responsible for the development of the medieval common law. It is the serjeants' opinions that fill the Year Books, the earliest 'law reports' that are available. Indeed, by the fifteenth century, it was the practice to appoint judges to the common law courts from the ranks of the order. Sir William Bereford CJCP, encountered above as a lively and creative chief justice of the Common Pleas, served first as a serjeant in the same Court. As reconstructed by Paul Brand, Bereford's career shows he emerged from a humble background to a legal career that spanned over 40 years.[103] Early on he appears in the records as an attorney, then as a busy serjeant working each term in the Court.[104]

The substance of the serjeants' practice declined in the sixteenth century, but the pretence was maintained by admitting all appointees to judicial office in the common law courts to the order of the coif before they were installed as judges. That meant that the judges

[98] Paul Brand, 'The Origins of the English Legal Profession' (1987) 5(1) *Law and History Review* 32.

[99] John Fortescue, *De Laudibus Legum Angliae* (Clark, New Jersey, Lawbook Exchange, 1999) 198.

[100] Paul Brand, 'An Irishman in Westminster Hall: William Skrene of Dundalk, King's Serjeant at Law' (c 1358–c 1420)' (1996) 31 *Irish Jurist 255.*

[101] Theobald Mathew, 'Decline and Fall of the Serjeants-at-Law' (1919) 35(3) *Law Quarterly Review* 264, 264–65.

[102] Edward H Warren, 'Serjeants-at-Law; The Order of the Coif' (1942) 28 *Virginia Law Review* 911, 935.

[103] Paul Brand, *The Earliest English Law Reports* (London, Selden Society, 1996) vol 2, xiii.

[104] *Ibid* xvi.

and the serjeants still in practice were technically equals, members of the same guild. The legacy survived in the nineteenth century. In Charles Dickens' *The Pickwick Papers* (1836), Serjeants **Buzfuz** and Snubbin represent the parties in a breach of promise case.

The serjeants-at-law had a monopoly on practice as advocates in the Court of Common Pleas, and the fortunes of the order followed those of that Court. The decline of the Court and the serjeants was slow. It began in the seventeenth century, as the Stuart kings tried to undermine the influence of the serjeants and the common law and, instead, began to elevate the status of King's Counsels. Five factors contributed to the weakening of serjeants-at-law as an elite group:

- The growing importance of the King's Bench and Chancery where, unlike the Common Pleas, there were no exclusive rights of audience for lawyers.
- The profitability of becoming a Crown law representative (for example an attorney general) from the sixteenth century onwards.
- King's Counsel (KCs or, in the reign of a Queen, QCs) ranking higher than serjeants from 1670.
- The opening of the Common Pleas to all barristers regardless of rank by statute in 1846.[105]
- The *Supreme Court of Judicature Act 1873* abolishing the requirement that judges be admitted to the order of serjeants.[106]

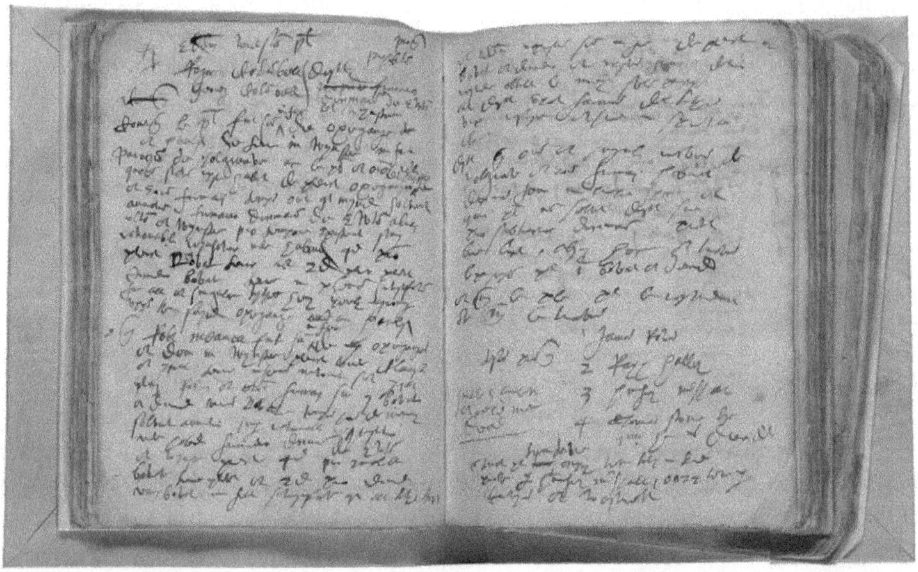

Figure 2.2 An Example of the Notes made by a Barrister as he Travelled on Circuit

Notebook of a barrister riding on the Midland Circuit [manuscript] (ca. February 1609–February 1610/11) 41–42. Call #: V.a.489.

[105] *Practitioners in Common Pleas Act 1846* (9 & 10 Vict c 54).
[106] 36 & 37 Vict c 66, s 8.

Barristers-at-law had their origins in the fifteenth and sixteenth centuries. At this time, new forms of legal work began to develop in the other courts in London, especially the Court of King's Bench and the Exchequer, and in the Court of Chancery. Here the serjeants and attorneys did not have a monopoly on practice. Any man who could conduct the litigation was able to do so in those courts.

A body of professional advocates subsequently emerged. By the mid-fifteenth century, four principal 'Inns of Court' survived out of the 20 or so Inns established in London, initially in property rented from religious orders:[107] Lincoln's Inn, Inner Temple, Middle Temple and Gray's Inn. The four Inns supervised up to nine 'Inns of Chancery'. The Inns were complex organisms. Their functions were social as well as educational. Their inhabitants were often notorious for their roistering and gaming rather than their studying. They participated in socially elite events such as masques, or elaborate theatrical entertainments performed before the royal family. They also attracted students who did not intend to practise law.[108] The corporate life of the Inn could involve more than instruction in law; in 1559 (as recorded in the Black Books of Lincoln's Inn) fellows of the house were informed they could not have a beard any longer than a fortnight's growth.[109] The Inns developed to provide the lawyers with chambers or accommodation, to share meals and for education. This environment meant that people studying at the Inns were deeply participative in the law, building up an emphasis on professional memory and the association between observation and interpretation.[110] They were a pathway for men from the shires to enter the legal profession and find a source of income not based on inherited land.[111]

The members of the Inns were apprentices-at-law, because their common life in the inn was to learn the law, starting when ready as there were no explicit age limits or academic entry qualifications.[112] To study common law a man went to the Inns rather than to university, whereas the civilian lawyers read Roman law at Oxford or Cambridge and knew both classical law and contemporary European treatises.[113] Men who proceeded to the Inns may well have matriculated to university first, but not to study the common law. For example, Sir Edmund Anderson CJCP studied first at Lincoln College Oxford before joining the Inner Temple. Sir Edward Coke CJCP and CJKB (see historical cameo below) first attended Trinity College Cambridge, then Clifford's Inn and finally the Inner Temple.[114] Sir Thomas Walmsley's knowledge of classical law indicates that he attended a university before joining Lincoln's Inn.[115] Education at the Inns derived from lectures or readings and moots. The readings were given by senior members of the Inn called readers and appointed annually

[107] RM Fisher, 'Inns of Court and the Reformation 1530–1580' (DPhil thesis, University of Cambridge, 1974) 3.

[108] Wilfrid R Prest, 'Legal Education of the Gentry at the Inns of Court, 1560–1640' (1967) 38 *Past and Present* 22.

[109] William Craddock Bolland, 'Two Problems in Legal History' (1908) 24 *LQR* 392, 396.

[110] Damian Powell, 'Coke in Context: Early Modern Legal Observation and Sir Edward Coke's Reports' (2000) 21(3) *Journal of Legal History* 33, 35.

[111] Eric Acheson, *A Gentry Community: Leicestershire in the Fifteenth Century, c 1422–c 1485* (Cambridge, Cambridge University Press, 1992) 74.

[112] Wilfrid R Prest, *The Rise of the Barristers: A Social History of the English Bar 1590–1640* (Oxford, Clarendon Press, 1991) 107.

[113] Richard Helmholz, 'The Origin of Holographic Wills in English Law' (1994) 15(2) *The Journal of Legal History* 97, 103.

[114] Edward Foss, *The Judges of England, From the Time of the Conquest* (London, Longman, Brown, Green, Longmans, and Roberts, 1857) vol 6, 51.

[115] John Snape, 'Sir Thomas Walmesley: An Elizabethan Judge' (1994) 3 *Nottingham Law Journal* 107, 109.

and were originally significant occasions in the life of the Inn.[116] The moots were intricate hypothetical problems, much more involved than the modern moot.

The moots gave the legal profession some of its distinctive terminology. The apprentices sitting inside the bar of the Inn for moots were 'inner barristers'. For about seven years, they would attend court and readings, but they could not plead in moots. Once this period of initial training was done, they were 'called to the Bar' of the Inn. They could now argue in moots and sit outside the Bar. The inner barristers thus graduated to the rank of utter (or outer) barrister. Senior members of the Inn, who sat on benches while hearing the moots, were benchers.

By the fifteenth century, the apprentices themselves conducted most advocacy in the Courts of King's Bench, Exchequer and Chancery and had established themselves as a separate professional class – *barristers*. By the sixteenth century, the judges of these courts made admission to the Bar of an Inn a precondition to practise as advocates before them.

There were separate but parallel developments in the civilian courts. These were the ecclesiastical courts, the Court of Admiralty, and the High Court of Chivalry. The civilian courts applied inherited canon law and Roman civil law – and not the common law or equity. The advocates in the civilian courts worked and lived in an Inn called Doctors' Commons at Blackfriars in London and owned a valuable library of continental legal works.

Advocates held doctorates in civil or canon law from Oxford or Cambridge. Though Henry VIII abolished canon law at the universities in 1535, the teaching of civil (Roman) law continued in both places. The Court of the Arches (a Church court) and the High Court Admiralty admitted civilians as advocates. The nineteenth century reforms to the English legal system saw the demise of civilians as a distinct branch of the legal profession and Doctors' Commons closed in 1865.

Australian courts preserve a divided profession, a legacy of the lower ranking law agents including the attorneys, solicitors and proctors. A class of lawyers practising in the Court of Common Pleas were attorneys and essoiners (whose role was to make an excuse for a defendant's failure to appear in court). Attorneys assumed the function of essoiners in the fourteenth century.

The attorney was the precursor to the modern solicitor. Their function as a branch of common lawyers was to undertake all legal work before the courtroom advocacy of the serjeants. The attorney acted as agent for a litigant. He did the preliminary work of litigation – having writs issued and entering pleas. He was treated as an officer of the court as access to administrative court records was an indispensable part of the job.

The class of solicitors developed between the fifteenth and mid-seventeenth centuries in the same courts as the class of barristers had: King's Bench, Exchequer and Chancery. Like attorneys, these men undertook general business. They acted as real estate agents and gave general legal advice. However, they took the name solicitor because they also solicited litigation conducted in those courts. Frequently, an attorney would act as a solicitor when undertaking work in those courts. Barristers would also undertake the work of solicitors: they would solicit litigation and arrange for it to be conducted in those courts. Solicitors and attorneys became peculiarly associated with the Court of Chancery where they had a great deal of exclusive business.

[116] Eric Ives, *The Common Lawyers of Pre-Reformation England: Thomas Kebell: A Case Study* (Cambridge, Cambridge University Press, 1983) 44.

The work of proctors paralleled that of attorneys and solicitors. Like advocates, however, proctors practised in the civilian courts and were educated in the universities. Proctors usually held a bachelor's degree and completed examinations in Latin and an additional seven-year period as an articled clerk. The *Judicature Act 1873* abolished the status of proctors. All proctors, like attorneys, became solicitors of the Supreme Court of Judicature.

Constitutional Detour

Gender Equality – Women Lawyers

While the capacity of women to enter legal practice in common law jurisdictions today is undoubted, that was not always the case. Until the start of the twentieth century, however, members of the legal profession were exclusively male in England, Australia, and most other common law jurisdictions. As the twentieth century progressed, the novelty of seeing a woman lawyer receded as their presence within the profession increased.

Ada Evans was Australia's first female law graduate. Evans graduated from Sydney Law School in 1902, but it took another 19 years before she was admitted to the Supreme Court of New South Wales as a barrister. The *Women's Legal Status Act 1918* (NSW) enabled Evans' admission to the still male-dominated legal profession.

A Victorian, **Flos Grieg**, had the distinction of being the first Australian woman admitted to practise law. Enabled by the *Women's Disabilities Removal Act 1903* (Vic), Grieg was admitted as a barrister in Victoria, in 1906. Other Australian jurisdictions followed suit.

Figure 2.3 Legislation Enabling Admission to Practise Law

Victoria	*Women's Disabilities Removal Act 1903* (Vic) (nicknamed the 'Flos Grieg Enabling Act')
Tasmania	*Legal Practitioners Act 1904* (Tas)
Queensland	*Legal Practitioners Act 1905* (Qld)
South Australia	*Female Law Practitioners Act 1911* (SA)
New South Wales	*Women's Legal Status Act 1918* (NSW)
Western Australia	*Women's Legal Status Act 1923* (WA)

Before enabling legislation was enacted, Australian courts interpreted the language of admission legislation narrowly. In *Re Edith Haynes*,[117] the Full Court of the Supreme Court of Western Australia determined that women could not be admitted to the legal profession in Western Australia. In 1900, the Western Australian Barristers' Board registered Edith Haynes as a student-at-law and approved her articles of clerkship. Edith Haynes would complete her articles of clerkship – a five-year period of apprenticeship – at her uncle's law firm. At the time of accepting her registration, the Board advised Haynes in writing that 'although the Board is of opinion (with some doubt) that women

[117] [1904] 6 WALR 209.

are eligible for admission under the **Legal Practitioner Act** .... The Board cannot guarantee such admission, even if you comply with all the provisions of the Act and of the regulations framed thereunder.'[118] On completion of her apprenticeship, Haynes would have to sit intermediate examinations with the Board but, in 1904, the Board refused. Edith Haynes sought a writ of *mandamus* from the Supreme Court, calling upon the Barristers' Board to show cause why the Board should not allow her to sit the intermediate examinations.

The Supreme Court found that the word 'person' in the relevant admission legislation, the *Supreme Court Act 1861* (WA), did not include 'woman'. In framing the statute, the legislature could not have contemplated the admission of women to the legal profession. Parker J remarked that '[t]he idea of women practising in the Supreme Court seems to me quite foreign to the legislation which has prevailed for years past, not only here but in the mother country'.[119]

None of the Supreme Court justices were prepared to set a precedent for the admission of women to the Bar, instead deferring to Parliament to legislate for this purpose. To confer this right on women, the legislature should use 'express language'.[120] The legislation, though it referred to 'every person', did not include women. Burnside J remarked: '[w]hen the Legislature in its wisdom confers the right on women, then we shall be pleased to admit them. But we must leave to the Legislature to decide on the desirability or otherwise of such legislation'.[121] Despite the promising note on which the Supreme Court judgment concludes, Western Australia was the last of the Australian states to allow women to practise law, in 1923. Haynes was never admitted to legal practice. She died in 1963.

In 2017, Susan Kiefel became the first female Chief Justice of Australia. Today, over 60 per cent of lawyers admitted to the Australian legal profession are women. There is still, however, a long way to go to achieve equality in the areas of salary, retention of female barristers, and appointments to senior legal positions.

Pause for Thought

The #MeToo Movement

At the time of writing, the Chief Justices of Australia and Queensland are women and females sit on the Supreme Courts of the United Kingdom and the United States of America. Yet proportionally the number of female lawyers on the bench, at the Bar as senior counsel and as senior partners of law firms is small. The profession is increasingly facing up to a once hidden but powerful culture of sexual abuse by mostly male senior lawyers against mostly female subordinates.

[118] *Ibid* 211.
[119] *Ibid.*
[120] *Ibid.*
[121] *Ibid* 213.

Questions to Consider

1. What structural inequalities govern the profession in ways that may influence these proportions?
2. To what extent does the decision-making credibility of judges depend on structural and cultural reform involving the treatment of women lawyers for the judges to retain credibility?

Law Reporting

Today, lawyers rely heavily on written law reports to identify the rule that was used to decide a case and that binds others – but this was not always so. Indeed, the common law can be 'unwritten law' and lawyers needed a good memory to practise. An emphasis on the written word has grown over the centuries: it is now a pervasive feature of the common law tradition. The entrenchment of the doctrine of precedent became possible with the emergence of written reports recording the arguments and decisions in past cases.

Judges and their clerks wrote in Latin, which is why the terminology referring to a judge's decision is in that language. These key terms express the impact of a judge's decision. The *ratio decidendi* (or the *rationes decidendi*) is an aspect of the doctrine of precedent. The Latin term refers to the rationale for a decision. However, the 'ratio' of the decision also points to the significance of the hierarchy of courts. An *obiter dictum* (or the *obiter dicta*) may be something expressed by the judge but is not the reason for the decision. It is something the judge expresses 'by the way'.

Under the English common law, three historical stages of law reporting can be identified: the Year Books, nominate reports, and authorised reports under the aegis of the Incorporated Council of Law Reporting (ICLR) for England and Wales.

The Year Books

The **Year Books** (so-called by their organisational principle of regnal year and then law term) dating from 1275 are our earliest case reports. Written in Law French, the Year Books differed markedly in purpose from modern law reports being fundamentally a tool for education. Law students distributed notes on discussions and exchanges between judges and counsel on matters of pleading and procedure that they considered important. The notes spread to other students and lawyers until, in the early fourteenth century, they were committed to manuscript – the Year Books. The arrival of the printing press in London in 1470 facilitated the widespread printing of these manuscripts. The discussions recorded in the Year Books gave rise to common law rules of pleadings. They are not an entirely different type of work to the reports. Some Tudor judges wrote reports that were akin to the Year Books, as well as keeping private notebooks.[122]

[122] Sir John Baker, 'Early Tudor Reports and the Plea Rolls' (1987) 18 *Cambrian Law Review* 25.

Nominate Reports

Nominate reports – private law reports written by individual lawyers and judges – succeeded Year Books. The first two nominate report series emerged in the second half of the sixteenth century, first with ***Edmund Plowden's Commentaries*** (1571) and then with Sir James Dyer's *Reports* in 1585. These later came into Edward Coke's possession and he actively used them in his own writings and public controversies, including with the High Commission.[123] Plowden's *Commentaries* (1571) are particularly noteworthy in these early reports for their accuracy as well as for the care taken in selecting cases to report. The most used nominate reports have been collected and republished in a series called the ***English Reports***, and they are freely available for present use and searching.

In 1600, Edward Coke published the first of 11 volumes of *Reports*. The authority of these *Reports* derives primarily from Coke's reputation as successively Attorney General, Chief Justice of the Courts of Common Pleas and of King's Bench rather than the quality or accuracy of the cases reported. Law French was the initial language of the nominate reports, but English replaced it. Nominate reports continued to be published in the centuries that followed; however, official reports appeared in response to the variable quality of nominate reports.

Official Reports

Formed in 1865, the ICLR for England and Wales saw the transformation of law reporting from a private enterprise to one state-administered venture. The ICLR introduced criteria to determine whether cases were worthy of publication – a practice that continues even today. The process of reporting involves law reporters attending court, taking note of the proceedings, and producing reports containing counsels' arguments and the judgments. The judges then check reports by the judges to allow for revisions or for approval before publication.

Historical Cameo

Sir Edward Coke

> 'What Shakespeare has been to literature, what Bacon has been to philosophy … Coke has been to the public and private law of England'.
>
> – Sir William Holdsworth, *Some Makers of English Law*

Sir Edward Coke (1552–1634) (pronounced 'Cook') was an English lawyer, judge and politician. His life and career spans the reigns of the Tudor Queen Elizabeth I and the Stuart kings, James VI and I and Charles I. He was successively Solicitor-General (1592–94), Attorney-General (1594–1606), Chief Justice of the Common Pleas (1606–13)

[123] Baker (n 52) 355.

and Chief Justice of the King's Bench (1613–16) during Elizabeth I's and James VI and I's reigns. He was the prosecutor in the trials of the Earl of Essex (1600) and Sir Walter Raleigh (1603). We already know of Coke's fame as a law reporter: Coke's *Reports* appeared in 11 volumes between 1600 and 1616. He also dabbled in textbook or 'treatise' writing with his four volume *Institutes of the Law of England*, which included another famous work, *Commentary on Littleton*.

Figure 2.4 Thomas de Littleton, whose Treatise on Tenures Received a Commentary from Edward Coke

R Vaughan, The true portraiture of Judge Littleton the famous English lawyer [graphic] (Great Britain?, late 17th to early 18th century?). Call #: ART File L781.2 no.1 (size XS).

As judge, Coke was unpopular with James VI and I. Several incidents did much to keep Coke's popularity at rock bottom. In one incident, in 1608, Coke told James that he had no authority to judge cases himself. That encounter closed with James threatening physical violence against Coke! That did not stop Coke from subsequently offending James. One incident in 1616 was the last straw. In 1616, James summoned Coke and 12 judges to Whitehall demanding an answer as to why they continued to hear a case in defiance of his command to halt it. Coke was the only judge not to seek James' pardon. He responded that a judge 'would do that which should be fit for a judge to do'. To halt the case would mean 'a delay of justice and therefore contrary to law and the Judges' oath'. James dismissed Coke a few months later.

Coke became a Member of Parliament (MP) (1620). Coke's return to politics was not without fuss. At one point Coke's conduct resulted in his imprisonment and arrest in the Tower of London (1622). The Honourable Patrick Keane's **Selden Society** lecture offers the thoughts of a modern judge on one of his predecessors.

Constitutional Detour

The Rule of Law, Coke and Dr Bonham's Case

In *Dr Bonham's Case*,[124] Coke CJCP held that an Act of Parliament was void if it was 'against common right and reason, or repugnant, or impossible to be performed'.[125] *Dr Bonham's Case* remains an important and hotly debated judgment to this day! This is the first time it is suggested that an Act of Parliament – legislation – might be 'void' because it did not meet some higher standard (such as being 'against common right and reason'). It has not been followed in England, and even in Australia it has been rejected as a principle of law. For example, in *Kable v Director of Public Prosecutions (NSW)*, Dawson J referred at length to Coke, not only to the judgment but to Coke's later reflections in the *Fourth Institutes*.[126] However, the idea that the rule of law might invalidate statutes if they do not comply with the national Constitution did eventually take on importance in the United States and Australia. *Dr Bonham's Case* also shows the dense and technical style of the older law reporting in even the highest quality of nominate reports.

Assumpsit Again: *Slade's Case* and the Law in Tudor England

This chapter has addressed in turn the evolution of actions and the emergence of a legal profession with distinct professional contours and education delivered by the Inns. Both these strands intersect in the person of Sir Edward Coke. Coke, whose cameo is above, is easily the most famous judge in English legal history, with his lengthy career beginning at the Inns of Court. He was a voluminous writer, and, amongst other things, he has influenced the Constitution of the United States of America. Appropriately he is immortalised on the great bronze doors of the Supreme Court in Washington DC.

Coke is significant for giving intellectual coherence to English law, including expanding on the idea of law as artificial reason or the distillation of centuries of thought, calling it the

[124] (1610) 8 Co Rep 113b; 77 ER 646.
[125] *Ibid* 118a, 652.
[126] (1996) 189 CLR 51.

'artificial perfection of reason'.[127] 'Artificial' carries no pejorative sense, but the artifice refers to the abilities of lawyers and the perfection to the artistry of the judges.[128]

Coke's career and writing reinforce further important points about the legal profession, with Coke asserting his belief that the profession comprised the combined talent and wisdom derived from its education. These points are exemplified by the technical complexity of the cases involving Coke as barrister and judge. The next section will look at one such case, ***Slade's Case***.

Slade's Case, 1597–1602[129]

The *Humber Ferry Case* could be the origin of modern contract law, but *Slade's Case* may take top honours.[130] It was a landmark legal ruling during Coke's tenure as Attorney-General.[131] In Common Pleas, if a plaintiff wanted a sum of money to be repaid, they needed a writ of action. By the Tudor period, it had become possible to bring *assumpsit* actions in the King's Bench, showing the emerging means of recovery. By the later part of the sixteenth century a plaintiff could sue in debt or in assumpsit.[132] The choice had consequences: bringing an action of *assumpsit* resulted in a jury trial but an action in debt meant the defendant could rely on compurgation (or waging law).[133] Choices remained limited. Notably, if the claim was for liquidated damages, technically the plaintiff needed to sue with a writ of debt.[134] *Assumpsit* was only available if the defendant had promised in express terms that a debt would be repaid.[135]

This course of action was unpopular by the Tudor period. Oath helpers received 12 pence each and would probably agree with the defendant. Despite what in hindsight may seem to be obvious limitations, the judges of the Common Pleas held firm against *assumpsit* because the writ of debt was an avenue for recovery. The points made about the Bill of Middlesex and the writ of *quo minus* indicated the competitive legal fictions judges used to bring cases into their courts. Aside from legal fictions, judges in one court, the Common Pleas, reversed decisions made by the King's Bench, meaning judges from different courts could sit together on the Assizes but disagree with each other.[136] The binary between the two courts should not be overstated. The Bill of Middlesex gave the King's Bench jurisdiction in cases of debt.[137]

[127] David A Sklansky, 'The Fourth Amendment and Common Law' (2000) 100 *Columbia Law Review* 1739, 1779; John Pocock, *The Ancient Constitution and the Feudal Law: Study of English Historical Thought in the Seventeenth Century: A Reissue with a Retrospect* (Cambridge, Cambridge University Press, 1987) 35.

[128] Allen Dillard Boyer, 'Understanding, Authority, and Will: Sir Edward Coke and the Elizabethan Origins of Judicial Review' (1997) 39 *Boston College Law Review* 43, 83.

[129] (1598) 4 Co Rep 92b; 76 ER 1074 (1602).

[130] Allen D Boyer, *Edward Coke and the Elizabethan Age* (Stanford, Stanford University Press, 2003) 125.

[131] Barbara Malament, 'The Economic Liberalism of Sir Edward Coke' (1967) 76(7) *Yale Law Journal* 1321, 1326.

[132] Boyer (n 132) 125.

[133] *Ibid* 126.

[134] James Ames, 'The History of Assumpsit: II – Implied Assumpsit' (1888) 2(2) *Harvard Law Review* 52, 58.

[135] Malament (n 133) 1326.

[136] Boyer (n 132) 127.

[137] Samuel Stoljar, *A History of Contract at Common Law* (Canberra, ANU Press, 1975) 77.

With that technical background, it is time to turn our attention to the dispute between two men in the city of Exeter towards the end of the sixteenth century. John Slade brought a claim of *assumpsit* against Humphrey Morley. In the original trial, the jury found that Morley had undertaken to buy wheat and rye from Slade, but he had reneged on the deal. From there, legal complexity ensued. John Popham CJKB referred it to all judges in the Exchequer Chamber, who argued for the next five years. Could there be *assumpsit* when a plaintiff could use a writ for debt? Edward Coke argued based on longstanding custom. Despite the opposition from the Common Pleas judges, this option had been available to plaintiffs for a long time.[138] As for the involvement of compurgators, Coke argued the borrower should ensure he had sufficient witnesses. Ultimately, it seems that allowing the *assumpsit* was a split decision, but the decision brought *assumpsit* into the realm of contract.[139] That took law down a path leading away from compurgation and the waging of law, leading to expectations that commercial obligations could be enforced.[140] As recounted in the reports of Sir Henry Yelverton, one of the judges involved:

> An Action on the Cafe on an Indebitatus Affumpfit lies well; for every Debt implies a Promife, and is a good Confideration in facto to found an Action upon. But for a Debt by Simple Contract due by the Teftator no Affumpfit lies againft the Executors; and this was openly deliver'd by Popham Chief Juftice 9 Nov 44 Eliz to be the Refolution of all the Juftices of England, and this to be a Precedent for all fubfequent Cafes'[141]

Historically, there had been tension between the two major common law courts for where *assumpsit* and debt overlapped with each other, a second promise could be relied on. The judges of the King's Bench did not expect proof of this promise, whereas the Common Pleas rejected that approach.[142] After *Slade's Case*, the Common Pleas judges accepted that a plaintiff could bring an action of *assumpsit* on an implied promise (where there was no proof). Further developments flowed from this decision. The case included arguments against the wager of law, which Coke argued was susceptible to perjury.[143] A further development was the courts no longer needing to insist on the line of separation between causes of action in debt and assumpsit. According to Ibbetson, 'any language or conduct from which a promise could be inferred was tantamount to an express promise'.[144] In *Slade's Case*, though, the issue was that Morley had entered a contract to buy corn. In other words, Morley had promised to pay the agreed price. The price was not paid. Slade could elect between an action of debt on contract or an action of *assumpsit* on the promise.[145]

This decision is a natural point to pause. The next chapter begins in the sixteenth century, and Sir Edward Coke reappears. *Slade's Case* concludes the discussion of the actions and technicalities this chapter has discussed as the courts and their personnel develop and mature over centuries, as does their education and their access to decisions in reports.

[138] Boyer (n 132) 127.
[139] *Ibid* 130, 132.
[140] Stroud Milsom, *Historical Foundations of the Common Law* (London, Boston, Butterworths, 1981) 354.
[141] *Reports of Sir Henry Yelverton* (E and R Nutt and R Gosling, 1735) 20.
[142] David Ibbetson, 'Sixteenth Century Contract Law: Slade's Case in Context' (1984) 4(3) *Oxford Journal of Legal Studies* 295, 315.
[143] Stoljar (n 139) 78.
[144] *Ibid* 297.
[145] *Ibid* 315.

Conclusion

This chapter has covered momentous legal activity filled with the vivid personalities of those involved and the details of their decision-making. This decision-making took place in the common law courts, as the legal profession itself gained coherence and character through education at the Inns of Court. Forms of actions (especially trespass, trespass on the case and assumpsit); legal fictions; the interaction between the court of equity or conscience; the common law courts and precedent; law reporting; and judicial review have all been explored. The next chapter will remain in the early modern period. Sir Edward Coke will reappear. It will feature dramatic legal events of the seventeenth century including the execution of one king and the deposition of another.

3

The English Revolutions: Parliament, the King and the Law Courts

Introduction

This chapter covers more than a century and a half of dramatic English history, including religious reformations in the sixteenth century and politico-religious crises in the seventeenth. In doing so it will follow a trajectory, as the profound changes to English religion that occur in the sixteenth century (the 'Reformation') set in train important changes to English national identity, framing that identity around being Protestant and anti-Catholic. That Protestant identity informs how events played out during the reign of James VI and I (reigned 1603–25 in England) through to the accession of William III and Mary II to the thrones of England, Scotland and Ireland in 1689. The execution of Charles I (1649), the Civil Wars (1642–51) and the 'Glorious Revolution' (1688) are three key events of the Stuart era. Historians call this period the 'Iron Century', in reference to the savage warfare that occurred in England, Scotland and Ireland and elsewhere in Europe. This violence provides the backdrop to fascinating legal history. This includes the trial and execution of Charles I, a momentous legal occasion raising procedural and human rights issues that continue to fascinate lawyers.

After examining the Church and the law in the sixteenth century, this chapter focuses attention on the seventeenth century conflicts between different branches of government. The most prominent of these were the changing relationships between the common law and the King, the common law and Parliament, and the King and Parliament. There were other issues concerning how the different courts related to each other when their judgments conflicted. Conflicts between different branches of government tended to focus on the extent and scope of 'the royal prerogative' – the personal legal and fiscal power of the King. The large questions of the period were whether the exercise of the royal prerogative power was superior to the common law or to legislation passed by Parliament. Much of this chapter sits in the domain of constitutional law, moving on from the coverage so far provided of property and contract law in chapters one and two.

Learning Resources

The content in this chapter is supported by:

Glossary
- Latin, Law French and Medieval English terms are defined

Chapter Overview
- The chapter begins with an overview explaining its intentions and focus

Historical Cameos
- Judge Jeffreys and the Bloody Asizes

Constitutional Detours
- The Petition of Right
- An Englishman's Home is his Castle
- The Trial of Charles I
- The Bill of Rights 1689 and the Rule of Law

Pause for Thought
- Swearin *Ex Officio*
- *Habeas corpus*
- Trying a Head of State

Chapter Overview

Place
- Kingdom of England

Time Period
- Tudor and Stuart dynasties

Dates
- 16th–17th centuries

Key Figures
- James VI and I
- Sir Edward Coke
- Charles I
- Oliver Cromwell
- James VII and II
- William III

Key Institutions
- King's Bench
- Common Pleas
- Chancery
- Court of Requests
- Star Chamber
- High Commission

Key Terms
- Reformation
- *Ex officio* oath
- Witchcraft
- Equity
- Whigs and Tories
- Seditious libel
- Glorious Revolution

Learning Outcomes

At the end of this chapter, readers should understand:

- Sixteenth-century interactions between law and religion.
- The notion of the 'ancient constitution' and its rhetorical importance to lawyers.
- Early assertions of judicial independence.
- The powers of the High Commission.
- The modern importance attached to the trial of a head of state.

Law and Religion: Sixteenth to Seventeenth Centuries

> Chantry (Middle English): an endowed chapel where masses are said for the benefactor

The medieval city of London burned down in 1666 in the Great Fire. Surviving topographical illustrations of the old city show it was full of churches dominated by St Paul's Cathedral (a victim of the 1666 fire), one of the largest buildings in Europe with the tallest spire in England.[1] The streets around it contained over 100 churches, perhaps one on each corner. In addition, there were **chantry** chapels and monasteries adding to the ambience of a social and political world dominated by its religion.[2] St Paul's visual dominance is a reminder that the legal history discussed here has a coterminous religious history. However, this religious history is not static and, towards the beginning of the sixteenth century, changes and revolutions in practice and doctrine now called the 'Reformation' convulsed English religion (as also happened elsewhere in Europe). This Reformation had legal implications.

Alongside the secular or temporal courts of the medieval period were the Church courts which investigated moral offences but also dealt with slander.[3] A Christian could be a sinner, whose sins would bring them to court for having committed a moral offence such as defamation, perjury, heresy, promiscuity or concubinage, offences concerning disruptions to social order and neighbourliness, or sexual misconduct, with canonists, the canon theologians, organising sins on a hierarchy. For example, fornication was not as bad as adultery, but rape was worse than adultery.[4] Gossiping, quarrelling, or working on the Sabbath or a Saint's Day were also offences which would also have brought a man or woman into a Church court.[5] The Church courts could also punish folk magicians, such as wise women and healers, and astrologers.[6]

The Church courts interacted with secular courts.[7] An ecclesiastical court would convict a person holding scandalously erroneous beliefs – a heretic – but a secular court would

[1] William Dugdale, *History of Saint Paul's Cathedral, in London, from its Foundation Etc with a Continuation and Additions* (Lockington, Hughes, Harding, Mavor & Jones, 1818) 190.

[2] Marie-Hélène Rousseau, *Saving the Souls of Medieval London: Perpetual Chantries at St Paul's Cathedral, c 1200–1548* (Aldershot, Ashgate, 2013) 137.

[3] Colin Morris, 'A Consistory Court in the Middle Ages' (1963) 14 *Journal of Ecclesiastical History* 150, 155.

[4] Andrew John Finch, 'Sexual Morality and Canon Law: The Evidence of the Rochester Consistory Court' (1994) 20 *Journal of Medieval History* 261, 261.

[5] Keith Thomas, *Religion and the Decline of Magic* (Harmondsworth, Penguin, 1971) 181.

[6] *Ibid* 434.

[7] See generally Bryan VanGinhoven, 'Margery Kempe and the Legal Status of Defamation' (2014) 49 *Journal of Medieval Religious Cultures* 20, 21.

punish them. A heretic would be executed but other punishments demeaned and degraded and imposed penitential pilgrimages.[8] A man might be compelled to ride bareheaded around his community in the marketplace, or to process with his legs bare, or to confess and make his penance in the local church.[9] Church authorities could also excommunicate a person, which barred them from participation in the sacramental life of the Church. Given they were members of a society based on the Church, the punishment also had the effect of an excommunication from social relations.

A bishop, the ordinary of his diocese, presided in a Consistory Court, assisted by a chancellor. An archdeacon is a priest, normally one assisting a bishop particularly in the enforcement of moral standards. The Archdeacons' Courts reveal themselves to legal history as the busiest local jurisdiction and an important point of connection between ordinary people and the worlds of law and religion. The officials presiding in an Archdeacons' Court encountered people accused of drunken behaviour, gambling, swearing, defamation, **usury**, mistreating children, adultery, fornication and masturbating. Understandably, with cases of this nature, people called these courts the 'bawdy courts'.[10]

Usury (Latin and Middle English): lending money at interest and immorally

While the Consistory and Archdeacons' Courts are Church courts, all law irrespective of jurisdiction upheld morality. In 1578, the municipal authorities in Bury St Edmunds passed municipal ordinances to compel jail for blasphemers and for the whipping of boys who were idle when they should have been listening attentively to a sermon. Other punishments included putting drunkards in the stocks as well as **scolds**, brawlers, and people who told ribald jokes.[11] At a more fundamental level, jurists and clergymen not only in England but around Europe understood portents and providences as signs of God's judgment in the world. Monstrous births, freaks, deformities and strange accidents indicated judgment occurring in this world not the next.[12] *The Theatre of Gods Iudgments*, written by the schoolmaster Thomas Beard in 1597 and re-issued many times, exemplifies an approach to understanding evil-doing and punishment that is eschatological (things concerned with supernatural judgment). For example, Beard narrated vividly the grotesque and smelly fate of a cruel gaoler:

Scold: a woman with a busy and disruptive tongue

> Alexander the Keeper of Newgate, a cruell enemy to thoſe that lay in that priſon for Religion, dyed very miſerably, being ſo ſwollen, that he was more like a monſter than a man, and ſo rotten within that homan could abide the ſmell of him.[13]

Beard incidentally educated Oliver Cromwell (discussed below).

The Consistory and Archdeacons' Courts predate the Reformation of the 1520s and 1530s but survived the Reformation. This Reformation is a complex and long lasting sixteenth century process. One cannot date a beginning or an end to it but, in broad terms,

[8] Finch (n 4) 266.

[9] James Masschaele, 'The Public Space of the Marketplace in Medieval England' (2002) 77(2) *Speculum* 383, 400.

[10] David Crawford, 'Courts of Conscience: English Archdeacons' Courts at the Time of the Reformation, c 1515–1558' (PhD thesis, University of Sydney, 1987) 123, 313; David Crawford, 'The Rule of Law?: The Laity, English Archdeacons' Courts and the Reformation to 1558' (1986) 4 *Parergon* 155, 158.

[11] Allen Boyer, *Sir Edward Coke and the Elizabethan Age* (Stanford, Stanford University Press, 2003) 61–62.

[12] See generally Jennifer Spinks, 'Wondrous Monsters: Representing Conjoined Twins in Early Sixteenth-Century German Broadsheets' (2005) 22 *Parergon* 77–112.

[13] Thomas Beard, *The Theatre of Gods Judgements* (1648) sig E3; Thomas (n 5) 109.

it entailed the Church in England separating economically and legally from the Church of Rome. Many of the impulses pushing the Church in England away from Rome were explicitly political and concerned the matrimonial concerns of Henry VIII (reigned 1509–47), who ultimately married six times. However, as this chapter suggests, the religious, the political and, for that matter, the legal, cannot be disentangled from each other. The next section of this chapter examines the Reformation as part of the legal fabric and tensions apparent between different types of lawyers. **The 'murder of Richard Hunne'** is discussed on the companion website as a microcosm of these tensions.

The Ecclesiastical High Commission

The Reformation of the Church in England meant more courts and more laws came into existence. These included the Court of Augmentations, a court established in 1536 by statute and then by Letters Patent to administer large amounts of property changing hands as Henry VIII dissolved the monasteries.[14] These monasteries had been major landowners and became a source of wealth and private estates. Other courts continued, especially those part of the moral community that enforced moral standards, the Archdeacons' Courts and Consistory Courts.

The existence of a body that regulated religion was not new to the sixteenth century; however, the powers of ecclesiastical courts had not always been consistent. In England, heresy became an offence pursuant to ***De Hæretico Comburendo***, a statute enacted in 1401.[15] It was a dual offence: a crime against the orthodox faith of the Church and treason against the Crown. After sentencing in a church court, a heretic went to the secular courts for execution.[16] Their property would **escheat** to the crown.

De Heretico Comburendo (Latin): on the burning of the heretics

The Reformation had involved the separation of English religion from the Church of Rome. Two provinces of western Christendom, Canterbury and York, each led by a primate became the Church of England. Henry VIII declared himself the Supreme Head of the Church. His daughter Mary I repudiated this power and returned English religion to the papal fold; her sister Elizabeth I in turn made herself the Supreme Governor of the Church, rather than Supreme Head. Section 8 of the *Act of Supremacy 1558*[17] remains law in the United Kingdom today, granting the English monarch:

Escheat (Latin and medieval French): the reversion of land to the king, a process overseen by the *escheator*

> suche Jurisdictions Privileges Superiorities and Preheminences Spirituall and Ecclesiasticall, as by any Spirituall or Ecclesiasticall Power or Aucthorite hathe heretofore bene or may lawfully be exerised or used for the Visitacion of the Ecclesiasticall State and Persons, and for Reformacion Order and Correccion of the same and of all maner of Errours Heresies Scismes Abuses Offences Contemptes and Enormities, shall for ever by aucthorite of this present Parliament be united and annexed to the Imperiall Crowne of this Realme.[18]

[14] Joseph Tanner, *Tudor Constitutional Documents AD 1485–1603 with an Historical Commentary* (Cambridge, Cambridge University Press, 1948) 336; William Hoskins, *The Age of Plunder: The England of Henry VIII 1500–1547* (London, Longman, 1976) 134.

[15] 2 Hen 4 c 15.

[16] Richard Burn, *The Ecclesiastical Law* (London, S Sweet, V and R Stevens, and GS Norton, 1842) vol 2, 305.

[17] 1 Eliz 1 c 1.

[18] *Ibid* s 8.

This post-Reformation Church of England was, and is, the established Church of England.

An important post-Reformation jurisdiction was the High Commission for Causes Ecclesiastical, a statutory body to uphold the established Church of England, first under Henry VIII and then with revival under Elizabeth I, established under Letters Patent.[19] The High Commission, enforced by the *Act of Supremacy 1558*, compelled obedience to the national Church. It had the authority to correct those who were schismatic in their religion, or disobedient to ecclesiastical authority.[20] It regulated the social fabric by, for example, punishing scolds, usurers and the sexually incontinent.[21]

The High Commission became widely disliked, especially by common law lawyers, for its use of inquisitorial procedures. Unlike a common law court, where the proceedings were (and are) seen to be done, the Commissioners worked behind closed doors. The *ex officio* oath was especially associated with the Commission. An *ex officio* oath was one an official administered by virtue of their office.[22] Apart from that circumstance, the High Commission's *ex officio* oath had more sinister implications as the testifier on oath did not know in advance what they were going to be asked and in that state of ignorance they swore a supernatural oath to tell the truth.

The dilemma and the threat that created was very real. People knew themselves to be living in a supernatural world. In being compelled to tell the truth, though in ignorance of the question, whatever the Commission asked them, could force them to give an incriminating answer, leading to punishment in this world. If they lied or perjured themselves – perhaps as an act of self-preservation – then their salvation was at stake. A testifier might be asked: did a mouse that ate a consecrated wafer eat the Body of Christ.[23] The answer could be a serious risk to the person in either this world or the afterlife.

Pause for Thought

Swearing Ex Officio

The section above indicated the very real dilemma of a testifier who would be administered the *ex officio* oath without knowing what they would be asked: would they incriminate or perjure themselves?

Questions to Consider

1. Are there any legal circumstances today when a person is required to swear an oath without knowing what they will be asked?
2. Is there any justification for placing this obligation on a witness or testifier?

[19] John Baker, *The Reinvention of Magna Carta* (Cambridge, Cambridge University Press, 2017) 133.

[20] Diana Newton, *The Making of the Jacobean Regime: James VI and I and the Government of England, 1603–1605* (Suffolk and Rochester, Boydell & Brewer, 2005) 57; Thomas Bayly Howell, *Cobbett's Complete Collection of State Trials and. Proceedings for High Treason and Other Crimes and Misdemeanors from the Earliest Period [1163] to the Present Time [1820]* (London, R Bagshaw, 1812) 439.

[21] Baker (n 19) 135.

[22] Boyer (n 11) 169.

[23] *Ibid.*

The Commission became a regular body, rather than being simply an executive instrument. It became stronger and larger over the sixteenth and seventeenth centuries. In 1611 it had 60 members; by 1625, 108. Other ecclesiastical courts lost cases to the High Commission as it dealt with matrimony, divorce, alimony, heresy, schism and nonconformity to the Church of England, as well as the punishment of clergymen who did not conform to Church discipline.[24]

As its powers increased so did opposition. A type of religious identity often called 'puritan' fell foul of the Commission, especially clergy who objected on principle to regulations imposed by the established Church of England. There was opposition from common law lawyers, including Sir Edward Coke. Coke, using his mastery of common law and statutory interpretation, interpreted the *Act of Supremacy 1558* in the narrowest possible way in an effort to limit the Commission. According to Coke's reading of the statute, the Commission ought only be empowered to deal with 'enormous' offences. Coke also objected to the use of *ex officio* oath, taking practical steps to oppose the Commission by using writs of prohibition and *habeas corpus*.[25]

The Crown and Common Law

The relationship between the common law and the King's authority was a central issue in the early years of James VI and I's reign after he succeeded Elizabeth I in 1603. The main question was whether the prerogative or personal powers of the King overrode the common law. This was squarely at issue in the *Case of Prohibitions*.[26] The case arose out of a jurisdictional dispute between the common law courts and the ecclesiastical courts, indicative of the tensions discussed earlier respecting the High Commission. The ultimate question was: *Could the common law courts prevent the ecclesiastical courts from hearing a case?* At this time, the ecclesiastical courts heard matters that today the secular courts deal with, including the probate of wills, marriage, the legitimacy of children, and offensive speech. The common law courts usually tried to prevent the ecclesiastical courts from hearing cases by an order called a writ of prohibition. Still in use today, courts use writs of prohibition to order a tribunal or inferior court not to hear a case. For example, this remedy is available in section 75(v) of the *Australian Constitution*. As Chief Justice of the Court of Common Pleas, Coke both wrote and acted against the Commission. His writings presented precedents from the sixteenth century to show the common law courts' rights to prohibit and arguing against the Commission's power to imprison people and to make them swear without knowing what they would be asked.[27]

[24] Cyndia Susan Clegg, *Press Censorship in Elizabethan England* (Cambridge, Cambridge University Press, 2004) 41.

[25] *Ibid* 610.

[26] (1607) 12 Co Rep 63, 77 ER 1342.

[27] Baker (n 19) 354.

Figure 3.1 Paperwork Generated by the Court of Common Pleas

Order from the Court of Common Pleas to Walter Bagot (sheriff) and Sir Walter Chetwynd (1604). Call #: L.a.1062.

If a common law court issued a writ of prohibition against an ecclesiastical court, it was claiming that the ecclesiastical court had no right to hear the action. The issue came to a head when the Archbishop of Canterbury, Richard Bancroft, approached James to resolve the dispute between the courts. James summoned together the ecclesiastical and common law judges to decide whether his prerogative power extended this far. In a subsequent second meeting, Sir Edward Coke disagreed with Archbishop Bancroft's claim that 'the King may himself decide it in his royal person; the Judges are but delegates of the King'.[28] James VI and I responded: 'he thought the law was founded upon reason, and that he and others had reason, as well as the Judges'.[29] What occurred next is famous; Coke strongly defended the independence of the courts and common law from interference from the King's personal powers. He provoked James' ire by denying that monarchs had the right to 'adjudge any case, either criminal or betwixt party and party; but it ought to be determined and adjudged in some Court of Justice, according to the law and custom of England'.[30]

James and Coke continued to spar. Coke (according to some reports, including his own) said to James:

> true it was, that God had endowed His Majesty with excellent science, and great endowments of nature; but His Majesty was not learned in the laws of his realm of England, and causes which concern the life, or inheritance, or goods, or fortunes of his subjects, are not to be decided by natural reason but by the artificial reason and judgment of law, which law is an act which requires long study and experience, before that a man can attain to the cognizance of it: that the law was the golden met-wand and measure to try the causes of the subjects.[31]

Effectively, the King could not decide the law even if he was not subject to anyone else. Only those trained in the law, who had gained 'artificial reason' through 'long study and experience',[32] had the skills and the expertise to decide cases.[33] The statement is an important one in terms of the professional identity of the law and of the lawyer, as Coke was stating a claim for a distinctively educated and expert body of people that comprised the legal profession. This excluded the King. In response, James VI and I threatened Coke with a closed fist. Coke, apparently weeping on all fours, begged James' forgiveness, although there are different versions of this story.[34]

Fuller's Case, decided in 1607, was a particular flashpoint of controversy.[35] The barrister Nicholas Fuller found himself imprisoned by the Commission after Fuller's vociferous defence of his clients and his attacks on the High Commission.[36] His criticisms of

[28] Edward Coke, *The Reports of Sir Edward Coke, Knt: In Thirteen Parts*, vol 6 (London, J Butterworth and Son, 1826) 281.

[29] Joseph Tanner (ed), *Constitutional Documents of the Reign of James I, AD 1603–1625* (Cambridge, Cambridge University Press, 1960) 187.

[30] Coke (n 28) 280.

[31] *Case of Prohibitions* (n 26). See also Roland G Usher, 'James VI and I and Sir Edward Coke' (1903) 18(72) *The English Historical Review* 664, 664.

[32] Edward Coke, *The First Part of the Institutes of the Laws of England: Or, A Commentary Upon Littleton: Not the Name of the Author Only, But of the Law Itself: Haec Ego Grandaevus Posui Tibi, Candide Lector* (London, J & WT Clarke, 1832) s 138.

[33] See chapter two of this volume.

[34] Catherine Drinker Bowen, *The Lion and the Throne: The Life and Times of Sir Edward Coke, 1552–1634* (London, Hamish Hamilton, 1957) 262.

[35] Coke (n 28) 254.

[36] Wilfrid R Prest, *The Inns of Court under Elizabeth I and the Early Stuarts* (New Jersey, Rowman and Littlefield, 1972) 211.

the Commission left him in contempt of court.[37] This same issue was re-agitated in the ***Case of Proclamations***.[38] By issuing royal proclamations, James prohibited the construction of new buildings in London and the making of starch from wheat. A breach of James' proclamation would result in criminal penalties. The House of Commons sought the opinion of Coke, then Chief Justice of the Court of Common Pleas, on whether this measure was legal. Coke and his fellow judges answered in the negative. They held, including on precedents adduced by Coke, that:

- The King could not grant himself new prerogative powers and could only use ones already recognised by the common law.
- Royal proclamation could not create criminal offences.[39]

The King

> by his proclamation or other ways, cannot change any part of the common law or statute law, or the customs of the realm … and the King cannot create any offence by his prohibition or proclamation which was not an offence before.[40]

Two key concepts – independence from royal interference and the King being subject to the law – emerge in these two cases. Seventeenth century court decisions determining the Crown's prerogative limits were, however, generally inconsistent with one another. The King and his officers still applied pressure to judges to decide in their favour, although these jurisdictional disputes and conflicts over royal authority presage many further conflicts during the seventeenth century.

Equity and the Common Law

Beyond the common law traditions were courts staffed by statutory officers, who also could exist in a state of tension with the common law courts and judges. These courts are distinct from common law method (procedure by writ) and used complaint or bill. The courts of equity were for occasions when the common law courts could not provide a remedy.[41] However equity is not a court; it is a principle that is expressed through courts.

Chancery

The Chancery was discussed in the context of the legal and administrative machinery of the Norman Conquest. The 'Latin side' of Chancery, the secretariat, was staffed by the

[37] See *The Argument of Master Nicholas Fuller in the Case of Thomas Lad and Richard Maunsell, His Clients: Wherein It Is Plainely Proved, That the Ecclesiasticall Commissioners Have No Power, by Vertue of Their Commission, to Imprison, to Put to the Oath Ex Officio, or to Fine Any of His Majesties Subjects* (1607).

[38] (1611) 12 Co Rep 74, 77 ER 1352.

[39] Rudolph W Heinze, *The Proclamations of the Tudor Kings* (Cambridge, Cambridge University Press, 1976) 36.

[40] Edward Coke, *The Reports of Sir Edward Coke, Knt. [1572–1617]: In English, in Thirteen Parts Complete; with References to All the Ancient and Modern Books of the Law*, vol 7 (London, J Rivington, 1777) 75.

[41] Ernest Jacob, *The Fifteenth Century 1399–1485* (Oxford, Oxford University Press, 1993) 455.

> *Cursitor* (Latin): clerk or messenger of the Chancery

cursitors who were under the masters or chief clerks and who prepared the Latin writs and charters (*clerici de cursu*).[42] As custodian of the Great Seal used to authenticate royal documents, the Chancellor was in charge of the King's clerks or secretariat. But the 'English side' of Chancery was the Chancellor's legal work.

To commence a common law action, litigants first purchased a writ from the clerks of Chancery. Litigants could only seek justice at common law if their claim was recognised in an existing royal writ. Earlier in its history, Chancery developed a practice of fashioning writs when existing royal writs were insufficient to cover a claim. Henry III's *Provisions of Oxford 1258* restricted that ability: only with the consent of the King's Council could the Chancery issue a new writ.

Due to the rigidity of royal writs, subjects increasingly presented bills of complaint (or petitions) to the King in Council to seek relief against common law injustices. The King's oath required the king 'to do equal and right justice and discretion in mercy and truth'.[43] Initially, the King or his Council heard these petitions but, by the fourteenth century, the King delegated to the Chancellor as 'Keeper of the King's Conscience'.[44] By the mid-fourteenth century, the Chancellor was hearing these petitions in the High Court of Chancery. This considered itself a 'court of conscience', and the rules it applied were 'equity'. The Lord Chancellor was technically the single judge of the Chancery but had masters in Chancery and the Master of the Rolls. Possible cases that the Chancery could hear included perjury, forgery, libel, slander, commercial fraud, trusts and uses.

The Chancery was enormously busy by the early 1500s hearing equitable cases and private litigation. The lawyers there were civil lawyers trained at university.[45] These lawyers possessed familiarity with civil Roman law and the notion of ***sinderisis***.[46] Equity is a process of adjudication beyond the common law courts. The way the Chancery functioned has implications for its archives. Courts of equity did not keep plea rolls as the action did not start with a writ.[47] The petition (a bill) preceded the process of formal adjudication. The involved and lengthy equity procedure included the exchange of written charges and denials between the parties and the examination of witnesses but in private rather than in court.[48]

> *Sinderisis* (Latin and Middle English): moral judgement of good and evil

To some, the work of the Chancery seemed fast and informal. When he was Lord Chancellor, Sir Thomas More sat in his own hall in his house in the afternoons, dispensing equitable jurisdiction.[49] More also received complaints from common law judges about

[42] Edward Foss, 'On the Origin of the Title and Office of Cursitor-Baron of the Exchequer. In a Letter addressed to Lord Viscount Strangford, FRS, VP' (1855) 36(1) *Archaeologia* 24.

[43] Frederic William Maitland, *The Constitutional History of England: A Course of Lectures Delivered* (Clark, New Jersey, The Lawbook Exchange, 2001) 99.

[44] John Campbell, *The Lives of the Lord Chancellors and Keepers of the Great Seal of England, from the Earliest Times Till the Reign of King George IV* (London, Lea and Blanchard, 1847) 27.

[45] Paul Tucker, 'The Early History of the Court of Chancery: A Comparative Study' (2000) 115(463) *The English Historical Review* 791, 794.

[46] Paul Vinogradoff, 'Reason and Conscience in Sixteenth-Century Jurisprudence' (1908) 24(4) *Law Quarterly Review* 378, 379.

[47] Geoffrey Elton, *England 1200–1640: The Sources of History* (Cambridge, Cambridge University Press, 1969) 57.

[48] *Ibid* 61.

[49] Tucker (n 45) 796.

interference, to which he riposted that they could try to be less rigorous themselves.[50] This small occasion of controversy between the Lord Chancellor and the common law judges belies the assumption that equity ought to be present in all courts.

Conflict between common law and the Chancery was long standing. In 1523 Christopher St Germain (1460–1540) published *Dialogus de fundamentis legum Anglie et de conscientia* (normally called *Doctor and Student* in English) and his dialogue between a Doctor of Laws and his pupil remained an influential source for understanding the conflicts between common law and Chancery and for discussion of conscience. Coke certainly knew it and used it.

Australian law still uses equity and famously uses equity in a more conservative form than England. *The Earl of Oxford's Case* sits at the foundation of that approach. That case resolved the sixteenth century and early seventeenth century jurisdictional conflict between common law courts and Chancery.[51] In this celebrated decision, King James VI and I held that equitable principles prevailed over the common law in cases of conflict. The King upheld the Court of Chancery's ability to grant injunctions prohibiting plaintiffs from bringing actions in the common law courts, or from enforcing a common law judgment, if the actions or judgments were inconsistent with the principles of equity applied in the Court of Chancery. These kinds of injunctions – effectively preventing the enforcement of common law rights – were called 'common injunctions' and were awarded right up to the 1870s.

The original case centred on land located at Covent Garden in London. There were a number of attempts to sell the land: (1) Magdalene College, Cambridge, owned it, but sold the land to (2) Queen Elizabeth I, who transferred it to (3) Benedict Spinola, who sold the land to (4) the Earl of Oxford. The question was whether Magdalene College or the Earl of Oxford owned the land. The legal issue was whether a statute of 1571 prohibited Magdalene College's sale of the land to Elizabeth I.

Sir Edward Coke, as Chief Justice of King's Bench, ruled in favour of the College and therefore considered that the statute of 1571 prohibited the sale to the Queen. The Earl of Oxford therefore petitioned the Lord Chancellor, Lord Ellesmere, for a common injunction so that the Earl could prevent the enforcement of the common law judgment. The College refused to answer the Earl's case and objected to Chancery hearing the matter. Ellesmere LC, who was no friend of Coke's, famously expounded Chancery's jurisdiction.[52] He pointed out that Chancery was there because:

> Mens Actions are so divers and infinite, That it is impossible to make any general Law which may aptly meet with every particular Act, and not fail in some Circumstances. The Office of the Chancellor is to correct Mens Consciences for Frauds, Breach of Trusts, Wrongs and Oppressions, of what Nature soever they be, and to soften and mollify the Extremity of the Law, which is called *Summum Jus*.[53]

Ellesmere held that equitable principles would give the Earl rights to the land. He then petitioned James VI and I personally to decide whether the Court of Chancery's decision

[50] *Ibid* 811.

[51] (1615) 1 Ch Rep 1; 21 ER 485.

[52] David Ibbetson, 'The Earl of Oxford's Case' in Charles Mitchell and Paul Mitchell (eds), *Landmark Cases in Equity* (London, Bloomsbury, 2012) 3.

[53] *Earl of Oxford's Case* (n 51) 486.

or the common law Court's decision had priority. James found in favour of Chancery, expressed in a decree from July 1616. Chancery was superior to the common law courts. Royal subjects should not have 'to perish under the rigor and extremity of our law'.[54]

The *Earl of Oxford's Case* established a fundamental principle of English law: where rules of equity and rules of the common law conflict, the rule of equity will prevail. As it had been in the *Earl of Oxford's Case*, this was dealt with by common injunction – the Court of Chancery prohibiting an action or the enforcement of a judgment at common law. In a clash of jurisdictions, equity (in the Court of Chancery) had priority over the common law (in the Courts of King's Bench, Common Pleas or Exchequer), and the priority was maintained by the common injunction. After merger of the Court of Chancery and the common law courts in the 1870s eliminated the clash of jurisdictions: there was then only a single superior court.[55] The priority of equity over the common law was therefore guaranteed instead by a rule. The Court should apply the rule of equity: 'Generally … in which there is any conflict or variance between the rules of equity and the rules of the common law with reference to the same matter the rules of equity shall prevail.' This was provided for in section 25(11) of the *Judicature Act 1873* (UK). It remains law in Australian jurisdictions.[56] These provisions effectively perpetuate James's decision in the *Earl of Oxford's Case*.

Star Chamber and Court of Requests

Besides the Chancery, there were other courts giving relief, in particular the Star Chamber and the Court of Requests. These were all newer than common law courts, although the Star Chamber had been in existence by the reign of Henry VII in the early sixteenth century. There is a reference in 1349 to a new chamber for receipt of exchequer, soon called the Star Chamber. A court whose name is now a synonym for cruel and arbitrary proceedings obtained its name from pretty decorations on the ceiling of the chamber where it met.[57] The Star Chamber therefore is the customary name given to the King's Council when that Council sat as a court, and which received petitions articulating grievances and was one of several prerogative jurisdictions.[58] Its records are patchy, but it is apparent the counsellors heard cases where one party contended against another. However, as a body with a jurisdiction flowing straight from the King, it 'acted as the king's tribunal of state, suppressing violence and keeping down men too great to be dealt with by the ordinary courts'.[59]

[54] James Spedding, Robert Leslie Ellis and Douglas Denon Heath (eds), *The Words of Francis Bacon* (London, Longman, Green, Reader and Dyer, 1869) vol 12, 395.

[55] See chapter six of this volume.

[56] The provisions are: *Judicature Act 1875* (Qld) s 5(11); *Civil Procedure Act 2011* (Qld) s 7(3); *Supreme Court Act 1986* (Vic) s 29(1); *Supreme Court Civil Procedure Act 1932* (Tas) ss 10–11; *Supreme Court Act 1935* (WA) ss 24, 25; *Supreme Court Act 1935* (SA) s 28; *Australian Capital Territory Supreme Court Act 1933* (Cth) s 25; *Supreme Court Act 1979* (NT) s 68.

[57] Albert Carter, 'Council and Star Chamber' (1902) 8(3) *LQR* 218.

[58] Geoffrey Elton, *The Tudor Constitution : Documents and Commentary* (Cambridge, Cambridge University Press, 1965) 158; Ryan Patrick Alford, 'The Star Chamber and the Regulation of the Legal Profession 1570–1640' (2011) 51(4) *American Journal of Legal History* 639, 645.

[59] Elton (n 58) 161.

It had a particular responsibility for the crime delineated as sedition.[60] John Baker cautions against calling the Star Chamber an actual court of equity, but as a body following a set of procedures that meant it could investigate and give equitable relief. It could order punishment, which could be fines but could also range from temporary to permanent humiliation. The Star Chamber could order people to the **pillory**, or to have their ears cropped off.[61] Such happened to William Prynne, a lawyer and prolific writer who published critical works about Charles I, his queen Henrietta Maria, and William Laud, the Archbishop of Canterbury. The Star Chamber punished Prynne for his sedition with gruesome physical punishment including cropping his ears and burning brands into his cheeks. On the scaffold the hangman 'burnt Prin in both the cheeks … and, because hee burnt one cheeke with a letter the wronge waye, hee burnt that againe. The haingman hewed off Prin's eares very scurvily, which putt him to much paine'.[62]

Pillory (Middle English): wooden frame locking a person's head and hands in place

The Lord Chancellor, discussed earlier in relation to the Chancery, was the guiding force in the Star Chamber. Cardinal Thomas Wolsey, one of Henry VIII's ministers, was Chancellor from 1515 to 1529 and referred to the 'new law of the star chamber'. Wolsey's biographer AF Pollard notes he was likely referring to the vigour with which he, and by extension the rest of the counsellors sitting in the Star Chamber, set about administering the law, especially over unruly great men. That included offences such as perjury and rioting.[63] Cases coming into the Chancellor included petitions from remoter parts of the kingdom, complaining that people of influence in the area were using their power to undercut or frustrate common law justice.[64]

If the Court of Star Chamber dealt with the aristocracy, the other end of the social spectrum came to the Court of Requests, known as the poor man's court. This Court lacked a formal establishment and instead existed ad hoc, as the poor would bring their complaints to the King.[65] Earlier impermanence gave way to a more settled institutional platform and by the reign of Henry VIII the Court of Requests sat permanently in Westminster. It is clear that there was a specialisation in the complaints of the poor by 1494 as well as a long association with **Lord Privy Seal**, with action taking place under the authority of the Great Seal.

Lord Privy Seal: an office of state

There is a notable feature of this Court; most English courts had jurisdiction over a class of action or a code of law such as common law, equity, the Church courts, or customary law. The Court of Requests, as Plucknett points out, is the odd man out with litigants determined by social class.[66] The complaints of the poor were of many types, such as

[60] Roger B Manning, 'The Origins of the Doctrine of Sedition' (1980) 12 *Albion: A Quarterly Journal Concerned with British Studies* 101.
[61] John Baker, *Oxford History of the Laws of England 1483–1558* (Oxford, Oxford University Press, 2003) 197–98.
[62] Samuel Rawson Gardiner, *Documents Relating to the Proceedings Against William Prynne, in 1634 and 1637: With a Biographical Fragment by the Late John Bruce* (Westminster, Camden Society, 1877) 87.
[63] Albert Pollard, *Wolsey* (Longmans, Green and Co, 1929) 75–76.
[64] Jacob (n 41) 458.
[65] Tim Stretton, *Women Waging Law in Elizabethan England* (Cambridge, Cambridge University Press, 2005) 71.
[66] Theodore Plucknett, *Concise History of the Common Law* (Union, New Jersey, Lawbook Exchange, 2001) 185.

testamentary, maritime and matrimonial matters.[67] The notion of the King consenting to hear the complaints of his poor subjects is a type of patriarchal justice.[68] Regardless of the court, equity involved lengthy processes. A petition to the King would require an answer by the defendant, followed by a replication by the plaintiff, and a rejoinder by the defendant.[69]

The Common Law and Parliament

The disagreements between Coke and King James VI and I and more broadly between different jurisdictions foreshadow ongoing sources of tension in the seventeenth century, including the involvement of the High Court of Parliament itself. In *Dr Bonham's Case*,[70] Coke CJCP held that an Act of Parliament was void if it was 'against common right and reason, or repugnant, or impossible to be performed'.[71] This is the first time that an Act of Parliament or legislation might be 'void' because it did not meet some higher but abstract standard, such as being 'against common right and reason'.

The idea of legislation being 'against common right and reason' sounds odd to modern observers, but common law was said to reflect 'natural law principles': that higher standard referred to earlier. In this context, Coke's suggestion that the common law was 'the golden met-wand whereby all men's causes are justly and evenly measured'[72] is less of a curiosity. Not all of Coke's contemporaries shared this view. Lord Ellesmere, for example, said that 'acts of parliament should be corrected by the same pen that drew them than to be dashed in pieces by the opinion of a few judges'.[73]

The King and Parliament

The relationship between the Crown and Parliament was tense in the seventeenth century. These tensions were root causes of the English Civil Wars (1642–51) and the decade-long abolition of the monarchy in the British Isles (1649–60). It was crucial that the King and Parliament stayed in harmony. While that certainly was not the case for Stuart England in the seventeenth century, the conflicts ushered in an age where notions of constitutional government could thrive.

As noted above, in 1603, James Stuart (or Stewart) – King James VI of Scotland – succeeded his cousin, Elizabeth Tudor (1558–1603), to the English throne as James VI of Scotland and I of England (1603–25). The English people had anticipated and welcomed James's accession to the throne. This popularity waned, leading to the fractured relationship James shared with Parliament and the common law courts on his death in 1625.

James' accession united the thrones of England and Scotland. Although he was King of England, Ireland and Scotland, these were still different countries, and each had its own

[67] Pollard (n 63) 87.

[68] Isaac Leadam, *Select Cases in the Court of Requests: AD 1497–1569* (London, Selden Society, 1898) xii.

[69] *Ibid* xxi.

[70] (1610) 8 Co Rep 113b; 77 ER 646.

[71] *Ibid* 652. See chapter two of this volume.

[72] Edward Coke, *The Fourth Part of the Institutes of the Laws of England Concerning the Jurisdictions of the Courts* (Clarke, 1817) 239.

[73] Cited in John Purdon (ed), *The Law Library* (Philadelphia, JS Littell, 1835) vol 9, 12.

Parliament and its own laws.[74] In chapter four the 'Union of the Crowns' is again discussed. To England, the new King brought with him the theory of the *divine right of kings* that was to mark the Stuart monarchs' reigns. It was James' view that the monarchy was a divine right, an absolutist theory that meant the monarch is appointed by God and is not subject to earthly authority. James by no means intended to break his coronation oath but his ideas were continental and perhaps jarred with English politics.[75] James VI and I was called by critics 'the wisest fool in Christendom'[76] owing to his lack of political acumen but his high scholarly achievement; James wrote several important works on political theory.

In *Daemonologie* (1597) James asserted not only his belief in **witchcraft and the preternatural** but made it a matter of politics and state, as he positioned witches as political threats to the divine persons and their divine authority. In *The True Lawe of Free Monarchies* (1598), James quoted from the Bible in support of the rights of kings.[77] In a speech to the English Parliament in 1610, James stated his position on the monarchy as 'the supremest thing upon earth, for kings are not only God's lieutenants upon earth and sit upon God's throne, but even by God himself they are called gods'. He added:

> Kings are justly called Gods, for that they exercise a manner and resemblance of divine power upon earth. For if you will consider the attributes of God, you shall see how they agree in the person of a king. God hath power to create, or destroy, make or unmake at his pleasure, to give life or send death, to judge all, and to be judges nor accountable to none. To raise low things, and to make high things low at his pleasure, and to God are both soul and body due. And the like power have Kings: they make and unmake their subjects: they have power of raising, and casting down: of life and of death: judges over all their subjects, and in all causes, and yet accountable to none but God only. They have power to exalt low things, and abase high things, and make of their subjects like men at the chess. A pawn to take a bishop or a knight, and to cry up and down any of their subjects, as they do their money. And to the king is due both the affection of the soul, and the service of the body of his subjects[78]

The Stuart monarchy's battles with Parliament took place against this theoretical backdrop.

Elizabethan parliaments were possibly more compliant. This was because members of Parliament were servants of the Crown, as the judges similarly tended to uphold the wishes of the central Government.[79] Elizabeth was an adroit politician herself. Her capacity tactfully and skilfully to get her way is demonstrated in her 'Golden Speech' of 1601. Parliament's submissiveness diminished following the new King's accession to the throne in 1603. James found himself unaccustomed to the practices and customs of English Parliament.

James mistakenly assumed that it would act as Scotland's two representative bodies did – *with obedience*. However, while James had exercised great control over Scotland's unicameral Parliament of 200 members and its Privy Council, he was unprepared for the much larger and more vocal English Parliament. For instance, the House of Commons alone had close to 500 members, more than double that of Scotland's Parliament. In addition, unlike in the Scottish Parliament, members of the English Parliament could freely speak without first seeking leave, as well as scrutinise and reject the monarch's proposals. This enraged James, for in

[74] Wales was part of the Kingdom of England.

[75] Sybil M Jack, '"A Pattern for a King's Inauguration": The Coronation of James I in England' (2004) 21(2) *Parergon* 67, 70.

[76] Hyman Shapiro, *Scotland in the Days of James VI* (London, Longman, 1970) 9.

[77] Daniel Fischlin and Mark Fortier (eds), *The True Law of Free Monarchies: And, Basilikon Doron* (Toronto, Centre for Reformation and Renaissance Studies, 1996) 57.

[78] Cited in David Wootton (ed), *Divine Right and Democracy: An Anthology of Political Writing in Stuart England* (Indianapolis, Hackett Publishing, 2003) 107 .

[79] James Cockburn, *A History of English Assizes 1558–1714* (Cambridge, Cambridge University Press, 1972) 202.

Scotland, Parliament 'heard [him] not only as a King, but, suppose I say it, as a counsellor'.[80] In England, there was 'nothing but curiosity from morning to evening to find faults with my propositions. There, all things warranted that come from me. Here, all things suspected'.[81]

In the *Form of Apology and Satisfaction* (1604), the House of Commons declared their parliamentary right to be the sole judge of elections.[82] The *Form* was an apology in name only. Though it was expressed in deferential language, the Commons strongly asserted that 'our privileges and liberties are our right and due inheritance, no less than our very lands and goods; that they cannot be withheld from us, denied or impaired, but with apparent wrong to the whole state of the realm'.[83]

However, monarchs, even before the Stuarts, summoned and dismissed parliament at their pleasure and parliament dissolved on the death of the monarch. With no obligation to summon Parliament regularly, the Stuart monarchs seldom did. The sitting of Parliament was thus an exceptional occurrence in the Stuart period. It was only when the monarchs, James VI and I and Charles I especially, were in desperate need of legislation or of funds – typically to finance military campaigns – that they called Parliament. James went without Parliaments between 1614 and 1621. He collected revenue using other strategies in order to reduce royal debt. Nevertheless, James was compelled to summon Parliament in 1621. James required a successful vote of supply so that he could contribute to military actions in Germany, when his son-in-law, the Elector Frederick V (whose family was the English Parliament's resort for a Protestant succession at the end of century, see discussion of the *Act of Settlement* in chapter four), was engaged in the Thirty Years' War (1618–48).

At first, Parliament responded positively by voting for two subsidies, but then it refused an additional money supply to James. James was quick to remind Parliament that waging war was within the royal prerogative. He received a protestation from the House of Commons in response. Echoing the 1604 *Form of Apology*, the 1621 *Protestation* reasserted:

> [t]hat the liberties, franchises, privileges and jurisdictions of Parliament are the ancient and undoubted birthright and inheritance of the subjects of England; and that the arduous and urgent affairs concerning the King, State and defence of the realm and of the Church of England, are proper subjects and matter of counsel and debate in Parliament; and that in the handling and proceeding of those businesses every member of the House of Parliament hath, and of right ought to have, freedom of speech to propound, treat, reason and bring to conclusion the same.[84]

At the 1621 sitting, the House of Commons began using the ancient procedure of impeachment to harass government ministers, reviving a process last used in 1459. It involved the House of Commons petitioning the House of Lords for the trial of government ministers for criminal offences.

Charles I succeeded to the throne on his father, James' death in 1625. Charles did not fare much better with Parliament. In fact, his dissatisfaction with the institution led him to adopt similar measures taken by his father. He barely summoned Parliament during

[80] Samuel Rawson Gardiner, *History of England from the Accession of James I to the Outbreak of the Civil War, 1603–1642* (Cambridge, Cambridge University Press, 2011) 191.

[81] David Colclough, *Freedom of Speech in Early Stuart England* (Cambridge, Cambridge University Press, 2005) 145.

[82] Cited in John Kenyon (ed), *The Stuart Constitution, 1603–1688: Documents and Commentary* (Cambridge, Cambridge University Press, 1986) 29.

[83] Paul L Hughes, *Crown and Parliament in Tudor-Stuart England: A Document Constitutional History, 1485–1714* (New York, CP Putnams & Sons, 1959) 159.

[84] Kenyon (n 82) 42.

his reign (1625–49). He did not summon Parliament for 11 years between 1629 and 1641. Without a parliamentary vote for money supply, he raised revenue without parliamentary approval.

Parliament and the Common Law

Parliament was – if not more – just as challenging for Charles I as it was for his father. Parliament proved uncooperative, particularly when the monarch was short of funds. The relationship between Parliament and Charles I deteriorated soon after the new King's accession in 1625. During the later years of James VI and I's reign, England was at war with Spain. The war with Spain was costly, disastrous, and unpopular with MPs. On his accession to the throne in 1625, Charles I renewed the conflict, and turned to Parliament to fund the campaign. To make matters worse, Charles I continued to favour his father's favourite and possible lover, the Duke of Buckingham, who unsuccessfully led a raid on Cadiz, a Spanish port, in late 1625. It was unlikely that, in these circumstances, the House of Commons would soon give in to Charles I's demands.

Tonnage and poundage: taxes on barrels (tuns) and the weight of goods

In 1625, the House of Commons granted **tonnage and poundage** to Charles for one year only in an effort to supervise the Crown's expenditure. Because parliament traditionally granted tonnage and poundage to a monarch for life, the House of Commons' refusal to vote for a longer period insulted Charles and the House of Lords. Parliament also voted for two war subsidies, but it was not enough to see Charles through the war. Dissatisfied with the amount granted, Charles I dissolved Parliament. In need of further funds to finance military campaigning, Charles I was forced to convene a second parliamentary sitting in 1626. The House of Commons and the House of Lords proved uncooperative. Charles I dissolved Parliament without Parliament having voted for tonnage and poundage or a war subsidy for a further year. With the Kingdom verging on bankruptcy, Charles I began to collect revenue without parliamentary approval. He collected tonnage and poundage by claiming a royal prerogative to do so. He declared a forced loan resisted by many nobles. Those who refused to lend money to the King, he either imprisoned or conscripted into the army.

By special command authorised by a Privy Council warrant, Charles I imprisoned 26 gentlemen and the Earl of Lincoln for their refusal to pay but they were not charged with any crime. Five knights sought a writ of *habeas corpus* from the King's Bench in a case known as *Darnell's Case* or *The Five Knights' Case* in 1627. *Habeas corpus* (meaning 'you may have the body') was an order that a person who was in prison should be freed and was the most important way that the common courts made sure that people were only imprisoned in accordance with the requirements of the law. The knights argued that, because the arrest was arbitrary and without cause, the Court should release them. The Court deemed the King's special command to be sufficient. They agreed with the Crown's argument that the King could imprison his subjects without due process of law based on a claim of national security. The result was to be expected. In Stuart England, the judiciary and the executive were contingent on the royal pleasure. The *Petition of Right 1627* declared illegal the royal prerogative power argued in *Darnell's Case*.[85]

[85] 3 Car 1 c 1.

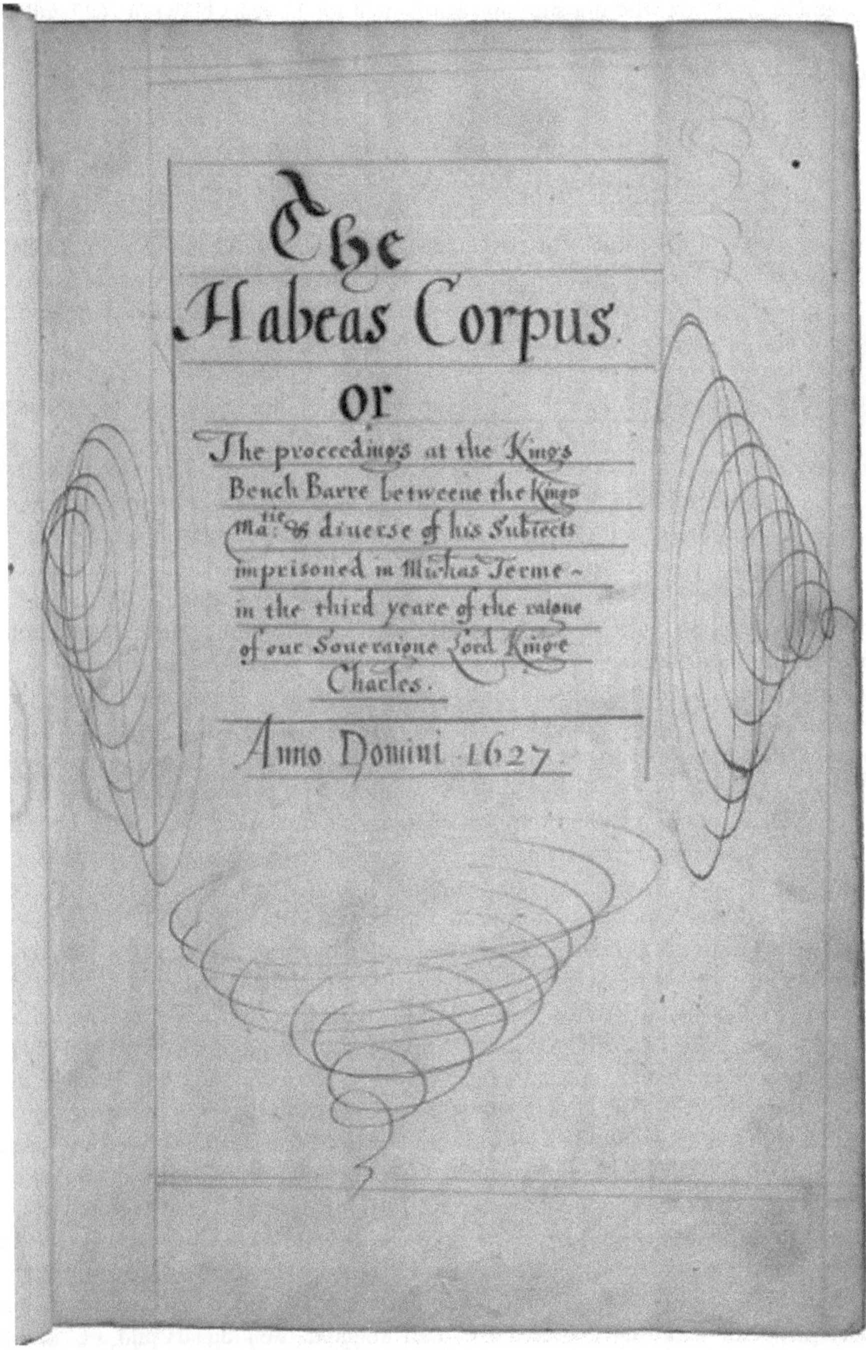

The
Habeas Corpus
or
The proceedings at the Kings
Bench Barre betweene the Kings
Ma:tie & diuerse of his Subiects
imprisoned in Michas Terme
in the third yeare of the raigne
of our Soueraigne Lord King
Charles.
Anno Domini 1627

Figure 3.2 Arguments from the Five Knights Case

T Darnell, *The habeas corpus, or, The proceedings at the King's Bench Bar between the King's Majesty and divers of his subjects imprisoned in Michaelmas term [manuscript]* (1627) title page. Call #: V.b.309.

Constitutional Detour

The Petition of Right

Charles I's subjects, including MPs in the House of Commons, found various ways to inform him of their concerns and displeasure, including sending him the *Petition of Right*. By 1628 Sir Edward Coke was an elderly man, whose judicial career was behind him (James VI and I dismissed him in 1616) but who remained active in the House of Commons, including as its Speaker. Coke's influence on the *Petition of Right* sent to the King is plain: the Magna Carta became the basis of Englishmen's liberties. The idea and the phrasing have Coke's imprint all over them. Coke had earlier told the Commons that 'Magna Carta is such a fellow that he will have no sovereign'.[86] The *Petition of Right* spoke with particular force against apparently felonious acts by the King and other acts deemed illegal, such as the use of martial law, the forced loans and the billeting of troops. Coke was an active participant, including proposing motions and negotiating with the House of Lords as the Commons framed this petition protesting against the King's actions.

The rhetorical force given to the age and authority of the common law contextualises the *Petition*. The so-called 'ancient constitution' is the notion that common law was immemorial. Once more, Edward Coke stands out as the intellectual and polemical leader for these ideas. Coke himself searched archives and used (and mis-used) historic documents. In teleological terms, he saw immemorial law as progressing to his own time with unbroken continuity. Much of what Coke said about these apparent continuities was plain wrong (one example was a claim that 30 different parliaments had confirmed the Magna Carta) but, as the best read and most prolific legal writer, who could have disagreed with him?[87] The *Petition of Right 1627*, the *Habeas Corpus Act 1640*, and the *Habeas Corpus Act 1679*[88] remain law in Queensland.[89] The *Habeas Corpus Act 1804*[90] is law in New South Wales.[91]

Pause for Thought

Habeas corpus

The writ of *habeas corpus* is a cherished right in common law countries but what actual and practical function does it still serve?

[86] David Sandler Berkowitz, *John Selden's Formative Years: Politics and Society in Seventeenth-Century England* (Washington, Folger Books, 1988) 180.

[87] John Pocock, *The Ancient Constitution and the Feudal Law: Study of English Historical Thought in the Seventeenth Century: A Reissue with a Retrospect* (Cambridge, Cambridge University Press, 1987) 46, 290.

[88] 31 Car 2 c 2.

[89] *Imperial Acts Application Act 1984* (Qld) sch 1.

[90] 44 Geo III c 102.

[91] *Imperial Acts Application Act 1969* (NSW) sch 1.

Questions to Consider

1. Are writs of *habeas corpus* still used or used successfully in English, Australian and American courts?
2. Based on your research, what circumstances have prompted any modern use of this ancient privilege?

Constitutional Detour

An Englishman's Home is his Castle

The *Petition of Right* shows Edward Coke engaged with the highest levels of state and society and discussing issues of deep constitutional significance. His reports also bring the reader down to earth with the humblest levels of society. The saying 'an Englishman's home is his castle' is a paraphrase from Coke's *Reports* that a man's private house is 'his castle and fortress, as well for his defence against injury and violence as for his repose'.[92] The case reported, *Semayne's Case*,[93] concerned a trespass on the case brought by Peter Semayne against Richard Gresham. Semayne had permission to take some of Gresham's property against a debt Gresham owed him, but he brought the action of trespass to gain entry to Gresham's house. The King's Bench upheld the privileges of householders against Semayne; 'the shutting of the door of his [Gresham's] own house was lawful'.[94] Although Coke's analogy of the private home with the castle is most often quoted, the significance of the reported case lies in the statement that the sheriff or other legal officer ought to 'signify the cause of his coming, and to make request to open doors',[95] rather than force entry on suspicion. The case has had a long afterlife, most obviously in the principles regarding warrants expressed in the Fourth Amendment to the *United States Constitution* and the Supreme Court's 1958 ruling in *Miller v United States*.[96]

The association of the private home with the castle has a particular resonance with Australian readers. The 1997 Australian comedy film, *The Castle*, involved a working-class family's fight to prevent the compulsory purchase of their modest suburban house to build an airport. Arguably the most popular depiction in Australian cinema of lawyers and judges arguing in the High Court of Australia, the film is remarkable: is there any other piece of Australian pop culture inspired by Sir Edward Coke?

[92] Coke (n 28) 186.
[93] (1604) 5 Co Rep 91a; 77 ER 194.
[94] Coke (n 28) 191.
[95] Coke (n 28) 188.
[96] George Robert Blakey, 'The Rule of Announcement and Unlawful Entry: *Miller v United States* and *Ker v California*' (1964) 112(4) *University of Pennsylvania Law Review* 499, 520.

Law and the English Civil Wars

In 1629, Charles I dissolved Parliament and did not call it again for 11 years – which, incidentally, sent Coke into retirement and he died in 1634. Religious conflicts with Scotland and Charles I's use of questionable measures to raise royal revenue marred this period of personal rule (1629–41). One of these measures was the ancient custom 'distraint of knighthood' dating from 1278. Men with landed income above £40 were fined for their failure to present themselves for knighthood at the King's coronation.

Another unpopular revenue-raising measure was 'ship money'. In 1634, Charles I taxed coastal counties to pay money in support of the Royal Navy. The following year this levy extended to inland counties, though ship money only traditionally applied to coastal areas. Those who did not pay were imprisoned. One of these acts of imprisonment led to the decision in *R v Hampden* or the *Ship Money Case*.[97] John Hampden and four other imprisoned nobles had their case heard before 12 judges of the Court of Exchequer Chamber. In a 7:5 decision, the common law judges found in favour of Charles I. However, Parliament itself then intervened and declared ship money illegal under the *Ship Money Act 1640*.[98] Much later, Article IV of the *Bill of Rights 1689* (Eng) made it illegal for the Crown to raise revenue without parliamentary approval. Article IV of the *Bill of Rights* is embodied in provisions across Australian jurisdictions.[99]

Meanwhile, Charles I's introduction of a Scottish version of the *Book of Common Prayer* (used to conduct Anglican services) to the Scottish church in 1637 triggered rebellion. The principal aim of it was to promote uniform worship between the Churches in England and Scotland. Scots' dissatisfaction with imposed religious practices had a chequered history. After Mary, Queen of Scots, abdicated in 1567, the Scottish church introduced Presbyterian government by elders and consistories (and not by bishops). James VI and I's attempts in 1618 to force the Five Articles of Perth, which changed Scottish worship practices, through the Scottish Assembly and Parliament were seen as an attempt to impose English worship upon them. Charles I's new attempts just conjured up the past for the Scots.

When the Scots rebelled in 1637, Charles I responded by raising levies in England for conscripts. Poorly supplied and armed, the English conscripts retreated at the Scottish border when faced with a stronger and better organised Scottish army. An equally disastrous second campaign against the Scots in 1640 followed the decisive Scots victory in 1639. The King had not summoned Parliament since 1629. But, to fund this second Scottish campaign, Charles I was required to summon Parliament for the first time in 11 years. The House of Commons rejected Charles' offer to repeal ship money in return for war subsidies.

[97] (1637) 3 St Tr 825.

[98] 16 Car 1 c 14.

[99] These provisions embody Article IV of the *Bill of Rights 1688* (Eng): *Australian Constitution* s 83; *Imperial Acts Application Act 1984* (Qld) sch 1; *Australian Capital Territory (Self-Government) Act 1988* (Cth) ss 57, 58; *Northern Territory (Self-Government) Act 1978* (Cth) ss 44, 45; *Constitution Act 1902* (NSW) ss 39, 45; *Constitution of Queensland 2001* (Qld) ss 64, 65, 66; *Public Finance and Audit Act 1987* (SA) ss 5, 6; *Public Account Act 1986* (Tas) ss 7, 8(2), 8(5); *Constitution Act 1975* (Vic) ss 89, 92; *Constitution Act 1889* (WA) ss 64, 72.

Charles dissolved Parliament on 5 May 1640, less than a month after he had summoned it. This parliamentary sitting became known as the 'Short Parliament' for obvious reasons. Charles I borrowed money at exorbitant rates of interest and conscripted subjects into the English Army. The failure of the second campaign resulted in Charles calling Parliament a second time in 1640.

The second sitting – aptly known as the 'Long Parliament' – began after summoning on 3 November 1640. The period between May and August 1641 was especially productive for Charles' opponents. Some key events of this sitting included:

- The attainder (the punishment and conviction of an individual without trial) and execution of the Earl of Strafford in May 1640. An advisor to Charles I, the Earl supported Charles' disastrous campaigns against the Scots.
- The abolition of 'the conciliar courts' of Star Chamber and High Commission.
- The expelling of bishops from the House of Lords, initiated by the *Root and Branch Petition*, which called for the abolition of the Government of the Church of England by bishops.
- Regular sittings of Parliament to be dissolved only with the consent of Parliament. Parliament had to be called every three years under the *Triennial Act*.[100]
- The illegality of ship money, distraint of knighthood, and levying tonnage and poundage without parliamentary consent.

Next, Parliament drew up and sent Charles I a list of demands: the Nineteen Propositions. If Charles I had agreed to these demands, it would have severely curtailed his powers with more responsibility given to Parliament. The Nineteen Propositions included demands that would have resulted in:

- A greater degree of parliamentary control over the appointment and approval of Crown councillors, officers and the tutors of Charles I's children.
- Church reform.
- Matters of public concern being debated in Parliament in all cases.
- Judges and Crown officers holding their position on the condition of good behaviour.

Charles I rejected these demands in his *Answer to the Nineteen Propositions*:

> There being three kindes of Government amongst men, Absolute Monarchy, Aristocracy and Democracy, and all these having their particular conveniences and inconveniencies. The experience and wisdom of your Ancestors hath so moulded this out of a mixture of these, as to give to this Kingdom (as far as humane Prudence can provide) the conveniencies of all three, without the inconveniencies of any one, as long as the Balance hangs even between the three Estates, and they run jointly on in their proper Chanell … The ill of absolute Monarchy is Tyranny, the ill of Aristocracy is Faction and Division, the ills of Democracy are Tumults, Violence and Licentiousnesse. The good of Monarchy is the uniting of a Nation under one Head to resist Invasion from abroad, and Insurrection at home: The good of Aristocracy is the Conjunction of

[100] 16 Car I c 1.

> Counsell in the ablest Persons of a State for the publike benefit: The good of Democracy is Liberty, and the Courage and Industry which Liberty begetts.[101]

As a result, the Civil War (1642–66) broke out. Parliamentary forces, led in part by Oliver Cromwell, defeated the Royalists in 1646. Parliamentary forces captured Charles I and, after fruitless negotiations, put him on trial for treason. On 30 January 1649, the Court convicted Charles I, and he was beheaded.

Constitutional Detour

The Trial of Charles I (1649)

The struggle between King Charles I and Parliament had a terminal conclusion with the execution of the King on 30 January 1649. Other trials of the King's ministers contextualise these momentous proceedings, including the trials and executions of the Earl of Strafford and Archbishop William Laud in 1641 and 1645 respectively. It is Charles' trial, though, which continues to command interest. Before 1649, heads of states from time to time had died in battle or from assassination but not because they had been executed by their own kingdom. While there was much that was novel in King Charles' trial, there were some legal continuities: as ever Westminster Hall was the scene of the legal activity and, as today, justice was seen to be done with a large crowd in the public gallery.

There was however much novelty. The ordinance establishing the Court was rejected by the House of Lords (itself soon to be abolished), but the English Parliament was in general terms behaving appropriately and had within its power the creation of new courts.[102] The Solicitor-General John Cook prosecuted and John Bradshaw presided. The trial proceedings were recorded in minute detail, even down to the furnishings in Westminster Hall, and therefore preserve much detail of the personal interactions lacking in accounts of other trials.[103] As such, it is clear that Charles rose to the occasion, speaking and acting with dignity, arguing firmly with Bradshaw, without his stutter.[104]

The Court charged Charles I with 'high treason and high misdemeanours … in the name of the commons of England'.[105] The charge placed responsibility for widespread

[101] *An Exact Collection of All Remonstrances, Declarations, Votes, Orders, Ordinances and Other Remarkable Passages Betweene the Kings Most Excellent Majesty, and His High Court of Parliament Beginning at His Majesties Return from Scotland, Being in December 1641, and Continued Untill March the 21, 1643. Which Were Formerly Published Either by the Kings Majiesties Command Or by Order from One of the Houses of Parliament* (London, Edward Husbands, T Warren, R Best, 1643) 320.

[102] Geoffrey Robertson, *The Tyrannicide Brief: The Story of the Man who Sent Charles I to the Scaffold* (London, Random House, 2010) 188.

[103] Joseph Muddiman, *Trial of King Charles the First* (Sydney, Butterworth, 1928) 75.

[104] *The Trials of Charles the First, and of Some of the Regicides: With Biographies of Bradshaw, Ireton, Harrison, and Others, and with Notes* (London, W Tegg, 1861) 72.

[105] *Ibid* 53.

bloodshed and death with him, including that he 'hathe caused and procured many thousands of the free peoples of this nation to be slain'.[106] In response, Charles denied the authority of the Court and any legal process not only against the King but without the King's participation and declared 'I would know by what power I am called hither. I would know by what authority, I mean lawful. There are many unlawful authorities in the world, thieves and robbers by the highway. Remember I am your King, your lawful King, and what sins you bring upon your heads, and the judgment of God upon this land; think well upon it, I say.'[107] From the beginning to the end, up to and beyond being found guilty, Charles refused to accept the 'Commons' comprised a court of judicature.[108]

Why does this trial continue to command interest, including from quarters such as modern constitutional and human rights law? Most famously, the Australian lawyer Geoffrey Robertson's *The Tyrannicide Brief* drew out the historical parallels between Charles I's trial and a modern war crimes trial of a head of state, down to features such as the deportment and presentation of the head of state. For instance, he notes that Slobodan Milosevic, the Serbian president tried at The Hague for war crimes, sat alone in the court room and presented as an isolated figure. Beyond studies on the seventeenth century, the trial of Charles I has an important place in the academic study of modern war crimes trials, not least for the questions it continues to raise about sovereign immunity and procedural questions about due process.[109]

Pause for Thought

Trying a Head of State

To put a head of state on trial is extraordinary, not least if the head of state is accepted as having been sacramentally upheld by God.

Questions to Consider

1. To what extent do you think the trial of Charles I can help to inform understanding of the mechanisms for but also the rhetorical importance of bringing a head of state to justice for crimes against their own people?

[106] Muddiman (n 103) 79.

[107] *Trials of Charles the First* (n 104) 31.

[108] Justice Michael Kirby, 'The Trial of King Charles I – Defining Moment for our Constitutional Liberties' (London, Anglo-Australasian Lawyers' Association, 22 January 1999), available at www.hcourt.gov.au/assets/publications/speeches/former-justices/kirbyj/kirbyj_charle88.htm.

[109] Robertson (n 102) 188; John Laughland, *A History of Political Trials: From Charles I to Saddam Hussein* (Oxford, Peter Lang, 2008) 21; Charles Anthony Smith, *The Rise and Fall of War Crimes Trials: From Charles I to Bush II* (Cambridge, Cambridge University Press, 2012); Robertson (n 102) in Morten Bergsmo, Cheah Wui Ling and YI Ping, *Historical Origins of International Criminal Law: Volume 1* (Torkel Opsahl Academic ePublisher, 2014).

The Interregnum, 1649–60

The monarchy and the House of Lords were abolished in 1649. England became a 'Commonwealth'. The 'Interregnum', meaning the period between kings, can be divided into four periods:

Figure 3.3 Parliaments and Authorities in Republican England

The Rump Parliament (1649–53)	**The Nominated Assembly (1653)**
• Remainder of the English Long Parliament	• This assembly is alternatively referred to as Barebone's Parliament after one of its extreme Puritan members, Praise-God Barebone
The Protectorate of Oliver Cromwell (1653–58)	**The Protectorate of Richard Cromwell (1658–59)**
• Oliver Cromwell led the country as Lord Protector until his death in 1658	• Richard succeeded his father, Oliver, as Lord Protector

In 1653, Oliver Cromwell dissolved the Barebone's Parliament. The executive Government subsequently legislated by ordinance under the *Instrument of Government*. The control of the common law courts had been a figurative battleground itself between the King and Parliament before and during the Civil Wars.[110] Radical members of the Barebone's Parliament wished to abolish the common law and replace it with the law of Moses; that is to say, 'Mosaic Law' from the Ten Commandments. At the same time, they passed innovative legislation establishing procedures for registering births, marriages and deaths; probate of wills; creditors' relief; and the incarceration of the mentally ill. The restoration of the monarchy swept all this away in 1660. In 1653, the Army presented Oliver Cromwell – the newly appointed Lord Protector – with England's *only* written constitution. The Cromwellian period had a policy of general religious tolerance, but that policy excluded Anglicans and Roman Catholics. Nevertheless, it still encouraged individuality in congregational practice, not seen again until after the *Toleration Act 1689*.[111]

The Interregnum is perhaps most widely remembered for its legislation enforcing standards of morality. For example, the *Commonwealth (Adultery) Act 1650* attached the death penalty to adultery and incest, and three months' imprisonment to fornication. Denying the Trinity, scriptural authority, the resurrection of Jesus, and the day of judgement likewise attracted the death penalty under the *Blasphemy Ordinance 1648*.[112] Over the six-month

[110] See generally Stephen F Black, 'The Courts and Judges of Westminster Hall during the Great Rebellion, 1640–1660' (1986) 7 *The Journal of Legal History* 25.

[111] 1 Wm & M c 18.

[112] Reid Mortensen, 'Blasphemy in a Secular State: A Pardonable Sin?' (1994) 17 *University of New South Wales Law Journal* 409, 410.

period of its existence, the Barebone's Parliament managed to offend lawyers, landowners and army officers with their suggested reforms, most of which involved taxation.

The Restoration (1660)

The monarchy was restored in 1660. Charles I's son, Charles II, took the throne. The new Royalist or Cavalier Parliament had three pressing items of business. In the first place, both Parliament and a monarch were required for the English Constitution to function. Second, religious conformity was necessary to suppress Puritans (as punishment) and Catholics (for past transgressions), and to establish a Church of England led by bishops as the national religion. Third, violence was a demonstrably ineffective weapon, as proven by the English Civil War, with the execution of Charles I, and throughout the Interregnum.

Charles II's 12 years of exile had produced a king who was pragmatic and shrewd about matters of state. The Cavalier Parliament restored Charles II to executive power. It granted him an extremely generous financial settlement to cover government costs. Though denied to his father, Parliament granted Charles II customs for life. Behind closed doors, Charles II secretly negotiated with Louis XIV of France to receive a handsome subsidy on the condition that he would declare himself Catholic at a convenient time.

The Glorious Revolution

In 1685, Charles II (1660–85) died. His brother, the Catholic James, Duke of York, came to the thrones of England and Scotland as James II and VII (1685–88). James II's reign was short. It ended with the 'Glorious Revolution', James II fleeing England, and new Protestant monarchs (William III and Mary II, James's daughter) on the throne.

Before the Revolution

To set the Glorious Revolution in context, four events took place in the last decade of Charles II's reign: the Popish Plot, the Rye House Plot, the Exclusion Crisis and the Monmouth Rebellion. A second reason for considering these events is to recognise the old religious prejudices exploited to promote fear and distrust of an absolutist Catholic monarchy.

The Popish Plot started in 1678. Titus Oates, a defrocked priest of highly questionable character, claimed that there was a Catholic plot to assassinate Charles II, install James as King, burn down London, and raise a Scottish and Irish rebellion against the Protestants to restore Roman Catholicism as England's official religion. The historian Edward Carpenter memorably recounts Oates' career as 'in turn Anglican vicar, naval chaplain, Roman Catholic student, embryonic Jesuit, Government pensioner, and finally zealous Baptist'.[113]

[113] Edward Carpenter, *The Protestant Bishop: Being the Life of Henry Compton, 1632–1713, Bishop of London* (London, Longmans, Green and Co, 1956) 43.

If that sounds like a tall tale, it was. In reality, there was no plot and Oates was later tried for perjury.[114] The Government was not initially convinced either, but two coincidences led to Oates' claims gaining greater momentum. First, the former secretary of James, the King's brother, had been secretly corresponding with the French court to reinstate Catholicism in England. The second coincidence was the still unsolved murder of Sir Edmund Berry Godfrey. Godfrey was the Justice of the Peace who had first interrogated Oates about his fanciful claims. The Popish Plot capitalised on anti-Catholic fear and distrust in England, and it worked. Distrust gripped England. Prominent Catholics at the royal court, including the Queen's servants, left the kingdom.[115] Well-known Catholics faced trial and were executed for high treason in trials presided over by Chief Justice Sir William Scroggs. Plots aside, the mere fact of being a Roman Catholic clergyman was a capital crime in seventeenth century England.

The Exclusion Crisis (1679–81) was next in the series of events that reached its climax with the Glorious Revolution. The Crisis comprised three attempts between 1679 and 1681 to exclude Charles II's Catholic brother, James, Duke of York, from the throne. Charles II dissolved Parliament twice to prevent the House of Lords from voting on the bill, and the House of Lords stopped one bill. The Rye House Plot (1683) was a total failure and led to the evaporation of the Whig case for James' exclusion. Evidence emerged of radical Whigs' involvement in plots to stir up rebellion, and to either kidnap or assassinate Charles II and his brother, James.

The Monmouth Rebellion is another notable antecedent of the Glorious Revolution. On his death in 1685, Charles II left a strong economy to his brother, James. Charles II had ruled without Parliament from 1681 and raised revenue through traditional (customs and exercise) and not so traditional routes (an annual subsidy from King Louis XIV of France). Although Charles II had no legitimate children with his wife, Catherine of Braganza, he had at least 14 bastards, to use the parlance of the era, with numerous mistresses. Under the law of succession, no illegitimate child could succeed to the throne of any of England, Ireland or Scotland. Charles II has many descendants alive today, often still holding titles, and with surnames like FitzCharles or FitzRoy – 'son of the king'. Charles' eldest illegitimate son was James Fitzroy or Scott (his wife's surname), Duke of Monmouth. As the king's eldest son and a Protestant, Monmouth was the focus of many who would have preferred a Protestant illegitimate son to take the throne instead of a legitimate brother who was a Catholic. His popularity was a threat to the new James II and VII, and on James' accession Monmouth went to the Netherlands in exile.

In late 1685, Monmouth landed in England with a tiny army to rebel against the Catholic monarchy. Though James II soon crushed the rebellion, two events are worth mentioning:

- The controversial dispensation of the first *Test Act* to appoint Catholic officers to James II's force based on emergency.
- The appointment of James II's Lord Chief Justice, Baron Jeffreys, to make an example of the Monmouth rebels, in what became known as 'the Bloody Assizes'.

[114] *A Complete Collection of State-Trials and Proceedings upon High Treason* (London, Printed for J Walthoe sen, 1730) vol 4, 1.
[115] John Kenyon, *The Popish Plot* (Harmondsworth, Penguin, 1972) 120.

Historical Cameo

Judge Jeffreys and the Bloody Assizes

Between 27 August and 23 September 1685, the Bloody Assizes wound its way through the counties of Hampshire, Dorset, Somerset and Devon in the southwest of England. In Somerset alone, Judge Jeffreys ('Hanging Judge Jeffreys') and five other judges heard 1,336 cases over a space of nine days. James II relished the daily reports he received of the Assizes. After a decisive victory over the Monmouth rebels (6 July 1685), James II executed his nephew the Duke of Monmouth. The execution was especially brutal; the executioner Jack Ketch needed several swings of the axe and finally hacking with a knife to complete the job.

The trials of his supporters commenced without delay and, indeed, justice. Jeffreys' aim was 'to breathe death like a destroying angel and to sanguine his very ermins in blood'.[116] It was claimed that Jeffreys 'was perpetually drunk or in a rage, liker a fury than the zeal of a judge'.[117] The link between Jeffreys and alcohol carries throughout his career. After the fall of James II, a crowd caught Jeffreys in a pub in Wapping. As a judge, he bullied, mocked and silenced those accused of high treason who, incidentally, were not entitled to legal representation. Representation by counsel was limited to treason and felony offences, but only after the *Treason Act 1695*.[118] Jeffreys hanged 320 rebels. Those not hanged suffered to varying degrees. Children under the age of ten were convicted of high treason, even though they had no awareness of the crime itself. Men, women and children were imprisoned, whipped, transported or fined. In all, 841 individuals were condemned to hard labour in the West Indies. Some even had their family's property confiscated. Each shire had to foot the bill for the executions, including erecting gallows and supplying kindling to burn the corpses. Blackened and ironed corpses swung from gibbets positioned by highways throughout the West Country. As thanks for Jeffreys' work, James II promoted him to Lord Chancellor on Jeffreys' return to London. This bloody episode destroyed any notion that James II might actually rule with fairness.

Jeffreys remains a byword for how a trial ought not to be conducted, invoked to shape the reputation of other 'hanging judges' including Sir John Pedder, the Chief Justice of Tasmania.[119] Nor was Jeffreys the only judge presiding at the Bloody Assize. Most trials followed the same procedures and all judges served at the King's pleasure.[120] Despite his reputation for drunkenness, aspects of his work show Jeffreys to have been an

[116] *The bloody assizes, or, A compleat history of the life of George Lord Jefferies, from his birth to this present time … to which is added Major Holmes's excellent speech, with the dying speeches and prayers of many other eminent Protestants: none of which were ever before publish'd* (J Dunton, 1689) 16.

[117] Gilbert Burnet, *History of the Reign of King James the Second* (OUP 1852) 65.

[118] See chapter four of this volume.

[119] Jacqueline Fox, 'A Tasmanian Judge Jeffreys?: John Lewes Pedder in Popular History' (2014) 19 *Tasmanian Historical Studies* 87–115.

[120] Eric Ives, *The Common Lawyers of Pre-Reformation England: Thomas Kebell: A Case Study* (Cambridge, Cambridge University Press, 1983) 232.

efficient judge.[121] Nonetheless, Jeffreys remains a derided figure and almost a bogeyman of English legal history. He is sufficiently notorious to have entered popular culture. He is a character in the subtly chilling ghost story 'Martin's Close', written by MR James in 1911. More luridly, the famous horror actor Christopher Lee brought him to life in the 1970 film, *The Bloody Judge*, presiding over the trials of witches for his own depraved gratification.

James II was an absolutist, modelled on the French example of Louis XIV: he demanded obedience. He did not attempt to conceal his Catholicism and, by royal prerogative, he re-established the Court of Ecclesiastical Commission abolished in 1641. Judge Jeffreys led it and controlled the Church of England's governance.[122] Though James II was a very capable administrator, he was not a good politician. This is best displayed through his interactions with Parliament. In late 1685, James II declared to Parliament that, not only would he maintain his army following the Monmouth Rebellion, but that he would keep his Catholic officers as well. Parliament responded by asking for the dismissal of Catholic officers. James II, in response to Parliament's request, packed the judiciary with judges sympathetic to his interpretation of the law.

This point is where the question of the dispensing and suspension powers arise. Can the king 'dispense' with the application of a law to a particular individual, or can the king 'suspend' the application of a law entirely? The question goes to the heart of the rule of law, because if the king can dispense with or suspend laws then the king (the government) is above the law. The question can be seen in the King's Bench decision in *Godden v Hales*.[123] The King's Bench had to decide whether the King could dispense with the application of the *Test Acts* for particular individuals. The packed bench of judges decided in favour of the King. It was an unsurprising result. This prepared the way for the appointment of Catholics and Dissenting Protestants to the army and civil government in England, Scotland and Ireland. Opponents focused on James' 'illegal' use of the dispensing power, rather than his religious convictions, as the primary justification for the later Glorious Revolution.

With the approval given in *Godden v Hales*, James II appointed Catholics and Dissenters to important positions by dispensing with the *Test Acts* and the penal laws that required oaths that were impossible for Catholics to swear. He appointed Catholics and Dissenters to positions in the militia, in universities – where traditionally both staff and students had to belong to the Church of England – and as justices of the peace. Further, James II used his prerogative power to suspend the *Clarendon Code*. He issued a Declaration of Indulgence in 1687, which allowed freedom of worship and removed disabilities on Catholics and Dissenters. James was wrong to think that Protestant Dissenters would support the first Declaration. High levels of fear and paranoia about Roman Catholicism were as common among Protestant Dissenters as among members of the Church of England.

[121] George Williams-Keeton, *Lord Chancellor Jeffreys and the Stuart Cause* (London, Macdonald, 1965) 495.

[122] Thomas Bayly Howell, *A Complete Collection of State Trials and Proceedings for High Treason and Other Crimes and Misdemeanors from the Earliest Period to the Year 1783* (London, TC Hansard for Longman, Hurst, Rees, Orme, and Brown, 1816) vol 11, 1127.

[123] (1686) 2 Show KB 475.

James II introduced other unpopular initiatives that did much to antagonise his remaining supporters. He modified local electorates to secure a parliament more favourable to his interests. He removed loyal Anglican Tories – conservatives – from public office and filled public offices with Dissenters. The few prominent Catholics left refused appointments for fear of causing offence to their Anglican neighbours. The political scene worsened. Henry Compton, the Bishop of London, refused to comply with James II's demand that anti-Catholic preaching stop. When James ordered the clergy to read the Declaration of Indulgence in May and June 1688, many resisted. Approximately 95 per cent of London clergy refused to comply because it would have meant endorsing toleration to their congregations and denying the Church of England's status as *the* national church to which all should belong. This expectation extended to the King as well. One outcome of the English Reformation was that the English King became the Supreme Head (later the title changed to Supreme Governor) of the Church of England, a position that was hopelessly paradoxical if the monarch happened to be, as James II was, a member of the Roman Catholic Church and hostile to the Church of England. Seven bishops, including the Archbishop of Canterbury (the Church's spiritual leader), William Sancroft, published a petition questioning the King's prerogative powers. James II had them charged with seditious libel and imprisoned in the Tower of London. A London jury in the King's Bench later acquitted the seven bishops, to public rejoicing.[124]

Rumours that James II's second wife was pregnant after 15 years of marriage caused further public anxiety. This intensified with the birth of a healthy baby boy, James Francis Edward, on 10 June 1688. The knowledge that the Prince of Wales would be raised Catholic spawned fears that Catholicism would again become England's official religion. James II had two Protestant daughters with his first wife Anne Hyde (the Earl of Clarendon's daughter): Mary Stuart, who married her cousin, William of Orange, Stadtholder of the Netherlands; and Anne Stuart. William's mother was the Princess Mary (who had died in 1660), sister of Charles II and James II. This meant that, before James Francis Edward was born, Mary was first in line to the thrones of England, Ireland and Scotland; Anne was second in line; and William of Orange (as James II's nephew) was third in line. Anne Hyde died in 1671. James married again in 1673 to a Catholic princess, Mary of Modena. A male Catholic heir, born after 15 years of marriage, secured the male Stuart line. A rumour spread that the Prince of Wales was an imposter smuggled into his mother's bedchamber in a warming pan ('the warming pan baby'), because the real child was stillborn. This allegation was clearly false: there were 42 witnesses present in the Queen's bedchamber while she gave birth. However, as we have already seen with the Popish Plot, high levels of paranoia existed among Protestants about Catholics.

After the Revolution

Three days before James Francis Edward's birth, seven nobles wrote to James II's son-in-law, William of Orange (part of what is now the Netherlands), urging him to invade England.

[124] William Gibson, *James II and the Trial of the Seven Bishops* (London, Springer, 2009) 124.

Conscious of the seriousness of the impending invasion, James attempted to retreat from reforms that he had introduced.

On 5 November 1688 (the anniversary of the Gunpowder Plot, a day celebrated throughout England with strongly anti-Catholic sentiments), William landed in southwest England. He had managed to assemble a force larger than the Spanish Armada exactly a century earlier. By the end of November, James II's two daughters, Mary and Anne, his other son-in-law Prince George, and loyal friends had change sides. When Anne Stuart defected, James II despaired: 'God help me … my own children have forsaken me'. In December, the Queen, Prince James Francis Edward and the King left England for France after throwing the seals of office overboard and suffering a nosebleed. This Revolution became the 'Glorious Revolution' because it was *apparently* bloodless and Protestant.

The Convention Parliament of 1689 met. Since the Earl of Rochester summoned it, and not the monarch, it was not a regular 'Parliament'. The assemblies considered whether James II had abdicated or abandoned the throne. They declared he had abdicated and the throne was vacant. The Whigs' position was that James had broken his contract with the people when he left the country; for them, the source of governmental authority was in contract. On the other hand, most Tories still supported the male Stuarts and the divine right of kings' doctrine. The Convention Parliament suggested that James II's eldest daughter, Mary Stuart, become monarch. William did not want 'to be his wife's gentleman usher' and threatened to leave England unless he received a title too – he had been, after all, third in line to the throne. Parliament offered the crown to William and Mary jointly, which they accepted as William III and Mary II. The *Declaration of Rights* they received on ascending the throne was the basis for the *Bill of Rights*.

Although anti-Catholic prejudices may have fuelled the Revolution, a greater irony lies in what the English Parliament achieved in 1689. This Parliament secured partial **religious toleration**: the *Toleration Act 1689* lifted most penalties imposed by the *Clarendon Code*. In addition, the *Bill of Rights 1689* clearly established that Parliament had supreme sovereign power in England. Parliament discussed preliminary issues of succession, but in the early eighteenth century they were re-examined when neither Mary II nor her sister, who later became Queen Anne, gave birth to a surviving heir (see chapter four).

Constitutional Detour

The Bill of Rights 1689 *and the Rule of Law*

A key constitutional document of the United Kingdom is the *Bill of Rights 1689*. Its 13 Articles settled many constitutional issues that had plagued parliaments throughout the seventeenth century, including whether it was legal for the monarch to personally suspend or dispense with the law. It established two important constitutional doctrines: the dominance of the rule of law and the supremacy of Parliament. Given its constitutional importance, it will certainly come as no surprise that its principles influenced the United States' Bill of Rights and international human rights instruments. It is still law in three states in Australia: New South Wales, Queensland, and Victoria. The *Bill of Rights* has three parts:

- A preamble, which describes all of James VI and II's wrongs.
- In answer to James VI and II's wrongs, 13 Articles setting out the rights of Parliament and subjects.
- A section which transfers the Crown to William III and Mary II and settles succession to the Crown.

Articles 1 and 2 make it illegal to suspend or to dispense with laws without the consent of Parliament. The Articles also include a prohibition on levying taxation without Parliament's consent. Article 9 protects free elections and freedom of speech within Parliament, ie parliamentary privilege and is incorporated into Australia's *Parliamentary Privileges Act 1987*. Parliament has to be frequent. Other Articles prohibit 'excessive bail', 'excessive fines', 'cruel and unusual punishment', and a standing army in times of peace without parliamentary approval.

The seventeenth century struggle for power between parliament, judges, and the king was a question of rights or, clearly, of power. The *Bill of Rights* restrained the monarch's power in order to prevent its arbitrary abuse. By placing restraints on what a monarch could personally do, Parliament was really governing by the 'rule of law'. This doctrine is fundamental to our legal system. At its heart is the idea that every person, including institutions and government, is subject to the law.

Conclusion

The legal history of the sixteenth and seventeenth centuries is nothing short of breathtaking. The early assertions of judicial independence made by Sir Edward Coke, the execution of Charles I, and the overthrow of James II stand without parallel in English history. The legal drama and the legal accomplishments of this era have never receded. The *Bill of Rights* remains law in Australia. The modern valorisation of the Magna Carta, which extended to the worldwide celebrations of its 800th anniversary in 2015, is in many ways a product of its forceful rediscovery and use in the seventeenth century. The legal dramas of the century continue to resonate. It is worth noting that, at a high point of drama in the United Kingdom's Brexit negotiations, the Government prorogued Parliament but the Supreme Court decided against the Government in *R (Miller) v Prime Minister (Lord Advocate intervening)* included the *Case of Proclamations*.[125] Baroness Hale read out the original seventeenth-century English claim that 'the King hath no prerogative, but that which the law of the land allows him'.[126] That case concerned responsible government and, in pursuit of this topic, the next chapter will go further forward in time to the eighteenth century.

[125] [2020] AC 373 (SC).
[126] *Ibid* 402.

4

Responsible Government, Law and Justice in Eighteenth-Century England

Introduction

Many modern constitutional arrangements had their origins in the aftermath of the Glorious Revolution. During the eighteenth century, a shift in political power from the royal court to Parliament occurred as the office of Prime Minister and cabinet government were established. The monarch's power gradually declined. By the 1760s, the dominance of the Whigs (or, broadly, liberals) in ministerial office had also declined after decades of dominance under the Hanoverian monarchs.

Under the guidance of Lord Mansfield, modern commercial law evolved. This chapter pursues these constitutional and legal developments, but also moves attention to the darker aspects of the period's legal history, including the theatre of public executions and autopsies, and trial procedures that to modern eyes seem startlingly unfair. From time to time, the chapter will break its chronology back to the seventeenth century, including a reappearance by Sir Edward Coke, to explore the administration of justice before the Glorious Revolution, to provide context for the administration of justice in the eighteenth century. Some of this chapter sits in the domain of criminal law, although other sections continue the focus on constitutional law in chapter three.

Learning Resources

The content in this chapter is supported by:

Glossary	Chapter Overview	Historical Cameos	Constitutional Detours	Pause for Thought
Latin, Law French and Medieval English terms are defined	The chapter begins with an overview explaining its intentions and focus	Lord Harwicke on Equity, Slavery and the Marriage Act 1753	Judicial Independence	Religion and the Head of State
		Lord Mansfield	Separation of Powers	Modern Slavery
		Sir William Blackstone	The 'Golden Thread of Criminal Law'	
			The Legal History of Rape	
			The Treason Trial of Sir Ambrose Rookwood and the Vulnerable Defendant	

Chapter Overview

Place

- Kingdom of England
- American and Caribbean colonies

Time Period

- Stuart and Hanoverian dynasties

Dates

- 17th–18th centuries

Key Figures

- William III
- William Blackstone
- Lord Mansfield
- Lord Hardwicke
- James Somerset
- Thomas Lewis

Key Institutions

- Bill of Rights
- Act of Union
- Marriage Act
- Cabinet and Junto
- Trial Act
- The Old Bailey

Key Terms

- Responsible government
- Separation of powers
- High treason and petty treason
- Presumption of innocence
- Tyburn
- Whigs and Tories
- Reception of English law
- Slavery

Learning Outcomes

At the end of this chapter, readers should understand:

- The importance of the *Habeas Corpus Act 1679* and the *Bill of Rights 1689*, including their application in modern Australia.
- The separation of powers, responsible government and judicial tenure.
- The origins of defence mechanisms, lawyers' participation in trials, and the presumption of innocence.
- The legal issues involved in the abolition of slavery in the British Empire.

The *Act of Settlement 1701*

The political and legal developments of the eighteenth century emerge from the religious tensions of the seventeenth, including the overthrow of the Catholic James II. The *Act of Settlement 1701* (as originally passed) secured the Protestant succession to the throne by excluding Roman Catholics, and those who marry Roman Catholics, from the line of succession. As will be discussed shortly, the *Succession to the Crown Act 2013* (UK) repealed the provisions that disabled those who might be in line to the throne from marrying Catholics.

The Protestant Succession

Mary II, daughter of James II and wife of William III, died in 1694 without any surviving children. After William III, the closest Protestant heir to the throne was William Duke of Gloucester, the son of William's sister-in-law Princess Anne – James II's daughter and Mary's sister. The Duke of Gloucester was Anne's only surviving child; however, he died in 1700 from multiple illnesses. After 18 pregnancies but no surviving children, Princess Anne was not expected to – nor did she – have another child.[1] With it unlikely that William III would marry again after Mary II's death in 1694, Parliament set about ensuring the Protestant succession to the throne to permanently exclude James II and his son. They did this in the *Act of Settlement 1701*.

Meanwhile the Catholic Stuarts deposed in 1688 had not vanished. James II, his son James Francis Edward Stuart (later dubbed the 'Old Pretender') and his grandson Charles Edward Stuart (known to history as 'Bonnie Prince Charlie') moved to the Continent and maintained their own court at St Germain, maintaining their claim on the throne and their Catholic faith. As such, Mary II and Anne's two younger and healthy half-siblings, James Francis Edward and Louisa Maria Teresa (children of the expelled James II and VII and Mary of Modena), were the next nearest competitors to the throne. Neither were a viable option because of their Catholicism. Parliament determined that the throne would pass

[1] Elizabeth Lane Furdell, *The Royal Doctors, 1485–1714: Medical Personnel at the Tudor and Stuart Courts* (Rochester, New York, University of Rochester Press, 2001) 231.

to the Protestant House of Hanover in northern Germany, who were the closest living Protestant relatives of the House of Stuart. The English Government had to go back three generations and down a female line (James I's daughter Elizabeth who had married into this line) to find a suitable Protestant heir.

The chosen heir presumptive – as only male children are heirs apparent – to the crowns of England, Wales and Scotland was Sophia, the Electress of Hanover. She was the Protestant granddaughter of James VI and I. Sophia died almost two months before Queen Anne's death in August 1714. Her son, Georg Ludwig of Hanover, the new Elector (or ***Princeps Elector***), inherited the throne as King George I of Great Britain and Ireland.

> *Princeps Elector* (Latin): the members of the electoral college of the Holy Roman Empire

Pause for Thought

Religion and the Head of State

The Australian head of state, the Queen (or King) of Australia, must be a member of the Church of England, even though Australia is a multicultural and pluralist society. While the *Succession to the Crown Act 2013* (UK) has removed other religious and gender-based limitations, this one remains. During the debate on the second reading of Australia's *Succession to the Crown Bill*, the then opposition leader Bill Shorten commented on the 'the anachronistic quality of this debate'; that included questions such as 'whether Australia's head of state can be the eldest princess, or whether they can be a Catholic, or indeed whether their marriage accords with an act passed in Westminster 243 years ago'.[2]

Questions to Consider

- Is there an anachronism in these questions and these constitutional circumstances?
- Where might the anachronism lie?

Constitutional Detour

Judicial Independence

The Act of Settlement fixed judicial salaries and based the holding of judicial office on 'good behaviour', instead of being at the monarch's 'pleasure'. By authorising judicial salaries, the *Act of Settlement* was a move closer to judicial independence. Judges no longer risked losing office or having their salary reduced for delivering a decision unfavourable to the Crown. In 1701, England had no inferior courts (county courts or circuit judges).

[2] Commonwealth, *Parliamentary Debates*, House of Representatives, 17 March 2015 (Bill Shorten, Leader of the Opposition) 2552.

Before the *Act of Settlement*, a monarch could dismiss a judge at will. It was the King's will that determined appointments and their termination. Edward IV dismissed Sir John Markham CJKB after he directed a jury in a 1468 treason trial contrary to Edward's wishes. In the last 11 years of Charles II's reign, he dismissed 11 judges. Over four years, James II dismissed 12 judges. By the *Act of Settlement*, however, the monarch is only able to dismiss a superior court judge for misbehaviour after petitions from both Houses of Parliament. In the United Kingdom, this has only occurred once: Sir Jonah Barrington, an Irish judge, was removed in 1830 for misappropriating litigants' money.

The *Acts of Union 1707*

Before the *Acts of Union 1707*, England and Scotland were independent countries with separate Parliaments and privy councils but a shared monarch. James VI of Scotland had merely united the English and Scottish thrones on his accession to the English throne in 1603 in his person. His attempts to achieve a closer union between the countries were in vain.

A century later, a much closer union between the two countries occurred. From 1 May 1707, the ***Act of Union*** merged England and Scotland as 'one kingdom by the name of Great Britain' and created a single Parliament. The English and Scottish Parliaments each passed an *Act of Union*. By respectively passing these, the two Parliaments voted themselves out of existence and merged into the Parliament of Great Britain at Westminster.[3] In 1701, the new Parliament had 16 Scottish peers and 45 MPs representing an overall Scottish population of over one million – only about 3,000 of whom were entitled to vote!

The *Acts of Union* had several significant implications. First, trade, customs and excise duties became uniform throughout Great Britain. Second, however, the separate legal and judicial systems of England and Scotland were preserved.[4] Scotland's highest civil and criminal courts remained the Court of Session and the High Court of Justiciary, respectively. None of the royal courts at Westminster would hear a Scottish cause of action (and to this day Scottish jurisprudence is notably different from English common law, owing more to European civil law). From 1711, however, the House of Lords developed appellate jurisdiction over Scottish civil matters. Third, England settled Scotland's official debts and Scotland received compensation for taking on a share of the English national debt. The compensation or the 'Equivalent' amounted to £398,085 – an extraordinary sum of money at the time. The true reason for the 'Equivalent' was to compensate victims of the failed Darien Scheme and save Scotland from the brink of bankruptcy.

In 1695, Scottish Parliament had set up the Company of Scotland Trading to Africa and the Indies to rival England's East India Company.[5] Over 25 per cent of Scotland's liquid assets

[3] Ireland remained separate until it became part of the United Kingdom of Great Britain and Ireland in 1801.

[4] Mark Godfrey, 'Parliament and the Law' in Keith M Brown and Alan R MacDonald (eds), *History of the Scottish Parliament: Parliament in Context, 1235–1707* (Edinburgh, Edinburgh University Press, 2010) 184.

[5] Frances G Davenport, *European Treaties Bearing on the History of the United States and Its Dependencies to 1648* (Clark, New Jersey, Lawbook Exchange, 2004) 117.

were sunk into the Company of Scotland's Darien Scheme. The aim was to establish a new colony in what is now Panama. The failure of that settlement almost bankrupted Scotland and induced the Scots to join with England as the United Kingdom of Great Britain.

Emergence of Responsible Government

If parliamentary sovereignty is the main achievement of the English seventeenth-century parliament, the achievement of the eighteenth century was responsible government. Over the course of the century, the monarch's power gradually declined. Constitutional conventions (parliamentary rules with no legal effect but nevertheless accepted and followed by politicians) on parliamentary practice developed.

Two broad political factions flourished but, for most of that century, the Whigs dominated. The Whigs, who strongly supported commercial interests, heavily populated ministerial positions between 1714 and the 1760s. The Tories were the party for landed gentry.[6] Responsible government is a system of government in which the executive (the administrative arm of government) is responsible to the legislature – the law-making arm of government. Ministers, who are also members of parliament, run the executive. Principles of responsible government are not contained in formal written rules.

The Office of Prime Minister

Even if he denied it, Sir Robert Walpole was the first British Prime Minister. During George I's reign, Walpole became the First Lord of the Treasury and Chancellor of the Exchequer and, as such, lived at Number 10 Downing Street, Whitehall, which remains the home of the UK's Prime Minister. Between 1721 and 1742, he held these offices continuously.[7]

From 1717, George I regularly absented himself from regular meetings of ministers (known as cabinet); however, the suggestion that he did so because of poor English is unfounded. Like other cosmopolitan and well-educated European men, George was multilingual, and he and Walpole conversed with each other in French.[8] He did however spend significant periods in Hanover where he was still Elector. From 1721, Walpole chaired these meetings in place of George I. Walpole also had effective leadership over the House of Commons and ensured it complied with his wishes. Walpole rose to power and gained the confidence of Parliament through his successful management of the South Sea Bubble of 1720, an unprecedented financial crisis for England. European wars, the Prince of Wales forming a coalition with the Tories, issues of royal succession abroad and a disastrous 1741 election all contributed to Walpole's resignation in 1741. He resigned because he lost the support on the floor of the House of Commons.

[6] Linda Colley, *In Defiance of Oligarchy: The Tory Party 1714–60* (Cambridge, Cambridge University Press, 1985) 5, 146.

[7] John M Beattie, *The English Court in the Reign of George I* (Cambridge, Cambridge University Press, 1967) 242.

[8] John Plumb, *The Growth of Political Stability in England, 1675–1725*, 1st edn (Harmondsworth, Penguin Books, 1967) 113.

Constitutional Detour

Separation of Powers

In 1731, the French lawyer Montesquieu published *De L'Esprit des Lois*. The book introduces the doctrine of the separation of powers, of importance to constitutional thinking ever since. Of the separation of powers, he wrote:

> There would be an end of everything, were the same man or the same body, whether of the nobles or of the people, to exercise those three powers, that of enacting laws, that of executing the public resolutions, and of trying the causes of individuals.

Montesquieu thought separate bodies should exercise these three powers: the legislature, the executive and the judiciary: the US Constitution was drafted to specifically integrate this doctrine.[9] Montesquieu compared the checks and balances that he thought he saw in the British Constitution with absolutist regimes in France and other European powers, where power was vested in the monarch and his advisers.

However, Montesquieu misunderstood the British system by dividing the King (the executive) too strongly from Parliament (the legislature) and failed to see that the ministers – the real executive – came from Parliament. Additionally, one party, the Whigs, controlled the Parliament in 1731, with leadership exercised by one man, Walpole.

Cabinet Government

Laws passed by Parliament require the monarch's assent before enactment. For some time after the Glorious Revolution, ministers were appointed and dismissed at the monarch's pleasure. Ministers were ultimately responsible to the Crown. Throughout the century, the monarch chose their ministers from the two political parties, the Whigs and the Tories. These terms however need considerable nuance related to a range of issues including voting consistency on the floor of the House of Commons, relations with dissenting and established religion, and the interactions between British parliamentarians and European treaties and alliances.[10]

During William III's reign, a group of ministers formed. Initially known as the **junto**, later the term 'cabinet' stuck. These ministers were responsible for national affairs. In time, the Prime Minister chose the cabinet – he advised the monarch who to appoint. Though the monarch could still choose ministers, this came to be a politically unwise move.

> Junto: the members of the Whig party leading government in the reign of William III

Much of this arose because only Parliament can raise taxes and authorise the expenditure of money. As the executive or 'government' (the King's ministers) needs money to govern, the practical necessity was for the King to choose his ministers from a group that had sufficient control of the Parliament to be able to have Parliament raise money and appropriate

[9] See chapter five of this volume.
[10] Geoffrey Holmes, *British Politics in the Age of Anne* (London, Macmillan, 1967) 57, 76–80, 102.

it for the Government of the kingdom. In time, it meant that the group that had a majority of seats in Parliament and that had 'the power of the purse strings' had to be appointed as government. The King took his advisers from the majority group in the Parliament. To this day, in 'Westminster systems of government', the group that holds the majority in the Parliament is the one that the Crown commissions as its government and which sits on the treasury benches.

Criminal Law and Criminal Trials in the Eighteenth Century

There were different implications cascading from the Glorious Revolution, the *Bill of Rights*, and the *Act of Settlement*. In addition to the developments in parliamentary and cabinet government and the notion of responsible government discussed above, these included developments in the administration of the law and the conduct of trials. Judicial tenure for good behaviour does predate the Glorious Revolution and expectations that royal officials and servants, including judges, held office contingent on their conduct is apparent from the medieval period.[11] However, the forceful statement of tenure itself has important implications for how judges acted during a trial. This next section examines the development of criminal justice from the end of the seventeenth century and into the eighteenth.

The opponents of James II and the instigators of the Glorious Revolution fixated on James's Catholicism and were part of a culture of paranoia about the Roman Catholic Church, but James's absolutist tendencies (ineluctably linked in popular minds with his Catholicism) was also a motivating factor for his opponents. That conduct provided justification for the Glorious Revolution and informed legal changes that came after it, owing to the justification that William of Orange's invasion was necessary to protect the English from arbitrary rule. The period immediately prior to the Glorious Revolution had already promoted legal safeguards. Chief among these was the ancient legal right of *habeas corpus*, re-stated in the *Habeas Corpus Act 1679*, passed by the Parliament held that year[12] *Habeas corpus* is traceable to at least the twelfth century. It is the right, and the insistence, to bring prisoners before court rather than suffer indefinite detention.

A number of the treason trials took place during the Restoration and during a period of heightened political and religious paranoia before the eighteenth century. These included the trial of the wholly innocent priests accused of the 'Popish Plot' and the victims of the 'Bloody Assizes'. At the treason trial of the Jesuits accused of the Popish Plot, Sir William Scrogg, CJKB was a bullying and hectoring presence on the bench.

[11] Ryan Rowberry, 'The Origins and Development of Judicial Tenure "During Good Behavior" to 1485' in Travis R Barker (ed), *Law and Society in Later Medieval England and Ireland: Essays in Honour of Paul Brand* (London, Routledge, 2018) 182.

[12] 31 Car 2 c 2 ss 1–8, 11, 15–19; George Clark, *The Later Stuarts 1660-1714*, 2nd edn (Oxford, Clarendon Press, 1955) 99.

Among other things, he and his fellow judges excused the lapses in memory of the Crown witnesses while making no similar allowances for the defendants.[13] Because the stakes were so high and they were so frequent, trials for treason are an excellent place to consider the emergence of the contours of a modern trial, including the evidentiary principle that someone is presumed innocent until proven guilty, the major operative principle of an Australian trial.

Constitutional Detour

The 'Golden Thread' of Criminal Law

The presumption of innocence is almost universal; however, it has a special association with English legal history. In 1935, the House of Lords heard the appeal of *Woolmington v Director of Public Prosecutions*.[14] Lord Sankey LC famously proclaimed that 'Throughout the web of the English Criminal Law one golden thread is always to be seen, that it is the duty of the prosecution to prove the prisoner's guilt'.[15] Sankey pointed to earlier cases where that principle was apparent, but his 1935 ruling remains the most coherent and celebrated articulation of this signature aspect of the English justice imported throughout the British Empire and Commonwealth. Perhaps most famously, the fictional barrister Horace Rumpole (the creation of John Mortimer QC) waxed lyrical about the 'golden thread' running through English justice and expanding to the law courts throughout the British Empire.[16] The actual barrister Sir Edward Marshall Hall KC (1858–1927), one of the greatest barristers in history and one of the models for Rumpole, would flamboyantly dramatise the presumption of innocence in closing speeches to the jury, turning an abstraction into a performance by swaying his body from side to side as he spoke and declaring of the scales of justice 'in the one scale, in the prisoner's scale, unseen by human eye, is placed that overbalancing weight, the weight of the presumption of innocence'.[17] Underpinning these affectionate notions are earlier statements recognised as William Blackstone's maxim (a ratio of 10:1) that it is better ten guilty persons go free than one innocent person be convicted. As commentators point out, this valorised ratio has a huge margin of error.[18] Neither was Blackstone saying anything new and acknowledged earlier jurists had made similar points about the weight placed on a person's presumed innocence.

[13] Lois G Schwoerer, 'The Attempted Impeachment of Sir William Scroggs, Lord Chief Justice of the Court of King's Bench, November 1680–March 1681' (1995) 38(4) *Historical Journal* 843, 859.

[14] [1935] 1 AC 462.

[15] *Ibid* 481.

[16] Brad Buchanan, 'A Nice Point of Blood: Race and Religion in Rumpole's Return' in Julie H Kim (ed), *Race and Religion in the Postcolonial British Detective Story: Ten Essays* (Jefferson, McFarland, 2005) 42.

[17] Edward Marjoribanks, *The Life of Sir Edward Marshall Hall* (Auckland, Pickle Partners Publishing, 2019).

[18] Jonathan Kertzer, *Poetic Justice and Legal Fictions* (Cambridge, Cambridge University Press, 2010) 119.

Constitutional Detour

The Legal History of Rape

The last detour observed the attachment of the English legal system and its colonial offshoots to the presumption of innocence – but where does that presumption become complex and, even, disturbing? One of the jurists whom Blackstone acknowledged as having earlier articulated something close to his ratio of ten innocent people and one guilty person was Sir Matthew Hale CJKB (1609–76).[19] Hale made other pronouncements on the presumption of innocence, including in cases of rape. Hale commented 'it must be remembered … that it [rape] is an accusation easily to be made and hard to be proved, and harder to be defended by the party accused, tho never so innocent'.[20] Hale had however delineated how rape was to be defined and recognised in law, as to 'make a rape there must be an actual penetration in *res or re* (as also in buggery) and therefore *emission seminis* is indeed an evidence of penetration, but singly of itself it makes neither rape nor buggery'.[21] As Gilbert Geis points out in his study of this particular aspect of Hale's career,[22] Hale's statement has endured in Anglo-American law though it is deeply problematic. Rape has a long legal history in English law, gaining statutory definition in the *Statute of Marlborough 1285*.[23] The case law on marital rape included the 1888 decision of the Court for Crown Cases Reserved in *R v Clarence*.[24]

The majority of *R v Clarence* quashed the convictions of a man who had knowingly transmitted gonorrhoea to his wife as a result of sexual intercourse. The husband was aware of his disease but had not informed his wife. The man's conduct was found not to have constituted an offence either of assault occasioning actual bodily harm or of unlawfully and maliciously inflicting grievous bodily harm. More broadly, marital rape immunity relied on Hale's writings. Hale's cool scepticism about rape is inversely related to his acceptance of witchcraft accusations in a trial at Bury St Edmunds in Suffolk in 1662.[25] As Geis further points out, the mode of proof Hale used in the witchcraft trial (a physical examination for the witch's mark) was one deployed in a rape trial where Hale presided but with precisely opposite results. The examination of the accused female witch found a mark; the examination of the man found his bowels had collapsed, his

[19] Jeffrey Reiman and Ernest Van Den Haag, 'On the Common Saying that it is Better that Ten Guilty Persons Escape than that One Innocent Suffer: *Pro* and *Con*' (1990) 7 *Social Philosophy and Policy* 226.

[20] Matthew Hale, *The History of the Pleas of the Crown: In Two Volumes, Volume 1* (Little Britain, T Payne, 1800) 634.

[21] *Ibid* 627.

[22] Gilbert Geis, 'Lord Hale, Witches, and Rape' (1978) 5 *British Journal of Law and Society* 26, 40.

[23] 52 Hen 3.

[24] (1882) 22 QBD 23. The ruling included the observation 'the husband's connection with his wife is not only lawful, but it is in accordance with the ordinary condition of married life. It is done in pursuance of the marital contract and of the status which was created by marriage, and the wife as to the connection itself is in a different position from any other woman, for she has no right or power to refuse her consent.'

[25] *A tryal of witches at the assizes held at Bury St. Edmonds for the count of Suffolk on the tenth day of March, 1664 [i.e 1665] before Sir Matthew Hale, Kt., then Lord Chief Baron of His Majesties Court of Exchequer / taken by a person then attending the court* (William Shrewsbery, 1682) sig E4.

genitals were scarcely visible, and Hale concluded he was incapable of raping someone.[26] Geis deftly reconstructs the social and religious forces building a web of misogynistic thinking about both witchcraft and rape. Hale's view that rape was easy to claim but hard to prove, and his encouragement of scepticism, was long lasting to the detriment of female victims of sexual assault. It was quoted as recently as 2009 in the House of Lords in *R v JTB*.[27]

Developments in Criminal Law

Precisely because it was the worst and the most serious crime, treason is a crime where important developments in the presumption of innocence, rules of evidence, trial procedure and the use of counsel are apparent. High treason was in fact one of the first common law crimes given a statutory basis in the *Treason Act 1351*,[28] which remains law in the United Kingdom and New South Wales.[29] As Edward Coke explains, high treason is so-called 'in respect of the royall majesty against whom it is committed'.[30] Convictions for high treason enforced the King's authority (as high treason was the reverse of allegiance) and the executions of traitors visibly rendered royal authority. English kings displayed the rotting heads and other body parts of traitors throughout the kingdom as exemplary warnings.[31]

Edward Coke graphically described the physical punishment meted out to traitors, interpolating that with the symbolic meaning underpinning the actions. Speaking with lip-smacking relish in front of the defendants accused of the 1605 Gunpowder Plot, Coke described how:

> He shall have his judgement to be drawn to the place of execution from his prison as being not worthy any more to tread upon the face of the earth whereof he was made: also for that he hath been retrograde to nature, therefore is he drawn backward at a horse-tail. And whereas God hath made the head of man the highest and most supreme part, as being his chief grace and ornament ... he must be drawn with his head declining downward ... For which cause also he shall be strangled, being hanged by the neck between heaven and earth, as deemed unworthy of both, or either .... Then he is be cut down alive and to have his privy parts cut off and burnt before his face as being unworthily begotten, and unfit to leave any generation after him. His bowels and inlay'd parts taken out and burnt, who inwardly had conceived and harboured in his heart such horrible treason. After, to have his head cut off, which had imagined the mischief. And lastly his body to be quartered, and the quarters set up in some high and eminent place, to the view and detestation of men, and to become a prey for the fowls of the air.[32]

[26] Geis (n 22) 40.
[27] [2009] 1 AC 1310.
[28] 25 Edw 3 St 5 c 5.
[29] See the *Imperial Acts Application Act 1969* (NSW) sch 1.
[30] Edward Coke, *The Third Part of the Institutes of the Laws of England: Concerning High Treason, and Other Pleas of the Crown and Criminal Causes* (Union, New Jersey, Lawbook Exchange, 2002) 19.
[31] Ernest Jacobs, *The Fifteenth Century 1399–1485* (Oxford, Oxford University Press, 1993) 53.
[32] *The Gunpowder Treason. Trials of the Conspirators: Extracted from Cobbett's Collection of State Trials: with Account of Their Arraignment and Execution. Also, History of the Gunpowder Plot, Written by King James, Extracted from the First Collection of His Works Published During His Life-time* (Northampton, J Taylor & Son, 1867) 19.

As treason was plotting against the King, kings took particular interest in the law, none more so than Henry VIII. In 1531, a cook called Richard Roose (a servant in the household of Bishop John Fisher) stood accused of putting poison in the household's food. Fisher was close to the royal court, and the case compelled Henry's personal attention and his insistence that both Houses of Parliament not only attaint Roose for high treason but make poisoning a treasonous offence. Perhaps ironically for a cook, Roose was then boiled to death. The significance here was that Roose did not receive a common law trial but his trial proceeded by the parliamentary attaint.[33] Roose was only a humble servant, but the greatest magnates in the land did not have protection from prosecution for treason.[34] In 1540, Henry VIII's great minister was attainted and executed with Henry left unmoved by Cromwell's frantic efforts to save his life, writing from the Tower of London: 'Most graycous prynce, I crye for mercye mercye mercye'.[35] People close to the monarch died after an accusation of treason, and Henry VIII's second wife, Anne Boleyn (mother of Elizabeth I) and his fifth wife, Catherine Howard, were tried, convicted and executed for treason.[36]

Where there was high treason there was also **petty (or petit) treason**. Coke defined it as 'when a servant slayeth his master, or a wife her husband, or when a man secular or religious slayeth his prelate to whom he oweth faith and obedience'.[37] A petit traitor, such as a wife who had killed her husband, was burnt at the stake, as happened in a case in 1662, when a woman killed her husband by stabbing him with a pipe stem.[38]

> **Petty or petit treason (French):** a subordinate murdering a superior

Treason, whether high or petty, resulted in the traitor's estate escheating to the Crown, rather than to their heirs. That possibility led accused persons to refuse to plead in a trial on a capital charge. If they refused, they were compressed, the physical torture intended to make them plead. This torture, called ***peine forte et dure***, meant the accused were stripped, tied on the ground, and compressed by heavy weights.[39] Social class and sex were no barrier to this treatment. Notable people pressed this way include Margaret Clitherow, now a saint, who was pressed in 1586 under her own front door after being accused of the felony (under an act against Jesuits) of harbouring Catholic priests.[40] Charles Stourton, 8th Baron Stourton, changed his mind about refusing to plead in a murder trial when threatened with pressing.

> ***Peine forte et dure* (French):** punishment hard and forceful

[33] Krista Kesselring, 'A Draft of the 1531 "Acte for Poysoning"' (2001) 116(468) *English Historical Review* 894.

[34] Michael Graves, 'Freedom of Peers from Arrest: The Case of Henry Second Lord Cromwell, 1571–1572' (1977) 21(1) *American Journal of Legal History* 1, 4.

[35] Robert Bigelow Merriman, *Life and Letters of Thomas Cromwell* (Oxford, Oxford University Press, 2000) vol 2, 273.

[36] Lacey Baldwin Smith, *A Tudor Tragedy: The Life and Times of Catherine Howard* (London, Reprint Society, 1961) 175.

[37] Coke (n 30) 19.

[38] Andrea McKenzie, *Tyburn's Martyrs: Executions in England 1675–1775* (London, Hambledon, 2007) 18.

[39] Andrea McKenzie, '"This Death Some Strong and Stout Hearted Man Doth Choose": The Practice *of Peine Forte et Dure* in Seventeenth- and Eighteenth-Century England' (2005) 23(2) *Law and History Review* 279, 280.

[40] 27 Eliz 1 c 2.

There may have been no such thing as a typical treason trial, but the many hundreds of cases collected in the *Complete Collection of State Trials* build up an impression of how they proceeded. There was some degree of awesome majesty involved. Kenyon likens a treason trial to a morality play, 'staged as a demonstration of government power'.[41] The customary exchange between the court and the accused at the start of a trial carried a supernatural resonance. The clerk would ask 'culprit, by whom will thou be tried?' The answer would be 'By God and my country', to which the clerk intoned 'God send thee a good deliverance'. Nor were the events completely a procedural free-for-all; for instance, defendants could challenge the empanelment and swearing of jurors.[42]

Trials from earlier in the seventeenth century give some impression of how events unfolded. Sir Walter Raleigh, the famous sailor, stood trial for high treason in the Great Hall of Winchester Castle in 1603, prosecuted by Edward Coke, then the Attorney General. As much as Coke is valourised as the doughty champion of common law against monarchy, his conduct as prosecutor remains notorious, largely for his almost complete absence of anything resembling evidence for a case and his reliance simply on ever more hysterical invective.[43] He seemed 'clownish and bitter' according to the contemporary observer John Aubrey.[44] 'Thou art a monster! Thou hast an English face but a Spanish heart!' is one of Coke's characteristic jibes at Raleigh. Coke also shouted 'thou traitor! I will prove thee the rankest traitor in all England!' It would seem even the judges were slightly embarrassed by Coke's performance and Chief Justice Popham excused Coke's behaviour as being 'zeal of his duty for the service of the King'.[45]

Coke together with jurist Sir Francis Bacon later participated in the trial of the Earl and Countess of Somerset in 1615, also known as the Overbury trial. Although a murder rather than a treason trial, it illustrates many features of a criminal trial still pertaining in the eighteenth century. In fact, this trial had it all. The background was a high society scandal at the court of King James I, whereby the Countess of Essex gained an annulment of her marriage to the Earl of Essex (alleging his sexual dysfunction) and married the Earl of Somerset. Meanwhile, Somerset's friend the poet Thomas Overbury was imprisoned in the Tower of London. He was charged with high treason after angering the King by refusing to become the ambassador to the Russian tsar[46] and died in the Tower. These events all occurred in 1613 but, by 1615, the Somersets had lost their place in King James' affections and the King tasked Coke and Bacon to investigate what had happened to Overbury, Somerset's friend, in the Tower.

[41] John Kenyon, *The Popish Plot* (Harmondsworth, Penguin, 1972) 132.

[42] For the trial of Lady Alice Lisle, see *A Complete Collection of State Trials and Proceedings Upon High Treason and other Crimes and Misdemeanours, from The Reign of King Richard II to the End of the Reign of King George I* (London, J Walthoe, 1730) vol 4, 106.

[43] Patrick Keane, 'Lecture One: Edward Coke' (Selden Society Lecture, Supreme Court of Queensland, 23 April 2015) [12], available at media.sclqld.org.au/documents/lectures-and-exhibitions/2015/Justice-Keane-Selden-Society-lecture-one.pdf.

[44] John Aubrey, *Brief Lives* (edited by Oliver Lawson Dick) (Harmondsworth, Penguin, 1972) 226.

[45] Catherine Drinker Bowen, *The Lion and the Throne: The Life and Times of Sir Edward Coke 1552–1634* (London, Hamish Hamilton, 1957) 167–69.

[46] Chester Dunning, 'The Fall of Sir Thomas Overbury and the Embassy to Russia in 1613' (1991) 22(4) *The Sixteenth Century Journal* 695, 695.

Figure 4.1 Thomas Overbury, a Poet whose Murder was the Basis of a Remarkable Trial

S van de Passe, *Viva effigies Thomae Overburii equitis aurati aetat. 32, veneno obit September 1613 [graphic]* (London, Compton Holland, 1614). Call #: ART File O96.6 no.3 (size M).

What followed in the trial of the Earl and Countess as well as their co-conspirators could be described as a legal freak show. One of the accused conspirators, Weston, only agreed to plea after being threatened with *peine forte et dure*. Evidence against other conspirators included puppets and magic spells, and another was accused of having given Overbury a poisoned tart. The Earl of Somerset declared he would not attend his own trial unless carried there in his bed.[47] A poem purportedly written by Overbury's ghost appeared in print.[48] Not all trials were as colourful, but the events in the Overbury case do distil some of the wildness and chaos of an English trial before important reforms.

[47] Gerald Chapin, 'An Historic Murder' (1906) 14(8) *American Lawyer* 343.
[48] *The Harleian Miscellany* (London, T Osborne, 1746) sig Y2.

After the Glorious Revolution and the *Bill of Rights*, a further legal landmark that shaped the eighteenth-century law is the *Trials Act 1696*.[49] It is worthwhile thinking in 'before' and 'after' terms for criminal trials. 'Before' defendants spoke for themselves (as did Walter Raleigh), were unable to prepare a defence in advance, and were not on oath. The Act created a number of legal safeguards, including the two-witness rule, insisting on two witnesses to corroborate that there had been a crime. Further, court granted the accused a defence counsel in the courtroom and the court would provide an attorney for them if the defendant could not source this support.[50] Additional changes included a statutory right to see the indictment five days before trial and for questioning witnesses under oath, meaning the jury could attach greater credibility to the defence case. These changes registered immediately in the treason trial of Sir Ambrose Rookwood in April 1696.

Constitutional Detour

The Treason Trial of Sir Ambrose Rookwood and the Vulnerable Defendant

Sir Ambrose Rookwood was part of a conspiracy to assassinate William III. The conspiracy failed and the conspirators, Rookwood among them, stood trial for high treason in April 1696. Rookwood's plea was not guilty, but he was found guilty and strung up at the Tyburn gallows. So far that could be a summary of almost all treason trials up to this point, but there is a difference in that Rookwood had a defence counsel to speak for him and test the prosecution case.[51] Bartholomew Shower, his counsel, held strong political opinions in sympathy with the Tory and Jacobite ideals that had inspired the assassination plot. However, before the King's Bench he was less assured, and the trial transcript in *State Trials* makes clear his awareness of his novelty in being a defence counsel and to assure the judges that they should not blame him for what his client did! Begging leave to speak, he explained 'we hope that nothing which we shall say in Defence of our Clients, shall be imputed to ourselves' and added that 'We come not here to countenance the practices for which the Prisoner stands accused'.[52]

These changes to the conduct of trials were a long-term process, some proposed for some time. These changes are more than technical and relate to the political landscape of the era, one dominated by Whigs whose political philosophy meant they wished to achieve a statutory framework for treason and for other capital crimes.[53] As noted above, judicial tenure was also more stable and by 1761 a judge's appointment no longer ended when the monarch died.[54]

[49] 7 & 8 Will 3 c 3.

[50] Lamar Hill, 'The Two-Witness Rule in English Treason Trials: Some Comments on the Emergence of Procedural Law' (1968) 12(2) *The American Journal of Legal History* 95, 95.

[51] Francis Young, *Rookwood Family Papers, 1606–1761* (Woodbridge, Suffolk, Boydell Press, 2016) xxxvi.

[52] *A Complete Collection of State-Trials and Proceedings upon High Treason* (London, 1730) vol 4, 651.

[53] Alexander H Shapiro, 'Political Theory and the Growth of Defensive Safeguards in Criminal Procedure: The Origins of the Treason Trials Act of 1696' (1993) 11(2) *Law and History Review* 218, 252.

[54] John H Langbein, *The Origins of Adversary Criminal Trial* (Oxford, Oxford University Press, 2003) 81, 82.

Historically, a defendant in an English trial was meant to be vulnerable. They were not on oath and their evidence was less credible.[55] In hindsight, unfairness is the most obvious feature of this arrangement. Counterintuitively perhaps to modern eyes, the more serious the offence, the more vulnerable was the defendant. Counsel was permitted for both the defence and the prosecution in civil cases and for misdemeanours but not for felonies (including treason) when a person's life was at stake.[56] There were jurisprudential reasons, as a judge could assist the defendant, including through exercising his power to include or exclude evidence.[57] The judges therefore were active participants in a trial, doing what in a modern trial the counsel would do, including conducting the cross-examinations but also bullying the defendants and the witnesses.[58]

John H Langbein has coined the 'Defendant speaks' mode of trial, and the point is to be taken literally. He refers to the historic arrangement whereby jailors brought the defendant up to the dock. The defendant heard the indictment read out and was expected to answer it. The legal theory behind this approach was that the person to speak in their defence was the defendant. Likewise, in legal theory the defendant was the person best positioned to interrogate prosecution witnesses.[59] These ideas were, by 1696, long standing. In the sixteenth century, Sir Thomas Smith described a trial as an altercation between an undefended accused and the accuser. Far from seeing that as unfair, Smith admired the purity and clarity of this approach, as the defendant would know the facts of the case and answer to them.[60] Jurisprudentially, it also speaks to an understanding of a trial as testing facts, not the law. William Hawkins' *Pleas of the Crown* (1721) regarded a trial as an occasion for speaking of facts, making the accused person the best lawyer.[61]

There was a further reason to have made the defendant vulnerable, which was the belief that a sure way to judge a person's guilt or innocence was to see their unmediated reaction to hearing the indictment. Images of the **Old Bailey** courtroom from the eighteenth century show that the internal arrangements made the defendant a visual centrepiece. The judge and jury would be able to see their face and watch their facial expressions. The accused sat beneath a large mirror above the dock that caught the light from high windows and shone it on the defendant's face. It enabled judge and jury to see the defendant's face and determine if they seemed honestly surprised by what they heard.[62]

The Old Bailey: the Central Criminal Court

[55] *Ibid* 48.

[56] Simon Devereaux, 'Arts of Public Performance: Barristers and Actors in Georgian England' in David Lemmings (ed), *Crime, Courtrooms and the Public Sphere in Britain, 1700–1850* (Farnham, Surrey, Ashgate, 2012) 108; Kenyon (n 41) 131.

[57] Langbein (n 54) 215.

[58] Kenyon (n 41) 133.

[59] Shapiro (n 53) 222.

[60] John H Langbein, 'The Privilege and Common Law Criminal Procedure: The Sixteenth to the Eighteenth Centuries' in *The Privilege Against Self-Incrimination: Its Origins and Development* (Chicago, University of Chicago Press, 1997) 84.

[61] Devereaux (n 56) 108.

[62] *Ibid* 109.

This theoretical basis of this mode of trial was in doubt by the 1680s and beyond. Doubts were not merely procedural or technical but spoke more deeply to political philosophies and the pretexts given for the Glorious Revolution. Whig politicians viewed this mode as inherently unfair. In theory, judges could assist defendants, but did not in practice.[63] Amongst other concerns and doubts were expressed anxieties about perjury, and the likelihood that courts would find an innocent man guilty. Political philosophies that espoused support for the Glorious Revolution and the Bill of Rights also spoke to the importance of freedom of speech, delivered in court with assistance from a defence counsel. The Glorious Revolution focused attention on the administration of justice to the extent that the safeguards emerging from the 1690s seemed a 'new bill of rights'.[64]

Beyond the intersection of the political context with trials, there was also a question emerging from natural law of the right to deny counsel to an accused person.[65] Langbein also directs attention to a most fundamental aspect of the lived experience of justice. As he points out, at the centre of many of the 'defendant speaks' trials would have been frightened and bewildered men and women lacking any skill or experience in public speaking who found themselves the sudden centre of attention. They most likely were also dirty, unwell from jail fever and hungry.[66] One lawyer who was prepared to enter these filthy environments was William Garrow (1760–1840) celebrated for his singular impact as counsel for the defence case. His ability to cross-examine witnesses and therefore test the prosecution case remains celebrated along with his defiance of judges.[67] He remains sufficiently well known that a period drama *Garrow's Law* appeared on the BBC between 2009 and 2011.

Earlier, a 'before' and 'after' in trial modes was suggested and this notion can be usefully reintroduced to consider the adversarial trial mode that is now the common Anglo-Australian mode. Underpinning this mode is an evidentiary principle: the presumption of innocence. The presumption of innocence points to where the burden of proof lies. This presumption also intersects with there being rules of evidence and the adversarial process to test the prosecution case. In this mode, the rules of evidence can include ones such as the character rule, the corroboration rule, and the hearsay rule, and the rule of materiality, with the jury being the arbiter. Further, the body of rules can be mobilised to exclude probative evidence from the proceedings.[68]

Philosophically, the presumption of innocence indicates a newer emphasis in political theory on individual rights. Structurally, there comes the change to adversarial mode with a defence counsel testing the prosecution case. The Tudor notion of the altercation

[63] Shapiro (n 53) 223.
[64] *Ibid* 251.
[65] *Ibid* 240.
[66] Langbein (n 54) 62.
[67] Andrew Watson, *Speaking in Court: Developments in Court Advocacy from the Seventeenth to the Twenty-First Century* (London, Palgrave Macmillan, 2019) 59.
[68] Langbein (n 54) 179, 237, 315; John H Langbein, 'Historical Foundations of the Law of Evidence: A View From the Ryder Sources' (1996) 96 *Columbia Law Review* 1168, 1172.

evolves into the interpretation and presentation of evidence in the 'crisp' division of the defence and prosecution.[69] This evolution is the 'lawyerisation' of trials, but it should not be overstated. Professional counsel cost money and, while there were some notable early defence counsels such as William Garrow, most trials in this period still did not have counsel involved. Nor was the involvement of defence counsel automatic to all crimes; it started with treason and moved to other felonies later.[70]

Public Execution and Justice

Regardless of the *Trials Act* and the lawyerisation of trials, a person brought to trial would likely die. Public executions were popular, and large crowds attended the executions at Newgate Prison and Tyburn (then a village in Middlesex, now near the junction of Marble Arch and Edgware Road in London). However, these crowds were raucous rather than solemn, and were able to come remarkably close to the condemned men and women. Executions were public spectacles in England until 1868 with the passing of the *Capital Punishment Amendment Act 1868*.[71]

Why had they been public? In theory, the person on the gallows should have a 'good death'. Unlike most, they knew when the moment of their death would be and would be able to prepare themselves; they would be spared a ***mors improvisa***.[72] The legal authorities intended crowds to see a penitent person who would endorse their sentence and provide an example and the public executions were one aspect of the administration of justice.[73]

Mors improvisa (Latin): a sudden and unplanned death

Other points explain the focus placed on public executions. There was no professional police force until the nineteenth century, making public deterrents necessary. Reality rarely matched theory. The eighteenth-century artist William Hogarth created the work 'The Idle Apprentice', showing a raucous crowd around the gallows at Tyburn. In this famous image, there is less emphasis on gallows and prisoner and more on the frank enjoyment of the crowd. Hogarth's moralistic series of prints also included 'The Reward of Cruelty', depicting the dissection and anatomisation of the executed criminal Tom Nero. Under the *Murder Act 1751*,[74] the bodies of hanged murderers were to be 'immediately conveyed' from the place of execution and delivered to Surgeons' Hall for use in the teaching of anatomy by autopsy. The demand for anatomical corpses saw executed people denied decent Christian burials. Hogarth shows the full extent of the post-mortem degradation facing anyone on trial on a capital charge, for they are not only dissected but dissected publicly.

[69] Langbein (n 54) 259.

[70] John H Langbein, 'The Historical Origins of the Privilege against Self-Incrimination at Common Law' (1994) 92(5) *Michigan Law Review* 1147, 1048.

[71] 31 & 32 Vic c 24.

[72] McKenzie (n 38) 160.

[73] Simon Devereaux, 'Recasting the Theatre of Execution: The Abolition of the Tyburn Ritual' (2009) 202 *Past and Present* 127, 129.

[74] 25 Geo 2 c 37.

The Reception of English Law Abroad

The preceding sections have considered legal developments on English soil. Coterminous with these was the overseas expansion of the British Empire, taking English people and their law abroad. The English went abroad for commercial gain and to seek commodities such as spices. Trade also included buying and selling human beings as slaves, which this section will consider as an aspect of legal history.

Reception is the process by which English law became part of the law of other countries. Other terms exist for this process – transmission, introduction, adoption and incorporation – but 'reception' is most commonly used. Where settled colonies were English in language and tradition, the process was more like a transplantation of the English law to the new environment.

According to William Blackstone, a coloniser could acquire a colony in three ways: by settlement, conquest or cession. The common view *before* Blackstone was that English settlers took the law overseas as part of their English birthright (the 'colonial birthright theory'). The Privy Council explained the birthright theory in *Case 15 – Anonymous* in the context of Barbados in the Caribbean:

> 1st, That if there be a new inhabited country found out by English subjects, as the law is the birthright of every subject, so wherever they go, they carry their laws with them, and therefore such new found country is to be governed by the laws of England … 2dly, Where the King of England conquers the country, it is a different consideration: for there the conqueror, by saving the laws of the people conquered, gains a right and property in such people; in consequence of which he may impose upon them what law he pleases.[75]

The notion that colonisers settled Australia as *terra nullius* was shattered in *Mabo v Queensland (No 2)*.[76] In English ideas of private land ownership, cultivation of the land and land ownership were intimately related. *Terra nullius* as a legal and philosophical principle does not mean that the land is empty, but that the land has no master.

From the fifteenth century, royal charters or letters patent authorised the creation of overseas territories. Judicial opinions and texts explored theories about the reception of English law. ***Calvin's Case*** (reported by Edward Coke),[77] established that the existing legal system of the conquered or ceded territory survived, but the monarch had an absolute royal prerogative – a personal power – to legislate over the territory and its subjects. The monarch could legislate in conquered territories. In other words, the law of conquered and ceded colonies remained 'in force until … altered by the conqueror'.[78] Within the royal prerogative was the power to import the English legal system into the conquered colony to alter or completely replace any pre-existing law it may have had. After 1689, Whigs progressively challenged the idea of an absolute royal prerogative.

The American colonies, which had gained independence as the United States after the American Revolution, were not the only British possessions in North America. Among the colonies acquired were Newfoundland, territories of the Hudson Bay Company, Nova Scotia,

[75] (1722) 2 P Wms 75; 24 ER 646.
[76] (1992) 175 CLR 1.
[77] (1608) 7 Co Rep 1a; 77 ER 377.
[78] *Campbell v Hall* (1774) 1 Cowp 204; 98 ER 1045.

Quebec, Upper Canada (now Ontario) and the West Indies, including Jamaica. These were all part of the North American colonial system. France ceded some West Indies possessions – including Grenada, Tobago, Dominica – to the British in 1763. Other Caribbean islands – such as Antigua, Barbados and Jamaica – had been in British possession for a longer period. In Caribbean colonies, English law in force was already confirmed – although some colonies delayed confirming this until the early nineteenth century.

English law came to India in a very limited sense from the early eighteenth century by means of royal charters, treaties, concessions, legislation and judge-made law. English law was not received wholesale into India. The East India Company, incorporated by a royal charter issued by Elizabeth I in 1600, had a monopoly of trade with the East Indies. This commercial venture saw English law received in trading factories established with the authority of local Indian monarchs.

From the early-eighteenth century, the colonial governments created special courts in Chennai (Madras), Kolkata (Calcutta) and Mumbai (Bombay) with jurisdiction at common law; in equity; and in admiralty, lunacy and ecclesiastical matters. These were restricted to Company employees and British subjects in areas in which the Company acquired sovereignty by conquest. Non-Europeans were restricted from accessing these special courts, which brought about clashes of jurisdiction and laws corrected in the late-nineteenth century.

Historical Cameo

Lord Hardwicke on Equity, Slavery and the Marriage Act 1753

Philip Yorke, 1st Earl of Hardwicke (1690–1764) was Lord High Chancellor of Great Britain for 19 years between 1737 and 1756. He was the longest serving lord chancellor of the eighteenth century. Before his time as Lord Chancellor, Lord Hardwicke served as Chief Justice of the King's Bench (1733–37), the country's Attorney-General (1724–33) and Solicitor-General (1720–24). The patronage of both Lord Macclesfield, himself a Chief Justice (1710–18) and a Lord Chancellor (1718–25), and the Duke of Newcastle gave Hardwicke a 'leg up' enabling his rapid rise through the ranks of the legal profession and Parliament.[79] This historical cameo discusses only three elements of Hardwicke's life, but ones with which he is most commonly associated: the emergence of modern equity, slavery and clandestine marriages.

The Emergence of Modern Equity

Lord Hardwicke refined the laws of equity. In the eighteenth century, the doctrine of precedent was not as we know it today. Past cases were not as binding. However, Lord Hardwicke still used past cases for the principles they established or as factual analogies. Through analogical reasoning, Hardwicke helped to give decisions consistency,

[79] George Harris, *The Life of Lord Chancellor Hardwicke: With Selections from His Correspondence, Diaries, Speeches, and Judgements, Volume 1* (London, E Moxon, 1847) 426–27.

legitimacy and the potential for future use. Though he often strictly followed 'precedent', Lord Hardwicke was more flexible in cases involving fraud, the mentally ill and the underage.

In one famous case, *Chesterfield v Janssen*, Lord Hardwicke classified five different types of fraud that equity would relieve against to prevent contractual unfairness. It was a novel approach because fraud, one of three traditional heads of equitable jurisdiction, had not until then received that sort of structure.[80]

Slavery and the Yorke-Talbot Opinion, 1729

Between the seventeenth and early-nineteenth century, England grew rich from trafficking in humans. The transatlantic slave trade saw many Africans enslaved and transported to the West Indies and North America to work as slave labour on sugar and cotton plantations. Liverpool, the major eighteenth-century slaving port, became prosperous on the back of this trade and slavery intersected with other industries and manufactories including shipwrights and cotton merchants.[81] The number of slaving ships departing from Liverpool for Africa increased from 15 a year in 1730 to over 50 during the 1750s. It was inevitable that legal questions about the status of slaves would confront English courts. During Hardwicke's time as Attorney-General, he penned the 1729 Yorke-Talbot opinion with Charles Talbot, the Solicitor-General. A West Indies lobby of slave-owners sought Yorke and Talbot's opinion on the legality of slavery in England out of concern that slaves might be free by stepping on English soil or becoming Christians. The Yorke-Talbot opinion was not a binding legal decision; rather, and perhaps startlingly for us, the opinion was offered to the slave-owner lobby after a dinner in Lincoln's Inn – one of the Inns of Court. Inconsistent decisions created the perfect storm for this particular slavery debate. In *Cartwright's Case* – a mid-sixteenth century ruling referred to in subsequent reported cases – an English court had apparently stated: 'England was too pure an Air for Slaves to breathe in'. Earlier, in *Calvin's Case*, Sir Edward Coke said that 'infidels' could be enslaved because they were 'perpetual enemies' of Christians.

Chief Justice Holt's (Chief Justice until his death in 1710) rulings included that:

- 'Slaves' were not property to be traded;
- English law did not know the state of slavery, but it did recognise 'slavish servants'; and
- 'As soon as a negro comes into England, he becomes free. One may be a villein in England but not a slave.'[82]

Based on Sir Edward Coke's decision in *Calvin's Case*, opponents of slavery reasoned that Christian baptism would free 'infidel' slaves. However, Yorke and Talbot disagreed.

[80] (1750–1) 2 Ves Sen 125; 28 ER 82.

[81] Eric Williams, *Capitalism and Slavery* (Chapel Hill, UNC Press, 2014) 58, 68.

[82] Holt's cases included *Chamberlain v Harvey* (1697) 1 Ld Raym 146 and *Smith v Gould* (1705–07) 2 Salk 666, quoted in *Somerset v Stewart* (1772) 98 ER 499.

Asked in their capacities as law officers for their opinion, which they delivered after a dinner at Lincoln's Inn, they concluded that a slave was not freed either by converting to Christianity or upon entering England.

> A Slave by coming from the West-Indies to Great Britain, doth not become free, and that his Master's Property or Right in him is not thereby determined or varied: And that Baptism doth not bestow freedom on him, nor make any Alterations in his Temporal Condition in these Kingdoms Slaves could be compelled to return to the colonies from whence they came.[83]

That however was an unreported decision, one made by law officers but not made as a ruling in a court and it was informally reported.[84]

Lord Hardwicke maintained this position in *Pearne v Lisle*.[85] He held that trover was available for slaves – a finding consistent with cases predating Holt. Trover is an old cause of action involving a plaintiff who, after losing property, finds it in possession of the defendant. The plaintiff sues the defendant, who refuses to hand the property back and instead 'converts' the property to his own use. In holding that an action in trover was available for the recovery of slaves, Lord Hardwicke was holding that slaves were property.

Lord Hardwicke's Act

To pause for a moment the discussion of slavery, other aspects of human life and experience were attended to by the law in the eighteenth century. *The Marriage Act 1753* (popularly referred to as **Lord Hardwicke's Act**) became law on 25 March 1754. The Act controlled irregular or clandestine marriages. There were various forms of clandestine or irregular marriage. A few examples of irregular marriages include marriage by a minister of religion and not in a church, marriage by a priest but not in a church, and marriage by a priest in a church but without 'banns' (public notice) having been read out loud several weeks beforehand, or a licence. The mischief that Lord Hardwicke's Act sought to correct were marriages celebrated in prisons by clerical inmates and in the prison surrounds. These marriages had caused 'great Mischiefs and Inconveniences' and were 'one of the growing evils introductive of much calamity and ruin to families'.[86] As the Lord Chancellor and, so, the judge in the Court of Chancery, Lord Hardwicke was exposed to irregular marriages, most typically involving wealthy heiresses. He wanted law reform to curb these marriages, 'which are not only introductive of great mischiefs, but put Courts of judicature under great difficulties'.[87]

[83] Anon, *The Trials of the Slave Traders, Samuel Samo, Joseph Peters, and William Tufft* (Cambridge, Cambridge University Press, 2014) 61.

[84] Srividhya Swaminathan, *Debating the Slave Trade: Rhetoric of British National Identity, 1759–1815* (Aldershot, Hampshire, Ashgate, 2009) 64.

[85] (1749) Amb 75; 27 ER 47.

[86] *Hervey v Aston*, West T Hard, 350, 426 (1737–38). *Reports of Cases Argued and Determined in the High Court of Chancery: From 1736 to July, 1739: from the Original Manuscripts of Lord Chancellor Hardwicke and the Contemporaneous Reports, Compared with and Corrected by Lord Hardwicke's Notes: with Notes and References Volume 1* (London, Joseph Butterworth and Son, 1827) 435.

[87] *Ibid* 197.

In one case, a 17-year-old ward of court was plied with alcohol until she was intoxicated and married in London's Fleet Prison. The Act required:

- The calling of banns on three successive Sundays before marriage in the church or chapel of the parish where the couple had resided for at least a month.
- Parental consent for minors, those under the age of 21.
- Two witnesses to the marriage ceremony.
- The public reading of Lord Hardwicke's Act from the pulpit on four occasions each year.

These requirements did not extend to Jews, Quakers, the Royal Family and Scotland. With the Act having limited territorial reach, places on the Scottish border, such as Gretna Green, became marriage havens for English couples. Scots law only required marriage *per verba de praesenti*, that is to say, the exchange of vows indicating the giving of present unconditional consent. As always, writers of fiction were keen observers of the laws of their times and in Jane Austen's *Pride and Prejudice*, Lydia Bennett and Mr Wickham elope and intend to make for Gretna Green.

Historical Cameo

Lord Mansfield

William Murray, 1st Earl of Mansfield (1705–93) was Lord Chief Justice of England from 1756–86. Legal historians credit him for developing English commercial law and for delivering two famous slavery decisions, *Somerset's Case*[88] and the *Zong Case* (*Gregson v Gilbert*).[89] Lord Mansfield's judgment in *Somerset's Case* is famously – albeit erroneously – associated with the end of slavery in England. Lord Mansfield remains one of the most eminent judges of the common law tradition. William Murray was born in Scotland in 1705. He was initially educated there but, as a 13-year-old, he went to Westminster School. In 1723, Murray matriculated at Christ Church, Oxford. After graduation, he was admitted to the Bar at Lincoln's Inn in 1730. During the 1730s, Murray gradually developed a strong practice in equity, colonial disputes and Scottish appeals to the House of Lords.

In 1742, he became a Member of Parliament to fill a vacancy that had opened for the position as Solicitor-General (in office 1742–54). He was the Attorney-General for England and Wales (1754–56) for a short time before serving for 30 years as Chief Justice of the Court of King's Bench (1756–86). On his swearing in, Murray became Baron Mansfield. As Chief Justice, Lord Mansfield expanded the jurisdiction of the Court of King's Bench. Using his experience as a Chancery lawyer, he borrowed from equity and introduced some equitable doctrines to the law.[90] In one case, Lord Mansfield made the plaintiff

[88] (1772) Lofft 1, 98 ER 49.
[89] (1783) 1 Dougl, 233 ER 629.
[90] James Oldham, *English Common Law in the Age of Mansfield* (Chapel Hill, University of North Carolina Press, 2005) 27–28;

disclose documents (the law calls this 'discovery') to the defendant.[91] He was by no means the first judge to do so. Matthew Hale's biographer Bishop Gilbert Burnet noted that Hale looked 'upon Equity as a part of the Common Law, and one of the Grounds of it'.[92]

Because Lord Mansfield ordered this equitable procedure, it meant the defendant no longer had to visit the Court of Chancery to obtain discovery. The Court of King's Bench heard some civil actions previously only heard in the Court of Common Pleas.

Development of Commercial Law

Throughout the Middle Ages, merchants had their own courts. Later on, common law judges consulted merchants to determine commercial practice. Lord Mansfield's innovation was to establish special juries comprising merchants to establish the commercial position. He considered that certainty and convenience were the two aims of commercial law because, as he expressed in *Metcalf v Hall*, 'nothing is more mischievous than uncertainty in mercantile law'.[93] Lord Mansfield put the law on bills of exchange, promissory notes and banknotes in order. He also helped to establish the law of insurance. For example, in *Carter v Boehm*,[94] Lord Mansfield examined principles underlying the legal doctrine of *uberrimae fidei* (or 'of utmost good faith'), observing in this case about insurance that:

> Insurance is a contract based on speculation. The special facts, upon which the contingent chance is to be computed, lie most commonly in the knowledge of the insured only: the underwriter trusts to his representation, and proceeds upon confidence that he does not keep back any circumstances in his knowledge, to mislead the underwriter into a belief that the circumstance does not exist, and to induce him to estimate the risque, as if it did not exist.[95]

The insured person's duty of disclosure is still of fundamental importance in insurance contracts. The duty of utmost good faith that Lord Mansfield brought to the English common law is still recognised as applying to all insurance contracts under Australia's *Insurance Contracts Act 1984* (Cth).

Somerset's Case

In 1772, Lord Mansfield heard his most famous case, *Somerset v Stewart*.[96] *Somerset's Case* was a test case brought by prominent abolitionists, one of whom was Granville Sharpe, to settle the question of slavery's legality in England. Before the case, significant weight attached to the Yorke-Talbot opinion that slavery was legal in England. The opinion, which was not a judgment delivered by a court, had great weight attached to it because of the eminence of the two lawyers who had delivered it. Charles Stewart, a

[91] *Ibid* 131.

[92] Gilbert Burnet, *The Life and Death of Sir Matthew Hale* (London, 1700) sig G3.

[93] *Reports of Cases Argued and Determined in the Court of King's Bench: In the Nineteenth, Twentieth, and Twenty-first [twenty-second, Twenty-third, Twenty-fourth, and Twenty-fifth] Years of the Reign of George III. [1778–1785]*, vol 3 (Reed and Hunter, 1831) 115.

[94] (1766) 3 Burr 1905; 97 ER 1162.

[95] *Reports of Cases Argued and Adjudged in the Court of King's Bench: During the Time Lord Mansfield Presided in that Court; from Michaelmas Term, 30 Geo II 1756, to Easter Term, 12 Geo III 1772* (A Strahan and W Woodfall, 1790) 1909.

[96] (1772) Lofft 1, 98 ER 499.

customs official, bought James Somerset in Boston, Massachusetts. In 1769, Stewart took Somerset to England as his personal servant. Two years later, Somerset escaped, but was recaptured and detained by Captain Knowles on the ship, the *Ann and Mary*, bound for Jamaica. Once there, Somerset would be sold. Lord Mansfield issued a writ of *habeas corpus*,[97] ordering the Captain produce Somerset for examination before the Court.

The case was heard over six hearings between January and May 1772. Lawyers paid for by a consortium of slave-owners represented Stewart. The lawyers of Somerset, chosen by anti-slavery campaigners, represented Somerset without charge. On 22 June 1772, after multiple failed attempts to have the parties settle, Lord Mansfield handed down judgment. At one of these six hearings, Lord Mansfield suggested that Stewart free Somerset. Lord Mansfield's delays were a result of understanding that freeing slaves *en masse* would have enormous financial consequences:

> The setting 14,000 or 15,000 men at once free loose by a solemn opinion, is much disagreeable in the effects it threatens. … £50 a head may not be a high price; then a loss follows to the proprietors of above £700,000 sterling.[98]

Thus, Lord Mansfield framed the legal issue for decision narrowly: 'the only question before us is, whether the cause on the return is sufficient? If it is, the negro must be remanded; if it is not, he must be discharged.'[99] He then said:

> So high an act of dominion must be recognized by the law of the country where it is used. The power of a master over his slave has been extremely different, in different countries. The state of slavery is of such a nature, that it is incapable of being introduced on any reasons, moral or political; but only positive law, which preserves its force long after the reasons, occasion, and time itself from whence it was created, is erased from memory: it's so odious, that nothing can be suffered to support it, but positive law. Whatever inconveniences, therefore, may follow from a decision, I cannot say this case is allowed or approved by the law of England; and therefore the black must be discharged.[100]

The decision did not declare slavery illegal and it did not free all slaves or even resolve the question of property in slaves. So, what was its legal effect? A master could not forcibly remove a slave from England. The campaign to abolish the slave trade was a hard fight over the decades following *Somerset's Case*. In 1787, abolitionists formed the Society for Effecting the Abolition of the Slave Trade. In 1807, 20 years later, the *Abolition of the Slave Trade Act* made it illegal to participate in the slave trade in the British Empire.

The Zong Massacre

Remarkably for the time, Lord Mansfield and his wife, Elizabeth, raised and educated two of their great nieces, Elizabeth Murray (the daughter of Murray's nephew, David Murray) and Dido Elizabeth Belle (the illegitimate child of another nephew,

[97] See chapter three.

[98] Thomas Bayly Howell, *Cobbett's Complete Collection of State Trials and Proceedings for High Treason: And Other Crimes and Misdemeanor from the Earliest Period to the Present Time … from the Ninth Year of the Reign of King Henry, the Second, A.D.1163, to [George IV, AD 1820]*, vol 20 (R Bagshaw, 1814) 79.

[99] *Ibid* 82.

[100] *Ibid* 81.

Sir John Lindsay, and an African slave). The film *Belle* (2014) explores the relationship between Dido and her great uncle, Lord Mansfield. The film also considers the Zong Massacre in which Captain Collingwood threw 133 Africans on the ship Zong overboard.

The *Zong Case* is the popular case name for *Gregson v Gilbert*.[101] In September 1781, the Zong left the west coast of Africa bound for Jamaica. On board this ship were approximately 440 Africans destined for a life of slavery. The ship was designed to hold only 200 souls. The captain, Luke Collingwood, hoped to retire on the profits made from the trip. Collingwood squeezed in and manacled as many Africans as he could on board. He was, however, inexperienced as a captain. This was to be his first and only trip. The Zong found itself stranded in the mid-Atlantic in an area colloquially referred to as 'the Doldrums' where there are few to no winds. Then, the crew mistook Jamaica for Haiti. In November, crew members and slaves began to die from scurvy, dysentery and other ailments. By the end of November, seven crew members and 60 slaves were dead. At this stage, Collingwood hatched a callous plan. The Zong's human cargo had been insured for £30 per head. Collingwood reasoned that it would be better to throw sickly and dying slaves overboard and claim insurance on them than to arrive in Jamaica with dead slaves and no money.

In England, the owner filed an insurance claim of £4000 for the value of the lost 'human cargo'. The case was first heard as a trial before a jury with Lord Mansfield as Chief Justice of the Court of the King's Bench presiding. The owners argued that a lack of water on board compelled the Captain to act as he did as a necessity. The First Mate contradicted Collingwood. The Zong may have had about 430 gallons of available drinking water on arrival in Jamaica. The insurer argued that 'a sufficient necessity did not exist for throwing the negroes overboard'.[102] In the first case, the jury found for the shipowners; however, the insurers applied for their verdict to be set aside and tried again. Lord Mansfield ordered a retrial. He had heard evidence of heavy rainfall over the three days the 'human cargo' went overboard. Two prominent abolitionists, Granville Sharp and Oloudah Equiano (the subject of another British film, *Amazing Grace* (2006)), tried to have charges laid against the Captain, the crew and the shipowners. The Solicitor-General refused to do this, stating:

> What is this claim that human people have been thrown overboard? This is a case of chattels or goods. Blacks are goods and property; it is madness to accuse these well-serving honourable men of murder. They acted out of necessity and in the most appropriate manner for the cause. … The case is the same *as if wood had been thrown overboard*.[103]

British commercial interests remained preeminent in law; however, Lord Mansfield's ordering of a retrial made the *Zong Case* famous and made it a cause célèbre for the anti-slavery movement. Parliament subsequently prohibited payment by insurance companies for slaves thrown overboard.

[101] *Gregson v Gilbert* (n 89).

[102] *Reports of Cases Argued and Determined in the English Courts of Common Law* (T & JW Johnson, 1853) vol 26, 159.

[103] *Ibid* 159 (emphasis added).

Abolition of the Slave Trade

In concluding the treatment of the slave trade, this section considers three pieces of early nineteenth-century legislation that achieved this end: the *Slave Trade Act 1807*,[104] the ***Slave Trade Felony Act 1811***,[105] and the *Slavery Abolition Act 1833*.[106] The *Slave Trade Act 1807* outlawed trading in slaves in most British colonies. Vessels fitted out to engage in the slave trade were forfeit. However, fines imposed by the 1807 Act did little to deter human trafficking. Indeed, when Parliament introduced the *Slave Trade Felony Bill 1811* to make the *Slave Trade Act 1807* more effective, the Member for Stockbridge Joseph Barham remarked that he was 'sorry to understand, that the illicit trade in slaves had so greatly increased, that if not effectually checked, it seemed as if it would shortly exceed that slave trade which had been abolished'.[107] The *Slave Trade Felony Act 1811* made slave trading a felony,[108] punishable by penalties of imprisonment and hard labour of between three to five years or 14 years' transportation.

On 28 August 1833, the *Slavery Abolition Act 1833* received royal assent and came into force on 1 August 1834. The aims of the Act were threefold. The first aim was to abolish slavery throughout the British colonies. Slaves in most British colonies including the British Caribbean, Mauritius and the Cape of Good Hope were emancipated.[109] The Act's operation excluded territories in possession of the East India Company, Ceylon (now Sri Lanka) and Saint Helena.[110] The Act also freed children under the age of six.[111]

The second aim was 'for promoting the Industry and securing the good Conduct of the Persons so to be manumitted'. Many formerly enslaved people continued to work for their former owners for four to six years as unpaid apprentices. They finally gained their freedom at midnight on 31 July 1838. The third aim was to pay 'a reasonable Compensation … to the Persons hitherto entitled to the Services of such Slaves for the Loss that they incur by being deprived of their Right to such Services'. The British Government borrowed £20 million, approximately 40 per cent of its total annual expenditure, to fund this compensation scheme.[112] The loan was finally repaid in 2015 following a loan restructure.

[104] 47 Geo 3 sess 1, c 36.
[105] 51 Geo 3, c 23.
[106] 3 & 4 Will IV, c 73.
[107] United Kingdom, *Parliamentary Debates*, House of Commons, 8 March 1811, vol 19, col 239 (Joseph Barham).
[108] *Slave Trade Felony Act 1811* (n 105) s 1.
[109] *Slavery Abolition Act 1833* (n 106) s 45
[110] *Ibid* s 64.
[111] But see s 13.
[112] Information Rights Unit, 'Freedom of Information Act 2000: Slavery Abolition Act 1833' (*HM Treasury*, 31 January 2018), available at https://assets.publishing.service.gov.uk/government/uploads/system/uploads/attachment_data/file/680456/FOI2018-00186_-_Slavery_Abolition_Act_1833_-_pdf_for_disclosure_log__003_.pdf.

Pause for Thought

Modern Slavery

Slavery, though legally abolished, is very much alive.

Questions to Consider

1. What are the modern circumstances that have given rise to slavery?
2. What modern safeguards exist to attempt to protect people from slavery?

Historical Cameo

Sir William Blackstone

Sir William Blackstone (1723–80) was a jurist, judge, poet, architectural enthusiast, politician and professor of law at the University of Oxford. He is widely known as the author of the *Commentaries of the Laws of England* (1765–70). Published in four volumes, the *Commentaries* comprehensively and systematically set out the common law of England, which Sir Edward Coke's *Institutes* had attempted about a century and half earlier. In the author's lifetime alone, the *Commentaries* received five separate republications. They were highly influential and popular in England and the colonies, especially in the United States, where judges still cite Blackstone regularly in judgments. A copy of Blackstone's *Commentaries* came to Australia with the First Fleet in 1788.

In 1758, Blackstone became the first Vinerian Professor of English Law, a chair that had just been established. He set about teaching English law in a series of lectures. This is significant because universities did not teach the common law until the nineteenth century. Cambridge and Oxford taught civil and Roman law. In 1770, Blackstone became a Justice of the Court of King's Bench before being elevated to Justice of the Court of Common Pleas the same year (1770–80). See more about him in the **Selden Society** lecture.

Conclusion

If the seventeenth century was the 'Iron Century', the eighteenth century is known as the era of the 'Bloody Code'. Many of the experiences of justice recounted in this chapter from the public executions to the commodification of human beings are not inspiring. This chapter has addressed a range of touch points for the legal history of the century, which in turn have intersected with different social layers. The notions of responsible government and the developments in contract law take attention to high-minded and intellectually adventurous developments in government and law. However, the brutality of trials and the human misery of slavery are critical elements of the legal history, and the history of slavery continues to resonate today.

5

The American Constitutional Settlement

Introduction

This chapter begins when the territory of the British North American colonies occupied 'only a skirt of coast along the shore of the Atlantic Ocean'.[1] Hemmed in by the Appalachian Mountains, colonists wrestled for land in the vast and fertile Ohio River Valley occupied by Native Americans and claimed by the French. Intent on preventing further westward incursions, the French constructed a line of forts in the disputed territory to consolidate their claim. So did the English.

In January 1754, the British commenced work on Fort Prince George, strategically located on the forks of the Ohio River where the Allegheny and Monongahela Rivers converge in modern-day Pittsburgh. Sitting at the gateway to the Ohio Valley, the unfinished fort fell to the French in April 1754. In its place, the French constructed the formidable Fort Duquesne. On 9 May 1754, just over three weeks after the fall of Fort Prince George, Benjamin Franklin's newspaper the *Pennsylvania Gazette* published an article and accompanying cartoon titled 'Join, or Die'. The cartoon depicted a snake cut up into eight segments labelled with initials representing British North American colonies and regions: New England, New York, New Jersey, Pennsylvania, Maryland, Virginia, North Carolina and South Carolina. Franklin's article, accompanying the famous political cartoon, urged the British North American colonies to unite for their 'common Defence and Security' in response to recent acts of aggression by the French. The appearance of Franklin's publication five weeks before the Albany Congress was almost certainly 'deliberate'.[2]

On 19 June 1754, representatives from seven of the British North American colonies assembled at Albany in New York. Franklin, as representative of Pennsylvania, presented his proposal of colonial union. While representatives agreed to Franklin's plan, neither the colonial assemblies nor British Parliament subsequently adopted it. Perhaps the time was not ripe for union because, in the meantime, a more pressing concern had emerged.

On 28 May 1754, the opening salvos of the French and Indian War (1754–63) – the North American theatre of the Seven Years' War – were fired in western Pennsylvania. The Virginia Regiment, led by 22-year-old Major George Washington, had finished constructing Fort Necessity when the Regiment received intelligence that a detachment of French soldiers were encamped nearby. Setting out from Fort Necessity, they ambushed the detachment and killed their leader, Ensign Jumonville. Washington and his men returned to Fort Necessity and strengthened its fortifications. Little over a month later Washington was forced to surrender Fort Necessity to a superior French and Indian force under the command of Louis Coulon de Villiers, Jumonville's older brother.

[1] RC, 'An Account of the French and English Colonies in North America', *The Universal Magazine of Knowledge and Pleasure for September 1755* (London, John Hinton, 1755) 84, 113.

[2] Karen Severud Cook, 'Benjamin Franklin and the Snake that would not Die' (1996) 22 *British Library Journal* 88, 98.

In the first few years of the war, British and colonial forces weathered defeat after defeat. The tide turned with the formation of the Pitt-Newcastle ministry in 1757. William Pitt (the Elder), the Secretary of State for the Southern Department, took control of war policy and increased military expenditure. From 1758, British forces won a series of victories against the French. The British captured strategically important strongholds in North America, West Africa and the Caribbean. In 1762, as French defeat looked imminent, Spain cast off its neutrality and joined France in a last effort to stave off British victory in North America. Britain soon captured the Spanish strongholds of Havana and Manila. In the meantime, political machinations had forced William Pitt to resign. George III appointed royal favourite John Stuart, the Earl of Bute, as British Prime Minister. Bute wanted peace with France and Spain.

Great Britain, France, and Spain signed the Treaty of Paris on 10 February 1763. The Seven Years' War (1756–63) and, for that matter, the French and Indian War were over. Under the Treaty, Great Britain gained territory in Canada, the Mississippi River Valley, Florida and some of the French West Indies. Bute, having concluded the Treaty of Paris, resigned. William Pitt's brother-in-law, George Grenville, took office, but the new Grenville ministry faced a crippling national debt exacerbated by the war.

Grenville's insistence that Americans pay for their defence sets this chapter on the American struggle for independence and the ensuing constitutional settlement in broader context. The next part of this chapter continues the story of American independence by considering how the financial consequences of the Seven Years' War contributed to the outbreak of the American War of Independence. The remainder of this chapter addresses the emergence of fundamental notions of constitutional law introduced with the foundation of the new American republic. The constitutional detours in this chapter add a further dimension to the Australian constitutional developments to be considered in chapters seven, ten and 11.

Learning Resources

The content in this chapter is supported by:

Glossary	Chapter Overview	Historical Cameos	Constitutional Detours
Terms are defined throughout the chapter	The chapter begins with an overview explaining its intentions and focus	James Madison	Thomas Paine's *Common Sense*
		Thomas Jefferson	Federalism
		John Marshall	Separation of Powers
			The Bill of Rights
			Judicial Review

Chapter Overview

Place	Time Period	Dates	Key Figures	Key Institutions	Key Terms
• Great Britain • British North American colonies • United States of America	• Georgian era	• 18th–19th century	• George III • George Grenville • William Pitt the Elder • Thomas Gage • George Washington • Thomas Paine • James Madison • Alexander Hamilton • John Adams • Thomas Jefferson • John Marshall	• British Parliament • Secretary of State for the Southern Department • East India Company • Virginia House of Burgesses • Stamp Act Congress • First Colonial Congress • Committees of safety • Supreme Court of the United States	• Drawback • Specie • Summarily • Internal tax • Intolerable Acts • Federalist • Anti-Federalist • Democratic-Republican • Judicial review • Original and appellate jurisdiction • Lame-duck session of Congress

Learning Outcomes

At the end of this chapter, readers should understand:

- The events contributing to the American War of Independence.
- The structure of the Constitution of the United States.
- Foundational concepts of constitutional law in federations including federalism, separation of powers and judicial review.

The *Stamp Act* Furore

The Seven Years' War had been extraordinarily expensive, thanks in no small part to its scale. Battles were fought on land and sea in North America, the Caribbean, Africa, India and continental Europe. Between 1755 and 1763, the nation's debt had almost doubled in size from £72,289,673 in 1755 to £122,603,336 in 1763,[3] carrying an annual interest of £4,409,797. One year later, the national debt had increased by another £7,000,000.[4] Peacetime would bring further expenses. Territories, once gained, required 'long-term investment'.[5]

[3] Edmund S Morgan and Helen M Morgan, *The Stamp Act Crisis: Prologue to Revolution* (Chapel Hill, University of North Carolina Press, 1995) 22.

[4] *Ibid.*

[5] *Ibid* 23.

For Great Britain that meant installing a standing army of 10,000 regular troops in America at a staggering annual cost of £220,000.[6] A standing army would guard against the chance of French repossession in the future.[7] At the conclusion of war, British expenditure outstripped revenue. Annual taxation in Britain averaged 26 shillings per person. In comparison the colonies were, in Grenville's opinion, 'grossly undertaxed'.[8] The average rate of taxation was one shilling per person.

The new Grenville ministry had to decide who was going to pay for the war, maintain the peace, and manage the newly acquired territories. The British North American colonies were to bear the brunt of Grenville's programme of reform. Tightening up the customs service was first on Grenville's agenda. Investigation into annual revenue of American customs revealed a smaller than expected return of £1,800 per year.[9] Royal customs officers were ordered to their colonial posts; otherwise, they would lose their jobs.[10] Colonial governors were instructed to report on contraband trade; the Royal Navy ordered to patrol American waters for smugglers.[11]

Apart from cracking down on officials' performance of duties, Grenville set his sights on generating revenue with a proposed new schedule of duties. A redraft of the *Molasses Act 1733*, the *Sugar Act 1764*[12] discontinued the **drawback** on foreign textiles exported from Great Britain and imposed new duties on non-British goods imported into the colonies. The colonies were banned from exporting their lumber and iron direct to Europe.[13] Duties were placed on sugar, indigo, coffee, Madeira wine, pimento and materials including silk, linen and calico. An existing six pence per gallon duty payable on foreign molasses was reduced to three pence. The six pence duty imposed by the *Molasses Act 1733* was habitually evaded through smuggling and bribery. Grenville thought a reduced duty would yield good income while also advantaging British sugar planters in the Caribbean.[14] Yet all the revised duties in the *Sugar Act 1764* had to be paid in specie (silver or gold coins),[15] and silver and gold were scarce in the American colonies. The means by which duties were to be collected and enforced under the *Sugar Act 1764* were strengthened by enlarging the powers of customs officials and creating a vice-admiralty court at Halifax in Nova Scotia. Violations of the 1764 Act would be tried summarily in the vice admiralty courts to avoid local colonial courts filled with 'sympathetic' judges and juries.[16] British Parliament further aggravated colonial resentment by enacting the *Currency Act 1764*. The Act forbade the colonies from issuing paper money

Drawback: refund of duties paid on goods imported that are subsequently exported

[6] *Ibid.*
[7] *Ibid.*
[8] *Ibid.*
[9] *Ibid.*
[10] *Ibid.*
[11] *Ibid.*
[12] 4 Geo 3 c 15.
[13] Morgan and Morgan (n 3) 29.
[14] *Ibid* 26, 27; John Phillip Reid, *Constitutional History of the American Revolution: The Authority To Tax* (Madison, University of Wisconsin Press, 1987) vol 2, 28, 29.
[15] Andrew David Edwards, 'Grenville's Silver Hammer: The Problem of Money in the Stamp Act Crisis' (2017) 104 *Journal of American History* 337, 344.
[16] Morgan and Morgan (n 3) 24.

as legal tender which, given the scarcity of specie, would force colonists to barter with what provisions they had.[17]

The colonial rumour mill soon went into overdrive with indications that Parliament were considering an **internal tax** to contribute to the cost of the standing army, the precise nature of which was anyone's guess.[18] By this point, Grenville was already committed to the idea of a stamp tax and sought advanced support from Parliament in March 1764. The measure was delayed for a year. In the interim, Grenville rejected entreaties for colonial self-taxation and reasserted Parliament's right to tax the colonies. He instructed Thomas Whately, Secretary to the Treasury, to draft a new American Stamp Act. Whately canvassed opinion from American acquaintances on the proposed tax, noting that '[i]t will be a principal objection of attention here to make this tax as little burthensome as possible'. Whately's acquaintances advised caution. Meanwhile, the Secretary of State for the Southern Department, the Earl of Halifax, wrote to the colonial governors with news of a proposed stamp tax and requested a schedule of instruments used in a range of transactions: 'in public transactions, law proceedings, grants, conveyances, securities of land or money within your government, with proper and sufficient descriptions of the same'.[19] This information would prove useful 'if Parliament should think proper to pursue the intention of the aforesaid resolution, they may thereby be enabled to carry it into execution, in the most effectual and least burdensome manner'.[20]

Internal tax: raising revenue directly from colonists as distinct from external taxes, ie customs duties on imports

On debating the Stamp Bill at Westminster, Grenville outlined the chief colonial objection 'is from the general right of mankind not to be taxed but by their representatives. This goes to all laws in general'.[21] At the Bill's second reading on 15 February 1765, the House of Commons refused to consider the colonists' petitions against the tax.[22] The proposed Stamp Act easily passed British Parliament and became law on 22 March. It was controversial because it assumed that the British Parliament had complete legislative authority over all colonies in the British Empire. The *Stamp Act 1765* imposed taxes on prescribed court documents, shipping papers, college degrees, appointments to public office, liquor licences, land transactions, newspapers, advertisements, pamphlets, almanacs, playing cards and dice.[23] They were to be 'written or printed on paper carrying a stamp embossed by the Treasury Office'.[24] The tax could only be paid in specie which was in short supply in the colonies.

By the end of May, news of the Stamp Act had arrived in the British American colonies. It provoked a wave of protest, starting in the **Virginia House of Burgesses**. On 30 May, a newly elected member of the House, Patrick Henry, introduced a series of resolutions against the Stamp Act,[25]

Virginia House of Burgesses: assembly of elected representatives in colonial Virginia

[17] *Ibid* 31.
[18] *Ibid* 34; Reid (n 14) 14.
[19] Cited in Morgan and Morgan (n 3) 58.
[20] *Ibid.*
[21] Reid (n 14) 16.
[22] Morgan and Morgan (n 3) 71–72, 92.
[23] *Ibid* 72.
[24] *Ibid.*
[25] *Ibid* 93–98.

and the Burgesses passed at least the first four.[26] The Virginia Resolves as they were known were soon reprinted and distorted in colonial papers.[27] Virginia's action inspired the colonial legislatures of Rhode Island, Connecticut, New York, Pennsylvania, Massachusetts and Maryland to pass their own resolutions.[28] In October, the Stamp Act Congress, comprising delegates of nine colonies, convened in New York and produced the Declaration of Rights and Grievances.[29] Adding pressure on Britain to repeal the Act were reports of physical resistance in Massachusetts, Rhode Island and New York. Local officials tasked with enforcing the Stamp Act, called stamp distributors, were physically threatened – some even resigned before the mob reached them.

With such fierce resistance, a new British government headed by Charles Watson-Wentworth, Marquis of Rockingham,[30] repealed the Stamp Act but also passed the Declaratory Act. *The Declaratory Act 1766* reinforced the supremacy of the British Parliament to legislate over the American colonies 'in all cases whatsoever'.[31] It made no reference to the heated topic of taxation. In England, Grenville opposed the repeal of the Stamp Act while Grenville's political rival, William Pitt the Elder, denied that the British Parliament had a general right of taxation and opposed the Declaratory Act.

The Boston Tea Party and the Intolerable Acts

The Boston Tea Party was a reaction to the *Tea Act 1773*. The British Government had enacted the Act to save the nearly bankrupt East India Company. From 1767, the Company had been unable to sell enough of its tea in the American colonies because the colonies boycotted all goods taxed by the Townshend duties. Named after the Chancellor of the Exchequer, the Townshend duties were designed to raise revenue and to humour the American colonists' distinction between internal taxes, which they opposed, and external taxes (customs duties on imported and exported goods), which they accepted as constitutionally permissible.[32] Duties were imposed on glass, paints, paper and tea.[33] By the end of 1770, the Townshend duties were repealed except for the duty on tea – left to symbolise Parliament's entitlement to raise taxes.[34] Patriots (against taxation), merchants (against monopolisation) and smugglers (against lower tea prices) combined to challenge these measures.[35] While the British Government maintained a duty on tea, a rebate ensured that the company's tea would be cheaper than smuggled tea. The Tea Act effectively gave the Company a monopoly to decide who could sell its tea in the American colonies.[36]

[26] *Ibid* 102.
[27] *Ibid* 98–102.
[28] *Ibid* 102–06.
[29] *Ibid* 108–18.
[30] The Marquis of Rockingham was the patron of Darcy Wentworth, a key figure in colonial New South Wales. See chapter eight of this volume.
[31] 6 Geo 3 c 12.
[32] Reid (n 14) 30.
[33] *Ibid* 31.
[34] David L Ammerman, 'The Tea Crisis and its Consequences, through 1776' in Jack P Greene and JR Pole (eds), *A Companion to the American Revolution* (Oxford, Blackwell Publishers Ltd, 2000) 195, 196.
[35] *Ibid.*
[36] *Ibid.*

In 1773, the East India Company shipped tea to Charles Town, Philadelphia, New York and Boston. Unloading that cargo proved problematic, especially in Boston where opposition turned violent and the tea was destroyed, rather than refused as had been the case in the other cities. On 16 December 1773, a group dressed up as Native Americans boarded three British vessels anchored in Boston Harbor and threw the tea overboard. The British Government reacted swiftly with four pieces of legislation. The American colonies described these Acts as the Coercive or Intolerable Acts, which:

1. closed the port of Boston;[37]
2. restructured colonial government in Massachusetts;[38]
3. changed the Massachusetts' justice system to protect government officials from local juries;[39] and
4. provided for the quartering or accommodation of British troops in unoccupied public buildings if colonial accommodation proved unacceptable.[40]

The colonists saw a fifth piece of British legislation, the *Quebec Act 1774*,[41] as an equally offensive and punitive measure. As part of the Treaty of Paris in 1763, France ceded New France to Great Britain. New France, redefined by the Quebec Act as the 'Province of Quebec', neighboured the 13 American colonies. The legislation guaranteed the freedom of Quebec's majority Catholic population to practise the Roman Catholic religion and to use the French language. It ensured the continuation of French civil law as the private law of Quebec and its seigneurial land tenure system. The usual oaths required for public office were waived. The Quebec Act also vested government in a governor and his advisory council. Many American colonists opposed the Quebec Act for compromising the Protestant hegemony and colonial land speculation. There was concern that the Quebec Act impaired common law traditions, such as civil trial by jury, in favour of the traditions of 'Catholic states of Europe' (see chapter four).[42] Others were convinced George III broke his coronation oath, particularly his obligation to uphold 'the Protestant reformed religion established by law', by supporting the Quebec Act.[43]

The First Continental Congress

The first Continental Congress met at Philadelphia in September and October 1774. A total of 56 delegates from 12 American colonies, except Georgia, adopted a declaration of rights and grievances and sent a Petition to the King demanding the repeal of the Intolerable Acts.

[37] *Boston Port Act 1774* (14 Geo 3 c 19).
[38] *Massachusetts Government Act 1774* (14 Geo 3 c 45).
[39] *Administration of Justice Act 1774* (14 Geo 3 c 39).
[40] *Quartering Act 1774* (14 Geo 3 c 54).
[41] 14 Geo 3 c 83.
[42] Vernon P Creviston, '"No King unless it be a Constitutional King": Rethinking the Place of the Quebec Act in the Coming of the American Revolution' (2011) 73 *The Historian* 463, 468.
[43] *Ibid* 470–79. For related reading on the British Protestant Whig tradition and the Franco-American alliance of 1778, see Brad A Jones, '"In Favour of Popery": Patriotism, Protestantism, and the Gordon Riots in the Revolutionary British Atlantic' (2013) 52 *Journal of British Studies* 79.

The Declaration of Rights and Grievances asserted the entitlement of colonists to 'all the rights, liberties, and immunities of free and natural-born subjects, within the realm of England' and the right to be represented in Parliament. Their grievances included taxation without representation and the keeping of a standing army in peacetime. Absent parliamentary representation, the colonists claimed the right 'to a free and exclusive power of legislation in their several provincial legislatures … subject only to the negative of their sovereign'.

Until British Parliament repealed the Intolerable Acts, the first Congress resolved to boycott British goods from 1 December 1774 through the Continental Association. Committees of inspection would be established in each colony to enforce the economic boycott. The colonies also pledged to embrace an austere and self-sufficient lifestyle. Later, the British Government rejected observations of the Governor of Massachusetts, Thomas Gage, on the strength of colonial resistance and the inadequacy of his forces to enforce the Coercive Acts; instead, they ordered him to show force.

On 18 April 1775, British troops marched on Lexington and Concord in Massachusetts, and destroyed military stores there. However, when the British troops retreated to Boston, they were faced with violent resistance from the colonials. The British were forced to withdraw. News of what had happened spread quickly to the other colonies. The colony of New York readily accepted the Continental Association and supported the upcoming second Congress. George Washington, a Virginian of aristocratic English descent, was given command of the American army.

Constitutional Detour

Thomas Paine's Common Sense

In the eight months following Lexington and Concord, the British colonies in America were not united on the question of independence from Great Britain. Public attitudes changed following the publication of the anonymously authored and highly popular book Common Sense (1776) in January 1776.[44] *Common Sense*'s author, Thomas Paine, estimated that approximately 125,000 copies were sold in its first year of publication.[45] Excerpts and full copies of the book were published in colonial, British and Continental newspapers.[46] *Common Sense* was Paine's argument for American independence. A notable revolutionary, Paine was English born but lived abroad in France and the American colonies. Paine had landed in Pennsylvania in November 1774 with a letter of recommendation from Benjamin Franklin.

[44] Thomas Paine, *Common Sense* (W and T Bradford, 1776). See generally Michael Everton, '"The Would-be-Author and the Real Bookseller": Thomas Paine and Eighteenth-Century Printing Ethics' (2005) 40 *Early American Literature* 79; Trish Loughran, 'Disseminating *Common Sense:* Thomas Paine and the Problem of the Early National Bestseller' (2006) 78 *American Literature* 1; Jonathon Charles Douglas Clark, *Thomas Paine, Britain, America, and France in the Age of Enlightenment and Revolution* (Oxford, Oxford University Press, 2018).

[45] Everton (n 44) 87–88.

[46] *Ibid* 88.

John Locke's ideas of the state of nature and the social contract are interwoven in the first part of Paine's 48-page pamphlet:

> Society in every state is a blessing, but government even in its best state is but a necessary evil; in its worst state an intolerable one; for when we suffer, or are exposed to the same miseries by a government, which we might expect in a country without government, our calamities is heightened by reflecting that we furnish the means by which we suffer. Government, like dress, is the badge of lost innocence; the palaces of kings are built upon the ruins of the bowers of paradise. For were the impulses of conscience clear, uniform and irresistibly obeyed, man would need no other lawgiver; but that not being the case, he finds it necessary to surrender up a part of his property to furnish means for the protection of the rest; and this he is induced to do by the same prudence which in every other case advises him out of two evils to choose the least. Wherefore, security being the true design and end of government, it unanswerably follows that whatever form thereof appears most likely to ensure it to us, with the least expence and greatest benefit, is preferable to all others.[47]

The second part was anti-monarchical. Paine rejected the monarchy – the idea of being ruled by one family for all time – and associated hereditary succession with original sin.[48] In the third part, Paine provided thoughts on American affairs,[49] arguing for independence by appealing to reason: '[e]very thing that is right or natural pleads for separation. The blood of the slain, the weeping voice of nature cries, 'Tis time to part.'[50] Paine finally outlined the strengths of America and called for a manifesto to set out their objections to the world.[51]

The Declaration of Independence

In June 1776, John Adams, Benjamin Franklin, Thomas Jefferson, Robert Livingston and Roger Sherman were appointed to a committee to draft a preamble to a resolution for independence. The Committee selected Jefferson, a young lawyer from Virginia, to write the document. This famous document, the Declaration of Independence, was to be submitted to the Colonial Congress. In the draft Declaration, Jefferson explained why the American colonies were seeking independence from Great Britain and outlined the philosophical bases for doing so. In the early nineteenth century, the aged Jefferson wrote that he drew on the writings of Aristotle, Cicero, John Locke and Locke's contemporary, Algernon Sidney, a seventeenth-century English republican.[52] The Declaration's preamble memorably begins by declaring: 'We hold these truths to be self-evident, that all men are created equal, that they are endowed by their Creator with certain unalienable Rights, that among these are Life,

[47] Paine (n 44) 7–8.
[48] *Ibid* 17–31.
[49] *Ibid* 31–58.
[50] *Ibid* 39.
[51] *Ibid* 59–76.
[52] Edward J Erler, *Property and the Pursuit of Happiness: Locke, the Declaration of Independence, Madison, and the Challenge of the Administrative State* (Lanham, Rowman & Littlefield, 2019) 12.

Liberty and the pursuit of Happiness'. Most famously the Declaration asserts, 'Governments are instituted among Men, deriving their just powers from the consent of the governed'. A century of Enlightenment debate among British, European and North American intellectuals had destroyed the notion of a spiritually ordained Divine Right of Kings. While the influence of Locke's *Second Treatise of Government* seems clear from the ideas of society and government expressed in the Declaration, some scholars disagree on the extent of that influence.[53]

On 28 June 1776, the final draft of the Declaration was submitted to the Congress. Clauses within the main body of the Declaration were changed. For example, a clause blaming George III for the perpetuation of the African slave trade in the colonies was struck out. No changes, however, were made to Jefferson's preamble, demonstrating the degree to which the political and philosophical underpinnings were accepted by the colonial delegates. On 4 July 1776, the second Continental Congress held in Philadelphia adopted the Declaration of Independence. Copies of the 'Unanimous Declaration of the Thirteen United States of America' were immediately sent to the colonies and reprinted. Seven years of war ensued but with the *Treaty of Paris* (1783), Great Britain finally recognised the United States' independence.

The Articles of Confederation

The first constitution of the United States, the Articles of Confederation and Perpetual Union, was adopted by the Continental Congress on 15 November 1777. A perceived need to explain the relationship between the Congress – a unicameral body to act as the national government – and the colonies motivated the drafting of the Articles in 1776–77. By February 1781, the Articles were ratified by all 13 states.

By Article 1, the new union would be styled the 'United States of America'. Government was divided between the Congress, which had complete control over war and foreign relations,[54] and the 13 states, which had complete legal authority over day-to-day life in their territories.[55] The Confederation had no power to tax or raise revenue; rather, it would issue requisitions to each state. Compliance with these requisitions was optional. States still had the power to levy their own taxes. The Confederation also had no power to create executive or judicial institutions. It could not make states or individuals obey its commands. To be effective, amendments to the Articles of Confederation had to be ratified by all 13 states. However, if Congress asked the states to adopt certain measures, the states had to comply. Discussions of the Articles at the 1776 Congress ended with issues of voting, expenses and territorial claims to western lands unresolved.

Despite its problems, the Confederation was instrumental in establishing American independence. The Confederation successfully negotiated the *Treaty of Paris* that ended

[53] See generally Garry Wills, *Inventing America: Jefferson's Declaration of Independence* (New York, First Mariner Books, 2002); Allen Jayne, *Jefferson's Declaration of Independence: Origins, Philosophy and Theology* (Lexington, The University Press of Kentucky, 1998).

[54] See Art 9.

[55] See Art 2.

the American War of Independence in 1783. Other achievements included the formation of a French alliance and the receipt of loans from European powers. In many respects, the Confederation was impotent.[56] It could not force the resolution of state disputes, raise revenue, or pay down interest on foreign loans incurred during the war. The national Government needed more authority than it presently had. George Washington, Alexander Hamilton and James Madison were advocates for a new government to replace the old. On 1 April 1789, the Articles were replaced by a new Constitution.

The Constitution of the United States

The Constitution of the United States was drafted at the Constitutional Convention of 1787, also known as the Philadelphia Convention or the Federal Convention. The Convention convened at the Pennsylvania State House in Philadelphia between 25 May and 17 September 1787.[57] The proceedings were 'secret': 'delegates met behind closed doors and windows with armed sentinels stationed both inside and outside the statehouse'.[58] Yet, secrecy was not unusual for parliamentary bodies of the time.[59] The Constitution was signed on the final day of the Convention. The argument for ratification had been presented in a collection of 85 essays, known as the *The Federalist Papers*, published between October 1787 and May 1788 under the pseudonym Publius. Publius was the collective pseudonym of Alexander Hamilton, James Madison and John Jay. By 26 July 1788, 11 states had ratified the draft Constitution. Nine was the minimum number required under the Constitution for the new government of the United States to form. The first Congress convened on 4 March 1789 at Federal Hall in New York City. North Carolina and Rhode Island became the final states to ratify the Constitution on 21 November 1789 and 29 May 1790 respectively.

- Primary source materials associated with the US Constitution
- Amendments 11–27

Since 1789, the Constitution has been amended 27 times. In its first 15 years, the Constitution was amended 12 times. In 1791, ten amendments known as the Bill of Rights were added to the Constitution. Three amendments were introduced between 1861 and 1870. The Convention envisaged a government where there were separate branches for the legislature, executive and judiciary. On the topic of representation, the delegates had to compromise. Representation in the Lower House would be based on state population but based on equal votes in the Upper House.[60]

The proposed Constitution, adopted by the delegates on 17 September 1787, vested government in a legislature, an executive and a judiciary. Vested with '[a]ll legislative Powers',

[56] For a similar conclusion, see the discussion on the Federal Council of Australasia in chapter eight of this volume.

[57] This is to be contrasted with the Federation debates in Australia, which were public: see chapter ten of this volume.

[58] John P Kaminski, *Secrecy and the Constitutional Convention* (Madison, University of Wisconsin-Madison, 2005) 7.

[59] *Ibid* 7–24. James Madison maintained thorough notes of the Convention.

[60] US Constitution Art I, § § 2, 3.

the Congress would consist of two houses: the Senate and the House of Representatives.[61] The composition, eligibility and election of the House of Representatives and Senate are outlined in Article I. Congress would have prescribed powers over a range of matters.[62] The Senate has 'the sole Power to try all Impeachments' including the trial of the President.[63] Article II deals with the executive power of the United States, which 'shall be vested in a President'.[64] According to Article II, Section 2, '[t]he President shall be Commander in Chief of the Army and Navy of the United States'. Article III focuses on judicial power which, by Section 1, is vested 'in one supreme Court, and in such inferior Courts as the Congress may from time to time ordain and establish'.[65] Judges appointed to these courts 'hold their Offices during good Behaviour'.[66] Washington was elected president and signed the Judiciary Act 1789 on 24 September 1789 to establish the federal judiciary and the office of Attorney-General. Where the US President is impeached, the Chief Justice is required to preside over the trial in the Senate.[67] However, the US Constitution demands a two-thirds majority of the members present in the Senate to secure a conviction in cases of impeachment.[68]

Constitutional Detour

Federalism

Federalism is a basic concept that lies at the heart of the US Constitution. The Constitution creates a form of federalism where power is balanced, or authority divided, between the federal government and states. It vests authority in the people of the United States. Sovereignty is shared between the federal government and the states, and some of this power is exclusive to each sphere. American federalism came about when the 13 colonies – as states – united under a federal government but on condition that they maintained separate identity and real political power. The federal polity has limited powers under Article I, Section 8, and the states have the residue of that power. When the federal polity legislates within these specifically enumerated powers, federal law is paramount.[69] The US Supreme Court has defined federalism incrementally since the Constitution's ratification. This process has produced conflicts, particularly in the interpretation of the Fifteenth Amendment's 'right to vote' clause (ratified in 1870).

[61] *Ibid* Art I, § 1.
[62] *Ibid* Art I, § 8.
[63] *Ibid* Art I, § 3.
[64] *Ibid* Art II, § 1.
[65] *Ibid* Art III, § 1.
[66] *Ibid.*
[67] *Ibid* Art I, § 3.
[68] *Ibid.*
[69] US Constitution Art VI.

Constitutional Detour

Separation of Powers

Figure 5.1 Three Branches of Government in the US Constitution

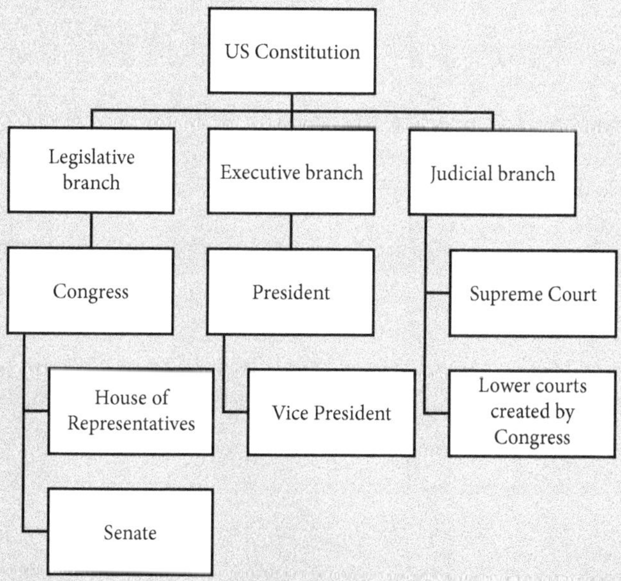

The text and structure of the US Constitution underscores another basic constitutional concept: the doctrine of separation of powers. The Constitution divides governmental power over three branches vesting legislative power in the Congress, executive power in the President and judicial power in the Supreme Court and lower courts created by Congress. This structure is embodied in the first three Articles of the US Constitution. It can be seen that the American constitutional framers consciously rejected the British cabinet model discussed in chapter four. In the United States, unlike in the United Kingdom (and Australia), members of cabinet are *not* also members of parliament. In other words, the executive cabinet is chosen from people who are not in the legislature.

The 'checks and balances' tool is part of the separation of powers doctrine. This tool was partly explained in *Federalist No 47* where James Madison wrote: 'where the WHOLE power of one department is exercised by the same hands which possess the WHOLE power of another department, the fundamental principles of a free constitution are subverted'.[70] Strict separation between the branches ensured 'PARTIAL AGENCY in, or … CONTROL over, the acts of each other'.[71] Each branch was 'connected and blended as to

[70] James Madison, 'The Particular Structure of the New Government and the Distribution of Power Among Its Different Parts' *New York Packet* (New York, 1 February 1788).

[71] *Ibid.*

give to each a constitutional control over the others',[72] but without encroaching on each class of power.

Making the exercise of power by the executive and the legislature subject to external check is central to 'checks and balances'. The president has the power to veto the Congress's law-making authority. Senate approval is needed for the appointment of senior officials to the president's administration. Congress may impeach and remove the president or the vice-president from office. Federal judges are not immune from Congress' reach either. Judicial appointments must be approved by Congress. Judges may also be impeached and removed from office. However, out of the three bodies, the judiciary has the upper hand with the ability to judicially review legislation. Federal judges can set aside actions of other bodies if that action violates the Constitution or other federal laws.

The phrase, 'separation of powers', is not mentioned anywhere in the US Constitution; however, the Constitution implies a separation or tripartite division. Madison's *Federalist No 37* explains the absence of an explicit 'separation of powers' standard: 'Experience has instructed us that no skill in the science of government has yet been able to discriminate and define, with sufficient certainty, its three great provisions – the legislative, executive, and judiciary.'[73] Adopting the tripartite structure of the US Constitution, the Australian Constitution is divided into Chapter I ('Parliament'), Chapter II ('The Executive Government') and Chapter III ('The Judicature').[74]

Constitutional Detour

The Bill of Rights

The first ten Amendments to the US Constitution, collectively referred to as the Bill of Rights (not to be confused with the English Bill of Rights, see chapter three), were the result of bargaining between the Federalists and the anti-Federalists over ratification of the proposed Constitution. The absence of a bill of rights in the proposed Constitution had become a burning issue for anti-Federalists who demanded it as a precondition to ratification. By June 1788, the promise of amendments had secured the Constitution's ratification in nine states, the threshold number required for constitutional government to take effect.[75] Federalist James Madison introduced a list of amendments to Congress. On 28 September 1781, President Washington sent 12 amendments, adopted by Congress three days earlier, to the states for ratification. Ten of the 12 amendments were ratified by three-fourths of the state legislatures on 15 December 1791. The Bill of

[72] James Madison, 'These Departments Should Not Be So Far Separated as to Have No Constitutional Control Over Each Other' *New York Packet* (New York, 1 February 1788).

[73] James Madison, 'Concerning the Difficulties of the Convention in Devising a Proper Form of Government' *Daily Advertiser* (New York, 11 January 1788).

[74] See chapter 10 of this volume.

[75] US Constitution Art VII.

Rights protects fundamental principles of liberty and self-government against incursion by Congress. The Amendments protect:

1. Freedom of religion, speech, press, assembly and petition.
2. The right to keep and bear arms.
3. Against the quartering of soldiers in people's homes.
4. Against unreasonable searches and seizures.
5. The rights of people accused of crimes including the right to due process and freedom from self-incrimination and double jeopardy.
6. Further rights of accused persons.
7. The right to a jury trial in civil cases.
8. Against the imposition of excessive bail and fines and the infliction of 'cruel and unusual punishments'.
9. People's rights not specifically listed in the Constitution.
10. The powers not delegated to the United States by the Constitution, reserving them to the States or to the people.

Two Early Political Factions: Federalists and Democratic-Republicans

During the presidency of George Washington (1789–97), two political factions surfaced. Washington, the first President of the United States, remained politically unaffiliated. In his farewell address in 1796, Washington warned 'in the most solemn manner against the baneful effects of the spirit of party generally'.[76] That advice was unheeded for, by this point, the Federalists and the Democratic-Republicans had developed as political parties.

Led by John Adams and Alexander Hamilton,[77] the Federalists supported a strong central government and a loose interpretation of the US Constitution. The interests of bankers, merchants and manufacturers were represented. The Federalists saw mob rule as the inherent danger of decentralised, state-centred government. Headed up by Thomas Jefferson and James Madison,[78] the Democratic-Republicans favoured states' rights and a weak central government. They supported a strict interpretation of the Constitution. Though the first three Democratic-Republican presidents were certainly wealthy and part of the elite, the Democratic-Republicans represented the interests of farmers and country folk. The party considered decentralised government as the ideal form of government. This would prevent the concentration of power in one body. Coupled with this position was the party's opposition to the Federalists' view that the elite should rule, which they saw as reminiscent of the monarchical rule they had shed after the War of Independence.

[76] George Washington, Washington's Farewell Address to the People of the United States (Joseph T Buckingham, 1812) 21.

[77] See generally Ron Chernow, *Alexander Hamilton* (London, Head of Zeus, 2017). The biography was adapted into the hugely successful Broadway musical, *Hamilton: An American Musical*.

[78] Jefferson was the main author of the Declaration of Independence while James Madison was the main author of the US Constitution.

In relation to foreign policy, the Federalists wanted to forge a better relationship with Great Britain and did not support the French revolutionary movement. Controversial legislation reinforcing that party platform was enacted during John Adams' presidency. In 1798, Congress enacted the Alien and Sedition Acts, which added to the difficulty of becoming a citizen and made seditious libel a federal crime. The *Sedition Act 1798* proved to be most provocative. It was illegal to oppose federal laws or to publish criticism of the American government. Only Democratic-Republicans were ever convicted of sedition under this Sedition Act. Opponents compared seditious libel to monarchical rule. Some argued that this legislation was unconstitutional because seditious libel – a common law doctrine (see chapter three) – was not within the limits of the *limited* government established under the Constitution. On the eve of Adams' presidential term ending, this Act expired. The Democratic-Republicans' position on foreign policy was the complete opposite. Between 1785–89, Jefferson served as US Minister to France and, witnessing the collapse of the French monarchy, he supported the Revolution. By the early 1800s, the Democratic-Republicans' emphasis on states' rights ensured political dominance over the Federalists.

The nomination of candidates occurred in the 1800 federal election. Polling in the states spanned from March to November.[79] Only 11 per cent of the population were entitled to vote, and voting was done in public.[80] The Federalists nominated two candidates: John Adams (presidential candidate) and Charles Pinckney (vice-presidential candidate) as did the Democratic-Republicans: Thomas Jefferson (presidential candidate) and Aaron Burr (vice-presidential candidate). The outcome of the state polls would result in the election of delegates to the Electoral College, which convened in December 1800. To form a government, 70 electoral votes were needed. Under the Constitution as it then stood, each elector had cast two votes for candidates without indicating who would take the position of president and vice-president. The candidate with the most electoral votes would be elected president with the runner-up awarded the vice-presidency. To secure Jefferson's election as president, at least one Republican elector 'had to remember to *not* vote for Burr'.[81] But, Jefferson and Burr each received 73 electoral votes.

Fortunately, the Constitution empowered the House of Representatives to choose which candidate would be president. The House of Representatives voted in favour of Jefferson. On 4 March 1801, Jefferson was inaugurated as president. The Twelfth Amendment ratified by three-fourths of the states in 1804 rectified the problem of the 1800 federal election. Now, a tie between candidates of the same political party in the Electoral College was out of the question. Electors had to vote separately for president and vice-president. The candidate with the most votes would occupy the presidency.

The Federalist Party collapsed around 1815. That left the Democratic-Republican Party as the remaining political party, which itself collapsed in 1824. Before that occurred, the Democratic-Republicans had splintered into factions. Out of these factions, modern US political parties emerged. In the 1830s, the Democratic Party was formed while, in 1854, the Republican Party was established on an anti-slavery footing. The Democrats and Republicans are the oldest surviving political parties in the United States and two of the oldest in the world.

[79] Jill Lepore, *These Truths: A History of the United States*, 1st edn (New York, WW Norton & Co, 2018) 162.
[80] *Ibid* 163.
[81] *Ibid* 164.

Figure 5.2 Political Affiliations of Early US Presidents

Unaffiliated	Federalist	Democratic-Republican
George Washington (1789–97)	John Adams (1797–1801)	Thomas Jefferson (1801–09)
		James Madison (1809–17)
		James Monroe (1817–25)
		John Quincy Adams (1825–29)

Historical Cameo

James Madison

James Madison (1751–1836) was a Democratic-Republican, the main architect of the US Constitution and the fourth President of the US (1809–17). Madison was responsible for drafting the Bill of Rights.

Madison was born to a family of Virginia planters. In 1771, he graduated from the College of New Jersey (now known as Princeton). He later practised law. During the 1770s, he helped draft the Virginia Constitution and was a delegate in the Virginia Congress. Before entering the Virginia legislature in 1784, he was a dyed-in-the-wool Federalist but his position moderated as his political experience grew. He came to appreciate the importance of states' rights. Madison encouraged a national convention to replace the Articles of Confederation with the US Constitution. Madison represented Virginia at the Constitutional Convention held at Philadelphia between May and September 1787. He drafted the Constitution and subsequently promoted its ratification.

After the Constitutional Convention, Madison, along with John Jay and Alexander Hamilton, wrote a series of 85 essays known as *The Federalist Papers* (1787–88) under the collective pseudonym of Publius to encourage the ratification of the proposed Constitution. The essays argued for a strong central government managed through a system of checks and balances. In one essay, Madison defended the doctrine of separation of powers by arguing that it allowed checks and balances on each branch of government:

> It may be a reflection of human nature, that such devices should be necessary to control the abuses of government. But what is government itself, but the greatest of all reflections on human nature? If men were angels, no government would be necessary.

While human fallibility made government necessary, Madison thought controls on government were necessary to prevent abuse.

Madison was elected President in 1808. He took office in 1809. Warfare characterised Madison's two terms in office. In his first year, Madison blocked trade with Great Britain and France. Congress authorised trade again on the condition that trade would be forbidden with the one country that did not accept America's neutrality. On the face of it, France accepted America's neutrality. In retaliation, Great Britain forced American sailors into naval service (called 'impressment'). They seized American cargoes. Madison declared war ('the War of 1812') against the British. The War of 1812 was a decisive victory for the US.

Historical Cameo

Thomas Jefferson

Thomas Jefferson (1743–1826) was the main author of the Declaration of Independence, Minister to France (1784–9), the United States' first Secretary of State, and the third President of the US (1801–09). He dabbled in the sciences and, like William Blackstone, was an architectural enthusiast.

Jefferson was born on his father's plantation, Shadwell, in Virginia. He studied at the College of William and Mary and later took articles of clerkship (the traditional form of training to be a lawyer) with a prominent Virginia attorney and signatory of the Declaration of Independence, George Wythe. After finishing articles, Jefferson practised as a lawyer. He was subsequently a member of the Virginia legislature. He joined the Continental Congress formed to discuss grievances against the British Government. There, he was appointed to a five-member committee that had the task of preparing a Declaration of Independence. The committee selected Jefferson to draft the Declaration, which was approved by Congress with only minor changes. One change was the deletion of a clause blaming George III for the slave trade.

After the Declaration, Jefferson participated in law reform in Virginia and served as Governor of Virginia for two terms. He was then appointed Minister to France (1784–89). When Jefferson returned from France, he retired from public life. Jefferson formally came out of retirement when the Republicans put him down as their presidential candidate; instead, he was elected Vice-President.

In 1800, Jefferson was elected President. Jefferson and his running mate, Aaron Burr, had actually tied even though Burr was his party's vice-presidential candidate. At the time, the Constitution was silent on the naming of candidates for president and vice-president. The stalemate was resolved by a vote in the House of Representatives. They elected Jefferson. During Jefferson's presidency, the Louisiana Territory (1803) was acquired. To explore the Louisiana Territory's western limits, Jefferson planned the Lewis and Clark expedition. Jefferson's second term was marked by war between Great Britain and France.

Jefferson resigned office consciously not taking a third term. This established an unwritten rule limiting presidential office to two terms (totalling eight years). Franklin Delano Roosevelt (1882–1945) was the first and only president (1933–1945) to break this two-term precedent. After Roosevelt's tenure, the Constitution was amended to restrict presidential office to two terms: see the Twenty-Second Amendment.

In retirement, Jefferson established the University of Virginia. He developed its modern curriculum and fulfilled his architectural plans for the campus. He could watch the University's construction from his Monticello plantation. Though Jefferson opposed slavery, and did so in the draft *Declaration of Independence*, he was a lifelong slave-owner. Jefferson also had a longstanding relationship with one of his slaves, Sally Hemings. Compelling evidence exists suggesting that Jefferson fathered at least one of Hemings' children.

Historical Cameo

John Marshall

John Marshall (1755–1835) was the fourth and longest serving Chief Justice of the US Supreme Court (1801–35). He was Jefferson's cousin.

The eldest of 15 children, Marshall was born to a prominent Virginian family in 1755. He and his siblings were home-schooled and had access to their father's (and his employer's) extensive library. Marshall's father, Thomas, bought a set of William Blackstone's *Commentaries on the Laws of England* (see chapter four) for his firstborn. By the age of 27, Marshall had read Blackstone's *Commentaries* at least four times. During the American War of Independence, Marshall joined a militia unit and actively served against the British. For four years, after accepting a commission as lieutenant, he fought alongside his father's friend, George Washington. Upon his discharge, Marshall studied law, developed a steady legal practice and entered politics as a Federalist.

Marshall was a spokesperson at the Virginia Ratifying Convention (1788). It was here that 168 delegates debated whether to ratify or reject the US Federal Constitution. In 1799, he was elected to the Congress on the urging of former President, George Washington. The incumbent President, John Adams, then nominated Marshall to be Secretary of State. In January 1801, two months before leaving office, John Adams nominated Marshall, then Secretary of State, to be the fourth Chief Justice of the Supreme Court. Marshall accepted the nomination and took office in early February 1801.

Constitutional Detour

Judicial Review

On 24 February 1803, the Supreme Court of the United States handed down its decision in the landmark case of *Marbury v Madison*.[82] The case articulates the fundamental principle of judicial review and established that the US Supreme Court has the power to declare Acts of Congress unconstitutional. As Fullagar J observed in *Australian Communist Party v Commonwealth*, 'the principle of *Marbury v Madison* is accepted as axiomatic' in Australian constitutional law.[83]

Thomas Jefferson, a Democratic-Republican and incumbent Vice-President, won the presidential election of 1800. He would not assume office until 4 March 1801. In December 1800, the outgoing President, John Adams, pushed the *Judiciary Act 1801* through the **lame-duck session of Congress**. Commencing in February 1801, the Act reorganised the Supreme Court, established a federal circuit court system, enabled the lifetime

Lame-duck session of Congress is one that convenes after the election of its successor but before the successor takes office

[82] 5 US 137 (1803).
[83] (1950) 83 CLR 1, 262 (Fullagar J).

appointment of judges, and increased the number of federal judges to 16. In February 1801, Adams appointed his Secretary of State, John Marshall, as the fourth Chief Justice of the Supreme Court. Marshall would assume office at the same time Jefferson was inaugurated as President. Marshall and Jefferson were distant cousins, fellow Virginians and political rivals. Adams used the remainder of his presidency to stack the judiciary with Federalists. The 58 judges appointed to the Federal Circuit courts and newly-created District of Columbia courts were referred to as 'midnight judges' because it is said that Adams signed their commissions until midnight on 3 March 1801, the day his term expired.[84] A total of 17 of Adams' judicial commissions were not delivered before Jefferson took office. This had been Marshall's responsibility. Jefferson instructed his new Secretary of State, James Madison, not to deliver the remaining commissions.

William Marbury, appointed as justice of the peace of the District of Columbia, sued Madison and, under the *Judiciary Act 1789*, asked the Supreme Court to issue a writ of *mandamus* – an order commanding an official to do or refrain from doing a particular thing – that would command Madison to deliver Marbury's commission of appointment. The Supreme Court is given original and appellate jurisdiction under Article III of the US Constitution. Original jurisdiction enables a litigant to bring a case directly before the Supreme Court where the case is heard for the first time. Appellate jurisdiction is engaged where the case is first argued and decided before lower courts and then appealed to the Supreme Court. Under Article III, section 2, clause 2 of the US Constitution, the Supreme Court had 'original jurisdiction in all cases affecting ambassadors, other public ministers and consuls, and those in which a state shall be a party. In all other cases, the supreme court shall have appellate jurisdiction.' The *Judiciary Act 1789* meanwhile authorised the Court 'to issue writs of mandamus … to … persons holding office, under the authority of the United States.' Here, the writ of *mandamus* would have forced Madison to deliver the commission. There was some delay before the case was heard before the Supreme Court. While the Jefferson administration had repealed the *Judiciary Act 1801*, it had by the repealing Act postponed the Supreme Court's next sitting to 1803.

In an opinion drafted by Marshall, the Supreme Court unanimously found that Madison was not required to deliver the commission to Marbury. While Marbury was entitled to his commission, the Supreme Court found that it did not have the authority to require Madison to deliver it. Put another way, the way the *Judiciary Act 1789* defined original jurisdiction exceeded the authority given to it by the US Constitution. By bringing the case directly before the Supreme Court, Marbury was engaging the Court's original jurisdiction in a dispute that did not concern ambassadors, public ministers or consuls. The Court could therefore not issue a mandamus directing Madison to deliver

[84] Kathryn Turner, 'Midnight Judges' (1961) 109 *University of Pennsylvania Law Review* 494; Jed Glickstein, 'After Midnight: The Circuit Judges and the Repeal of the Judiciary Act of 1801' (2012) 24 *Yale Journal of Law & Humanities* 543, 544.

Marbury's commission. In claiming the power of judicial review for the Supreme Court, Marshall CJ wrote that:

> [i]t is emphatically the province and duty of the judicial department to say what the law is. Those who apply the rule to particular cases, must of necessity expound and interpret the rule. If the two laws conflict with each other the court must decide on the operation of each.[85]

The Supreme Court was entitled to declare ordinary laws repugnant to the Constitution void, else that 'would subvert the very foundation of all written constitutions … giving to the legislature a practical and real omnipotence, with the same breath which professes to restrict their powers within narrow limits'.[86]

Marbury v Madison adds a dimension to the rule of law that is unique in countries with a fixed, written constitution such as the United States and, later, Canada and Australia where parliamentary sovereignty is qualified.[87] In other words, parliament is not sovereign in that it only has the powers given to it by the constitution. The courts can assess whether laws passed by the legislature are made in accordance with the constitution and, if finding that they have *not* been, can invalidate or 'strike down' those laws. Legislation that violates the constitution is not law – but the courts decide that; the legislature itself (Congress or Parliament) does not. Judicial review of legislation is important in federations where all legislatures – the central (in Australia, the Commonwealth) parliament and the regional (in Australia, the states) parliaments – are all of limited power. It needs an independent decision-maker – the courts – to decide whether legislatures have made laws within their relevant powers.

Conclusion

This chapter diverted attention from Great Britain to North America to consider the American War of Independence and resulting constitutional settlement. The ways in which the United States' founders changed thinking about law, government and human rights was enormously influential. A century later, it helped to shape the writing of the Australian Constitution as covered in chapter ten on the Australian federation. In chapter six, consideration turns to nineteenth-century legal and parliamentary reform in the United Kingdom.

[85] *Marbury v Madison* (n 82) 177.

[86] *Ibid* 178.

[87] See generally Suri Ratnapala, *Australian Constitutional Law: Foundations and Theory* (Oxford, Oxford University Press, 2002) 193–94; Nicholas Aroney et al, *The Constitution of the Commonwealth of Australia: History, Principle and Interpretation* (Cambridge, Cambridge University Press, 2015) 32.

6

Reform of British Parliament, Society and Courts in Nineteenth-Century England

Introduction

Victorian England (1837–1901) is the 'Age of Reform'. While this label could fasten itself to any number of targets, such as social or moral reform, this chapter focuses principally on reforms of a legal and political nature. It does however provide wider context of how the law impinged on society and how social forces changed the law and examines nineteenth-century reform to two institutions: Parliament and the courts. The introduction of new courts and the significant court reforms of the 1870s are set against reform in Parliament and in society. It examines the Reform Acts's achievement of a limited franchise. But a wider vision also presents itself. Catholic and Jewish emancipation, attempts to legislate for and about women and the law's attempts to understand and punish different types of sexual activity are important aspects of a century considered as a period of law reform.

Learning Resources

The content within this chapter is supported by:

Glossary	Chapter Overview	Historical Cameos	Constitutional Detours	Pause for Thought
Latin, Law French and Medieval English terms are defined	The chapter begins with an overview explaining its intentions and focus	Lord Eldon Jeremy Bentham The trial of Oscar Wilde	The Legal History of Homosexuality	Sex and the Law

Chapter Overview

Key Figures	Key Institutions	Key Terms
• Lord Eldon • Jeremy Bentham • Robert Peel • Benjamin Disraeli • Charles Dickens • Oscar Wilde	• Chancery • Court for Divorce and Matrimonial Causes • Supreme Court of Judicature	• Slavery • Judicature • Reform Acts • Tamworth Manifesto • Contagious Diseases Acts • Married Women's Property Acts • Criminal Law Amendment Act • Whigs and Tories • Codification • Feme covert

Learning Outcomes

At the end of this chapter, readers should understand:

- Historical dimensions of law reform, political reform, religious emancipation, and legislating about human sexuality.
- Developments that have shaped current legal education.
- Criticisms of the law and outlets for these critics.

Reform of the Courts

The Court for Divorce and Matrimonial Causes

The *Matrimonial Causes Act 1857*[1] arguably revolutionised divorce under English law. Before this time a marriage was capable of dissolution only by a private Act of Parliament. The church courts had granted only **annulments**, but they could not grant divorces. The 1857 Act authorised a secular court to dissolve a marriage without the involvement of the church courts or, indeed, Parliament. In stripping the matrimonial jurisdiction from the church courts, the Act established in its place a court of record called the Court for Divorce and Matrimonial Causes. As part of these reforms, the probate jurisdiction of the church courts transferred to a new Court of Probate, one that dealt

Annulments (Latin): declarations that a marriage had not existed in law

[1] 20 & 21 Vic c 85.

with wills and intestate estates. The new Court for Divorce and Matrimonial Causes had jurisdiction to grant a decree of divorce where:

- the husband proved his wife's adultery; or
- the wife proved her husband's adultery together with an act of 'aggravated enormity', such as bigamy or incest, on the husband's part.[2]

The dissolution of marriage by judicial means rather than by private Act of Parliament might have expedited the process of divorce and made it relatively cheaper, but hardships continued. The costs associated with divorce proceedings still placed divorce beyond the means of most.[3] Petitioners were upper and middle class and, given the Divorce Court's location in London, drawn from London and the Home Counties – the counties surrounding London.[4] While adultery alone supported the husband petitioner, the grounds on which women could obtain divorce were conservatively framed. The *Matrimonial Causes Act 1857* maintained a 'double moral standard' for women.[5] A wife had to prove the husband's adultery coupled with an act of 'aggravated enormity', which included incest, bigamy, cruelty and two years' desertion. The *Matrimonial Causes Act 1923* removed that double standard, allowing a woman to petition for divorce because of her husband's adultery.[6]

Historical Cameo

Lord Eldon

John Scott, 1st Earl of Eldon (1751–1838) was born at Newcastle-upon-Tyne, the youngest of six surviving children to William Scott, a successful coal factor, and his second wife, Jane.

Lord Eldon, though bound for holy orders in the Church of England, eloped with a wealthy Newcastle banker's daughter in 1772. The ensuing family scandal set off a chain of events leading to a career in law. His older brother, William Scott (1745–1836), later Lord Stowell, had a distinguished legal career, serving as a judge of the High Court of Admiralty for 30 years. At age 15, John Scott entered Oxford University. He graduated in 1770 with a Bachelor of Arts degree and received a Master of Arts degree in 1773.

At the end of November 1772, he eloped with Elizabeth (Bessie) Surtees. They married in Scotland. Though William Scott and Bessie's father initially disapproved of the match, they relented and settled generous trusts on both. The marriage lasted until Lady Eldon's

[2] See Henry Kha and Warren Swain, 'The Enactment of the *Matrimonial Causes Act 1857*: The Campbell Commission and the Parliamentary Debates' (2016) 37(3) *Journal of Legal History* 303, 305.

[3] William Cornish et al (eds), *Law and Society in England, 1750–1950*, 2nd edn (London, Hart Publishing, 2019) 365. See also Kha and Swain, *ibid* 305.

[4] Cornish et al, *ibid* 366.

[5] Ann Sumner Holmes, 'The Double Standard in English Divorce Laws, 1857–1923' (1995) 20(2) *Law & Social Inquiry* 601, 601.

[6] 13 & 14 Geo V c 19.

death in 1831. Lord Eldon followed seven years later. Marriage disqualified Scott from a fellowship – an academic position – at Oxford. Soon after marriage, he wrote to a friend: 'I have married rashly, and have neither house nor home to offer my wife; but it is my determination to work hard to provide for the woman I love, as soon as I can find the means of doing so'.[7]

In 1773, he enrolled as a student at the Middle Temple and was called to the Bar in early 1776. Scott's first few years at the Bar were hard, but his fortunes turned in 1780. In an appeal over a property transfer, his arguments impressed Lord Chancellor Thurlow. In 1783, he became King's Counsel. That year, having secured the Lord Chancellor's patronage, John Scott entered Parliament. He was Solicitor-General (1788–93) and Attorney-General (1793–99). For a short time, he was the Chief Justice of the Court of Common Pleas (1799–1801). In 1799, he became Baron Eldon. In 1801, he became Lord Chancellor (1801–06; 1807–27). Lord Eldon's work as Chancellor largely involved real property litigation. Chancery also had protective power over minors, 'idiots' and 'lunatics'. He would have heard lawsuits concerning charities and bankruptcy.

To aid administrative work, the Lord Chancellor had 12 Masters to whom he delegated factual issues to investigate and decide, but their orders were not binding. The Masters were answerable to the Master of the Rolls, who could only hear and decide cases in the Lord Chancellor's absence. In any case, decisions of the Master of the Rolls could be appealed to the Lord Chancellor. When a Vice-Chancellor position was created in 1813, his decisions could also be appealed to the Lord Chancellor. These two judicial positions did little to reduce the glut of cases. Below the Masters were the Six Clerks, who unnecessarily duplicated litigants' documents to increase their fees. Sixty Clerks assisted the Six Clerks. A range of other offices existed. Litigation in Chancery was expensive; the administrative clerks charged fees for each procedural step.[8]

Effectively Chancery had only two judicial staff – the Chancellor and the Master of the Rolls – but ultimate responsibility rested with the Chancellor. This lack of judicial staff contributed to delays in hearing and resolving complex legal cases in Chancery and undoubtedly prompted calls for reform. Despite his apparent tendency for indecision (Jeremy Bentham nicknamed him 'Lord Endless'[9] and 'the Lord of Doubts'),[10] Lord Eldon is best remembered for systematising and bringing certainty to equitable rules and principles. He was thorough and, as one contemporary Sir Samuel Romilly noted, 'his fault was over anxiety to do justice in each particular case, without considering how

[7] Horace Twiss, *The Public and Private Life of Lord Chancellor Eldon, with Selections from his Correspondence* (Philadelphia, Carey and Hart, 1844) 54–55.

[8] Michael Lobban, 'Preparing for Fusion: Reforming the Nineteenth-Century Court of Chancery, Part I' (2004) 22(2) *Law and History Review* 389, 396.

[9] Chris Riley, 'Jeremy Bentham and Equity: The Court of Chancery, Lord Eldon, and the Dispatch Court Plan' (2018) 39(1) *Journal of Legal History* 29, 45, quoting Stephen Conway (ed), *The Correspondence of Jeremy Bentham* (Oxford, Clarendon Press, 1988) vol 8, ix, 230.

[10] *Ibid*; John Bowring, *The Works of Jeremy Bentham under the Superintendence of His Literary Executor John Bowring* (Edinburgh, William Tait, 1838–43) vol 10, 177.

many other causes were waiting to be decided'.[11] Wishing to avoid 'the reproach that the equity of this Court varies like the Chancellor's foot',[12] Lord Eldon said in *Gee v Pritchard* that:

> The doctrines of this Court ought to be as well settled and made as uniform almost as those of the common law, laying down fixed principles, but taking care that they are to be applied according to the circumstances of each case. I cannot agree that the doctrines of this Court are to be changed with every succeeding judge.[13]

Lord Eldon was probably the greatest equity judge ever, but he became a symbol of the Court of Chancery's appalling delays and described himself as 'cunctative',[14] or prone to delays.

Charles Dickens mocked these delays in Chancery in *Bleak House* (1853). Dickens placed the characters in *Bleak House* around litigation in the Court of Chancery in the great, but fictional, case of *Jarndyce v Jarndyce* – a dispute over an estate that lasted so long legal fees swallowed the whole estate. Dickens however did not base the Lord Chancellor in *Bleak House* on Lord Eldon but Lord Lyndhurst, Lord Chancellor from 1827–30, 1834–35, and 1841–46.

Lord Eldon remains an esteemed jurist and his judgments are actively cited in equity. The editors of *Meagher, Gummow and Lehane's Equity: Doctrines and Remedies* hold Eldon in high regard.[15] As recently as 2015, the High Court of Australia in *Lavin v Toppi* used Eldon LC's judgment in *Craythorne v Swinburne*, a Chancery decision of 1807.[16] As Andrew Stumer observes, the 'principle laid down so clearly by Lord Eldon 208 years earlier provided the correct answer to the question in law, and one might add, in justice'.[17] See more about Lord Eldon in the **Selden Society** lecture about him.

Courts of Common Law and Equity

This subsection focuses on the fused administration of law and equity in the late nineteenth century. By the beginning of the nineteenth century, delay and expense typified litigation in English courts. The complexity of existing court structures and available avenues of appeal

[11] Andrew Stumer, 'Lord Eldon – John Scott' (Selden Society Lecture, Supreme Court of Queensland, 23 July 2015) [57], available at https://media.sclqld.org.au/documents/lectures-and-exhibitions/2015/Andrew-stumer-lecture-three.pdf, quoting Rose A Melikan, *John Scott, Lord Eldon, 1751–1838: The Duty of Loyalty* (Cambridge, Cambridge University Press, 1999) 307.

[12] *Gee v Pritchard* (1818) 2 Swan 408, 36 ER 670, 674.

[13] *Ibid.*

[14] Sir John Baker, *An Introduction to English Legal History*, 4th edn (London, Butterworths, 2002) 113.

[15] Stumer (n 11) [2].

[16] (2015) 254 CLR 459, 472 [44], quoting *Craythorne v Swinburne* (1807) 14 Ves Jun 160; 33 ER 482, 483–84 (Lord Eldon LC).

[17] Stumer (n11) [65].

added to the need for major court reform. Charles Dickens and other nineteenth century writers responded with critical attacks on the law and its administration. *Bleak House* was inspired by Chancery litigation that had gone on for over 20 years, and in the novel the case of *Jarndyce v Jarndyce* was 'no nearer to its termination now than when it was begun'.[18] The novel famously begins with a description of the Chancery sitting in Lincoln's Inn Hall surrounded by heavy fog, which serves as a metaphor for what Dickens calls the 'groping and floundering' of the Chancery lawyers lost in their legal fog.[19]

The starting point for reform is the *Uniformity of Process Act 1832*.[20] This 1832 Act introduced a single uniform process for personal actions and replaced the variety of writs used to start litigation in Chancery. The *Common Law Procedure Act 1852*[21] removed the requirement for the common law courts that a writ had to mention any form of action. In the first half of the nineteenth century, ancient 'sinecure' offices – offices that involved little work but had a secure salary – were either reorganised or abolished. The creation of new judicial offices reduced Chancery's workload. Chancery only had two judicial officers in its later history, but it had an endless supply of administrative support. Ultimate responsibility rested with the Lord Chancellor. By the early 1850s, the Government paid the salaries of court personnel – not court fees.

Gradually, each reform improved public confidence in Chancery. The remaining cause of disagreement was the inefficiency of having two systems of legal rules administered in separate jurisdictions – the common law and equity. The following example explains the complications that this system produced. A plaintiff might have litigation in a common law court, but he might require an equitable remedy. To get that equitable remedy, the plaintiff would have to bring another set of proceedings in the Court of Chancery. Equally, if the defendant had an equitable defence, he could not plead that in the common law courts. He had to obtain that remedy from the Court of Chancery. To apply for discovery of evidence from an opponent, a litigant would have to seek an order of discovery from Chancery. Common law courts were unable to grant equitable remedies, and vice versa. A litigant needing both equitable and common law damages had to go to both courts for relief. Following the reforms, Chancery could award some common law remedies, and some equitable remedies were possible in the common law courts.

These reforms were a positive change, though it did not remove all problems of delay and cost. New courts added to the complex system of courts. In 1857, legislation stripped the probate jurisdiction from the church courts to make way for a new Court of Probate. The former matrimonial jurisdiction of the church courts went to the new Court for Divorce and Matrimonial Courts under the *Matrimonial Causes Act 1857*. This removed all civil jurisdictions from the church courts.

[18] Charles Dickens, *Bleak House* (London, Bradbury and Evans, 1853) viii.
[19] *Ibid* 1.
[20] 2 Will IV c 39. Also known as the *Process in Courts of Law at Westminster Act 1832*.
[21] 15 & 16 Vic c 76.

The Judicature Acts

The **Judicature** Acts 1873–75 corrected many inefficiencies by restructuring the English court system. The 1873 Act abolished most of the old superior courts. It created one court – the High Court of Justice – with five divisions based on the old courts: Queen's Bench Division; Exchequer Division; Common Pleas Division; Chancery Division; and Probate, Divorce and Admiralty Division.

Judicature (Latin): judges collectively administering justice

In 1880, the Common Pleas and Exchequer divisions ended, leaving the High Court of Justice divided into three divisions: Queen's Bench Division, Chancery Division and Probate, Divorce and Admiralty Division. The point of this was that *any* civil proceedings or prosecution could be brought in the High Court, but it would be allocated to the division that specialised in that kind of matter by the court administration. For instance, a judge and jury in the Queen's Bench Division tried all criminal matters and claims in contract (which are common law claims) would also be dealt with there. A judge in the Chancery Division heard claims for an **injunction**.

Injunction (Latin): an equitable remedy and order to undertake an action or refrain from action

However, all divisions of the Court could apply all laws, and so an equitable defence would be available to a common law action heard in the Queen's Bench Division. The idea was that the divisions represented expertise in different parts of the High Court, but all divisions could apply any aspect of the law. The Probate, Divorce and Admiralty Division was renamed the Family Division in 1971.[22] The Court of Appeal in Chancery and the Court of Exchequer Chamber became the Court of Appeal.

The Judicature Acts naturally had to bring other reforms. If the High Court had all of the jurisdiction of the former Courts of Chancery and Common Pleas, how would it decide a case if it had inherited a rule of equity (Chancery) that conflicted with a rule of common law (Common Pleas). There were similar reforms in British colonies. Queensland was one of the first to follow, and Attorney-General Samuel Griffith had a Judicature Act put through the Queensland Parliament in 1876.

The creation of a single Court of Appeal streamlined the appeal process. Appeals in civil cases went to a single Court of Appeal. A Court of Criminal Appeal came into existence in 1907. For the first time, a right to appeal lay against conviction or sentence for serious criminal offences. The House of Lords sat at the top of the hierarchy. In 2009, the judicial functions of the House of Lords transferred to the Supreme Court of the United Kingdom.

As mentioned, regardless of origin, any High Court division could award all doctrines and remedies. If there were a conflict between a legal and an equitable rule, the equitable rule would prevail. Most Australian colonies were quick to adopt the Judicature Acts 1873–75 (with the notable exception of New South Wales). Until 1972, New South Wales had a separate court of equity in the Supreme Court. Bear in mind that, though the same court could administer law and equity, it did not alter the substance of the law. It is still useful to

[22] The Admiralty Court is not part of the Family Division but remains part of the High Court of England and Wales.

remember the classification of a rule as a common law rule or an equitable one because each principle has distinct requirements.

When the reform of the courts was taking place in the 1870s, reformers overlooked one old superior court because it had not heard any litigation since 1737. The High Court of Chivalry, a civil law court, dealt with the law of arms (heraldry and the entitlement to coats of arms). As a result, the High Court of Justice under the Judicature Act 1873 did not receive its jurisdiction. It was forgotten! In 1954, when the City of Manchester wanted to prohibit a theatre in Manchester from using the city's coat of arms, the High Court of Chivalry was reconvened and Lord Goddard, the Lord Chief Justice, appointed to constitute the Court in *Manchester Corporation v Manchester Palace of Varieties Ltd*.[23] The High Court of Chivalry has not sat since the *Manchester Corporation* case.

Historical Cameo

Jeremy Bentham

Jeremy Bentham (1748–1832) was an English philosopher. He was born in London to a wealthy family and was reportedly a child prodigy.

At the age of 12, Bentham began study at Oxford University. It was here that he heard Sir William Blackstone deliver his lectures on English law. That prompted him to train as a lawyer. Bentham was called to the Bar in 1769; however, he soon quit legal practice. For the rest of his life, he devoted himself to social, penal, legal and political reform. His ideas for reform found more success after he died.

Bentham's first published work, *A Fragment on Government*, was a criticism of Blackstone's adored common law. He referred to the common law as 'dog law': 'When your dog does anything you want to break him of, you wait until he does it, and then beat him for it'.[24]

In his next publication, *An Introduction to the Principles of Morals and Legislation*, he promoted the principle of utility or utilitarianism. Utilitarianism is the philosophy – widely held today – that the greatest happiness of the greatest number is the proper end to action. During the mid-1780s, Bentham proposed a model prison, *Panopticon*, in which inmates would be under constant observation without their knowledge. Bentham's Panopticon was circular in design. Cells lined the circumference. Prisoners were isolated from one another by a wall separating each cell. A prison guard was stationed in a central observation tower.

In later works, he turned his attention to the **codification** of law. After Bentham's death, reforms of the court system took place to improve its procedure. The creation of local courts in 1846 aided access to justice.

Many of Bentham's works remained unpublished during his lifetime. Some only surfaced towards the end of the twentieth century. One famous Bentham quote appeared after his

[23] [1955] P 135.

[24] Jeremy Bentham, *Benthamiana, Or, Select Extracts from the Works of Jeremy Bentham: With an Outline of His Opinions on the Principal Subjects Discussed in His Works* (Philadelphia, Lea & Blanchard, 1844) 148.

death when *Anarchical Fallacies* was published in 1843: 'Natural rights is simple nonsense: natural and imprescriptible rights, rhetorical nonsense – nonsense upon stilts.'[25]

In Bentham's will, he left instructions that his corpse be preserved and displayed in a wooden cabinet. The University met these wishes – though his head did not fare well during the embalming process! Bentham sits in a corridor of the University College London together with a fake wax head. Bentham's development of the principle of utility as a means of driving reform – for the greatest number – ushered in the Age of Legislation.

One final point about Bentham: one of his closest companions 'bore no other name than the Reverend Doctor John Langborn'.[26] Langborn was a cat. Their closeness and Bentham's eccentric naming of the cat, and awarding him a doctorate of Divinity, testifies to the regard with which Bentham held animals (and his low regard for religion). In his work *An Introduction to the Principles of Morals and Legislation*, Bentham asserted 'The question is not, Can they *reason*? Nor, Can they *talk*? But, Can they *suffer*?'[27] His assertion and more broadly his discussion of rights for animals based on an understanding they had an inner emotional life continues to inform modern animal rights campaigns and legislation. For more about Bentham, see University College London's **Jeremy Bentham Project**.

Reform of the British Parliament: Modern Political Parties

The Tamworth Manifesto of 1834 entrenched a constitutional convention with which we are familiar in modern Australian politics. The Manifesto established the convention that the party carrying a majority in the House of Commons forms government. This was a shift from the idea of having the *confidence* of the monarch to the necessity of maintaining the *confidence* of the House of Commons. Parliament, rather than the monarch, holds ultimate sway in forming and maintaining government. This had grown out of the idea that the Government (executive or monarch) could only raise or spend money with the consent of Parliament, and so it was important for the monarch to ensure that the group (or party) that controlled the Parliament would provide the ministers who *were* the Government.

The Manifesto was an address by Sir Robert Peel to his Tamworth (Staffordshire) electorate. Peel was seeking re-election to his seat, having not long before secured the Prime Ministership. It affirmed the commitment of Peel and the Conservative Party (the Tories) to take a middle road on reform: 'a careful review of institutions … undertaken in a friendly temper, combining with the firm maintenance of established rights, the correction of proved abuses, and the redress of real grievances'.[28]

[25] Jeremy Bentham, *The Works of Jeremy Bentham* (Edinburgh, W Tait, 1843) vol 2, 501.

[26] Johannes Kniess, 'Bentham on Animal Welfare' (2019) 27(3) *British Journal for the History of Philosophy* 556, 558.

[27] Jeremy Bentham, *An Introduction to the Principles of Morals and Legislation* (Oxford, Clarendon Press, 1879) 311.

[28] 'Sir Robert Peel's Address to the Electors of the Borough of Tamworth' (February and April 1835) 58 *Quarterly Review* 261.

Catholic Emancipation and Jewish Relief

The topic of Catholic emancipation spans over a century of history from the Glorious Revolution to the early nineteenth century. The Clarendon Code and the *Act of Settlement 1701*,[29] discussed in chapter four, were leading examples of disabling measures introduced against Catholics. From the Restoration until the early-nineteenth century, Catholics were unable to purchase land, hold civil or political office, hold seats in Parliament, inherit property, or freely practise their religion without incurring penalty. These disabilities impacted more than two million Catholics in Ireland. The first *Relief Act 1778*[30] allowed Catholics to hold property. In 1791, Catholics could freely practise their religion. The campaigning of an Irish lawyer, Daniel O'Connell, forced the British Prime Minister, the Duke of Wellington, and the Home Secretary, Sir Robert Peel, to pass the *Emancipation Act 1829*.[31] Catholics could now enter Parliament and some public offices.

The move towards Catholic emancipation was gradual; however, it was not without disquiet. The Gordon Riots erupted in 1780 in response to the newly enacted first *Relief Act 1778*, which, as mentioned, made it legal for Catholics to hold property in Britain. In 1828, Parliament repealed the Test and Corporation Acts.[32] Another consequence of Catholic emancipation reform was Tory disintegration.[33] Though long opposed to Catholic emancipation, Wellington and Peel allowed the reform to avoid the prospect of civil war in Ireland, where approximately 90 per cent of the population were Catholics. This concession split Protestant voters and the Tory party (to which Wellington and Peel belonged). The *Universities Tests Act 1871*[34] abolished religious tests for 'taking lay academical degrees or holding lay academical or collegiate offices' at the Universities of Oxford, Cambridge and Durham, meaning they could enrol at and take degrees from these universities.[35]

In the nineteenth century, legal restrictions against the English Jewish population also gradually eased. King Edward I expelled all Jews from England in 1290, and Oliver Cromwell (see chapter three) had received back a Jewish population. Jewish people's social and economic lives remained restricted to certain areas and certain types of activities, including money lending, but the easing of restrictions on Catholics to worship, to attend university and to sit as members of parliament paralleled similar measures for English Jewry including the *Jews Relief Act 1858*.[36] These measures however did not prevent strongly expressed anti-Semitism including in the East End of London, where a large population of Jews lived after Russian anti-Jewish **pogroms**. One notable manifestation of this anti-Semitism was the widely repeated rumour that the serial killer Jack the Ripper was a Jew.[37]

Pogrom: the targeting and destruction of an ethnic group

[29] 12 & 13 Wm 3 c 2.
[30] 18 Geo III c 60.
[31] 10 Geo IV v 7.
[32] See chapter three of this volume.
[33] The leadership of Sir Robert Peel partly resuscitated the fortunes of the Tories. By the mid-1830s, they were known as Conservatives with a position expressed in Peel's Tamworth Manifesto.
[34] 34 & 35 Vic c 26.
[35] *Ibid* s 3.
[36] 21 & 22 Vic c 49.
[37] Donald Rumbelow, *The Complete Jack the Ripper* (Harmondsworth, Penguin, 1987) 136.

The *Great Reform Act 1832*

Parliamentary reform was an ongoing issue of several radical political societies in the decades leading up to the ***Great Reform Act 1832***. The harsh economic realities during and following the Napoleonic Wars did much to further these reformist tendencies. The two Reform Acts discussed in this section reorganised existing constituencies, or electorates for seats in Parliament, and created new ones. The 'franchise' (the people who could vote in elections for Parliament) was cast wider with each Reform Act. Universal male suffrage, though not achieved by the close of the nineteenth century, was bound to happen – it became a matter of 'when'. The *Representation of the People Act 1918* secured universal male suffrage and introduced the vote to women, but only for those over the age of 30 who met a property qualification. Electoral equality was obtained ten years later.[38]

To begin in the 1830s, several members of the British Parliament were leading figures of the Evangelical movement within the Church of England, which having finally won the abolition of slavery pressed for further reforms. They idealistically believed that it was possible to have humane imperialism and their policies had considerable influence on the colonies. The most important initiatives from an Australian perspective were select committees to inquire into the convict system (usually referred to as the Molesworth Committee) and the treatment of Indigenous peoples throughout the Empire. The former led to the decision in 1840 to abolish transportation and the latter to the appointment of 'protectors' for Aboriginal people. They were less successful in opposing the Corn Laws that kept the price of bread in Britain and Ireland expensive, a serious issue for the working poor of Britain and Ireland.

In the first quarter of the nineteenth century, radicals frequently described the British political system as 'Old Corruption', 'Corruption', 'the System' or 'the Thing'.[39] Throughout the 1810s and 1820s, segments of the press began advocating for universal, rather than limited, male suffrage. By lowering the prices of these publications, publishers hoped to attract a larger audience. Large public meetings assembled. In these venues, pro-reformers campaigned to extend male suffrage. By the 1820s, the argument for reform had 'become an accepted creed' among British society.

The *Great Reform Act 1832* brought about modest reforms to the parliamentary system in England, three of which are significant:

1. The franchise extended to men owning household worth over £10.
2. It abolished rotten and pocket boroughs or electorates (see below).
3. To ensure fairer representation, the boundaries of electorates (called 'constituencies') were redistributed to take in industrial cities with booming populations, which had either not been represented or had not been fairly represented in Parliament.

The impact of reform was far more dramatic in Scotland. In the early 1830s, other largescale reforms, like the emancipation of slaves in the West Indies, also became law.

Although this Act did not achieve universal suffrage, because of the Act half a million men could vote in Britain and Ireland. The Act led to the introduction of a system of annual

[38] *Representation of the People (Equal Franchise) Act 1928* (UK).

[39] Philip Harling, 'Parliament, the State, and 'Old Corruption': Conceptualizing Reform, c 1790–1832' in Arthur Burns and Joanna Innes (eds), *Rethinking the Age of Reform: Britain 1780–1850* (Cambridge, Cambridge University Press, 2003) 98, 100.

voter registration. Only those whose names were on the register could vote, and local activists took it upon themselves to ensure that those eligible to vote were registered. Political associations used this voting base to canvass their party position. In addition, the professionalisation of the political system made it more desirable for a member of parliament to attach himself to an established political party than run as an independent.

Rotten boroughs – parliamentary constituencies with little to no voters (and controlled by either the Crown or an aristocratic patron) – were relics of the Middle Ages. Famous among the rotten boroughs were Old Sarum in Wiltshire, Dunwich in Suffolk and East and West Looe in Cornwall where voters numbered in the single figures. The boundaries of these constituencies were unchanged for centuries so that, in many respects, representation was neither fair nor balanced. Aside from the very small boroughs, there were other boroughs with insignificant voter numbers – perhaps a few hundred – and elections were rare.

A problematic feature of the old system was that each borough could elect two members to the House of Commons. The lack of representation was a particularly acute concern for highly populated counties in the north of England, where populations had boomed due to the Industrial Revolution. Lancashire – the heart of the industrial north – sent 13 members to Parliament compared with 44 in the less populated county of Cornwall. The whole of Scotland, including large industrial cities like Glasgow, had only 45 MPs.

Rotten boroughs received memorable definition in the series *Blackadder the Third* (1987), where the constituency Dunny-on-the-Wold contained the following residents: three cows, a Dachshund, a middle-aged hen and one human voter. The comedy in *Blackadder* keenly drew on historical realities. For example, Old Sarum, once a busy town in the early Middle Ages, had very few residents by the eighteenth century. In fact, it had no *resident* voters in the eighteenth century.[40] By then, the Pitt family controlled the land, decided their next member of Parliament, and acted as patron to the two MPs sent to Parliament. William Pitt, the Elder (father) and William Pitt, the Younger (son) were prominent members of the Pitt family, both of whom served as Prime Minister. Patronage meant the patron could assert undue and unrepresentative influence over the MP as well as in the House of Commons.

The Great Reform Act's reforms were modest. It did not provide for shorter parliaments, secret ballots, or universal male suffrage. It did not eliminate a property qualification, but this was not the object of the reform. Parliament only had a limited extension of the franchise in mind to respond to voter concerns over the representativeness of existing constituencies. The efforts to reform the body politic were far from popular in all quarters. Many opposed the Bill, including some of the highest subjects in the land. The Archbishop of Canterbury, William Howley opposed reform of Church and State and urged the Government to preserve some of the old boroughs. In response, large crowds turned on him and other high-ranking opponents of reform.[41] More far-reaching reforms were to come later that century. Undue influence over MPs through powerful borough patrons, and undue influence over voters through bribery or intimidation, remained. However, one of the Great Reform Act's main achievements was to promote a position agitating for greater parliamentary reform.

[40] Ronald Quinault, 'The Industrial Revolution and Parliamentary Reform' in Patrick K O'Brien and Ronald Quinault (eds), *The Industrial Revolution and British Society* (Cambridge, Cambridge University Press, 1993) 187; HJ Hanham (ed), *The Nineteenth-Century Constitution 1815–1914: Documents and Commentary* (Cambridge, Cambridge University Press, 1969) 256.

[41] James Garrard, *Archbishop Howley, 1828–1848* (London, Routledge, 2016) 47; Robert Saunders, 'God and the Great Reform Act: Preaching against Reform, 1831–32' (2014) 53(2) *Journal of British Studies* 378, 389.

The reform created an environment in which contested elections and partisan politics were more common.

It would be remiss not to briefly mention a number of other significant statutory reforms introduced in the 1830s and 1840s. Through these reforms, the existing poor law system was radically changed, county police forces came into existence – a consequence of Sir Robert Peel's *Metropolitan Police Act 1829*[42] – and local government rationalised. Borough councils, as established under the *Municipal Corporations Act 1835*,[43] were more likely to address the immediate needs of their electors – local ratepayers – because they had responsibility over important public works such as drainage and sewerage. Even after local government legislation, sanitation was still inadequate in densely populated areas like London. A notable example of London's sanitation problems is the 1854 Broad Street cholera outbreak, in which 616 people died from cholera transmitted in contaminated water taken from the Broad Street pump.

The Second Reform Acts of 1867–68

Since the Great Reform Act only achieved partial reform, radical MPs campaigned for more far-reaching reforms: a secret ballot and shorter parliaments. However, peaks and troughs (mainly troughs) were characteristic of the reform movement between the 1830s and the 1860s, culminating in the Second Reform Acts of 1867 and 1868. Though MPs regularly introduced bills for political reforms, Parliament had knocked them back. More than anything else, Parliament simply could not agree upon what type of reform was best.

When reform returned as a serious issue on the parliamentary agenda, the political parties (Conservatives and now Liberals rather than Whigs) hoped to shore up the 1832 reform and increase the electorate by targeting 'respectable' voters. To Victorians, 'respectability' had a special meaning. It usually meant those with gainful employment, conformed to the Church, had savings, and were otherwise financially competent. The MPs made a crude – but for them important – distinction between 'respectable' voters and 'the residuum' (or the 'dangerous classes'). The franchise was not to be extended to 'the residuum', which embraced unemployed or unvirtuous men. While the reform movement had a moral tone to it, a reduced financial qualification soon gained more favour.

In the early 1850s, the Liberals had floated the idea of 'fancy franchises'. The idea was that men would be eligible to vote if they had a set amount of savings, a government pension of a set amount, a professional qualification, or a university degree. This reform proposal failed, but so did quite a few other proposals.[44]

[42] 10 Geo 4 c 44. British police officers are referred to as 'Peelers' or, more commonly, 'Bobbies', in reference to Sir Robert Peel's creation of a professional police force in London. Under the *Metropolitan Police Act 1829*, constables received a paid appointment to maintain order in London. The original Peeler uniform comprised a blue tailcoat and a top hat. Peelers were armed with a wooden truncheon, handcuffs and a rattle to gain attention, which was later replaced with a whistle. The London police force model was extended to counties and towns in the late 1830s: see *County Police Act 1839* (2 & 3 Vict c 93).

[43] 5 & 6 Wm IV c 76.

[44] Francis Smith, *The Making of the Second Reform Bill* (Cambridge, Cambridge University Press, 1966) 229; Robert Blake, *Disraeli* (London, Doubleday, 1968) 445.

The reforms introduced by the *Reform Acts 1867* and *1868* doubled the number of eligible voters. These Acts were, perhaps unexpectedly, the achievement of a Conservative Government led by Benjamin Disraeli. Disraeli, a novelist as well as a politician, was of Jewish descent but eligible to sit in Parliament as his family had converted to Christianity. The overriding principle that he managed to persuade his party to accept was 'one household, one vote, whatever the rental, with appropriate restrictions of time and residence'.[45] Following the Act, over a million working class men could have their names added to the electoral register. The constituency of Stoke-upon-Trent increased from 3,000 to 18,000 voters, demonstrating the magnitude of these reforms in rural areas. In Glasgow, the electorate more than doubled from 18,000 to 47,000. In townships, the franchise extended to:

- Male house owners aged over 21.
- Male lodgers who paid annual rent of £10 or more.

In counties, the right to vote extended to:

- Male house owners with property worth over £5 per year.
- Men who paid annual rent of £12 in England and Wales, and £15 or more in Scotland.

Later Nineteenth-Century Reforms

Later nineteenth century statutes extended the male franchise even further. The *Representation of the People Act 1884* (or the Third Reform Act) extended the voting entitlements of the boroughs (introduced in 1867) to all parliamentary boroughs and counties.[46] All men who paid an annual rent of or whose land was valued at £10 could vote. Following the 'Australian Ballot' model, the United Kingdom adopted the secret ballot in 1872. The secret ballot is a mainstay in Australian politics. In fact, the Australian colonies (the first was Victoria in 1856) introduced a secret ballot well before the US or even the UK did. The *Ballot Act 1872* abolished voting by public declaration. Before the Ballot Act, voters had to declare their candidate in a public forum, often accompanied by political rallies and public drinking. That meant that rioting – sometimes resulting in deaths – was common on Election Day.

Before the *Ballot Act 1872* and the *Corrupt Practices Act 1883*[47] became law, voting could be violent and dangerous for the average voter. In addition, corrupt practices prospered. Some political candidates would 'wine and dine' the public to buy votes before elections. Other candidates paid money to their electorates to secure votes. The *Corrupt Practices Act 1883* prohibited candidates from buying food or drink for voters and limited the expenditure of each candidate during election season.

In 1885, the *Redistribution of Seats Act*[48] saw the restructuring of constituencies. Scotland gained another 12 seats. Towns with a certain population (50,000–165,000) now had two MPs. In 1918, all adult males (over 21) and women over 30 became entitled to vote.

[45] Andre Maurois, *Disraeli* (translated by Hamish Miles) (Alexandria, Virginia, Time-Life Books, 1936) 232.
[46] 48 & 49 Vic c 3, s 2.
[47] 35 & 36 Vic c 33 and 46 & 47 Vic c 51.
[48] 48 & 49 Vic c 23.

Women over the age of 21 finally achieved that right in 1928. In 1948, business and university votes were abolished; by which point, the principle of one-person-one-vote was firmly entrenched.

Codification Movement

Jeremy Bentham coined the term 'codification'. He saw the benefits of making codes, as in European countries, to state what the law is in certain areas of law. Bentham despised the common law and having to identify what the law was by looking at a series of cases (and hoping the right ones were found). The law would become rational, and easier to understand, if collected in one systematic and well-arranged book of legislation. The Pandectist movement was also of some influence in England and the British Empire, often amongst Liberals who admired Bentham's philosophy. It had a small effect in English civil law. Four pieces of late-nineteenth and early-twentieth century legislation are characteristic of the movement:

- *Bills of Exchange Act 1882*[49]
- *Partnership Act 1890*[50]
- *Sale of Goods Act 1893*[51]
- *Marine Insurance Act 1906*[52]

Each piece of legislation codifies a particular area of law. It was often necessary first to identify in a systematic way what the common law in an area was. This came through scholarly efforts in writing the first major textbooks in English law. The late nineteenth century therefore saw the first major textbooks published on a large scale, some of which remain in print today in later editions. An example is in the work of Lord Lindley (1828–1905), who as a barrister practising in the Court of Chancery became a keen Pandectist. In 1860, Lindley published the *Treatise on the Law of Partnership* – which added a section in 1862 for the newly developed area of company law. This eventually became two texts: *Lindley on Companies* and *Lindley on Partnership*. The *Partnership Act 1890* later codified the principles so elegantly stated in *Lindley on Partnership*. The modern textbook, and small efforts at codification, arose hand-in-hand. Much of this legislation came to the British colonies. Queensland also had a supportive Pandectist in its Liberal Attorney-General and Premier, Sir Samuel Griffith. The colony saw a number of these statutes adopted, such as the *Partnership Act 1891* and the *Sale of Goods Act 1896*. Commonwealth Parliament adopted the *Bills of Exchange Act 1909*. These statutes are still in force.

There were also attempts at comprehensive codification in criminal law. In England itself, repeated unsuccessful efforts took place during the nineteenth century to codify the criminal

[49] 45 & 46 Vic c 61.
[50] 53 & 53 Vic c 39.
[51] 56 & 57 Vic c 71.
[52] 6 Edw 7 c 41.

law. Again, the influence of textbooks was important. Sir James Fitzjames Stephen's *Digest of Criminal Law* (1863) formed the basis of a code proposed, again unsuccessfully, in 1880. There was greater success in the colonies, most notably the *Indian Penal Code 1860* (or 'the IPC') drafted by the Whig politician Thomas Babington Macaulay (1800–59). Lord Macaulay's Code came into force in 1862 and remains the basis of India's criminal law. Stephen's Criminal Code, though unsuccessful in England, had some influence on the development of a criminal code for the whole of Canada. The Canadian *Criminal Code*, which is also still in force, was enacted in 1892.[53] More importantly, for this course, 'the Stephen Code' also had some influence on Sir Samuel Griffith, who drafted a criminal code after his appointment as Chief Justice of Queensland. Griffith also seems to have drawn on criminal codes from New York and Italy. The *Queensland Criminal Code* came into force in 1900, and was adopted elsewhere in Australia and its territories: namely, Western Australia (1903), British New Guinea (1903) and Nauru (1921). It is still in force in Papua New Guinea. The *Griffith Code* was also adopted in Nigeria, Bermuda, Cyprus and Israel – which was part of the British colony of Palestine before independence, although it is no longer in force in Israel. Additional cameos on **AV Dicey and John Austin** on the website expand discussion of codification and the law's intellectual development.

Law and Society in the Nineteenth Century

This chapter has primarily focused on the reform of legal institutions and their political context, but nineteenth-century law was no more or less divorced from or impactful on its contextual society than any other period. Victorian legislation articulated official attitudes to different social demographics, including children, the poor and vagrant, the mentally ill, women and homosexuals. On the cusp of the Victorian age, the *Vagrancy Act 1824*[54] made public begging a criminal offence, along with sleeping on the streets, as it remains to this day in Britain.

Further legislative steps included the *Vagrancy Acts of 1838* and *1898*, which extended the notion of vagrancy to include showing obscene works and prostitution on the streets.[55] The *Poor Law Amendment Act 1834* gave a commission powers over paupers.[56] The *Lunacy Act 1845* regulated the treatment of the mentally ill.[57] Hanging over the poor, the vagrant and the sick was the hideous possibility of going to the workhouse. Few institutions are so darkly Dickensian in popular imagination as these. They inhabit the same theoretical domain as Bentham's panopticon and utilitarian principles; in reality, they were horrendous places, fully deserving the dark reputation they have carried into the present day, assisted by their grim fictional presentations in works such as Charles Dickens' *Oliver Twist* (1838) and Thomas Hardy's *Far From the Madding Crowd* (1874). Based on an underlying supposition that paupers were idlers, the workhouse conditions and regime struck 'terror among the

[53] See Criminal Code, RSC 1985, c C-45.
[54] 5 Geo 4 c 83.
[55] 1 & 2 Vic c 38 and Vic 61 & 62 c 39.
[56] 4 & 5 Wm 4 c 76.
[57] 8 & 9 Vic c 100.

able-bodied population'.[58] Commissions came into existence because of both the Lunacy and Poor Law Acts, giving commissioners the power to investigate and regulate.

'Victorian' is often and stereotypically used as a pejorative adjective to mean stuffy, strait-laced or prudish, exemplified by a grimly unamused Queen Victoria. But the period was alive with fascination in and about sexuality. Queen Victoria herself enjoyed sex and spoke about it in frank terms. Victorian law engaged with different types of sexualities. Especially notorious today were efforts to regulate female sexuality through the *Contagious Diseases Acts 1864*,[59] *1866*,[60] and *1869*.[61] The diseases in question were venereal diseases, especially syphilis contracted by British soldiers. However, it was not the male soldiers affected by the Acts but female prostitutes. The Acts enforced compulsory genital inspection on women believed to be prostitutes, if they were near military barracks. Infected women were confined to Lock Hospitals, 'pseudo-medical prisons for whores'.[62] They provoked a strong repeal campaign led by charismatic female reformers including Josephine Butler.[63]

The *Married Women's Property Act 1882* also affected women.[64] A married woman was a **feme covert**, whose husband subsumed her legal identity. As ever Charles Dickens was a shrewd and observant writer on English law in his fiction. In *David Copperfield* (1849–50) Dickens depicts the reality of being a *feme covert* when the young widow Mrs Copperfield marries the forceful Mr Murdstone and finds every aspect of her life and her domestic economy pass from her control to her husband's. Dickens adds the additional darkness of Murdstone's emotional manipulation and destruction of his wife's personality and identity. Many non-fictional analogues of Mrs Copperfield campaigned for improvements to property rights, finally achieved in some measure by the Married Women's Property Act. Before this legislation passed, the common law and equity devised methods to relieve against the harshness of coverture. Married women had no legal personality under the English common law. A husband's legal status covered his wife's ('coverture') and, so, a wife was legally dependent upon her husband and all her property became his upon marriage. Married women could not enter contracts, sue or be sued, execute wills, or own personal property. In relief, first, women from affluent backgrounds circumvented coverture using marriage settlement contracts. In equity, women could lawfully enter marriage settlements with certain property settled on them for their own separate use during marriage. The soon-to-be husband could not touch this property. Second, widows with children had a right to dower at common law. This meant two things:

> *Feme covert* (French): the legal status of a married woman

1. A right to property brought into the marriage.
2. A life interest in one-third of the deceased husband's land.

[58] David Englander, *Poverty and Poor Law Reform in Nineteenth-Century Britain, 1834–1914: From Chadwick to Booth* (London, Routledge, 2013).

[59] 27 & 28 Vic c 85.

[60] 29 & 30 Vic c 35.

[61] 32 & 33 Vic c 96.

[62] Nickie Roberts, *Whores in History: Prostitution in Western Society* (London, HarperCollins, 1993) 248.

[63] Judith R Walkowitz, *City of Dreadful Delight: Narratives of Sexual Danger in Late-Victorian London* (London, Virago, 1994) 91.

[64] 45 & 46 Vic c 75.

Constitutional Detour

The Legal History of Homosexuality

The section above considered where law and female sexuality and identity engaged. English law historically responded punitively to 'unnatural' sexual activity by men, including the 1533 statute against the 'detestable and abominable Vice of Buggery committed with mankind or beast'.[65] The Tudor nobleman Lord Hungerford was convicted 'as it was said, for buggery', in 1540. However, the statute law is not straightforward. Hungerford's conviction was for 'unnatural offences', and his act of buggery was not only unnatural but treasonous.[66] The ecclesiastical courts discussed in chapter three also punished sexual immortalities. Buggery, with another man or with an animal, was punished by execution until 1836.[67] The *Offences Against the Person Act 1861* made buggery or attempted buggery an offence punishable by imprisonment.[68] Among those prosecuted under this Act were the cross-dressing Thomas Boulton and Frederick Park, who had the female alter egos Stella and Fanny, prosecuted in the Court of Queen's Bench in 1870. Notwithstanding the prosecution's aggressive pursuit of evidence, including brutal medical examinations of both men while in police custody for signs of anal sex and a prosecution led by the Attorney General and the Solicitor General, the case failed but did exemplify Victorian law's determined pursuit of the 'abomination' of buggery.[69] Under the *Criminal Law Amendment Act 1885*,[70] the offence of 'gross indecency' attracted two years' hard labour. The Act only ever referred to sexual activity between men, although the story that the Act omitted lesbianism because Queen Victoria refused to believe it existed is not true.[71] Wider moral panics about child and adult sexual pathologies and activities contextualised the passage of the 1885 Act. The sensationalist journalist WT Stead had published a series of lurid articles titled the 'Maiden Tribute of Modern Babylon', alleging white girls were being sexually trafficked to Europe.[72]

[65] 25 Hen 8 c 6.

[66] John Bellamy, *The Tudor Law of Treason (Routledge Revivals): An Introduction* (London, Routledge, 2013); Baker (n 14) 531.

[67] John Bellamy, *Criminal Law and Society in Late Medieval and Tudor England* (New York, St Martin's Press, 1984) 150; Michael Kirby, '*The Sodomy Offence: England's Least Lovely Criminal Law Export?*' *Human Rights, Sexual Orientation and Gender Identity in The Commonwealth: Struggles for Decriminalisation and Change* (Institute of Commonwealth Studies, School of Advanced Study, University of London, 2013) 63.

[68] 24 & 25 Vic c 100.

[69] Judith Rowbotham, 'A Deception on the Public: The Real Scandal of Boulton and Park' (2015) 36 *Liverpool Law Review* 123, 124.

[70] 48 & 49 Vic c 69.

[71] Caroline Derry, *Lesbianism and the Criminal Law: Three Centuries of Legal Regulation in England and Wales* (Cham, Springer Nature, 2020) 1, 234.

[72] Matthew Sweet, *Inventing the Victorians* (London, Faber, 2002) 64.

Historical Cameo

The Trial of Oscar Wilde

The 1895 trial, conviction and imprisonment of the Irish writer **Oscar Wilde** (1854–1900) brings together various aspects of Victorian legal and social approaches to sexuality as it sought to understand but also control human sexuality. Wilde, a successful playwright who was married with two sons, commenced a libel action against the Marquis of Queensberry in April 1895. The Marquis had left a calling card in Wilde's club, accusing the writer of being a 'posing somdomite [sic]'; Wilde had been having an affair with Queensberry's son Lord Alfred Douglas. ***The Libel Act 1843*** required Queensberry to prove his claim that Wilde had committed a homosexual act.[73] The Marquis of Queensberry succeeded in doing so, using private detectives to build evidence of the literal truth of his claim: that Wilde had committed sodomy. Not only did Wilde lose his libel case, but the authorities then arrested and tried him for gross indecency under the Criminal Law Amendment Act. During a particularly lethal cross-examination by Edward Carson QC, the barrister asked Wilde if he had kissed a boy. Wilde denied it, because: 'He was a particularly plain boy, unfortunately ugly'. In that moment Wilde realised how harmful his answer had been to his case when Carson then asked if he would have kissed a pretty boy. *R v Wilde* was actually two trials. The first ended inconclusively; the second ended with Wilde guilty of gross indecency. Among the evidence were faecal and Vaseline stains on some bedsheets from the Savoy Hotel, claimed by the prosecution to be clear signs of buggery. His sentence was two years' hard labour, pursuant to the Criminal Law Amendment Act. The Marquis of Queensberry held a party to celebrate.[74]

Pause for Thought

Sex and the Law

Over centuries the law has sought to regulate human bodies and sexualities and the trials of Oscar Wilde are one aspect of that regulation. That regulation has often taken the form of prohibiting and criminalising types of sexual activity that extend to the sexualities informing them. Most obviously English, American and Australian law has criminalised homosexual activity between men, whether consenting or otherwise and regardless of an age of consent. Law codes contained references to sexual activity using historically pejorative language such as sodomy and buggery. Tasmania decriminalised homosexual activity in 1997.

Questions to consider

1. What has driven different processes of criminalising and decriminalising sexual activities and changes to the age of consent?
2. To what extent are law and morality intertwined?

[73] 6 & 7 Vic c 96.
[74] Richard Ellmann, *Oscar Wilde* (Harmondsworth, Penguin, 1987) 448–49.

Conclusion

This chapter concludes the section of this book concerned with England and, latterly, the United Kingdom. The next chapters move geographically to Australia. The nineteenth century is a natural springboard for this transition. Many of the legal reforms and much of the legislation discussed in this chapter expanded to Australia, including Australian versions of the Judicature Acts, the Contagious Diseases Acts and the *Married Women's Property Act 1882*.[75] The preceding chapters have overviewed many centuries of legal activity, including foundational achievements that have directly shaped the Australian legal system. While the reception of English law into Australia is an important part of these chapters, teleologically these next chapters do not propose a straightforward chronology, instead disrupting that with the ancient presence of Indigenous law.

[75] See generally Judith Smart, 'Sex, the State and the "Scarlet Scourge": Gender, Citizenship and Venereal Diseases Regulation in Australia during the Great War' (1998) 7 *Women's History Review* 5.

7

The Reception of English Law in Australia

Introduction

On 21 November 1789, just 21 months since the female convicts of the First Fleet had been disembarked, Ann Davis was tried before the Court of Criminal Jurisdiction in Sydney for the theft of shirts, waistcoats, handkerchiefs and other goods and chattels. The Court found her guilty and pronounced sentence of death at which point the 32-year-old 'pleaded the belly', 'declar[ing] that she was with child'. As had been the practice in English law for more than 400 years, a jury of matrons was empanelled to determine if she was more than three months' pregnant ('quick with child'), or whether the hanging could proceed. Sadly for Ann Davis, the leading matron reported to the Court, 'Gentlemen! she is as much with child as I am' and Ann became the first woman hanged in New South Wales on 23 November 1789.[1]

This is a dramatic reminder that the First Fleet did not just bring people to the shores of Sydney Harbour; it also brought their experiences of English law at home and in other colonial settings and their eighteenth-century ideas about the rule of law. This set up an interesting dynamic. Although New South Wales was founded as a convict colony, both free settlers and convicts began to contest their rights using the rhetoric of law. This chapter will consider the problems with the system of criminal justice introduced to New South Wales, the extraordinary powers given to governors and how the community evaded them, and how the colony's first Chief Justice interpreted the limits of English law in this new setting. This was Chief Justice Sir Francis Forbes who is the subject of a historical cameo. The aim is to understand how the idea of the rule of law was championed in a new political context, the origins of Australia's court system, and the development of its constitutional arrangements.

[1] New South Wales Capital Convictions Database: Francis Forbes Society for Legal History (2013) research. forbessociety.org.au/record/13: Ann Davis – 1789. For Ann's age and original Old Bailey conviction, see John Cobley, *The Crimes of the First Fleet Convicts* (Sydney, Angus & Robertson, 1970) 71.

Learning Resources

The content in this chapter is supported by:

Glossary	Chapter Overview	Historical Cameos	Pause for Thought
Convict-era terms are defined throughout the chapter	The chapter begins with an overview explaining its intentions and focus	Sir Francis Forbes	Convict Legal Status Rule of Law in a Penal Colony

Chapter Overview

Place	Period	Dates	Key Figures	Key Institutions	Key Terms
• Eastern Australia to 135° E • Primarily Sydney and Hobart	• Late Georgian, Regency and Early Victorian	• Eighteenth to early nineteenth centuries	• Governors Bligh, Macquarie and Darling • Deputy Judge-Advocate Collins • Judges Ellis and Jeffery Bent • Chief Justice Francis Forbes • Robert Wardell and William Charles Wentworth	• Convict system: transportation and attaint • Convict economy • Power of governors • Military juries or panels • Court of Criminal Judicature • Supreme Court of New South Wales • Colonial legal profession	• Transportation • Commutation of sentence • Emancipation • Convict Attaint • Indictable Offence

Learning Outcomes

At the end of this chapter, readers should understand:

- The Bloody Code and its direct connection to the founding of Botany Bay.
- Ideas concerning the rule of law and experiences of eighteenth-century court rooms which were brought to the convict colonies by both the guards and the guarded.
- How, even in a convict colony, the autocratic power of governors was resisted.
- Demands for a separation of powers between governors and courts which finally led to an independent legal system.

The Eighteenth-Century Context: Idealism and Slavery

Chapter four discussed the dramatic legal developments flowing from the Bill of Rights after the Glorious Revolution. The idea of responsible government and more radical ideas of government as a social contract inspired intellectuals in Europe and in the American colonies. These seventeenth-century ideals contributed to American independence and its Constitution.[2] This same body of ideas was brought to New South Wales by the officers of the First Fleet, many of whom had served in the American War of Independence.

A fuller insight into English law in Australia, however, requires understanding of the darker results of seventeenth-century constitutional developments. The Whigs who came to dominate eighteenth-century politics built their fortunes in Britain's slave colonies abroad and defended their newfound property at home through the Bloody Code, the body of legislation which made more than 200 offences, often property offences, punishable by death. While one part of the elite proudly debated ideas of constitutional reform, political liberty and innate and natural rights, its predominant business arm was profiting from slavery and depending on public displays of punishment to deter the poor from questioning the growing and visible inequality among classes. These contradictory impulses were manifested in legal and constitutional developments in the Australian colonies.

One measure of the wealth and power that slavery brought Britain was the intransigence of the British Parliament towards abolition. The first petition to Parliament calling for an end to slavery was presented in 1783 but it would take another 50 years and numerous public petitions before slavery was finally abolished throughout the British Empire. Advocates in favour of slavery had immense political and economic power and supporters in both Houses of Parliament. The third son of George III, who in 1786 had befriended planters when stationed in the West Indies on naval duties, was a prominent supporter of slavery. As the Duke of Clarence and St Andrews, he had a seat in the House of Lords and used his position to speak against the abolition movement. He later became William IV, following the death of his father, George III, in 1820 and older brother George IV in 1830.

[2] Discussed in chapter five of this volume.

Even when the issue was finally won, the slaves were not immediately freed but forced to undertake a system of indenture to minimise the hardship on their owners. Although they received no recompense for their enslavement, the British Government did compensate slave owners to the tune of more than £20 million for the loss of 670,000 slaves.[3]

The forces in favour of a slave-based economy provide insight into the class power of those who supported the Bloody Code at home and, in turn, introduced the system of convict transportation to settle New South Wales. In 1688, 50 offences had been punishable by death under English law but by 1800 this had increased to 220 offences, an overwhelming proportion of which were concerned with the defence of private property. Grand larceny was defined as theft equivalent to 12 pence (one shilling).[4] This system was designed to defend the growing property of the elite and to terrorise the poor who lost traditional rights to graze cattle, collect firewood and hunt on what were now private estates and forests.[5] By attaching the death penalty to minor offences (such as stealing five shillings), the intention was to terrorise the population into becoming law-abiding subjects and maintain general order in the face of extreme inequality.

The English Criminal Justice System and Convict Transportation

Public displays of power were an integral part of the success of English criminal justice. The aim of punishment was physical pain to the body and public humiliation by exhibiting its infliction. In complete contrast to today's thinking, time in prison seemed cruel and unnatural and was limited to those awaiting trial, short sentences of four months or less, and to debtors who were held until their debts had been paid. Most gaols were privately run and on completion of their sentence inmates had to pay a '**turnkey**' for their release.[6] Bodily punishment was cheap and offered a range of punishments from time in the stocks or pillory to flogging at the village whipping post through to hanging on gallows erected in a public place.

> **Turnkey:** an eighteenth-century term for a gaoler or prison guard

Crowds came to view the spectacle, drawing satisfaction when a murderer or a thief was punished. There were times, however, when the crowd supported the person in the pillory or regarded the condemned as unfairly treated; then there could be riots, threats to the hangman and clergyman, the gallows overturned, and order established only by calling out the military. The proverbial action of 'reading the Riot Act' had a literal meaning of a justice

[3] Legacies of British Slave Ownership, University College, London (Department of History, 2019), available at www.ucl.ac.uk/lbs/.

[4] Proceedings of the Old Bailey Online: Crimes Tried at the Old Bailey (HRI Online & Sheffield University UK), available at www.oldbaileyonline.org/static/Crimes.jsp.

[5] Douglas Hay, 'Poaching and the Game Laws on Cannock Chase' in Douglas Hay, Peter Linebaugh, John G Rule, Edward P Thompson and Cal Winslow, *Albion's Fatal Tree: Crime and Society in Eighteenth Century England* (London, Penguin, 1977). See also Edward P Thompson, *Whigs and Hunters* (Harmondsworth, Penguin, 1977).

[6] Michael Ignatieff, *A Just Measure of Pain: The Penitentiary in the Industrial Revolution 1750–1850* (New York, Columbia University Press, 1980) 30–34.

of the peace attempting to disperse an unruly crowd by reminding them of the law. In eighteenth-century London, it was common for the procession of the condemned through the streets to **Tyburn** to be accompanied by armed cavalry to suppress rioting.[7] Governments saw the emotion and unruliness as appropriate to this awful theatre but as the century progressed the potential for disruption and for the crowd to challenge authority led to this ritual being increasingly questioned by social critics. In the aftermath of American independence and the French Revolution, the irrationality of the mob then began to disturb the authorities. Jeremy Bentham's ideas that punishment should be certain, consistent and any pain inflicted measurable[8] began to gain attention among critics who were disturbed by the debasing aspects of punishment rituals. In the meantime, commuting death sentences by replacing them with transportation eased social tensions.

Tyburn: the place of London executions until 1783

Transportation was consistent with the idea of bodily punishment; it represented the middle ground between time in the pillory and hanging. The idea was to extract the labour of the body of the convicted. Exile or banishment had been an old idea in criminal justice but in 1717 a new Act[9] introduced seven years transportation to commute a sentence of death. After the Duke of Monmouth's rebellion in 1685 (see chapter four) convicts had been transported and now under this Act convicts were sent to colonies in America and the West Indies.[10]

Commutation of sentences was integral to the English political system. Majesty, justice, and mercy were treated as three ideological planks of the criminal law. The first stage – the majesty of the law – was sentencing the prisoner to death. The second stage – justice – was the attention paid by an assize judge to a prisoner's rights for 'it is an exercise of compassion that costs nothing, and is sure to gain the applause of vulgar hearers'.[11] It also ensured scrupulous attention to formalities. A prosecution could fail on a technicality; a wrong date, name, or occupational description in the writ were fatal. While seemingly trivial, avoiding conviction on a technicality demonstrated that the judge and prosecutor were not above the law. The notion that all were equal before the law reinforced the ideology among the poor. Mercy – the third and most powerful weapon of the criminal law – ensured the political structure's survival. Pardons were common, and hangings selective. Justices of the peace through to High Court justices and the Secretary of State had the same discretion to pardon a prisoner convicted to death.

Commutation of sentences was a means of social control. Authorities selectively applied the 'King's mercy' to soften the horrors of the legal code and gain the consent of the mass of the working poor. Cultural effects were pervasive as each level of society sought to use the law but also to intervene, resist, negotiate and accommodate its processes and limit its dire consequences.[12] The authorities were conscious that, if they did not apply the King's

[7] Peter Linebaugh, 'The Riot against the Surgeons' in Hay et al, *Albion's Fatal Tree* (London, Penguin, 1977) 98–102.

[8] Ignatieff (n 6) 75–76.

[9] *Transportation Act 1717* (4 Geo I c 11).

[10] Emma Christopher, *A Merciless Place: The Lost Story of Britain's Convict Disaster in Africa and How it Led to the Settlement of Australia* (Crows Nest, New South Wales, Allen & Unwin, 2010) 31–34. See also Jacobite Rebellion of 1745 database, available at www.jacobites.net/jacobite-lists.html.

[11] John Hawkins, *The Life of Samuel Johnson LLD* (London, 1787) 522.

[12] Peter King, *Crime, Justice and Discretion in England, 1740–1820* (Oxford, Oxford University Press, 2000) 373.

mercy judiciously, a revolutionary situation could easily develop and had European examples before their eyes as warnings.

In the aftermath of the war with the American colonies, the number of prisoners awaiting transportation on crowded prison '**hulks**'[13] had begun to expand exponentially. In 1779, the House of Lords established a committee to investigate new destinations for convicts. Joseph Banks, the botanist, and James Matra, a midshipman, on Captain James Cook's first expedition suggested a settlement at Botany Bay. In April 1770, Cook had proclaimed the eastern third of the continent of New Holland for George III. He had landed on an island in Torres Strait, raised the British flag and read a proclamation. His instruction had been to do so 'with the consent of the natives' and his reasoning on this point will be discussed in later chapters. The Dutch had already claimed the western two-thirds of the continent. However, if the British Government did not follow with actual occupation then other European powers could usurp this claim. So, Botany Bay was chosen after attempts to send convicts to West Africa had proved disastrous.[14]

Hulks: unseaworthy, rotting warships (floating on the Thames and in Portsmouth harbour and other waterways) that were used to house prisoners

Figure 7.1 AL Garneray, *Prison Hulks in Portsmouth Harbour* (1812–1814). BHC1924
National Maritime Museum, Greenwich, London, Caird Collection (CC BY-NC-ND), https://creativecommons.org/licenses/by-nc-nd/2.0/.

Historians have continued to debate whether this was the only reason or whether there were secret motives of imperial strategy or trade. The fact that there were no established sea routes, that the journey would take nine months and the extensive government funding and planning required, *merely to deal with convicts*, has led scholars to continue to question the real reasons behind the decision. There was also opposition by members of Parliament and no known return trade to offset the massive costs.[15] Whatever the grounds, new legislation,

[13] Ignatieff (n 6) 80–81.
[14] Christopher (n 10) 321–32.
[15] Sir Nathaniel Wraxell's and the East India Company's opposition are covered in L Evans and P Nicholls, *Convicts and Colonial Society 1788–1853* (Stanmore New South Wales, Cassell, 1976) 32–35. Jeremy Bentham's

the *Transportation Act 1784*[16] authorised the Privy Council to designate places within or outside the British colonies to transport convicts.

With Botany Bay chosen, Captain Arthur Phillip received his first commission on 12 October 1786. By this commission, Phillip was appointed Governor of the territory of New South Wales. This territory ranged up to Cape York and to the west. Phillip had charge of the whole of eastern Australia to the 135th meridian of longitude. In theory, all Aboriginal peoples living within this vast claim were now British subjects without sovereignty or political independence. As is covered in later chapters, governors soon appreciated that the legal situation was not so simple, and it was some decades before local officials would mistakenly assert that both Aboriginal title and Aboriginal law no longer existed.

Other commissions had to be issued. David Collins was appointed Deputy Judge-Advocate, recognising that, despite the potentially totalitarian powers of the governor, a legal system would also be required in this colony of soldiers, civilian officials, freed felons and felons. His title was however a military title and his commission required him 'to observe and follow' orders and directions from the Governor;[17] so this make-do legal system was not independent of the governor. In line with the *Transportation Act 1784*,[18] orders for the transportation of certain male and female offenders were made.[19]

Two naval vessels, *HMS Supply* and *HMS Sirius*, and nine convict ships left Portsmouth, England bound for Botany Bay on 13 May 1787. The ships reached Botany Bay on 19 January, but they soon relocated. On 25 January 1788, this First Fleet sailed into Port Jackson. The following day – 26 January 1788 – the British flag was raised, and a volley of shots fired. Of the 1,336 people who landed at Sydney Cove, 732 were convicts. On 7 February 1788, the Judge-Advocate David Collins read the Governor's two commissions, the *Courts Act*, and the Letters Patent to an assembly of convicts.[20]

Convict transportation lasted for more than 80 years. During that time, approximately 162,000 convicts arrived in the Australian colonies, excluding South Australia.[21] South Australia was the only Australian colony not to participate in convict transportation, but some former convicts settled there. The bulk of convicts arrived in the 1820s and 1830s, after the end of the Napoleonic wars, although criminal law reform in England was beginning to reduce the number of offences that attracted the death penalty. The criminal justice system was being reformed from one based on deterrence and little regulation of rowdy public spaces to a system intended to be professional in preventing, prosecuting and punishing

continuous disapproval is summarised in John Hirst, 'The Australian Experience' in Norval Morris and David J Rothman (eds), *The Oxford History of the Prison* (New York, Oxford University Press, 1995) 274–75. The debate about the Botany Bay decision is covered in detail in Ged Martin (ed), *The Founding of Australia* (Sydney, Hale & Iremonger, 1978) and was further extended when scholars investigated Spanish and French archives: see Robert J King, *The Secret History of the Convict Colony* (Sydney, Allen & Unwin, 1990); Colin Dyer, *The French Explorers and Sydney 1788–1831* (St Lucia, UQP, 2009).

[16] 24 Geo III c 56 sess 2.

[17] John F Nagle, *Collins, the Courts and the Colony: Law and Society in Colonial New South Wales 1788–1796* (Sydney, UNSWP, 1996) 16.

[18] *Transportation Act 1784* (n 16).

[19] A 1795 list of crimes punishable by transportation is provided in Evans and Nicholls (n 15) 105–06.

[20] *New South Wales Act 1787* (7 Geo III c 2); Nagle (n 17) 16.

[21] John Hirst gives a higher figure of 187,000 in 'The Australian Experience' (n 15) 266. George Rude draws on earlier work by Manning Clark and Lloyd Robson to provide a summary and profile in George Rude, *Protest and Punishment* (Melbourne, Oxford University Press, 1978) 240.

crime – one suited to elevated levels of public order for a modern state. As part of this process the decision to build a new English prison, Pentonville, in 1840[22] made possible the decision to cease transportation to New South Wales with the last convicts arriving in that year, although they continued to be sent to Van Diemen's Land until 1850[23] and Western Australia until 1868.[24]

Criminal processes that are valued and held as essential today, such as the right to defence counsel, to testify or to remain silent, are comparatively recent additions to English legal proceedings.[25] The enactment of the *Prisoners' Counsel Act* in 1836 enabled prisoners to be represented by defence counsel in felony trials. Until the *Criminal Law and Evidence Amendment Act 1891* (NSW),[26] an accused had no right to testify – and this was only available at trials for **indictable** offences. The right to speak could be 'the difference between sentence of death and sentence of transportation'.[27] Under this flawed process, less than five per cent of convicts ever returned to Great Britain and their families again.

Indictable: a more serious offence tried in a superior court, such as the District or Supreme Court, with a jury

Convicts' Rights

The convict system operated for more than eight decades and in that time reflected Britain's home and imperial interests. Convicts were sent from all parts of the British Empire. There were French Catholics following the Canadian Rebellions of 1837–1838, African slaves who came via Mauritius after 1810, and Maori and Pakeha New Zealanders.[28] The majority however came from England and Wales and up to one-third from Ireland. Another surprising aspect of the convict profile was that they were literate, or at least had a higher rate of literacy than the English working class at home.[29] This is important context for understanding how convicts reacted to and shaped their experiences of servitude, a system which nineteenth-century critics repeatedly categorised as a form of slavery.

[22] Randall McGowen, 'The Well-Ordered Prison' in Norval Morris and David J Rothman (eds), *The Oxford History of the Prison* (New York, Oxford University Press, 1995) 101.

[23] Evans and Nicholls (n 15) 233–39; Hamish Maxwell-Stewart, 'Convicts' in *The Companion to Tasmanian History* (Centre for Tasmanian Historical Studies, 2006), available at www.utas.edu.au/library/companion_to_tasmanian_history/C/Convicts.htm.

[24] The usual date given for cessation to Western Australia is 1868 but David Rothman gives the date of January 1869 for the last arrival of convicts, David J Rothman, 'The Victorian Prison' in Morris and Rothman (eds) (n 22) 135.

[25] See chapter four of this volume.

[26] *Criminal Law and Evidence Amendment Act 1891* (NSW) s 6.

[27] *Azzopardi v The Queen* (2001) 205 CLR 50 [141].

[28] Cassandra Pybus and Hamish Maxwell-Stuart, *American Citizens, British Slaves: Yankee Political Prisoners in an Australian Penal Colony* (Carlton South, Melbourne University Press, 2002); Cassandra Pybus, *Black Founders* (Sydney, University of New South Wales Press, 2006); Krysten Harman, *Aboriginal Convicts: Australian, Khoisan and Maori Exiles* (Sydney, NewSouth, 2012).

[29] Stephen Nicholas and Peter R Shergold, 'Convicts as Migrants' in Stephen Nicholas (ed), *Convict Workers: Reinterpreting Australia's Past* (Cambridge, Cambridge University Press, 1989) 43, 75–76.

At common law, persons sentenced to death for felony were attainted. In practical terms, that meant that holding property and suing or giving evidence in court was an impossibility for attainted persons under the common law of England. As it turned out, that was not the position in New South Wales. Convicts were able to sue, give evidence in court, and own property in New South Wales. This made sense in a community where the early courts had to repeatedly draw on convict witnesses who constituted 75 per cent of the population in its founding years.[30] The effect of this decision was remarkable.

The first convening of the Court of Civil Judicature in Australia was at the behest of two convicts.[31] Their civil action commenced before the Judge-Advocate, David Collins, on 1 July 1788. Henry and Susannah Kable were successful in recovering £20 in damages from the master of the ship *Alexander* for losing their luggage on the journey. Because Henry and Susannah had been sentenced to death, the Kables should have been treated as attainted. By deciding in favour of the Kables, Collins ignored the common law rule. In *Cable v Sinclair*,[32] court documents described Henry Kable as a labourer.[33]

On arrival, initially, convicts could only work for the Government for there were no free settlers. With the arrival of small numbers of settlers in the 1790s, convicts could be assigned to settlers or to government for work. The introduction in 1801 of the ticket of leave system was an indulgence that rewarded well-behaved convicts by allowing them to find their own employment within a specified district.[34] However, the system underwent significant change over eight decades. By 1819 the British Government was receiving complaints that the convict system was no longer sufficiently feared by the English poor and appointed JT Bigge to inquire into the system. His three-volume report, which was finalised in the years 1822–23, recommended increased controls over convicts at the same time as the courts began to reimpose **convict attaint**.[35]

Convict attaint: a condemned felon was 'civilly dead'; this meant that their property was forfeited to the Crown and they could not give evidence in a court of law or initiate action in a court of law

Convicts and **emancipated convicts** were central to the commercial life of early New South Wales and this had only been possible because the law of felony attaint had not been enforced. The economy rested not only on cheap convict labour but also on their small businesses. In 1820, when local courts for the first time held that the full law of attaint applied, it caused considerable economic destabilisation. Naturally convicts and emancipists resisted this attack on their property and commercial rights and found innovative ways around it. It took 20 years of campaigning before some of these rights were restored.[36]

Emancipated convicts: convicts who have served their sentences

30 Nagle (n 17) 60.

31 David Neal, *The Rule of Law in a Penal Colony: Law and Power in Early New South Wales* (Cambridge, Cambridge University Press, 1991) 6.

32 [1788] NSWKR 7.

33 Bruce Kercher, *Debt Seduction and Other Disasters: The Birth of Civil Law in Convict New South Wales* (Leichhardt NSW, Federation Press, 1996) Introduction.

34 Bruce Kercher, *An Unruly Child: A History of Law in Australia* (St Leonards NSW, Allen & Unwin, 1995) 29.

35 *Ibid* 35.

36 *Ibid* 36.

Pause for Thought

Convict Legal Status

The local courts' decision to ignore convict attaint had important repercussions for the economy of early New South Wales.

Questions to Consider

1. Reflect upon some of the practical advantages it gave convicts. How might emancipist businesses have survived its removal in 1822? You might like to think about convict family life when answering this question.

Governors encouraged convicts to marry and the birth-rate was high. Unlike the system of slavery, where the children of slaves were born into slavery, the children of convicts were legally free. In the first three decades, settlers did not have to own land to have assigned convicts so small businesspeople could apply for convict servants; for example, a free woman married to a convict could apply for her husband to be assigned to her.

The Governor's Powers

Distance and time were insurmountable obstacles for the supervision of this colony from London. As a result, the British Government gave the governors extensive powers under commissions issued by the Crown. An officer of the First Fleet, American-born Jacob Nagle, recorded his amazement that so much power could be invested in any governor of a British colony.[37] Although the Letters Patent used the phrase 'colony and civil government', Arthur Phillip was also given the title of 'captain-general' usually used for commander-in-chief of an army.[38] All the early governors from Arthur Phillip to George Gipps (recalled in 1846) were either navy or army officers.

Figure 7.2 Governors of Early New South Wales and their Terms of Office

Governor	Period in Office
Captain Arthur Phillip	7 February 1788–10 December 1792
Captain John Hunter	11 September 1795–27 September 1800
Captain Philip Gidley King	28 September 1800–12 August 1806
Captain William Bligh	13 August 1806–26 January 1808
Major-General Lachlan Macquarie	1 January 1810–1 December 1821
General Sir Thomas Brisbane	1 December 1821–1 December 1825
General Sir Ralph Darling	19 December 1825–21 October 1831
General Sir Richard Bourke	3 December 1831–5 December 1837
Sir George Gipps	24 February 1838–11 July 1846

[37] See comments in Nagle (n 17) 16–17.
[38] *Ibid* 15.

Their commissions contained instructions on how to act but as the colony developed governors found their authority repeatedly challenged. Governors' instructions were to reform convicts through farming while the self-interest of the officers and later free settlers was to maximise their access to cheap convict labour for their own personal prosperity. Written powers giving almost absolute or autocratic rule, but which could not be enforced without the consent of the officers would repeatedly come up against their determined economic interest. The governor's superior was the British Government, but a year of travel was required to get news to Westminster. Though responsible to the Crown, Governor Bligh responded to a legal argument by saying, 'the law Sir! Damn the Law; my will is the law, and woe unto the man that dares to disobey it'.[39]

In many respects Bligh was correct: no separation of powers was possible under the autocratic structures of the early colony. The governors were representatives of the monarch in the colony – but with no local parliament or responsible ministers to exercise power for them. In the absence of such a local legislature, governors issued orders and proclamations. The early governors controlled all arms of government: the judiciary, the legislature, and the executive. David Collins was commissioned the Deputy Judge-Advocate to oversee the colony's legal system, but he was also instructed to obey all instructions and directions 'from our Governor … according to the rules and discipline of war'.[40] Despite these limitations, free colonists, military officers, and convicts soon found ways to use the courts to contest the governor's powers.

Early Colonial Legal System

The Court of Criminal Judicature

Without a legislature to debate the orders and proclamations of the governor, officers and settlers turned to the courts despite their lack of independence. The *New South Wales Courts Act*[41] had been enacted in 1787. It provided for the establishment of a court of record, the Court of Criminal Judicature, 'on the Eastern Coast of New South Wales and the points adjacent'. In 1791, a similar tribunal was established in Norfolk Island.

The *New South Wales Courts Act* and the *First Charter of Justice* provided detail on the Court's jurisdiction and procedure. The Deputy Judge-Advocate could only preside with six fellow 'officers of his majesty's forces by sea or land'[42] who attended in military dress and with 'the sash and the sword'. Although none of these officials had any legal training, the court had 'authority to proceed in a more **summary** way than is used within this realm [ie, Great Britain] according to the known and established laws thereof'.[43] In this situation, the members of the tribunal determine all questions of fact and law. In England at the time, the jury system required a unanimous verdict of guilty from 12 jurors; the

[39] Cited by Kercher (n 33) *10*.

[40] Cited in Nagle (n 17) 16. This instruction was included in the commissions of the first three Judge-Advocates; see Neal (n 31) 93.

[41] 27 Geo III c 2.

[42] Cited in Nagle (n 17) 52.

[43] *Charter of Justice 2 April 1787* (UK), Museum of Australian Democracy at Old Parliament House & National Archives of Australia (2011), available at www.foundingdocs.gov.au/item-sdid-70.html.

Court of Criminal Judicature only required a four-member majority, including that of the Judge-Advocate. No appeal against conviction was available, but cases were appealed to the governor who could commute sentences. Criminal appeals were not introduced until the *Criminal Appeal Act 1907* (UK) more than a century later.

The Court of Criminal Judicature had the power to hear, determine (or oyer and terminer, see chapter one) and to punish 'Misprision … Murders Felonies Forgeries Perjuries Trespasses and other Crimes whatsoever'. It would meet

> from time to time as occasion may require … for the trial and punishment of all such outrages and misbehaviours as i[f] committed within this realm would be deemed and taken according to the laws of this realm to be treason or misprision thereof felony or misdemeanour.[44]

The Court's procedure was specified in the *Courts Act*. The written charge against the accused was to be exhibited to the Judge-Advocate. Witnesses and offenders would be examined on oath. Capital punishment could not be carried out 'unless five persons present in such court' agreed or the monarch's approval had been obtained. Death for capital offences and corporal punishment for non-capital offences were the only two punishments the Court could impose. The Judge-Advocate's role in criminal hearings clearly generated conflicts of interest. Not only did the Judge-Advocate act as prosecutor, he led the Court and delivered judgment with the six other members.

Summary trial: a court without a jury such as a magistrates' court

The Court of Civil Jurisdiction

The Court of Civil Jurisdiction was also established under Letters Patent known as the First Charter of Justice. Whether this Court was properly established was a topic from time to time broached in the colony's early years. The *Courts Act* only specified that a criminal court be established. It did not authorise a civil court, which the First Charter of Justice (made in accordance with the *Courts Act*) did. The civil Court, comprising the Judge-Advocate and 'two fit and proper persons inhabiting the said place', had power to hear matters involving real property, personal actions,[45] and deceased estates. The Court could enforce its own judgments. From this civil Court, litigants had the right to appeal to the governor. For claims over £300, a further right of appeal to the Privy Council in London was available.

Between 1788 and 1823, the administration of civil justice in New South Wales was arguably simpler than in England. The jurisdictions of the three common law courts in England – the Courts of Kings Bench, Common Pleas and Exchequer – coincided in many respects. The ecclesiastical courts, the High Court of Admiralty and the Court of Chancery were separate jurisdictions. This civil Court was modelled after the Court of Common Pleas. Moreover, the authority given in the First Charter to grant probate on **testate** and **intestate** estates in the colony were matters traditionally dealt with in the ecclesiastical courts.

Testate: dying leaving a will

Intestate: dying without leaving a will

[44] *New South Wales Courts Act 1787* (UK), Museum of Australian Democracy at Old Parliament House & National Archives of Australia (2011), available at www.foundingdocs.gov.au/resources/transcripts/nsw3i_doc_1787.pdf.

[45] Debt, contracts and trespass.

Small civil claims were handled by magistrates from at least 1791. No equivalent existed in England enabling English magistrates to act as early New South Wales' magistrates did.

For British subjects schooled in basic legal knowledge of the eighteenth century, including William Blackstone's extensive legal writings,[46] much about these courts was an affront to their understanding of how English law ought to function. Governors Hunter, King and Bligh all complained to the Colonial Office about the court structure and begged for trained legal staff and law books.[47] As the colony grew, the presence of military in civilian courts was distasteful to British subjects of all classes who associated it with the repression of the English Civil War. Governor Bligh pointed out that their form and character was too close to courts martial.[48]

In their own unique way, however, they had become a site of opposition power. Military officers who had grown wealthy in the colony controlled the courts and used them as a bloc against governors. The decisions of these courts could be appealed to the governor and, in theory, governors could overturn decisions; they certainly amended sentences. However, governors needed the support of free settlers, military personnel, and convicts for their proclamations to be carried into effect. Decisions of the Court could not be ignored or overturned by governors if they were viewed as legitimate by the community. With no trained legal personnel in the colony, the governors had only the Judge-Advocate for legal advice on the very cases that the Judge-Advocate had prosecuted and presided over. In 1803 Governor King complained that he had had to turn to a convict, George Crossley, the only trained attorney and solicitor in the colony, for legal advice.[49] In the governors' famous struggles with serving and ex-military officers over the rum monopoly much of the conflict played out in the courts; only once Governor Bligh had legally trumped John Macarthur (former captain and regimental paymaster of the New South Wales Corps) was the recourse to arms taken.[50]

Pause for Thought

The Rule of Law in a Penal Colony

For contemporary readers, the notion that residents of a penal colony expected rule of law principles to apply is somewhat surprising.

Questions to Consider

1. Using knowledge gained from earlier chapters, reflect upon what emancipist convicts meant when they talked of their 'birthright'. Why did the absence of rule of law principles in governing the early colony affront serving military officers?

[46] See chapter four of this volume.

[47] Neal (n 31) 92.

[48] *Ibid* 93.

[49] *Ibid.*

[50] *Ibid* 94; Gregory D Woods, *A History of Criminal Law in New South Wales 1788–1900* (Sydney, Federation, 2002) 31–34 has a good summary, drawing on Evatt's *Rum Rebellion*, of the use of the Court in the dispute between Governor Bligh on the one hand and Macarthur and the New South Wales Corps on the other.

The First Supreme Court of New South Wales

These complaints were eventually heard by the Colonial Office in London, especially after the extraordinary events of 26 January 1808 when the New South Wales Corps overthrew Governor Bligh. In February 1814, the Second Charter of Justice was issued.[51] The Second Charter was limited to civil matters. It abolished the Court of Civil Jurisdiction and replaced it with the first Supreme Court of New South Wales. Like the First Charter, no jury was allowed; however, the military no longer had any direct part in the judgments of the Court.

A Supreme Court judge (the title remained Judge-Advocate) appointed by commission and two governor-appointed lay magistrates heard matters relating to the common law and, for the first time, equity. The Charter specified that the Supreme Court had power to 'administer Justice in a summary manner according or as near as may be to the Rules of our High Court of Chancery in Great Britain'. However, there were still no juries for New South Wales or Van Diemen's Land, a colony founded in 1803. An appeal to the governor existed as of right for claims above £300. The right to appeal to the Privy Council was even more closely defined. Only claims over £3,000 could go up to the Privy Council. Besides that, the appellant had to provide security[52] double the amount being claimed.

Nonetheless, for the first time a professionally trained lawyer, Ellis Bent, was appointed Judge-Advocate and arrived with Governor Macquarie in 1810. They worked together amicably until the extraordinary powers of the Governor of New South Wales began to concern Bent. He was nonetheless instructed by Bathurst, Secretary of State for the Colonies, 'to set an Example of due obedience' to the governor's authority.[53] The Cambridge-educated 'barrister of some eminence' argued for the independence of the judiciary from the executive and for the rule of law.[54]

The Second Charter created two other courts: the Governor's Court and the Lieutenant-Governor's Court. The jurisdiction of each court was not as extensive as the Supreme Court. It could hear disputes up to £50. The two courts had limited power over common law actions like those previously heard in the old Civil Court. Equity could not be administered in either court. The Lieutenant-Governor's Court was limited to Van Diemen's Land (Tasmania). A Judge-Advocate and 'two fit and proper persons' appointed by the Governor constituted the Lieutenant-Governor's Court.

The problem of the courts not being fully independent of the governor was compounded by the colony's lack of solicitors and barristers. By the 1810s, George Crossley had been joined by two other former convicts with legal training and Ellis Bent allowed these three men to act, not as attorneys per se, but as special agents in the Court of Civil Judicature. In 1814 when a second judge was to be appointed to the colony, Ellis Bent recommended his brother, Jeffery Bent. It was a poor choice. While Ellis had protested the independence of the courts as a principle, his brother was pre-occupied with his elevated personal status. Once Jeffery Bent was sworn in by Governor Macquarie in August 1814, among other complaints,

[51] Letters Patent to establish Courts of Civil Judicature in New South Wales 2 April 1814 *Historical Records of Australia*, Series III, vol I.

[52] See chapter two of this volume on payment of securities.

[53] Bathurst cited in Neal (n 31) 96.

[54] Charles H Currey, 'Bent, Ellis (1783–1815)' in *Australian Dictionary of Biography*, vol 1 (Melbourne, Melbourne University Press, 1966), available at adb.anu.edu.au/biography/bent-ellis-1772/text1985.

he refused to allow emancipist attorneys to appear in his court and therefore refused to open the court. When he finally consented to open the court in May 1815, Jeffery argued with the two lay magistrates with whom he was required to sit and consequently declined to take his seat. Supreme Court business ground to a halt until October 1816. Governor Lachlan Macquarie intervened to try to resolve the problems, which Jeffery Bent rebuffed as political interference in the rule of law.

The irony was that Macquarie was trying to increase the legal services available in the colony for himself, for the courts and for settlers. The emancipists in turn were using the rhetoric of ancient constitutional liberties to press for their rights as 'freeborn Englishmen' to be restored to them so that they could not only practise law, but also be appointed magistrates and sit on juries.[55]

In the end, Lord Bathurst removed Jeffery Bent while at the same time asserting the principle of judicial independence to Governor Macquarie.[56] In 1817, Barron Field replaced Bent. Field soon drafted rules for the Supreme Court that met the approval of Macquarie. For the first time, the Supreme Court was sitting regularly, although the shortage of trained lawyers, limited court business and delays continued to beset the first Supreme Court.

In Van Diemen's Land, the £50 jurisdictional limit of the Lieutenant-Governor's Court produced its own problems for litigants there. Many were disinclined to take the hazardous journey to Sydney to resolve disputes. Court fees paid the salaries of court officers. By closely following English court procedures, the colonial court experienced similar delays. As in England, the length of court documents determined the fees paid to lawyers and court officials: the longer the greater the fee. Brevity was not a prized virtue. Its first judge was a military man who, reputedly, boasted that he could 'not be bothered with the law'.[57] Legal historians Bruce Kercher and Alex Castles both describe the continued amateur administration of law in Tasmania in these years as 'frontier law' which was not resolved until the Third Charter of Justice was enacted in 1824.[58]

The *New South Wales Act 1823*, the Third Charter of Justice and the Supreme Court of New South Wales

For 35 years, politics in the colony centred on demands by emancipists and settlers for the rule of law and checks on executive power. When British Parliament finally passed the *New South Wales Act 1823*[59] it was a momentous piece of legislation which, by Letters Patent or Charters of Justice to New South Wales and Van Diemen's Land, granted the separation of the two colonies. It also attempted to provide a check on the powers of the Governor of New South Wales by establishing a Legislative Council, although those councillors were

[55] Neal (n 31) 102–03, 167–87.

[56] *Ibid* 103, Woods (n 50) vol 1, 42–43. Ellis Bent had died 10 November 1815, Currey (n 54).

[57] Kercher (n 34) 59.

[58] *Ibid* 59–60; Alex Castles, 'Law without Full Order' in Alex Castles, Stefan Petrow and Kate Ramsay (eds), *Lawless Harvests or God Save the Judges: Van Diemen's Land 1803–1855, A Legal History* (Melbourne, Australian Scholarly, 2003) 30–38.

[59] 4 Geo IV c 96.

appointed not elected. Additionally, proposed new legislation was to be placed before the Chief Justice to certify whether it was 'not repugnant to the Laws of England'.[60]

The position of Chief Justice was newly created for the Third Charter of Justice, issued under the *New South Wales Act*, which established the current Supreme Court of New South Wales. The old position of Deputy Judge-Advocate acting as both judge and prosecutor was no more. The law would now be administered independently of the governor, and judges were paid a salary rather than rely on court fees. In other respects, however, this legislation disappointed emancipist settlers, judges, and governors – trial by jury had again been rejected by London, and military panels continued to decide criminal cases although they were now restricted to deciding matters of fact only.[61] The first Chief Justice of the New South Wales Supreme Court, Sir Francis Forbes, publicly read the Third Charter on the day of his swearing-in.

Figure 7.3 Watercolour of Sydney Looking North along Elizabeth Street towards the Supreme Court and St James' Church, 1842. Hyde Park appears on the right J Rae, *Supreme Court and St James Church, from Elizabeth Street* (1842).

Dixson Galleries, State Library of New South Wales, DG V/Sp Coll/Rae/1.*

[60] Alex Castles, *An Australian Legal History* (Sydney, Law Book, 1982) 130–31; Kercher (n 34) 70.
[61] Woods (n 56) 48–50; Kercher (n 34) 72–73.

The Third Charter of Justice also created the Supreme Court of Van Diemen's Land and 30-year-old John Pedder was appointed its first Chief Justice on 10 May[62] and Pedder opened the Court that same day. This sitting was prior to New South Wales' first session, making the Supreme Court of Tasmania Australia's oldest continuous superior court by one week.[63]

Despite the letter of the law, judges in both colonies discovered that the separation of powers still had to be fought for. Francis Forbes' responsibility to check any new laws proposed by the governor did not harm his relations with Governor Brisbane but his successor, General Ralph Darling, resented the limited powers and checks that the Legislative Council and Chief Justice held. Darling's lack of sympathy for the rule of law came to the fore in a very public case. Two Privates of the 57th Regiment, Joseph Sudds and Patrick Thompson, were found guilty of stealing 10 pence worth of cloth, ostensibly doing so deliberately so that they would be dismissed from the army and able to remain in New South Wales. The Court of Quarter Sessions sentenced them to seven years' transportation but Governor Darling, who wanted to make an example of them, 'commuted' (**commutation**) the sentence to seven years in a chain gang and ordered that special iron collars be forged for their chains, each set of chains weighing more than six kilograms. Stripped of their uniforms, dressed in prison garb and iron collars, the two men were paraded and drummed from their Regiment under a Sydney November sun. Sudds died five days later, and local newspapers took up their cause. Only at this point did Darling seek legal advice. Forbes CJ informed him that his actions in overturning the Court's decision was illegal. Relations between Chief Justice and Governor worsened when Darling tried to pass legislation enabling him to close the newspapers critical of him and, again, the Chief Justice had to advise him that his powers were limited.[64]

Commutation: an act of mercy by the governor who had the power to reduce the sentence imposed by the courts

When the temporary *New South Wales Act 1823* was replaced by the *Australian Courts Act 1828* (UK),[65] any Supreme Court judge, not just the Chief Justice, could raise repugnancy issues relating to legislation proposed by the governor. Furthermore, Supreme Court decisions could no longer be appealed to the governor. These provisions, recommended by Francis Forbes and Attorney-General Saxe Bannister, strengthened judicial checks on executive power.[66]

Historical Cameo

Sir Francis Forbes

Sir Francis Forbes (1784–1841) was the first Chief Justice of the Supreme Court of New South Wales (1823–37). By the time he left office, Forbes had set the foundations for

[62] Peter A Howell, 'Pedder, Sir John Lewes (1793–1859)' in *Australian Dictionary of Biography*, vol 2 (n 54), 1967), available at adb.anu.edu.au/biography/pedder-sir-john-lewes-2542/text3457.

[63] Tasmania: Charter of Justice 13 October 1823 (UK) Museum of Australian Democracy, available at foundingdocs.gov.au/item-sdid-118.html.

[64] On appeal to London, Thompson was ordered to be released. See especially Castles (n 60) 159–60, 153, fn 6; Currey (n 54); Kercher (n 34) 35–36, 82–86; Neal (n 31) 110–13.

[65] 9 Geo 4, c 83.

[66] Kercher (n 34) 75–76.

judicial review of executive decisions and encouraged the emergence of the rule of law in the young colony.

Forbes was born in Bermuda where his father was a medical doctor, but later studied law in London. In 1812, he was called to the Bar of Lincoln's Inn. He was appointed Attorney-General of Bermuda (1812), King's Advocate in the Vice-Admiralty Court of Bermuda (1813), and Chief Justice of the Supreme Court of Newfoundland (1816). Here, he proved his willingness to use the courts to check excessive gubernatorial power.[67]

Illness prompted Forbes to seek leave from the Newfoundland chief justiceship in 1822. He left for England with his wife and three sons. Despite their conflicts, the Admiral-Governor of Newfoundland, Sir Charles Hamilton, was anxious for Forbes to return to attend to criminal matters that were pending trial. Forbes, however, was offered and accepted the position of Chief Justice of a new Supreme Court in New South Wales.

Figure 7.4 Portrait of Sir Francis Forbes
Mitchell Library, State Library of New South Wales, ML 14, IE3258574.

As part of his official inquiry into New South Wales, Commissioner Bigge reported only briefly on New South Wales' legal system. In a private letter to the Secretary of State for War and the Colonies, Bigge made clear that colonial administration in New South Wales required complete refurbishment. Thus, before Forbes' formal appointment, the Colonial Office engaged Forbes and counsel to the Colonial Office, James Stephen, to

[67] CH Currey, 'Forbes, Sir Francis (1784–1841)' in *Australian Dictionary of Biography*, vol 1 (n 54), available at adb.anu.edu.au/biography/forbes-sir-francis-2052/text2545.

draft legislation to overhaul the system. Bigge thought highly of young Forbes despite their contrasting personal values; Forbes who had been sent to school in the United States was said to have 'political opinions of the freest tendency'.[68]

Letters Patent, known as the Third Charter of Justice, were sealed in 1823 and proclaimed in Sydney in 1824. The Third Charter established the Supreme Court of New South Wales, which possessed both civil and criminal jurisdictions. The Chief Justice was the second highest ranked officer in New South Wales. Only the governor (or the acting governor) held a higher rank. The Supreme Court could hear bankruptcy, lunacy and probate matters. The Letters Patent set out the procedure for the admission of practitioners to the Court. The *New South Wales Act 1823*, replaced by the *Australian Courts Act 1828*, placed the Third Charter of Justice on a more secure footing.

In 1824, Forbes and his family arrived in Sydney whereupon Forbes embarked on raising the professional standard of the administration of justice in the colony. He ordered the indictments of three judicial officers for imposing an illegal sentence in a situation where a prisoner had confessed due to being flogged. To safeguard the untrained and unpaid justices of the peace who underpinned the local magistrates' courts, an *Act of Indemnity* had to be passed in 1825 to the dissatisfaction of John Macarthur's nephew, Hannibal Macarthur.[69]

The rise of talented men in the legal profession and the beginnings of a free press provoked several constitutional struggles during Forbes' time as Chief Justice. Roger Therry, later also a judge of the New South Wales Supreme Court, described Forbes as 'the model of an excellent judge' for his imperturbability and knowledge of legal principles.[70] Exhausted by successive controversies however, Forbes became ill in 1834. The Colonial Office finally granted him leave in 1836 but then called on him for further legal advice while he was on leave in England. His poor health continued and in 1837 he applied for retirement. Forbes had advised four governors and between 1823 and 1837 had directly shaped 'all three of the first basic constitutional instruments'[71] for New South Wales. He returned to Sydney and died in Newtown in 1841.

The Legal Profession in New South Wales: 1788–1859

'The people are taught by the papers to talk about the rights of Englishmen and the Free Institutions of the Mother Country, many of them forgetting their actual condition', Governor Darling complained to the Colonial Office in February 1827.[72] The disagreements between Chief Justice Francis Forbes and Governor Darling about the rule of law in early New South Wales reflected a major cleavage in colonial New South Wales between a wealthy elite who styled themselves as 'Exclusives' and the growing body of wealthy emancipists whose rights were under attack in the 1820s. The rhetoric of law was used to full effect in these political struggles which were enhanced by the arrival of legal professionals in the colony.

[68] *Ibid.*
[69] Woods (n 56) 60–61. See also chapter eight of this volume.
[70] Cited in Currey (n 67).
[71] *Ibid.*
[72] Darling cited in Neal (n 31) 27.

The first Attorney-General for New South Wales, Saxe Bannister, had been appointed in 1823[73] but he was no match in the court room for the two leading barristers in private practice, Robert Wardell[74] and William Charles Wentworth.[75] The *Catholic* **Emancipation** *Act*,[76] which enabled Catholics to take the oaths of office required for membership of the civil service and parliament, brought two new barristers to the colony in 1830 and 1831, Roger Therry (later Sir Roger) and John Plunkett. Both men were Irish and Catholic but with aristocratic connections which made them very much part of the elite. Their Irish experience gave them both strong grounding in notions of rights and, within a short time, both had public impact: Therry standing up for convict rights against the magistracy and Plunkett insisting on Aboriginal rights, both themes taken up in a later chapter.

Emancipation: winning legal freedom by slaves, convicts and repressed religious adherents such as Catholics, Dissenters and Jews

Their traditional legal training, however, made them side with local barristers over their status. The stratified English model of attorney and solicitor was adopted in most of the Australasian colonies. The English legacy of the divided profession often remained in the formal designation of lawyers admitted as 'barristers and solicitors'. In the main, this was because the first lawyers in the colony were attorneys, and the populations were too small to replicate the arrangements that existed in London. Several attorneys had been transported to the early penal colony and practised in the Courts of Civil and Criminal Jurisdiction before and after their emancipation.

After the controversy of Jeffery Bent's refusal to allow emancipist attorneys to practise in his court, the Third Charter of Justice for the Supreme Court was passed in 1823, and clause 10 provided:

> AND WE DO hereby authorize and empower the said Supreme Court of New South Wales to approve admit and enrol such and so many persons having been admitted Barristers at Law or Advocates in Great Britain or Ireland or having been admitted Writers [a writer is a Scottish solicitor] Attornies or Solicitors in one of our Courts at Westminster Dublin or Edinburgh or having been admitted as Proctors in any Ecclesiastical Court in England to act as well in the Character of Barristers and Advocates as of Proctors Attornies and Solicitors in the said Court ... and we do ordain and declare that in case there shall not be a sufficient number of such Barristers at Law Advocates Writers Attornies Solicitors and Proctors within the said Colony competent and willing to appear and act for the Suitors of the said Court then and in that case the said Supreme Court of New South Wales shall and is hereby authorized to admit as many other fit and proper persons to appear and act as Barristers Advocates Proctors Attornies and Solicitors as may be necessary according to such general rules and qualifications as the said Court shall for that purpose make and establish.

[73] Castles (n 60) 145–46. Joseph T Gellibrand was appointed Attorney-General for Van Diemen's Land, later replaced by Alfred Stephen. See further Peter C James, 'Gellibrand, Joseph Tice (1792–1837)' in *Australian Dictionary of Biography*, vol 1 (n 54), available at adb.anu.edu.au/biography/gellibrand-joseph-tice-2088/text2621.

[74] Charles H Currey, 'Robert Wardell (1793–1834)' in *Australian Dictionary of Biography*, vol 2 (n 54), available at adb.anu.edu.au/biography/wardell-robert-2773.

[75] Charles H Currey, 'Bannister, Saxe (1790–1877)' in *Australian Dictionary of Biography*, vol 1 (n 54), available at adb.anu.edu.au/biography/bannister-saxe-1738/text1919; Neal (n 31) 176–77; Michael Persse, 'Wentworth, William Charles (1790–1872)' in *Australian Dictionary of Biography*, vol 2 (n 54), adb.anu.edu.au/biography/wentworth-william-charles-2782/text3961.

[76] See chapter six of this volume.

These provisions were confirmed in the *Australian Courts Act 1828*, and the *Australian Constitutions Act 1842*.[77] Therefore, under the Third Charter of Justice the Supreme Court could admit lawyers to practise as barristers, advocates, proctors, attorneys, and solicitors – and did. The intention was therefore to amalgamate all those distinct types of lawyers into one, as happened in other colonies.

The amalgamated status of the profession was confirmed by the first Chief Justice of New South Wales, Sir Francis Forbes, in the *Bar Monopoly Case*.[78] In that case Dr Robert Wardell and William Charles Wentworth were admitted as barristers of the Supreme Court. They, together with the Attorney-General and the Solicitor-General, made a total of four barristers for the colony. Within days, the four barristers moved for the exclusion of attorneys from the Bar. The attorneys resisted this though, according to the report, not because they were keen to practise as advocates. They thought it was discourteous that they were being forced out of the Court. Chief Justice Forbes held that the Third Charter of Justice did not permit the exclusion of attorneys from the Bar.[79]

Despite the intention to have an amalgamated profession in New South Wales, colonial administrations and assemblies were more inclined than most in the Empire to mimic the legal arrangements made in England. In June 1829 the Supreme Court judges (Forbes CJ and Stephen and Dowling JJ) concluded 'that it is most expedient to divide the duties of the profession' and stated a rule that all lawyers admitted in New South Wales to that date would have to opt to practise as either a barrister or an attorney (and see chapter two).[80] Uncertainties about the legality of this arrangement, however, led the Court to suspend the operation of this rule until the King's opinion on the question was known. The rule also provided that, from that time, no man would be admitted as a barrister of the Court unless he had already been admitted as a barrister or advocate in England, Scotland or Ireland.

It was later confirmed that a barrister or advocate would even take precedence according to the date on which he was admitted in the United Kingdom in the *Precedence of Barristers Case*.[81] Under the Court's 1829 rule, a person could be admitted as a solicitor or attorney if 'actually admitted as Solicitors, Attornies, Proctors, or Writers to the Signet [a class of Scottish solicitor], in some one or other of the King's Supreme Courts within the United Kingdom of Great Britain or Ireland'. Irish lawyers were legally required to read in London, and they had formed the King's Inn Society in the mid-sixteenth century to gain admission.[82] *The Australian* newspaper, originally founded by Wardell and Wentworth but now under new ownership, opposed this stricture, decrying its potentially negative effect on the independence of the Court:

> the whole practise can scarcely fail in a little time, and in a distant Colony circumstanced as this, to degenerate into the hands of a few, to whose sole discretion, however clever, and independent, and honorable, … is not desirable for the properties and liberties of the community … the same power which the Bar keeps in a tolerably wholesome check at present, would find ample room for corrupting a majority, if not the entire of the few Barristers, who would have the privilege of

[77] 5 & 6 Vic c 76.
[78] [1824] NSWSupC 17.
[79] *Sydney Gazette* (Sydney, 16 September 1824) 2.
[80] *Division of the Legal Profession Case* [1829] NSWSupC 34; *Sydney Gazette* (Sydney, 8 September 1829) 2; *Sydney Gazette* (Sydney, 1 October 1829) 3.
[81] [1832] NSWSupC 77; 'Law Intelligence' *Sydney Herald* (Sydney, 18 October 1832) 1.
[82] Tony Earls, *Plunkett's Legacy* (North Melbourne, Australian Scholarly, 2009) 14.

> pleading, and whose self-interest would best be answered by siding with the House, and not with the People.[83]

The concession that was won in 1846 was the creation of a local Barristers' Admission Board in 1846 so that locally trained lawyers would no longer have to read at one of the four London Inns of Court.[84]

London approved the division of the profession in New South Wales in 1834[85] whereas in Van Diemen's Land the Supreme Court admitted solicitors and barristers on a single roll.[86] In South Australia too, the first Chief Justice, Charles Cooper, refused division in that colony so that by the time of Federation only New South Wales and Queensland had a divided profession.[87]

Reception of English Law

Francis Forbes' term as Chief Justice coincided with significant reforms to criminal justice in England and the application of these laws to New South Wales would be one more point of contention between the Supreme Court and the governor.[88]

On 7 February 1788, the Letters Patent instructing the first Governor of New South Wales, Captain Arthur Phillip, to establish a penal colony were read out to the European population. But did English law apply from this date? In the first volume of his *Commentaries*, William Blackstone said: 'For it hath been held, that if an uninhabited country be discovered and planted by English subjects, *all English laws then in being, which are the birthright of every subject, are immediately there in force*.'[89] Free settlers and emancipist convicts certainly argued staunchly for this birth right when it came to matters such as a check on executive authority and an independent legal system and the emancipists for trial by jury. For them, as for Forbes, 'the essence of the law was British freedom'.[90] Blackstone had said that there was one important qualification, however: settled colonies received 'only so much of the English law, as is applicable to their own situation and the condition of an infant colony'.[91] It was unclear whether a particular rule or doctrine had become law in New South Wales. Posing another difficulty was the reception of the common law and of statute.

Section 24 of the *Australian Courts Act 1828* sought to resolve the problem of which English law was applicable. It provided that:

> all laws and statutes in force within the Realm of England at the time of passing of this Act [ie, 25 July 1828] … shall be applied in the administration of justice in the Courts of New South Wales and Van Diemen's Land respectively, so far as the same can be applied within the said colonies.

[83] 'Proposed Rules of Practice' *The Australian* (Sydney, 7 October 1829) 3.
[84] Kercher (n 34) 95.
[85] *Ibid.*
[86] Castles (n 60) 280.
[87] Kercher (n 34) 96.
[88] *Ibid* 74–75. On other disputes re criminal law, see Bruce Kercher, *Outsiders: Tales from the Supreme Court of NSW 1824–1836* (Melbourne, Australian Scholarly, 2006) 20.
[89] William Blackstone, *The Oxford Edition of Blackstone's: Commentaries on the Laws of England: Book I: Of the Rights of Persons* (Oxford, Oxford University Press, 2016) 327.
[90] Kercher (n 34) 83.
[91] Blackstone (n 89) 327.

The date of reception for New South Wales and Tasmania was 25 July 1828. The date was chosen so that Sir Robert Peel's criminal law reforms, discussed in chapter six, were part of the received law. The reception date is the same for states that were once part of New South Wales: Queensland and Victoria. South Australia and Western Australia have different reception dates. For South Australia, that date was 28 December 1836 while the date of reception in Western Australia was 1 June 1829.

How the reception of English law worked in practice is evident in *Cooper v Stuart*,[92] a case that was appealed to the Privy Council. In 1882, a park was created in Sydney from ten acres of a 1400-acre land grant made in 1823. The grant included a clause 'reserving to His Majesty … any quantity of land not exceeding ten acres and in any part of the said grant as may be required for public purposes'. The issue before the Privy Council was whether that reservation was valid. Cooper argued that it was not because it infringed **the rule against perpetuities**. The nominal defendant, Stuart, argued that the rule against perpetuities was not part of the law of New South Wales in 1823. Lord Watson, on behalf of the other Privy Council members, said that:

> **Rule against perpetuities:** a common law rule preventing the tying up of property forever

> The extent to which English law is introduced into a British Colony, and the manner of its introduction, must necessarily vary according to the circumstances. There is a great difference between the case of a Colony acquired by conquest or cession, in which there is an established legal system, and that of a Colony which consisted of a tract of territory practically unoccupied, without settled inhabitants or settled law, at the time when it was peacefully annexed to the British dominions. The Colony of New South Wales belongs to the latter class. In the case of such a Colony the Crown may by ordinance, and the Imperial Parliament, or its own legislature when it comes to possess one, may by statute declare what parts of the common and statute law of England shall have effect within its limits. But, when that is not done, the law of England must (subject to well-established exceptions) become from the outset the law of the Colony, and be administered by its tribunals. In so far as it is reasonably applicable to the circumstances of the Colony, the law of England must prevail, until it is abrogated or modified, either by ordinance or statute. … The often-quoted observations of Sir William Blackstone appear to their Lordships to have a direct bearing upon the present case.[93]

This is a famous passage as it claimed Australia was peacefully settled and thereby denied Aboriginal title. However, the plaintiff lost this case and was ordered to pay costs since the Privy Council ruled that the law of perpetuities was not suited to colonial conditions of 1823. The question of peaceful settlement is the theme of later chapters.

Conclusion

This chapter explored the darkest aspects of Britain's eighteenth-century legal system to place the decision to colonise New South Wales in context. One of the most remarkable aspects of the new colony was that convicts who had experienced law's harsh realities

[92] (1889) 14 App Cas 286.
[93] *Ibid* 291.

nonetheless sought to use it for their own ends. Both the guards and the guarded contested the strictures of imperial power in early New South Wales. Remarkably it was the rhetoric of law, and their expectations of how English law and authority should operate, that enabled early settlers of New South Wales and Van Diemen's Land to challenge military authority, to demand professionally trained legal officers and an independent court system.

This chapter introduced the political system of early New South Wales to show how its flaws led to campaigns for legal and political reform. These campaigns bore fruit less than seven decades after the colonies were founded; these constitutional developments are the subject of chapter eight.

8

Self-Government and Law in Colonial Australia

Introduction

In 1843, Australia's first legislative elections took place in New South Wales. The elections would return 24 members to the 36 strong Legislative Council. The first day of polling in Sydney on 15 June 1843 'commenced at the usual hour' with great excitement but, by the time polls closed at four, had descended into drunken chaos.[1] Two days earlier, the five candidates for Sydney, which would elect two members to the partly elected, partly nominated Legislative Council, had been announced publicly. They were William Charles Wentworth, Dr William Bland, Captain O'Connell, Robert Cooper and Mr Hustler. Candidates plied their supporters with free food and drink to buy votes. Electors meanwhile had to write down the name of their preferred candidate and publicly declare for whom they voted.

At 11am, a running tally showed Wentworth and Bland leading the polls. Incensed by their early leads, 'a mob of four or five hundred persons, with Captain O'Connell's colours, rushed up to the polling places of Gipps Ward, tore down Wentworth and Bland's colours, and made a furious attack upon their supporters, who fled in all directions'.[2] The mob, 'armed with clubs, sticks, paling, and other weapons',[3] broke windows, damaged property and intimidated Wentworth-Bland supporters. As bedlam reigned, mounted police and soldiers were called out to disperse the mob. A man named Finney died from injuries received during the riots.[4] While 'a large portion of the electors … were prevented from giving their votes',[5] Wentworth and Dr Bland were duly elected as representatives of Sydney.[6] Governor George Gipps, seemingly unfazed, reported to the Colonial Office that: 'The Election in general went off very well.'[7]

This chapter concentrates on colonial judicial and legislative reforms resulting in representative and responsible government in all Australian colonies. The end of convict transportation to the eastern colonies in 1853 signalled that the time was ripe for self-government. Most Australian colonies, with the notable exception of Western Australia,[8]

[1] 'Sydney Election' *Sydney Morning Herald* (Sydney, 16 June 1843) 2.
[2] *Ibid* 2.
[3] 'Sydney Election Riots' *South Australian Register* (Adelaide, 8 July 1843) 3.
[4] 'The Election Disturbances' *Australasian Chronicle* (Sydney, 20 June 1843) 3; 'The Election Riots' *The Australian* (Sydney, 23 June 1843) 2; 'Inquest on the Man Killed in the Election Riots at Sydney' *The Teetotal Advocate* (Launceston, 10 July 1843) 2.
[5] 'The Electioneering Riots' *Sydney Morning Herald* (Sydney, 17 June 1843) 3.
[6] 'City Election' *Sydney Morning Herald* (Sydney, 20 June 1843) 2.
[7] For a similar account, see Judith Brett, *From Secret Ballot to Democracy Sausage: How Australia Got Compulsory Voting* (Melbourne, The Text Publishing Company, 2019) 11–13.
[8] Western Australia was granted self-government in 1890.

achieved this status during the 1850s. Beginning with the end of convict transportation, this chapter proceeds to discuss the early use of, and the economic and political power wielded by, paid magistrates in the Australian colonies. The development of responsible government and Privy Council appeals are next explored. The chapter concludes by considering the 'federal idea' in colonial Australia, which was taking on a definite form in the 1880s. In this regard, a forerunner to Commonwealth Parliament, the Federal Council of Australasia, is discussed.

Learning Resources

The content in this chapter is supported by:

Glossary	Chapter Overview	Historical Cameos	Constitutional Detours	Pause for Thought
Latin and other legal specific terms are defined	End of Convict Transportation The Colonial Magistracy Representation in Colonial Legislatures Path to Responsible Government	Sir Richard Bourke William Charles Wentworth Alfred James Peter Lutwyche	Universal Manhood Suffrage and the Secret Ballot	Innovation in Colonial South Australia

Chapter Overview

Place	Time Period	Dates	Key Figures	Key Institutions	Key Terms
• The Australian colonies	• Late-Georgian, Regency and Victorian eras	• 19th century	• Lachlan Macquarie • William Charles Wentworth • Sir William Molesworth • Sir Richard Bourke • Ulrich Hübbe • Judge Boothby • Judge Lutwyche and Chief Justice Cockle	• The Molesworth Committee • Colonial parliament • Colonial courts	• Select committee • Radical • Convict assignment • Sunset clause • Naturalised • Indefeasibility of title

Learning Outcomes

At the end of this chapter, readers should understand:

- The economic and political power of the amateur magistracy.
- Liberal political rights won by settlers.
- Significant constitutional developments up to the 1880s.

The End of an Era: Convict Transportation

During the 1830s, agitation against transportation was gathering momentum not only from new immigrants wanting regular employment, but also from radicals and Whigs in Great Britain.[9] Not all were opposed to transportation continuing in New South Wales because, first, it was the foundation upon which the colony was built and, second, abolition would shrink the supply of free convict labour to the colony's apparent 'ruin'.[10] In 1837, British Parliament appointed a **Select Committee** on transportation to look 'into the System of Transportation, its Efficacy as a Punishment, its Influence on the Moral State of Society in the Penal Colonies, and how far it is susceptible of Improvement'.[11] The man who urged the establishment of the Committee and its ultimate chair, the 26-year-old Sir William Molesworth, was a **Radical**. Like others of his ilk, Molesworth strongly opposed transportation. Evidence was given by handpicked witnesses.[12]

> **Select Committee:** a small legislative committee appointed to investigate and report on a specific issue

> **Radical:** a group allied with the Whigs that sought to extend the franchise following 1832's Reform Act

After 16 months, the Select Committee handed down its findings in August 1838. Considering Molesworth's personal opposition to transportation, the Committee's scathing findings were hardly surprising. The Committee concluded that transportation was an insufficient punishment and an expensive system to run.[13] The system did not deter people from crime.

Australian writer Robert Hughes argued that the Molesworth Committee, far from being objective as claimed, 'was in fact a heavily biased show trial designed to present a catalog of **antipodean** horrors'.[14] Even before the Committee was formed,

> **Antipodean:** concerning Australia or New Zealand

[9] Alexander Clifford Vernon Melbourne, *Early Constitutional Development in Australia* (St Lucia, University of Queensland Press, 1963) 230.

[10] *Ibid* 229.

[11] Sir William Molesworth, British Parliament, *Report of the Select Committee of the House of Commons on Transportation* (London, Henry Hooper, 1838) 7.

[12] Philip Harling, 'The Trouble with Convicts: From Transportation to Penal Servitude, 1840–67' (2014) 53 *Journal of British Studies* 80, 84.

[13] Molesworth (n 11) iv.

[14] Robert Hughes, *The Fatal Shore: A History of the Transportation of Convicts to Australia, 1787–1868* (London, Collins Harvill, 1987) 493. See also Harling (n 12) 83.

abolition was a *fait accompli*.[15] Molesworth was a friend and admirer of Edward Gibbon Wakefield who, while in Newgate Prison for the abduction of and attempted marriage to a teenage heiress, conceived a system of systematic colonisation of Australia through free immigration. He proposed the sale of Crown land at a 'sufficient' price,[16] the proceeds of which would be used to subsidise immigration. Preference for migrants would be given to 'young persons only, and especially young couples of both sexes'.[17] When South Australia was founded using Wakefield's blueprint, opposition to transportation swelled among supporters of free emigration.[18] Press in New South Wales viewed the final Report with suspicion, seeing it as a conspiracy of 'the South Australian colonizationers [*sic*]' to lift the price of land and labour in New South Wales.[19]

Molesworth, the main author of the Report, condemned transportation as 'inefficient, cruel, and demoralizing a punishment' and recommended its abolition.[20] He associated convictism with slavery, using language strikingly reminiscent of the abolitionist debates. The colonies were characterised as hotbeds of prostitution, sodomy, drunkenness and profligacy[21] – 'vice is the rule and virtue the exception'.[22] The **convict assignment** system was denounced as a 'mere lottery':[23] a convict had no way of knowing whether his or her assigned master would be kind or of good character. Molesworth remarked that a convict sent to New South Wales or Van Diemen's Land:

Convict assignment: a system by which convicts were assigned to work for free settlers or into government service in return for accommodation, food and clothing

> might be a domestic servant, well fed, well clothed, and well treated by a kind or indulgent master; he might be fortunate in obtaining a ticket of leave, or a conditional pardon, and finish his career by accumulating considerable wealth. Or he may be the wretched praedial slave of some harsh master, compelled by the lash to work, until driven to desperation, he takes to the bush, and is shot down like a beast of prey; or for some small offence is sent to work in chains, or to a penal settler, where having suffered till he can endure no longer, he commits murder in order that he may die. Between these extremes of comfort and misery, there are innumerable gradations of good and evil, in which the lot of a convict may be cast.[24]

Accounts of good fortune from 'persons who have been fortunate in the lottery of punishment' may have driven those looking for better prospects than they had at home to crime, only for them to find the opposite on arrival.[25]

The Report condemned the common practice of flogging as degrading to its convict recipients, as well as bringing about an indifference in settlers ('till the heart of the emigrant

[15] Hughes, *ibid*. See also Melbourne (n 9) 231; John Ritchie, 'Towards Ending an Unclean Thing: The Molesworth Committee and the Abolition of Transportation to New South Wales, 1837–40' (1976) 17(67) *Historical Studies* 144, 144.

[16] Edward Gibbon Wakefield, *A Letter from Sydney, the Principal Town of Australasia* (London, Joseph Cross, 1829).

[17] *Ibid* 180.

[18] Melbourne (n 9) 222–23.

[19] *Ibid* 246–7.

[20] Molesworth (n 11) iv.

[21] *Ibid* 20, 30, 35.

[22] *Ibid* 23.

[23] *Ibid* 11.

[24] *Ibid* 20.

[25] *Ibid*.

is gradually deadened to the sufferings of others, and he becomes at last as cruel as the other gaolers of these vast prisons').[26] One petition to the Committee wrote that 'the whole system of Transportation violates the feelings of the adult, barbarizes the habits, and demoralizes the principles of the rising generation, and the result is, to use the expression of a public newspaper, "Sodom and Gomorrah".'[27] The Committee's Report recommended the 'immediate discontinuance' of convict transportation to New South Wales and Van Diemen's Land.[28] Prior to the Molesworth Committee, the Whig Government was already agitating for the abolition of convict transportation in favour of penitentiaries at home.[29] The findings made in the Molesworth Committee's Report against New South Wales outraged exclusives and emancipists alike.[30]

The assignment system was replaced with a system of probation in Van Diemen's Land and Norfolk Island and a ticket of leave system continued in New South Wales.[31] The end of transportation was altogether much more gradual. In May 1840, an Order-in-Council was issued removing New South Wales as a place of convict transportation.[32] The United Kingdom continued to send convicts to Van Diemen's Land. The Whig Government of the time sought to complement imprisonment at home with transportation abroad.[33] Before being transported, convicts would undergo a period of solitary confinement and religious instruction followed by a period of hard labour.[34] The idea was to instil 'religious and work discipline'.[35] This reformed transportation system was insufficient to remove the stigma associated with transportation in the colonies.[36] Subsequent British efforts to resume convict transportation to New South Wales triggered a public protest at Circular Quay in Sydney in 1849. These convicts were nevertheless diverted to Brisbane, Ipswich and the Darling Downs.

By 1840, a healthy population of free settlers and native-born individuals encouraged public agitation for reform of the existing unrepresentative system of government in New South Wales. In 1853, transportation to Van Diemen's Land ceased. Vandemonians were increasingly resentful of the Colonial Office for reducing their colony to 'a huge cesspool, in which all the criminal filth of the British empire was to be accumulated'.[37] And, in 1855, Van Diemen's Land was renamed Tasmania. In comparison, the colony of Western Australia petitioned for convict transportation in 1849 to combat 'chronic labour shortages'.[38]

[26] *Ibid* 36.
[27] *Ibid* 37.
[28] *Ibid* 40.
[29] Hughes (n 14) 3.
[30] Harling (n 12) 84.
[31] See also Anne McKay, 'The Assignment System of Convict Labour in Van Diemen's Land 1824–1842' (MA thesis, University of Tasmania, 1958); Richard Tuffin and Martin Gibbs, '"Uninformed and Impractical"? The Convict Probation System and its Impact upon the Landscape of 1840s Van Diemen's Land' (2020) 17 *History Australia* 87; Richard Tuffin and Martin Gibbs, 'The Archaeology of the Convict Probation System: The Labor Landscapes of Port Arthur and the Cascades Probation Station, 1839–55' (2020) 24 *International Journal of Historical Archaeology* 589.
[32] Melbourne (n 9) 246.
[33] Harling (n 12) 87.
[34] *Ibid* 87–88.
[35] *Ibid* 88.
[36] *Ibid* 89.
[37] *Ibid* 94.
[38] Winston Gregory McMinn, *A Constitutional History of Australia* (Oxford, Oxford University Press, 1979) 34.

The colony had started life as the free Swan River Colony in 1829,[39] but was converted to a penal colony at the settlers' insistence in 1849.[40] Economic progress weighed more heavily on the minds of Western Australia's settlers than the achievement of self-government.[41] Despite the objections of Western Australia, the UK Government abolished penal transportation in 1865 and the last convict ship arrived in January 1868. The cessation of convict transportation, particularly in the eastern colonies, would be used to justify the introduction of responsible government to the colonies. As long as the system remained, the convict colonies were penal settlements first and foremost,[42] and responsible government was incompatible with it.[43]

The Amateur Magistracy in the Colonies

The English tradition of appointing amateur magistrates from the gentry was adopted in New South Wales. The position of magistrate or justice of the peace was a prestigious one, affording 'prized symbolic, practical and strategic advantages to those who could secure it'.[44] Following the English model of decentralised policing, colonial magistrates were directly connected with the administration of justice at a local level.[45] Lay magistrates organised and controlled the police. They exercised extensive jurisdiction over summary criminal offences as well as convict administration and discipline. The governor had the sole power to appoint and dismiss magistrates.

Between 1788 and 1810, magistrates carried out a coronial function investigating sudden, unexplained, and suspicious deaths. From 1814, they had the power to deal with small civil claims, an area in which English magistrates had no power. Governor Lachlan Macquarie appointed former convicts to the magistracy to the consternation of **exclusives** in the colony. In hearing minor criminal matters, magistrates could and did impose some heavy penalties – 500, 800 or 1,000 lashes.

Exclusives: a colonial elite of free settlers and officials who maintained rigid caste barriers against anyone with a convict connection

In England, magisterial functions were traditionally undertaken by an unpaid magistrate or justice of the peace. The considerable power the holder possessed over county districts was a significant benefit to them. Against this context, the exclusives' objections to emancipist magistrates were to some extent understandable. The position enabled the holder to participate in public life and to achieve a heightened degree of social respectability. The first stipendiary magistrate in New South Wales was Darcy Wentworth, who was appointed by Lachlan Macquarie in 1810. The appointment was not universally well-received. Darcy left London in 1790 under a cloud. As a young Irish surgeon living in

[39] The colony was renamed the Colony of Western Australia in 1832.
[40] McMinn (n 38) 34.
[41] *Ibid.*
[42] Melbourne (n 9) 227.
[43] *Ibid* 228.
[44] David Neal, 'Law and Authority: The Magistracy in New South Wales, 1788–1840' (1985) 3 *Law in Context* 45, 45–46.
[45] *Ibid* 52.

London without a private fortune, Darcy resorted to gambling and **highway robbery** to fund his lifestyle. He was tried and acquitted of highway robbery on several occasions at the Old Bailey. Darcy was discharged from a fourth charge in December 1789 because he accepted a position as assistant surgeon on the Second Fleet.[46] Concerned family and friends helped. The receipt of a government salary was the only aspect that differentiated Darcy Wentworth's commission from the commissions of other colonial magistrates. In his official role as Police Magistrate, Darcy presided over a court handling minor criminal offences. As well as being Police Magistrate, he was also Superintendent of Police in Sydney.

Highway robbery: robbery committed on or near a public road

The appointment of stipendiary magistrates was a relatively recent addition to the English legal system. It was not a very common practice in 1800. The few stipendiary magistrates that were appointed in England were all located in London. The practice of paying magistrates for their services emerged to reduce corruption among magistrates in built-up areas. By 1821, the number of appointed magistrates presiding over New South Wales and Van Diemen's Land were few. This was unfortunate, given the rising population in the colonies and the isolation of settlements from main centres. New South Wales had 26 appointed magistrates, whereas Van Diemen's Land had eight. By the 1830s, the use of paid magistrates had grown.[47]

The enormous power wielded by amateur magistrates was the subject of reform in New South Wales in the 1820s and 1830s. The creation of Courts of General or Quarter Sessions in 1823 gave magistrates jurisdiction over non-capital and convict disciplinary offences.[48] Meanwhile, single magistrates in session courts could punish convict 'misbehaviour' or 'disorderly conduct' through 'moderate punishment' of 50 lashes or three months' hard labour.[49] Single magistrates in remote districts possessed the same jurisdiction as the session courts.[50] Accusations of brutality and illegal behaviour urged the passing of legislation to indemnify magistrates from prosecution.[51] Legislation passed in 1830 tripled the number of lashes a single magistrate could order to 150 while stripping magistrates' authority to adjudicate non-capital crimes.[52] In separate legislation of the same year, magistrates could detain individuals indefinitely on the suspicion they *might* be convicts at large.[53] This confusing array of legislation was consolidated in Governor Richard Bourke's *Punishment and Summary Jurisdiction Act 1832* (NSW).[54] The 1832 Act, for example, restricted sentencing by magistrates sitting alone and reduced the maximum number of lashes that could be inflicted by a single magistrate from 150 to 50.

[46] *Ibid* 64.

[47] Alex C Castles, *An Australian Legal History* (Sydney, Law Book Co, 1982) 373.

[48] *New South Wales Act 1823* (Imp) (4 Geo 4 c 96). For an overview of this legislative history, see David Andrew Roberts, 'The "illegal sentences which magistrates were daily passing": The Backstory to Governor Richard Bourke's 1832 Punishment and Summary Jurisdiction Act in Convict New South Wales' (2017) 38 *Journal of Legal History* 231; Lisa Ford and David Andrew Roberts, 'The Convict Peace: The Imperial Context of the 1833 Convict Revolt at Castle Forbes' (2020) *Journal of Imperial and Commonwealth History* 1, 2.

[49] *Felons Absconding Act* (NSW) (6 Geo 4 no 5).

[50] *Transportation Act 1825* (Imp) (6 Geo 4 c 69).

[51] Roberts (n 48) 238; Ford and Roberts (n 48) 9.

[52] *Felons Punishment Act 1830* (NSW) (11 Geo 4 no 12); *Quarter Sessions and Justices of the Peace Act* (NSW) (11 Geo 4 no 13).

[53] *Bushranging Act 1830* (NSW) (11 Geo 4 no 10).

[54] 3 Wm 4 no 3.

Accusations of abuse of authority by local elites and dissatisfaction with the newly consolidated jurisdiction of magistrates boiled over following the Castle Forbes revolt in November 1833. On 5 November 1833, six convicts assigned to the Castle Forbes estate, owned by James Mudie, revolted. Mudie's property was located on the Hunter Valley, a frontier where relations between local elites and convicts had progressively deteriorated.[55] The convict workforce at Castle Forbes were 'served inedible meat and blackened wheat, driven too hard in their work and verbally abused and sometimes beaten by their managers'.[56] Convicts could hardly complain or expect justice when settler-magistrates colluded with fellow neighbour masters.[57] Egged on by this situation, six Castle Forbes convicts looted the station and made an attempt on the life of Mudie's overseer and son-in-law, John Larnach. The convicts took to the bush until they were caught several days later by Larnach and a group of mounted police.

Represented by Irish-born Roger Therry at trial, the convicts claimed 'that by the bad treatment, flogging and bad provisions they had to endure, they were driven to desperation, and brought to this unhappy end'.[58] They pointed to the willingness of magistrates, often pastoralists and employers of convict labour themselves, to acquiesce to pastoralists' demands for punishment.[59] Five were hanged, and the sixth exiled to Norfolk Island for life. Governor Richard Bourke instituted an inquiry into the discipline of convicts at Castle Forbes and the conduct of magistrates in the Hunter Valley. Mudie and Larnach were exonerated of ill-treatment but were criticised for the quality and quantity of rations supplied to convicts. The Castle Forbes revolt and its aftermath reinforced the importance of appointing stipendiary magistrates who were 'personally unconnected' with the district and loyal to the interests of colonial government (not local elites).[60] The use of stipendiary magistrates was harshly criticised by the Hunter Valley elite, including Mudie. Later becoming a strident critic of Bourke's administration, Mudie attributed the leniency of the 1823 Act to the revolt.

The Path to Responsible Government: 1823–50

As explored in chapter seven, New South Wales and Van Diemen's Land (the name of which changed to Tasmania in 1855) were autocratic colonies in their foundation years. Until 1823, the colonies had no form of legislature; instead, governors issued Orders and Proclamations that served as legislation. With the British Government so far away, governors exercised almost absolute control over the colonies because the governor's actions could not be immediately reviewed. At least a year's worth of travel was required before despatches were received. This section will explore the decline of the governor's autocracy and the emergence of responsible government with a particular focus on the oldest colonies. New South Wales and Van Diemen's Land.

[55] Ford and Roberts (n 48) 8.
[56] *Ibid.*
[57] *Ibid* 8–9.
[58] *R v Hitchcock* [1833] NSWSupC 114.
[59] Ford and Roberts (n 48) 2.
[60] *Ibid* 10.

Figure 8.1 Timeline of Legislation Contributing to Responsible Government in New South Wales

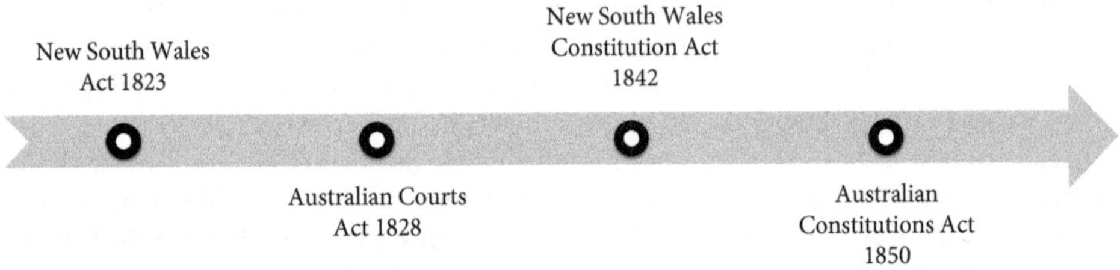

The *New South Wales Act 1823*

The *New South Wales Act 1823*,[61] authorising the Third Charter of Justice, received royal assent on 19 July 1823. It was drafted by Francis Forbes, previously Chief Justice of Newfoundland, and James Stephen of the Colonial Office. The 1823 Act, introduced in chapter seven, ushered in reforms that ended the governors' autocracy, remodelled the colonial judicial system and authorised the establishment of the first Legislative Council of New South Wales.

The Third Charter created, by Letters Patent, a Supreme Court of New South Wales and a Supreme Court of Van Diemen's Land as courts of record.[62] Each court would have 'one judge or chief justice'.[63] The Supreme Court of New South Wales would be constituted by a single Chief Justice of five years' standing, who would be entitled to an annual salary of £2,000.[64] By section 8, Francis Forbes was appointed first Chief Justice of the Supreme Court. The number of judges for either court could be increased from one to three where 'expedient'.[65] The courts would comprise other officers – including a registrar, **prothonotary**, master and keeper of records – that were 'necessary for the administration of justice'.[66]

Prothonotary: principal clerk of a court

The Act clarified the criminal and civil jurisdiction of these two courts.[67] The Supreme Courts would 'have cognizance of all pleas, civil, criminal, or mixed, and jurisdiction in all cases whatsoever' as fully as the courts at Westminster.[68] They were 'courts of Oyer and Terminer, and general gaol delivery'.[69] By section 3, the courts had jurisdiction to hear 'all treasons, piracies, felonies, robberies, murders, conspiracies and other offences of what nature or kind soever committee'. Section 4 provided that 'all crimes, misdemeanors, and offences cognizable in the said courts … shall be prosecuted by information in the name of his Majesty's attorney-general, or other office duly appointed for such purpose by the governor'. Significantly, prosecutions would be brought by the attorney-general, and not by the Judge-Advocate. Moreover, criminal trials would be in the presence of the Chief Judge

[61] 4 Geo 4 c 96.
[62] *New South Wales Act 1823* (UK) s 2.
[63] *Ibid* s 1.
[64] *Ibid* ss 1, 2 and 5.
[65] *Ibid* s 1.
[66] *Ibid* s 9.
[67] *Ibid* ss 2, 3, 9, 10, 11.
[68] *Ibid* s 2.
[69] *Ibid.* See chapter two of this volume.

and a jury of seven commissioned military officers.[70] The office of Judge-Advocate, who acted as prosecutor and judge, was no more. Civil actions were to be tried by the Chief Judge and two assessors 'being magistrates or justices of the peace in and for the said colony'.[71] The Supreme Courts were given equitable and ecclesiastical jurisdiction together with jurisdiction in debt.[72]

The 1823 Act established limited legislatures for New South Wales and Van Diemen's Land. The Legislative Council would consist of five to seven members appointed by the King.[73] The Act empowered the governor 'to make laws and ordinances for the welfare and good government of the said colony'.[74] Nevertheless, governors carried immense power under this Act with few restraints. Only the governor could introduce legislation. He could also bring that legislation into force, even if only one Council member agreed, should that be required for the 'peace and safety' of the colony.[75] Still, the Chief Justice had the power to veto proposed legislation that he considered repugnant to the laws of England. Before colonial legislation became law, the Chief Justice had to certify that 'such proposed Law is not repugnant to the Laws of England, but is consistent with such Laws, so far as the Circumstances of the said Colony will admit'.[76] All laws and ordinances had to be laid before British Parliament, which had a power of disallowance to be exercised within three years of enactment.[77] The governor had to consult the Legislative Council but could in exceptional circumstances (specifically, 'rebellion and insurrection' having 'broken out') act without the Legislative Council's advice.[78]

Section 44 provided for the separation of Van Diemen's Land from New South Wales. The 1823 Act contained a five-year **sunset clause**,[79] which was extended for one year.

Sunset clause: a legislative provision providing that a piece of legislation will expire on or by a certain date or time

Historical Cameo

Sir Richard Bourke

Sir Richard Bourke (1777–1855) was Acting Governor of the Cape of Good Hope (1826–28) and the eighth Governor of New South Wales (1831–37). As a colonial administrator, Bourke had a reputation as a humanitarian with liberal Whig sympathies. Modern historians have, however, portrayed Bourke in a more nuanced way;[80]

[70] *Ibid* s 4.
[71] *Ibid* s 6.
[72] *Ibid* ss 9–11.
[73] *Ibid* s 24.
[74] *Ibid.*
[75] *Ibid.*
[76] *Ibid* s 29.
[77] *Ibid* ss 30, 31.
[78] *Ibid* s 25.
[79] *Ibid* s 45. It continued in force until 1 July 1827.
[80] Frank Bongiorno, 'Sir Richard Bourke (3 December 1831–5 December 1837)' in David Clune and Ken Turner (eds), *The Governors of New South Wales: 1788–2010* (Federation Press, 2009) 167, 167.

for example, his paradoxical treatment of Indigenous peoples in Africa and Australia have been highlighted.

Born in Dublin to a Protestant Irish family, Bourke was educated at Westminster School, London and at Oriel College and Exeter College, Oxford. In 1798, he graduated with a Bachelor of Arts from Oxford. Though he read for the Bar, Bourke joined the British Army in November 1798. Rising through the ranks, he was promoted to Lieutenant and Captain (1799), to Major (1805) and to Lieutenant-Colonel.

Figure 8.2 Portrait of Sir Richard Bourke
Mitchell Library, State Library of New South Wales, P2/355, IE3283042.

Bourke's wife, Betsy, experienced bouts of ill health throughout his career, prompting Bourke to seek appointments to warmer climates. In one case, Bourke disappointed the Duke of Wellington, Sir Arthur Wellesley, by returning to England to care for his sick wife.[81] After the Peninsular War ended, Bourke retired from the British Army on **half pay** and withdrew to his Irish estate. He educated his children, managed and improved his estate, and engaged in public life. By 1825, however, Bourke was seeking an appointment to a better climate not only for Betsy's health but to enlarge his income.[82]

Selected for a military post in Malta, Bourke was instead appointed as Lieutenant-Governor of the Eastern Cape in South Africa. This appointment had been brought on by the Cape Governor's autocratic administration of the colony. The Governor, Lord Charles Somerset, had returned to London to defend himself. In 1826, Bourke arrived in the Cape Colony as Acting Governor. Bourke instituted several administrative and legislative reforms. Bourke's predecessor, Somerset, had stifled freedom of the press.[83] The legal system was reformed. Roman-Dutch law, subsisting after British rule returned in 1806, and the common law now worked alongside one another.[84] A jury system was brought in. Inferior civil and criminal courts were established. Not all

Half pay: British army and naval officers, who were either retired or not on active service, received half their original pay

[81] *Ibid* 169.
[82] *Ibid.*
[83] *Ibid* 170.
[84] *Ibid.*

were happy with Bourke's reforms. The Afrikaaner population were enflamed by Bourke's 'native policy', which aimed to limit frontier violence.[85] Bourke left the Cape Colony in September 1828. He returned to his Irish estate, but later accepted an appointment as Governor of New South Wales.

On 3 December 1831, Bourke arrived in Sydney to excited crowds. Betsy, who had been in poor health on the voyage over, died in May 1832. Despite opposition from exclusives, Bourke's casting vote on a bill permitting emancipists to sit as jurors in civil trials passed into law in July 1833.[86] The *Summary Punishment Act* or 'Fifty Lashes Act' was also introduced to streamline convict punishment and the summary jurisdiction exercised by colonial magistrates.[87] The Act restricted the sentence that could be imposed by a single magistrate to 50 lashes. Apart from 50 lashes, magistrates could punish convicts with the **treadmill**, two months' imprisonment with hard labour, or solitary confinement on bread and water for two weeks – still harsh by any measure![88]

Treadmill: a device introduced to Sydney in 1823 as a form of convict punishment. Convicts would work the treadmill or treadwheel by continuously stepping on a series of wooden planks to power wheels often used to grind grain or pump water

Bourke's approach to Aboriginal Australians brought together, as Bongiorno wrote, 'Christian piety, humanitarianism, paternalism and faith in the virtues of capitalist enterprise and the British Empire'.[89]

He believed Aboriginals could scale up the social hierarchy through intermarriage with 'lower class whites'.[90] Despite that, Bourke responded to news of violence against Aboriginals by issuing proclamations and launching inquiries. He warned settlers that violence and killings would not be tolerated nor would the sexual exploitation of Aboriginal women – endemic in remote districts.[91]

Following a row over the candidate for chair of the Quarter Sessions, Bourke resigned his governorship. He left New South Wales in late 1837. He returned to his estate in Ireland where he died in 1855.

Australian Courts Act 1828

Following its expiration on 1 July 1828, the *New South Wales Act 1823* was replaced by the *Australian Courts Act 1828* (Imp).[92] The 1828 Act, though largely concerned with the judicial system, included provisions touching on the legislative and executive functions of

[85] *Ibid* 170.
[86] *Ibid* 172–73.
[87] *Offenders Punishment and Justices Summary Jurisdiction Act 1832* (3 Wm IV, No 3). See also Roberts (n 48) 237
[88] Bongiorno (n 80) 174.
[89] *Ibid* 177.
[90] *Ibid.*
[91] *Ibid* 177–78.
[92] 9 Geo 4, c 83.

government in the colony (as well as the imposition of taxes and appropriation of revenues).[93] The Governor and Legislative Council were authorised to make laws and ordinances for the 'peace, welfare and good government' of the colony.[94] The number of Legislative Council members was increased to between ten and 15 members appointed by the Crown.[95] Seats would be apportioned between official and non-official members at the Crown's discretion.[96] In practice, non-official members of the Legislative Council were selected from the exclusive caste of colonial society, though this had not been the Colonial Secretary's 'pious hope'.[97] Still, the new Act encouraged public discussion of legislative proposals before the Council.[98] The Governor was required to advertise legislative proposals in the press 'at least eight clear days' before he presented them to the Council.[99] Special urgency was the only exception to this requirement.[100] The Governor no longer had the power to pass laws without the Legislative Council's consent; a majority of Council members could veto the Governor's proposed legislation.

Moreover, the earlier requirement of the Chief Justice's certificate was substituted with the less divisive requirement that all legislation be enrolled and recorded at the Supreme Court within seven days of its enactment.[101] At this point, the three judges constituting the Supreme Court had 14 days within which to protest its repugnancy to the laws of England.[102] The Governor was required to suspend the operation of the law and present it to the Legislative Council for revision.[103] The Council could reject the protest and re-enact the legislation, subject to the decision of Imperial Government.[104]

Trial by jury was placed on a surer footing by the 1828 Act. The Supreme Court was given the discretion to allow trial by jury in civil matters upon the application of either party.[105] In criminal matters, though, trial by jury was suspended in the Court of Quarter Sessions until it was established in the Supreme Court.[106] Military juries for criminal trials, provided for in the 1823 Act, continued.[107] Importantly, the Governor received authorisation to introduce trial by jury in criminal matters in the future.[108] This occurred in 1833 in New South Wales. Further changes were made to the colonial judicial system. Appeals to the Supreme Court were to be taken to the Crown-in-Council as opposed to the Governor.[109] Sections 17 and 18 enabled the Governor and Legislative Council to create Courts of Requests and Courts of General and Quarter Sessions.[110]

[93] Melbourne (n 9) 152.
[94] *Australian Courts Act 1828* s 21. See also Melbourne (n 9) 153–54.
[95] *Ibid* s 20.
[96] Melbourne (n 9) 153.
[97] McMinn (n 38) 26; Melbourne (n 9) 157.
[98] *Ibid.*
[99] *Australian Courts Act 1828* s 21. See also McMinn (n 38) 26; Melbourne (n 9) 153.
[100] Melbourne (n 9) 153.
[101] McMinn (n 38) 26; Melbourne (n 9) 158.
[102] *Ibid.*
[103] *Australian Courts Act 1828* s 22. See also Melbourne (n 9) 158.
[104] *Ibid.*
[105] *Australian Courts Act 1828* s 8.
[106] Melbourne (n 9) 162.
[107] *Australian Courts Act 1828* s 5.
[108] *Ibid* s 6. See also Melbourne (n 9) 161.
[109] *Ibid* s 15. See also Melbourne (n 9) 161.
[110] Melbourne (n 9) 162.

New South Wales Constitution Act 1842

Two years after the cessation of convict transportation, New South Wales was given a form of representative government under the *New South Wales Constitution Act 1842* (Imp).[111] The 1842 Act granted the colony a partly elective legislative body but not full responsible government. Indeed, the Governor held the 'purse strings'.[112] The 1828 Act set out what sums would be set aside from the consolidated revenue for public 'services and purposes' as outlined in annexed schedules.[113] Under the *Waste Lands Act 1842*, land revenue was 'appropriated and applied' to the public service, placing it outside the hands of the Legislative Council, and one half of the proceeds appropriated to defray the cost of emigration.[114]

The Legislative Council, first established under the 1823 Act, would now comprise 36 members, 12 of whom would be Crown-appointed and 24 elected.[115] Of the remaining elected members, five would be from the Port Phillip District in Victoria and one from the town of Melbourne. To stand for Parliament, a candidate had to 'be of the full age of twenty-one years', a natural-born or **naturalised** British subject and meet certain property requirements.[116] The property requirements were set at either possession of freehold worth £2,000 or £100 per year.[117] Men over the age of 21 were qualified to vote if they possessed freehold valued at £200 or occupied a house worth £20 per year.[118] However, this qualification had to be held for at least 'six calendar months' before the date of election.[119] Only British subjects were qualified to vote.[120] Convicts who were yet to receive a pardon or finish their sentence could not vote.[121]

Naturalisation: a non-British person resident in the Australian colonies could become a citizen on application to the appropriate colonial authorities

At least one session of the Legislative Council was to be held annually.[122] The time and place of the meeting would be determined by the Governor,[123] who was given the power to **prorogue** or dissolve the Legislative Council.[124] The Council was required to appoint its own Speaker, subject to the Governor's supervision,[125] and develop its own standing rules and orders 'for the orderly conduct of business', subject to the Governor's approval and the Crown's confirmation or disallowance.[126] The Governor and Legislative Council were empowered 'to make laws for the peace welfare and good government of the said colony' provided the law was not repugnant to the laws of England

Prorogue: to terminate a current session of Parliament

[111] 5 & 6 Vic c 76.
[112] Melbourne (n 9) 272–73.
[113] *New South Wales Constitution Act 1842* ss 33–38.
[114] *Waste Lands Act 1842* (5 & 6 Vic c 36) s 19.
[115] *New South Wales Constitution Act 1842* s 1.
[116] *Ibid* s 8.
[117] *Ibid.*
[118] *Ibid* ss 5–6.
[119] *Ibid* s 7.
[120] *Ibid* s 6.
[121] *Ibid.*
[122] *Ibid* s 21.
[123] *Ibid* s 20.
[124] *Ibid* s 21.
[125] *Ibid* s 23.
[126] *Ibid* s 27.

nor interfere with the sale or appropriation of Crown land or revenue 'thence arising'.[127] The Governor was empowered to submit bills to the Council for its consideration and suggest amendments to bills of the Legislative Council.[128] When presented with a bill for royal assent, the Governor could assent, withhold assent, or reserve bills 'for the signification of her Majesty's pleasure thereon'.[129] Bills meeting a certain description were specifically reserved, including bills 'altering or affecting' electoral divisions.[130] The Crown could disallow colonial legislation within two years of enactment.[131] Other provisions of the 1828 Act dealt with government expenditure, salaries of government officials, local government, and anticipated the future subdivision of New South Wales.[132] The Act had no application to Van Diemen's Land, unsurprisingly given that convict transportation continued there for another decade. In contrast to New South Wales, Van Diemen's Land still had a nominated Legislative Council.

Historical Cameo

William Charles Wentworth

William Charles Wentworth (1790–1872) was an explorer, landowner, barrister and politician. He was born to a female convict, Catherine Crowley, in August 1790. Darcy Wentworth, a young Irish surgeon, acknowledged William Charles as his son. Darcy narrowly avoided a charge of highway robbery by joining the Second Fleet as Assistant Surgeon. Despite the patronage of William Wentworth, 4th Earl Fitzwilliam (a distant relative), Darcy was excluded from exclusive society – a slight that apparently wounded William Charles for the rest of his life.[133] After Catherine's death in 1800, Darcy sent his three sons by this union to England for their education.

Figure 8.3 J Anderson, *William Charles Wentworth* (1872)

Mitchell Library, State Library of New South Wales, ML 411, IE3241368.

William Charles returned to Sydney in 1810. In 1813, he crossed the Blue Mountains together with William Lawson, Gregory Blaxland, a party of convicts and Aboriginal guides, opening up land to grazing.[134] Wentworth returned to England in 1816. In 1817, it emerged that Wentworth was responsible for satirical verse lampooning the colony's Lieutenant-Governor, Colonel Molle,

[127] *Ibid* s 29.
[128] *Ibid* s 30.
[129] *Ibid* s 31.
[130] *Ibid.*
[131] *Ibid* s 32.
[132] Melbourne (n 9) 271–74.
[133] Melbourne (n 9) 63. See also McMinn (n 38) 16.
[134] Melbourne (n 9) 65.

published shortly after his departure from Sydney. Wentworth entered Middle Temple in 1817 to qualify as a barrister. Once his training was complete, Wentworth intended to practise in New South Wales. He was called to the Bar in 1822, studied at Cambridge for a short time, and returned to New South Wales in 1823.

Historians traditionally divide early colonial society into two opposing factions: the exclusives and the emancipists. The exclusives were free immigrants, many of whom occupied non-official positions of power and enjoyed substantial land grants. The emancipists were ex-convicts, their families and supporters. By population, the emancipists substantially outnumbered the exclusives. By the 1830s, many of the emancipists' leaders were educated radicals and professionals. Because of their radicalism, the leaders had reached a point of no return with important colonial and British figures. Tainted by their pasts, ex-convicts were generally excluded from positions of power and opportunities for advancement afforded to the exclusives. The exclusives opposed the appointment of ex-convicts to official positions, such as membership on juries or the magistracy. The two factions found common ground in opposing the autocratic power of the Governor.

In 1819, Wentworth published his first book, *A Statistical, Historical, and Political Description of the Colony of New South Wales*. Wentworth argued for a bicameral legislature, trial by jury, and representative government in New South Wales. He slammed the colony's exclusives, describing them as

> a party in the colony, by whom the very notion of granting such a privilege [standing for parliament] to a class of men who have been subject to the lash of the law, would be treated as a chimera pregnant with the most fatal consequences to this infant community.[135]

The sentiment was to treat convictism as a 'hereditary deformity', passed 'down from father to son … an eternal barrier of separation between their offspring, and the offspring of the unfortunate convict'.[136] Wentworth published subsequent editions of the book. In the third edition, Wentworth criticised the inadequacies of the 1823 Act, condemning its Crown-appointed Legislative Council as a 'wretched mongrel substitute for a Legislative Assembly'.[137] While Wentworth was convinced New South Wales was ready for responsible government, it would take many more years for this to be achieved.

In 1824, Wentworth partnered with his Cambridge friend and fellow barrister, Dr Robert Wardell, to found the colony's first independent newspaper, *The Australian* (1824–48). Neither Wentworth nor Wardell sought official permission to publish the newspaper. The new Governor Sir Thomas Brisbane allowed the 'experiment', thinking freedom of the press 'has been productive of more benefit than disadvantage to the public'.[138]

[135] William Charles Wentworth, *A Statistical, Historical, and Political Description of the Colony of New South Wales*, 1st edn (London, G & WB Whittaker, 1819) 346.
[136] *Ibid* 348.
[137] William Charles Wentworth, *A Statistical Account of the British Settlements of Australasia*, 3rd edn (London, Geo B Whittaker, 1824) 323. See Melbourne (n 9) 126.
[138] Melbourne (n 9) 128.

The Australian's nearest competitor, *The Sydney Gazette*, started as a government publication in 1803 and was heavily censored.[139] Wentworth and Wardell's paper, which consistently poured scorn on colonial and imperial authority, paved the way for other colonial newspapers to be established.[140] The next Governor, Ralph Darling, was not as receptive of the free press.

In 1825, Wentworth represented the daughter of two ex-convicts, Sarah Cox, in the first Supreme Court action for a breach of a promise to marry against Captain John Payne. Cox succeeded. The case gained notoriety for another reason altogether: it became apparent that Wentworth and Cox were lovers and Cox was carrying Wentworth's first child, Thomasine. Before marrying in 1829, Wentworth and Cox had a second child together. A month before the wedding, Wentworth published a poem for Sarah in *The Australian*: 'For I must love thee, love thee on, 'Till life's remotest latest minute'.[141] Sarah Wentworth was, at the time of the marriage, eight months' pregnant with the third of the couple's ten children. Sarah and her daughters were socially ostracised, encouraging the Wentworths to leave New South Wales for England from 1853 to 1861.[142] Within months of marrying Sarah,[143] Wentworth fathered a son by Jemima Eagar, the wife of emancipist solicitor Edward Eagar who had abandoned her and their children in 1823.

In 1835, Wentworth made possible the establishment of the London-based Australian Patriotic Association to lobby, among other things, for representative government and land legislation.[144] In 1840, Wentworth withdrew from public life, humiliated that Governor George Gipps invalidated his transaction to buy all of New Zealand's South Island 'at the rate of four hundred acres for a penny'.[145] He returned to political life only after the *New South Wales Act 1842* was enacted and Parliament reconstituted under the statute assembled. Despite early challenges with the colony's exclusives, Wentworth lamented the 'spirit of democracy' permeating New South Wales after the *Australian Constitutions Act 1850* (Imp) extended the franchise.[146] By 1850 Wentworth was the wealthiest man in New South Wales. He narrowly won an election in 1851 but, according to Governor Fitzroy, alienated himself from newly enfranchised voters with his 'high and offensive' tone and contempt for the 'lower class of voters'.[147] In 1853, Wentworth chaired a select committee to draft a constitution for responsible self-government in New South Wales. The proposed constitution envisaged a bicameral parliament with an elected lower house, the Legislative Assembly, and a nominated upper house, the Legislative Council.

[139] *Ibid.*
[140] *Ibid.*
[141] William Charles Wentworth, 'To Sarah' *The Australian* (Sydney, 23 September 1829) 3.
[142] Sarah and her daughters preferred London society over the 'viperish nastiness' of Sydney's social scene. See Peter Cochrane, *Colonial Ambition: Foundations of Australian Democracy* (Melbourne, Melbourne University Press, 2006) 398–99.
[143] And seemingly incongruent with his public declarations of love for Sarah!
[144] Melbourne (n 9) 207–09.
[145] New South Wales, *Parliamentary Debates*, Legislative Chamber, 9 July 1840, 30 (Sir George Gipps).
[146] 13 & 14 Vic c 54. See Melbourne (n 9) 381–82.
[147] Melbourne (n 9) 381–82.

The use of a nominated upper house was controversial as was Wentworth's enthusiasm for a hereditary peerage scheme. The proposal was lambasted as 'a bunyip aristocracy'.[148] Fully responsible government was granted in 1856.

Wentworth died in England. His body was returned to Sydney and interred in the family vault at Vaucluse House.

Australian Constitutions Act 1850

Demands from the Port Phillip District for separation from New South Wales and colonists in Tasmania and South Australia for representative government precipitated the passage of the *Australian Constitutions Act 1850*. The 1850 Act provided for the separation of the Port Phillip District from New South Wales to form the separate colony of Victoria.[149] This separation took effect on 1 July 1851. The 1850 Act extended the form of government introduced to New South Wales by the 1842 Act to Van Diemen's Land, South Australia and Victoria. The Governors and Legislative Councils of these colonies were authorised to make laws for the 'Peace, Welfare, and good Government' of the colony with the usual repugnancy condition.[150]

Statutory provisions concerning the appropriation of government revenue for public services were an enduring point of contention for some New South Wales inhabitants.[151] The members of its colonial legislature expected revenue earned in New South Wales would be the subject of legislative supervision in New South Wales.[152] For years, frustrations had been brewing in New South Wales over land laws and the cost borne by the colony for police and jails.[153] The 1850 reforms were not enough to sate the settlers' desire for responsible government.

The 1850 Act expanded the franchise and increased the powers of the Legislative Council. The qualifications and disqualifications of electors and elective members of the Legislative Council were maintained.[154] The levels of the 1842 franchise were, however, halved. Thus, in the four colonies, electors were qualified to vote with £100 worth of freehold or occupation of a house worth £10 per year. In addition, holders of depasturing licences and leaseholders of a certain value (£10 per year) and duration (more than three years left) were entitled to vote.[155] The existing legislatures of Van Diemen's Land and South Australia were authorised to establish Legislative Councils of 24 members, two-thirds of whom would be elected.[156] Western Australia would be able to establish a similar Legislative Council on the petition

[148] This was the moniker used in a speech given by Daniel Deniehy on 15 August 1853. Deniehy mocked the scheme's promoters as 'these harlequin aristocrats, these Botany Bay magnificos, these Australian Mandarins'.
[149] *Ibid* s 1.
[150] *Ibid* s 14.
[151] *Ibid* ss 14–19.
[152] Melbourne (n 9) 380.
[153] McMinn (n 38) 39.
[154] *Australian Constitutions Act 1850* s 12.
[155] *Ibid* s 4.
[156] *Ibid* s 7.

of one-third of its inhabitants.[157] Provision was made for the separation of the northern part of New South Wales.[158] Control over local government, the judiciary and the scale of tariffs were three areas over which the colonies' Legislative Councils were granted increased power.

Most importantly of all, the new legislatures were entitled to pass laws to change the composition of the Legislative Council and 'to establish … instead of the Legislative Council, a Council and a House of Representatives, or other separate Legislative Houses'.[159] The bills introducing these measures would be reserved for the Crown's consideration. In December 1852, the new Colonial Secretary, Sir John Pakington, wrote to the Governors of New South Wales, Victoria and South Australia persuading them to draft constitutions with bicameral legislatures. Bills were submitted to London for approval. When the colonial constitutions came into effect in October 1856, each provided for a bicameral legislature – a legislature divided between two chambers. All but one colony chose an elected, rather than nominated, upper house. To protect landed interests, New South Wales settled upon a nominated Upper House. The remaining four colonies were to have elected Legislative Councils. The Constitutions afforded greater autonomy over land and finance in the colony. These Constitutions paved the way for this system of government to apply to Western Australia and the proposed colony of Queensland.

Representative and Responsible Government from 1850

In early 1851, gold was discovered near Bathurst in New South Wales. The resulting gold rush improved government coffers and substantially increased the colonial population. Responsible government beckoned. Now, the Colonial Office was more prepared than ever before to relinquish control over land policy and revenue from land sales to the colonies. By 1859, five of the six separate British colonies in Australia had achieved responsible government.

Colonial governance was placed on a similar footing to British political arrangements. The Governor acted as the British Crown's representative. He constituted an Executive Council comprising Members of Parliament who were also Ministers of the Crown. Second, the colonial constitutions created parliaments with two chambers: an upper house (the Legislative Council) and a lower house (the Legislative Assembly or House of Assembly). The lower houses in New South Wales, Victoria, Tasmania and South Australia were elected by voters satisfying certain property or educational qualifications. Eligibility to vote was set at a higher level for the upper house. In New South Wales, members of the upper house were appointed. Patterns of membership and the franchise were key differences between the colonial constitutions. The power of colonial parliament, though enlarged, was still limited by the doctrine of repugnancy to the laws of England. That did not prevent colonial legislatives from introducing progressive legislation including, for example, legislation protecting widows and children from disinheritance.

[157] *Ibid* s 9.
[158] *Ibid* s 34.
[159] *Ibid* s 32.

Pause for Thought

Innovation in Colonial South Australia

In January 1858, South Australia's first parliament under its *Constitution Act 1856*[160] passed the *Real Property Act 1858*.[161] All land transferred in South Australia after 1 July 1858 was to be registered under this new regime.

The Government was to maintain a central register recording all changes to land title. Registration secured **indefeasibility of title** subject to limited exceptions.[162] The system, commonly called Torrens title after one of its chief architects, was soon adopted in all other Australian colonies.

Indefeasibility of title: a central characteristic of Torrens title meaning that a registered proprietor's interest in land is not liable to be set aside subject to limited exceptions including fraud.

The old system of land transfer required an unbroken chain of title deeds as evidence of title. It was a cumbersome, expensive and, by no means, secure way of transferring title. Robert Torrens, the sponsor of the 1858 Act, had been exposed to the inefficiencies of the old system as Registrar-General of Land in South Australia. Australian historians largely agree that Dr Ulrich Hübbe, a German lawyer from Hamburg and South Australian emigrant, provided the model for the Torrens system.[163] Esposito argues that Hamburg's land law was the main model for the Torrens system, though inevitably adapted to better suit South Australian conditions.[164] German settlers in South Australia celebrated the Torrens system as 'a German child'.[165]

Figure 8.4 Men, Women and Children at the Tanunda Real Property Act Festival

T Muller, *An albumen paper carte de visite photograph showing part of the Tanunda Real Property Act Festival, held on 30 October 1862* (1862).

State Library of South Australia, B 77783.

[160] *Constitution Act 1857* (SA).
[161] *Real Property Act 1858* (SA).
[162] *Ibid* s 33.
[163] Antonio Esposito, 'Ulrich Hübbe's Role in the Creation of the Torrens System of Land Registration in South Australia' (2003) 24 *Adelaide Law Review* 263, 269–70, 301–03. See generally Antonio Esposito, 'A Comparison of the Australian (Torrens) System of Land Registration of 1858 and the Law of Hamburg in the 1850s' (2003) 7 *Australian Journal of Legal History* 193; *cf* Greg Taylor, 'Is the Torrens System German?' (2008) 29 *Journal of Legal History* 253; Greg Taylor, 'The Torrens System – Definitely Not German' (2009) 30 *Adelaide Law Review* 195.
[164] Esposito, 'A Comparison' (n 163) 211, 228–29.
[165] *Ibid* 266.

Putting the thorny question of authorship to one side, the system was revolutionary because:

1. Title to land passed by its registration on a State-maintained public register as opposed to the execution of deeds.
2. Evidence of title was proved through a certificate of title not, as it had been, by an unbroken chain of deeds.
3. The original certificate remained with the Registry; the registered owner received a duplicate copy from the register book.
4. Once registered, the title of the registered proprietor was indefeasible.
5. Innocent dealers in registered land were assured their interest in that land or monetary compensation.

Issues with the South Australian scheme demanded amendments in 1858, 1860 and 1861.[166] Queensland, the first of the Australian colonies to follow the Torrens scheme, adopted South Australia's unreformed real property legislation in 1861.[167] Victoria, Tasmania and New South Wales embraced the second tranche of Torrens' reforms.[168] Western Australia followed in 1874.[169] Two South Australian judges, Mr Justice Benjamin Boothby and Justice Gwynne, resisted the Torrens system. Boothby remains the only South Australian judge to be dismissed from office.

Bicameralism

A bicameral legislature is a characteristic feature of the Westminster system of government. When invited to draft constitutions, the Australian colonies chose to be governed by an elected lower house and, by and large, an elected upper house. The nominated upper houses of New South Wales and Queensland were designed to operate as a check on the actions of the elected lower house and to protect the interests of the landed elite. The use of nominated upper houses in these colonies was clearly modelled after the House of Lords,[170] comprising unelected hereditary peers. Although that remains the case, today not all hereditary peers are entitled to membership of the House of Lords. Membership is restricted to 92 hereditary peers.[171]

Separation, Responsible Government and Unicameralism in Queensland

In 1859, Queensland separated from New South Wales. British officials and convicts had arrived in the region now known as Queensland as far back as 1824 when the Moreton Bay

[166] *Real Property Law Amendment Act 1858* (SA); *Real Property Act 1860* (SA); *Real Property Act 1861* (SA).

[167] *Real Property Act 1861* (Qld).

[168] *Real Property Act 1862* (Vic); *Land Titles Act 1862* (Tas); *Real Property Act* 1863 (NSW).

[169] *Transfer of Land Act 1874* (WA). The Northern Territory and the Australian Capital Territory were not established until 1911 and 1910 respectively.

[170] Justin Harding, 'A Tale of Two Chambers: Bicameralism in Queensland 1860–85' (2000) 17(6) *Journal of the Royal Historical Society of Queensland* 247, 248.

[171] See *House of Lords Act 1999* (UK).

penal settlement was created as a place of secondary punishment. Because Moreton Bay was a penal station, settlers were specifically banned until 1842. Following the settlement's closure in 1842, the Moreton Bay area was opened to free settlers. Judges and magistrates were soon appointed to the Northern Districts or Moreton Bay District of New South Wales. The *Moreton Bay Supreme Court Act 1857* (NSW) set up a permanent Supreme Court at Moreton Bay. The groundwork for establishing Queensland and its government was laid by New South Wales' 1842, 1850 and 1855 Constitutions. The 1842 Act provided that separate colonies could be established within the existing boundaries of New South Wales using letters patent issued by the Privy Council.

This provision was maintained in section 7 of the 1855 Act. On 6 June 1859, the Privy Council issued an Order-in-Council and Letters Patent by which a new colony named Queensland was founded.[172] Sir George Ferguson Bowen was appointed as the new colony's Governor. The Letters Patent described the borders of Queensland. The Order-in-Council established a bicameral legislature that reflected the system in New South Wales and defined the authority of the Governor who was invested with the power 'to make laws, and to provide for the administrative of justice in the said Colony'. Queensland's new Parliament was given the power to make laws for the peace, welfare, and good government of the colony. Formal separation occurred on the publication of Letters Patent in New South Wales on 1 December 1859 and Queensland on 10 December 1859. On 10 December 1859, the first Governor of Queensland, Sir George Ferguson Bowen, arrived in Brisbane to proclaim the new colony. The Order-in-Council and Letters Patent were publicly read. The Supreme Court of Queensland was established under the *Supreme Court Constitution Amendment Act 1861. Queensland's Constitution Act 1867* consolidated the earlier New South Wales legislation, the 1859 Order-in-Council and other Queensland legislation to clear up issues surrounding the colonial legislature and gubernatorial power.

Queensland has the distinction of being the only State parliament in Australia with a unicameral parliamentary system. Between 1859 and 1922, Queensland had two Houses of Parliament: an elected Legislative Assembly and a nominated Legislative Council. The Legislative Council was abolished under the Theodore Labour Government in 1922. The Legislative Council abolished itself. The first members of the Legislative Council were initially appointed for five years with all subsequent appointments made for life. Because it was unpaid, Council membership was restricted to moneyed settlers capable of affording the necessary trips to and from Brisbane. Early in the life of the Queensland Legislative Council, its members were described in an anonymous letter to the editor as 'brainless gobemouches, political drones, and servile renegades, tools of the ministry, or hangers-on to the skirts of the Governor – needy vampires waiting to suck the nation's blood'.[173]

From the early twentieth century, the Labour Party moved to abolish the nominated Legislative Council. During the term of Labour Premier TJ Ryan (1915–19), the Council routinely rejected or substantially amended bills originating in the Legislative Assembly. Bills attempting to reform or abolish the Legislative Council were likewise futile because, unsurprisingly, they were rejected in the upper house. A referendum held in 1917 to abolish this chamber failed. Ryan's replacement, 'Red' Ted Theodore, adopted a different, and ultimately effective, strategy to abolish the Legislative Council. Once the Theodore Labour

[172] These documents are available on the foundingdocs.gov.au website.

[173] 'Letters to the Editor' *The Courier* (Brisbane, 12 August 1861) 2.

Government had swamped the Council with Labour members, the new nominees, describing themselves as the 'suicide club',[174] passed the Constitution Act Amendment Bill 1922. The Legislative Council was no more. In 1934, Queensland Parliament passed the *Constitution Act Amendment Act 1934* making it extremely difficult to reinstate the Legislative Council. A referendum is required.[175]

Historical Cameo

Alfred James Peter Lutwyche

Alfred Lutwyche (1810–80) was the Resident Judge at Moreton Bay (1859–61), Justice of the Supreme Court of Queensland (1861–80) and Acting Chief Justice of the Supreme Court of Queensland (1879). Lutwyche was, by most accounts, 'a good Judge'.[176]

Born in London to a prosperous leather merchant, Lutwyche was educated at Charterhouse and Oxford. In 1831, he was admitted to Middle Temple. Reading law at Gray's Inn, Lutwyche was called to the Bar in 1840. He practised as a barrister on the Oxford circuit. During the 1830s, he was a law reporter on the staff of the *Morning Herald*. He also reported on parliamentary debates. Due to declining health, Lutwyche accepted a position as the *Morning Chronicle's* correspondent in Sydney. In June 1853, he sailed for Australia on the *Meridian*. On the journey to Australia, however, the *Meridian* was shipwrecked on Amsterdam Island in the southern Indian Ocean.[177] The *Meridian* survivors were taken to Mauritius. On 30 December 1853, Lutwyche finally arrived in Sydney. Upon being admitted to the colonial Bar, he relinquished his correspondent position. He soon became Solicitor-General (1857) and Attorney-General of New South Wales (1858–59). In 1855, he married a widow, Mary Morris, at Sydney. On 21 February 1859, Lutwyche was appointed resident Supreme Court judge at Moreton Bay.

After the separation of Queensland, Lutwyche's early years in the colony were marked by hostilities with the legislature and executive. He was quick to point out the executive's errors following separation. The Order-in-Council establishing Queensland had, for example, removed the right to vote for men over 21 (see Detour below) and reduced Lutwyche's salary from £2,000. In response, the Queensland legislature withdrew Lutwyche's commission substituting it with another, setting his salary at £1,200. After some political jockeying, Lutwyche's salary was returned to £2,000.

On 23 February 1863, James Cockle took his seat as first Chief Justice of the Supreme Court of Queensland. Cockle's wise counsel to his new colleague, Lutwyche, probably

[174] 'The Suicide Club' *Brisbane Courier* (Brisbane, 13 March 1922) 6.
[175] Constitution Act Amendment Act 1934 (Qld) s 3.
[176] John Michael Bennett, *Sir James Cockle: First Chief Justice of Queensland, 1863–1879* (Annandale, Federation Press, 2003) 19.
[177] Alfred JP Lutwyche, *A Narrative of the Wreck of the* Meridian, *on the Island of Amsterdam* (Sydney, Waugh & Cox, 1854).

saved the latter's judicial career. On 25 May 1863, Lutwyche published an address to the constituents of East Moreton during final days of campaigning for the Queensland colonial election. It was his belief that judges could publicly express their political views. In his address, Lutwyche supported the colonial legislature's dissolution. He expressed his lack of support for the three candidates in his electorate, writing that:

> I have no confidence in them, collectively or individually. I look upon them *as the agents of despotism cloaked in the guise of responsible government.* What the people want is a constitutional Ministry, who will have a policy of their own, and who will be sufficiently independent in character and position to stand or fall by it.[178]

Offended by Lutwyche's publication, the Queensland legislature pressed for the judge's removal from the Supreme Court bench. Aware of this, the new Chief Justice, James Cockle, approached Governor Bowen and the first Premier of Queensland, Sir Robert Herbert, offering to talk Lutwyche to his senses.

On 10 August 1863, Cockle wrote to Lutwyche encouraging him not to continue publicising his political views:

> I have seen a motion on the Council papers which causes me considerable pain. I should be sorry to lose the benefit of your learning, experience, and ability, and of the constant and cordial cooperation you have afforded me since my arrival in the colony.[179]

Cockle commented that Lutwyche's public opinions 'might affect your impartiality as a Judge'.[180] The letter clearly struck a chord with Lutwyche, who replied:

> I know that yours is a dispassionate judgment, and I should be sorry to do anything which might cause suspicion, however unfounded, of partiality on the bench. Much as I value, therefore, a privilege which is the birthright of every Englishman, I shall forego its exercise in future, so long as I remain a Judge.[181]

Lutwyche kept his word for the rest of his judicial career, ending with his death in office in 1880.

In a quirk peculiar to Queensland, the Legislative Council President was appointed administrator or Lieutenant-Governor in the Governor's absence. In New South Wales, the Lieutenant-Governor was the Chief Justice of the Supreme Court, as is the case in most other Australian jurisdictions. The Queensland custom apparently emerged from unfavourable views that were formed of Lutwyche's wife, whom Sir Alfred Stephen, Chief Justice of New South Wales, described to a friend as 'unfit … for the circle into which her husband's rank must place her'.[182] A rumour had circulated in colonial society that Lutwyche's wife, Mary, was formerly his mistress and had given birth to his children

[178] Alfred JP Lutwyche, 'To the Electors of the District of East Moreton' *Sydney Morning Herald* (Sydney, 15 June 1863) 8 (emphasis added).
[179] Bennett (n 176) 55.
[180] *Ibid.*
[181] *Ibid* 56.
[182] *Ibid* 20.

outside of wedlock. Lutwyche and his wife had no children together. The more traditional course would have been to give Lutwyche a dormant commission to administer government in the Governor's absence. In any case, there is no longer a Legislative Council in Queensland – nor a President of such. Following the New South Wales model, the Chief Justice of Queensland is now inevitably also the Lieutenant Governor and acts as Governor when the Governor him or herself is absent.

Colonial Laws Validity Act 1865

Much has been written about the motivations and effect of the *Colonial Laws Validity Act 1865*.[183] The 1865 Act was enacted by British Parliament to clarify when a colonial law would be void for repugnancy with the laws of England. The conduct of South Australian judge, Benjamin Boothby, provided the catalyst for the new statute. Boothby, first appointed to the Supreme Court of South Australia in 1853, nurtured an antipathy towards legislation passed by the newly responsible South Australian Government, particularly the *Real Property Act 1858*. He was not alone in resisting the Torrens legislation but, as John M Williams observes, 'it is usually Boothby who is singled out for rebuke'.[184]

In three early cases interpreting South Australia's innovative Torrens legislation, the Supreme Court allowed purchasers of land transactions to look behind the registration to investigate title – defeating one of the central purposes of the scheme.[185] In subsequent cases, Boothby concluded that the Torrens legislation was void for repugnancy and, in cases of the early 1860s, South Australia's Full Court invalidated parts of the legislation.[186] Boothby also questioned whether the Court of Appeal, established in 1837 and constituted by the Governor and Executive Council, was consistent with the grant of responsible government under South Australia's *Constitution Act 1856*.[187] Boothby's objections intensified, fixing attention on other pieces of colonial legislation and the question of repugnance.[188] South Australia's legislature were constrained: 'there seemed no limit to the laws declared invalid through careless drafting or through repugnancy'.[189] Probably the worst aspect of Boothby's tenure was his attitude towards the colonial profession and his judicial colleagues.[190]

British Parliament enacted the Colonial Laws Validity Act to, as stated in the preamble, 'remove Doubts as to the Validity of Colonial Laws'. The Act applied not only to South Australia but to other British colonies. Colonial legislatures were only bound by British

[183] 28 & 29 Vic, c 63 See generally Alex C Castles, 'The Reception and Status of English Law in Australia' (1963–66) 2 *Adelaide Law Review* 1; Enid Campbell, 'Colonial Legislation and the Laws of England (1964–67) 2(2) *University of Tasmania Law Review* 148; David Clark, 'The Struggle for Judicial Independence: The Amotion and Suspension of Supreme Court Judges in 19th Century Australia' (2013) 12 *Macquarie Law Journal* 21, 36–46.

[184] John M Williams, 'Justice Boothby: A Disaster that Happened' in George Winterton (ed), *State Constitutional Landmarks* (Sydney, Federation Press, 2006) 21, 30.

[185] *Ibid* 30.

[186] Clark (n 183) 38; Williams (n 184) 37, 39–40, 43.

[187] Williams (n 184) 31.

[188] *Ibid* 32.

[189] Castles (n 183) 25.

[190] Clark (n 183) 40.

legislation that was directly applicable to their colony and, thus, had paramount force. Section 2 provided that a colonial law was not repugnant to British legislation unless by 'express words or necessary intendment' the legislation extended to the colony. Section 3 stated that a colonial law could only be repugnant if it related to British legislation. Under section 1, imperial statutes were 'said to extend to any Colony when it is made applicable to such Colony by the express "Words or necessary Intendment of any Act of Parliament"'.

Manner and Form

Section 5 of the Act introduced a 'manner and form' requirement that provided:[191]

> every representative legislature shall, in respect to the colony under its jurisdiction, have, and be deemed at all times to have had, full power to make laws respecting the constitution, powers and procedure of such legislature; *provided that such laws shall have been passed in such manner and form as may from time to time be required by any Act of Parliament, Letters Patent, Order in Council, or colonial law for the time being in force in the said colony.*[192]

Manner and form requirements enable a state legislature to protect or entrench important pieces of legislation – usually fundamental constitutional principles – from being amended or repealed by ordinary legislation. By entrenching law in this way, parliament binds its successors. It does this by imposing special procedures on the manner and form in which repeal or amendment can take place. The reinstatement of the Legislative Council in Queensland is the subject of a doubly entrenched manner and form provision.

The Federal Idea and the Federal Council of Australasia

At two conferences in 1880 and 1881, Sir Henry Parkes proposed that a Federal Council be established. At the second conference in 1881, Parkes submitted a draft bill with a memorandum hoping the establishment of a Federal Council would 'pave the way to a complete federal organization'. However, it was not until 1883 that more decisive action took place. External affairs and defence contributed to a renewed interest in federation. The activities of France and Germany in the south Pacific prompted action. The colonies saw themselves as vulnerable to attack and erected fortifications along the Australian coastline. In South Australia, Fort Glanville was constructed at Semaphore Park in Adelaide between 1878 and 1882 to defend against perceived threats of foreign attack. Friendly visits of Russian ships in the late 1800s compounded these fears. Queensland was uneasy about the intentions of Germany over New Guinea. On 4 April 1883, the Queensland Premier, Sir Thomas McIlwraith, attempted annexation of eastern New Guinea to keep it out of Germany's grasp. The British Parliament disallowed the annexation. In light of these events, McIlwraith and James Service of Victoria proposed an inter-colonial convention.

Held in 1883, the convention was attended by representatives of New Zealand, Fiji and the six Australian colonies. The convention adopted a bill drafted by Samuel Griffith to

[191] See *Australia Act 1986* (Cth) (UK) s 6.
[192] Emphasis added.

create a Federal Council of Australasia. Excluding New South Wales and New Zealand, the Australian colonies and Fiji requested the creation of limited federal authority through the draft bill. It was passed by imperial Parliament as the *Federal Council of Australasia Act 1885* (UK), and the body was convened for the first time in 1886. Section 15 of the Act set out the express legislative powers of the Federal Council and left scope for power to be referred to it by the Queen or 'two or more colonies'. Section 5 provided that the Council would consist of two representatives from each self-governing colony, including New Zealand, and one representative from the two Crown colonies of Fiji and Western Australia.[193] The process by which representatives were appointed was left to the colonies.[194] Once described as a 'contemptible phantom',[195] the Council was less effective than had been imagined. Meetings took place in Hobart every two years from 1886 to 1899. Participation was voluntary, and a colony could join or withdraw from the Council at will.[196] New South Wales did not participate. South Australia participated between 1889 and 1890. The Council had no means by which to generate revenue or to enforce its decisions.

The concern of foreign attack is reflected in s 51(xxx) of the *Australian Constitution*, which provides that the Commonwealth has legislative power with respect to 'the relations of the Commonwealth with the islands of the Pacific'. It has very rarely been relied upon.

Constitutional Detour

Universal Manhood Suffrage and the Secret Ballot

The Australian colonies broke ground in the 1850s, being among the first places in the world to introduce universal manhood suffrage and the secret ballot. The abolition of **plural voting** was a more gradual affair. In abolishing plural voting, colonial and state upper houses were much more dilatory than the lower houses. Victoria abolished plural voting for lower house elections in 1899 and for upper house elections in 1937.[197] This was the sequence followed in Western Australia. Western Australia abolished plural voting for the lower house in 1904, but it continued in the upper house until 1964.[198]

Plural voting: refers to the ability of electors to vote in all the constituencies in which they held land

Universal Manhood Suffrage

South Australia was the first colony to introduce universal manhood suffrage – extending the right to vote to all adult males – in 1856. Male British subjects over 21 years of age could enrol to vote, but this only applied to elections for the lower house. In 1857, Victoria followed South Australia's lead as did New South Wales in 1858. Victoria had

[193] *Ibid* s 5.
[194] *Ibid* s 6.
[195] Scott Bennett, *The Making of the Commonwealth* (Melbourne, Cassell, 1971) 66.
[196] *Federal Council of Australasia Act 1885* ss 30–31.
[197] *Constitution Act Amendment Act 1899* (Vic) s 4; *Constitution (Reform) Act* 1937 (Vic) s 7.
[198] *Electoral Act 1904* (WA) ss 15–16; (WA); *Electoral Act Amendment Act 1964* (WA).

already made some progress in extending the franchise to men. In 1854, Victoria broadened the franchise to men possessing a miner's right valued at one pound.

The Secret Ballot

By 1860, five of Australia's six colonies had introduced the secret ballot. The secret ballot was so-called because the written ballot, officially published by the state, was cast secretly in a locked box until the official closing of polling. In the Australian colonies, voting by secret ballot replaced open voting and the use of partisan written ballots which could, as explored in chapter six and the introduction to this chapter, leave voters open to undue pressure from campaigning parties, their supporters and employers.

There had been campaigning for the secret ballot in Britain from at least the 1780s. Though momentum for it built in the 1830s, voting by secret ballot was not achieved in the United Kingdom until 1871. Voting became a private act rather than one motivated by community interests and responsibility. Colonists could vote for who they wanted without the fear of repercussions from their employer, landlord or neighbour.

Of the colonies, Victoria's bill introducing voting by secret ballot received royal assent first in 1856. Victoria became the first place in the world to conduct an election using the secret ballot system. During the first years of it being introduced, the secret ballot was referred to as the 'Victorian ballot', the 'Australian ballot' or the 'kangaroo ballot'. Tasmania was not far behind Victoria. The South Australian legislature added the secret ballot to its Electoral Bill in late 1855. The Bill passed on 12 February 1856, and royal assent was obtained on 24 June 1856. It was introduced to New South Wales in 1858. The next year, Queensland followed only to have it reversed by its new constitution. Queensland men aged over 21 did not regain the right to vote until 1 January 1873. In 1879, Western Australia adopted the secret ballot.

Conclusion

This chapter has mapped out the development of representative and responsible government in colonial Australia, opening with an account of Australia's first parliamentary election in 1843 where bribery and disorder ruled. The chaotic scenes of this election were not to be repeated after the Australian colonies introduced the secret ballot. It was necessary to backtrack to chronicle successive legislative enactments that afforded colonial governments more power to govern their internal affairs. However, the devastating impact of colonisation on Indigenous Australians in the nineteenth century was not explored. The next chapter is devoted to exploring the gulf that existed between the parliamentary and legal developments achieved by Australian colonists, explored in this chapter, and the fate of Indigenous Australians.

9

Indigenous Australia and the Law in the Colonial Period

Introduction

When an Aboriginal man known by Europeans only as Jackey was questioned by Chief Justice Forbes (see chapter seven) before the New South Wales Supreme Court in 1834, he asked for a jury of 'Blackfellows'. It was a reasonable request not only given the principle of being tried by a jury of one's peers in English law but also because judgment by one's community had been the practice of Aboriginal Australia for thousands of years.[1] Given that there were more than 250 First Nations in Australia and the Torres Strait in 1788 the successful imposition of English law is anomalous and inconsistent with other parts of the British Empire where existing local law was recognised. This chapter discusses the impact of the British occupation of the Australian continent and its surrounding islands on the First Peoples of Australia, Aboriginal and Torres Strait Islanders. It begins with an overview of Aboriginal Australia before European contact. The British arrived on a continent inhabited for thousands of years by cultures with a deeply embedded sense of law and correct behaviour.

The British Government's decision to claim different parts of the continent did not take place in a vacuum. For local governors the concern was the loss of settlers' lives and property as a result of Aboriginal resistance. For the Home Government it was initially the international community's response to Britain's claims that mattered, whether other European powers might challenge any territorial claim and, therefore, whether it could be justified under international law. At other periods it was domestic politics which influenced British Government decisions, especially when concern about the morality of slavery and mistreatment of Indigenous peoples was at its height. As a result, this chapter also delves into the history of international law governing the acquisition of territory by settlement, conquest or cession and historical debates about its interpretation in the late eighteenth century.

Judge Willis, the first resident judge at Port Phillip (now Victoria), made one of the clearest statements regarding Aboriginal sovereignty and the limits of English law's **jurisdiction** in 1841. He is the subject of this chapter's historical cameo as he is also significant for illustrating the problems that arose when judges could not be dismissed. This chapter concludes with the Melanesian or Pacific Island labour trade which had a profound impact on First

> Jurisdiction: where a legal system can be applied and enforced

[1] In New South Wales in 1834 the option was for a military jury or a civil jury. When Forbes CJ further explained this to Jackey his response was 'no soldier'. Aboriginal Australians were not eligible to serve on juries in 1834. See John N Molony, *An Architect of Freedom: John Hubert Plunkett in New South Wales 1832–1869* (Canberra, ANU Press, 1973) 134–35.

Peoples in Australia's neighbouring Pacific islands and also triggered the 1870s annexation of the Torres Strait Islands to the colony of Queensland.

Learning Resources

The content in this chapter is supported by:

Glossary	Chapter Overview	Historical Cameos	Pause for Thought
Latin legal and Australian colonial terms are defined	The chapter begins with an overview explaining its intentions and focus	Judge John Walpole Willis	Conquest or Cession? *R v Kilmeister* Slaves or Contractors?

Chapter Overview

Place	Period	Dates	Key Figures	Key Institutions	Key Terms
• All Australian colonies • Kimberley Coast • Torres Strait • Southwest Pacific	• Late Georgian to Edwardian eras	• 1838 • 1901 • 1908	• Emer de Vattel • Hugo Grotius • Judges Forbes, Burton and Willis • Attorney-General Plunkett • Edward Landor • Bishop Patteson	• Supreme Court of New South Wales • Governors Phillip, Arthur and Gipps • Queensland Native Police • Royal Navy	• Customary law • Terra nullius • Jurisdiction • Sovereignty • Pacific Islands labour trade • South Sea Islander community • British annexation of Fiji • Queensland annexation of Torres Strait Islands

Learning Outcomes

At the end of this chapter, readers should understand:

- There were many languages, nations and legal systems in Australia in 1788.
- The basis of British claims to Australia under international law and the grounds on which they are contested.
- Why humanitarian insistence that British law applied on Australian colonial frontiers failed to protect Aboriginal subjects and why colonial authorities used police, not military, to quell Aboriginal resistance.
- The vulnerability of traditional peoples from the Kimberley coast of Western Australia to the islands of the south-west Pacific in the late nineteenth century as Europeans moved into tropical environments.

Aboriginal Australia before European Contact

Aboriginal and Torres Strait Islander peoples' occupation of the lands now known as Australia reaches back into deep time. Recent archaeological studies place the length of time Aboriginal people have lived on the Australian continent to at least 65,000 years, but some archaeologists believe it could be even further back in time. Aboriginal traditional belief is that they have been on their country since the beginning of time. Archaeological evidence affirms that the first Australians survived and flourished through immense geological and climate change that saw the continent's volcanoes fall dormant, its climate become drier, megafauna die out, the shoreline dramatically re-shaped, and the islands of Tasmania and Torres Strait created after the ending of the last mini ice age.[2]

Not surprisingly, given that the Australian landmass is as large as Europe, more than 250 languages and over 700 dialects have been estimated to have been spoken in 1788. There were as many nations as there were languages and these operated on extraordinarily egalitarian and decentralised principles. Yet the system was remarkably orderly because everyone in Aboriginal society knew their identity and place within their kinship system and from an early age were taught their legal obligations to others. Elders who knew and enforced the law held great status, not least because law was spiritually ordained. Aboriginal law was passed down from ancestors and was part of a philosophy known as the Dreaming. Ancestral law covered all aspects of life hence why many Aboriginal people prefer to use the term 'lore' to encompass both the regulations that governed daily life and the spiritual element that underpinned them. Law determined the 'proper' relations that governed people, personal property and territory. As one Aboriginal person defined

[2] For an overview of how Australian archaeology has developed in the last 50 years, see Billy Griffiths, *Deep Time Dreaming: Uncovering Ancient Australia* (Melbourne, Black Inc, 2018).

it for the Western Australian Law Reform Commission, **customary law**:

> connected people in a web of relationships with a diverse group of people; and with our ancestral spirits, the land, the sea and the universe; and our responsibility to the maintenance of this order.[3]

Customary law: traditional Aboriginal law connecting Aboriginal Australians in a web of relationships with a diverse group of people; and with ancestral spirits, the land, the sea and the universe; and responsibility to the maintenance of this order

The 250 language or national groups are charted in a map (2013) developed by the Australian Institute of Aboriginal and Torres Strait Islander Studies (AIATSIS). Not included in the pictorial representation are smaller groupings – clans or dialects – existing within these 250 larger groupings. The map confirms the diversity of languages and the division of the whole Australian continent, Tasmania and Torres Strait into national groups.

It is astounding to First Nations that the authority of their long connection – longer than any other people on earth – has not been respected and recognised, especially given the clear evidence of their jurisdiction. When the Australian Law Reform Commission conducted an Inquiry into Recognition of Aboriginal Customary Laws some 200 years after first white settlement, it acknowledged that 'Aboriginal customary laws and traditions continue as a real controlling force in the lives of many Aborigines'.[4] In many parts of Australia, customary law continues to have jurisdiction over Aboriginal people even if the official court system does not recognise it.

Disputes in Indigenous society were resolved through communal gatherings of those affected by a violation; at other times they were resolved privately according to kinship rules; more serious offences could be decided by a council of elders and punished publicly before the whole community and finally there were actions which violated sacred knowledge, objects or behaviour which could be punished secretly. Affected families, communities and elders not only deliberated on the gravity of an offence but had a say in its punishment.

Indigenous kinship systems vary across the country and are complex. Interpersonal relationships within a community were traditionally guided by kinship rules, which determined the rights and duties owed by one person to other members of the group. The definition of one's brothers and sisters in Aboriginal Australia is much broader than the western biological definition and includes one's 'skin' brothers and sisters as well as relations who would be termed cousins in western nuclear family terms. Frequently, when British officials and settlers first appeared on Aboriginal land, local people would assign them a 'skin' which was intended to help them know their place in Aboriginal law and to govern their behaviour while on Aboriginal land – an obligation which they invariably breached.

The practice was not only historic – it remains a strong element of First Nations' relationships today. This system impacts on Aboriginal people's obligations and responsibilities under customary law, as it 'largely dictates the way people behave towards one another,

[3] Aboriginal respondent cited in Law Reform Commission of Western Australia, *Aboriginal Customary Laws: The Interaction of Western Australian Law with Aboriginal Law and Culture: Final Report* (No 94, 2006) 64.

[4] Australian Law Reform Commission, *Recognition of Aboriginal Customary Law: Report* (ALRC No 31, 1986) para 38.

Figure 9.1 *Cum la watum Ba a native of the Coal River* (1810–1822)

An Aboriginal man from the Hunter River wears the ornate headdress and head band of his people. His status is denoted by his collar and scarring.

Pictorial material and regalia of the Macquarie family, 1800–1844 Series 04, Item 09.

Mitchell Library, State Library of New South Wales, P2/425, IE1602059.

prescribing dominance, deference, obligation or equality as the basis of the relationship'.[5] An injury to one person might oblige uncles or brothers to take action on their behalf so that incorrect behaviour becomes a matter for families rather than the individualist approach of Australian law.

The British Government in 1786 knew nothing about the system of government and law that regulated First Nations but they did have knowledge of other hunter-gatherer societies and directed Arthur Phillip to collect information so that they might either gain Aboriginal consent to their 'overlordship' or to purchase some of their lands. To understand these initial steps, it is important to place the views of the British Government in the context of international law as it had developed by the eighteenth century.

[5] Tonkinson cited in H McRae, G Nettheim and L Beacroft (eds), *Indigenous Legal Issues: Commentaries and Materials*, 2nd edn (North Ryde New South Wales, LBC Information Services, 1997) 83.

Figure 9.2 J Lycett, Fishing by Torchlight (1820–1822), as displayed on a sign in Glades Bay Park, Gladesville, Sydney

Joseph Lycett, a convict artist, painted Aboriginal women fishing at night while friends and family gather on shore. *National Library of Australia, PIC MSR 12/1/4 #R5677, nla.obj-138499378.*

International Law by 1787

In contrast to the ancient law of Aboriginal Australia, the idea of international law is very recent. It is a body of thinking that developed in response to the Reformation (see chapter three) in the sixteenth and seventeenth centuries. New Protestant powers such as England and Holland wanted to usurp the claims of Spain and Portugal to colonial territories which had been granted to them by the Pope in the Treaty of Tordesillas in 1494. The idea of international law was given added stimulus by the Thirty Years' War which ravaged parts of continental Europe from 1618 to 1648; this conflict between Protestant and Catholic states resulted in an estimated eight million deaths through combat and accompanying famine and disease. Reacting against this horror, a Dutch scholar, Hugo Grotius, published *De Jure Belli ac Pacis* [*On the Law of War and Peace*] in 1625 in which he argued that law between nations was essential to limit bloodshed and recourse to warfare.[6] The origins of international law were thus both pragmatic and idealistic, as well as driven by European imperial conquest of what was, to them, the 'new world'. It evolved from the self-interest of Europeans who sought to invade and exploit other peoples in the new world on the one hand but, on the other hand, some scholars began to use natural law principles to argue nobly for reason and the rule of law to oppose war and provide order among the international community.

[6] Hugo Grotius, *Hugo Grotius on the Law of War and Peace* (Cambridge, Cambridge University Press, 2012).

Grotius' ideas concerning natural law were an important influence on the English philosopher John Locke (see chapter five), as well as leading North American thinkers of the eighteenth century. The North American experience was of course the main guide for British administrators of the Australian colonies.

Settlement, Conquest and Cession

Australian historians have argued that the British followed international law, which had further evolved from Grotius's time, when they laid claim to eastern Australia. The British view was that as long as no other European power had laid claim to a territory then they could legitimately obtain it in one of three ways. The first was to persuade the Indigenous people already living there to submit to Britain's overlordship. This was one of the factors behind British alliances with Native American peoples. The British Government wanted traditional owners to cede their sovereignty to them rather than their French rivals who also wanted to acquire lands in the eighteenth century. Second, British settlers could purchase land and the right to settle it from the Indigenous people. This was what happened in parts of North America and in New Zealand. Lastly, Great Britain could take unilateral possession on the basis of first discovery and occupation. According to Alan Frost, the historian whose account of this process has been very influential, this was why Captain James Cook only claimed the eastern third of the Australian continent – the British recognised the Dutch claim to all the remaining land which they referred to as New Holland.[7] To this end, after sailing and charting the entire length of the east coast, Cook landed on Bedanug Island in Torres Strait, which he re-named Possession Island, allegedly climbed a hill, hoisted the Union Jack and ceremoniously declared the whole eastern portion of the continent the possession of George III. This legal proclamation could have been challenged by other European powers had it not been followed by subsequent occupation in 1788.[8]

The problem with the third position is that it is done in opposition to other European powers but does not take into account the Indigenous people already occupying the lands. Frost argued that the British used ideas from the Bible, Grotius, other European jurists, John Locke and Blackstone to argue that Aboriginal people did not legally own the land. This approach emphasised the failure of the First Nation peoples to cultivate, enclose or otherwise mix their labour with the land in order to deny them any legal title.[9] This is the origin of the idea that in 1788 Australia was *terra nullius* – land owned by no one or by no master as discussed in chapter one. Frost acknowledges that no one in the British Government or

[7] The British continued to use the name New Holland for the continent until after Matthew Flinders' circumnavigation of the continent. On his recommendation the name 'Australia' – taken from the Latin 'Australis' for 'southern' – was adopted and entered common use after 1817.

[8] This was also the position taken earlier in 1971 by Alex C Castles, *An Introduction to Australian Legal History* (Sydney, Law Book Co, 1971) 14–15. Frost's influential interpretation was first published in 1981 and updated in 2011, see Alan Frost, 'New South Wales as *Terra Nullius*: The British Denial of Aboriginal Land Rights' (1981) 19 *Historical Studies* 513; Alan Frost, 'Claiming Pacific Lands: Late Eighteenth-Century and Nineteenth-Century Approaches' (2011) 17 *Journal of Commonwealth and Post-Colonial Studies* 187.

[9] Aboriginal and historical scholarship has refuted all of these misplaced claims. See especially Bruce Pascoe, *Dark Emu, Black Seeds: Agriculture or Accident?* (Broome, Magabala, 2014); Bill Gammage, *The Biggest Estate on Earth: How Aborigines made Australia* (Crows Nest New South Wales, Allen & Unwin, 2011).

in the early settlement used this term which only entered international legal debates in the late-nineteenth century. Nonetheless, the idea allegedly existed at common law and in international law.[10]

This account has been questioned by a number of historians in recent years. Applying the term *terra nullius* to the eighteenth century has been criticised by many scholars as anachronistic. Although Roman law used the phrase ***res nullius*** to apply to ownership of things, it did not cover land. Instead, the term *terra nullius* was constructed and applied in nineteenth and twentieth century disputes about the right of nations to claim Arctic and Antarctic lands which were, in fact, uninhabited. Furthermore, international jurists at the time did not agree that it could be used to justify colonisation.[11]

> *Res nullius* (Latin): something nobody owns

Whether eighteenth-century English jurists believed that Indigenous Australians had no sovereignty or legal rights to their land has also been disputed. Danish historian Merete Borch re-visited the works of William Blackstone (see chapter four) as well as European jurists such as Christian Wolff and Emer de Vattel to show that there was no eighteenth-century legal doctrine that inhabited lands could be ownerless. Although Edward Coke had famously decreed in *Calvin's Case* in 1608 (see chapter four) that Christian conquest of the lands of 'infidels' and denial of their laws was justified, a view used to justify usurpation of lands in Virginia and a position which Blackstone had accepted, the legal position of the American colonies was that the land belonged to the Native Americans until 'they give it or sell it, though it be not improved'.[12] This decision of a royal commission was also a view shared by Lord Northey who as Attorney-General in 1703 had said of the Charter of Connecticut 'that it was not intended to dispossess the Indians who before and after the Grant were owners and possessors of [their lands].'[13] Then in 1774 Chief Justice Lord Mansfield (see chapter four) refuted Coke's position that the law of infidels could be disregarded; this was the 'mad enthusiasm of [the] Crusades' and affirmed that Native American law remained in force, after conquest, until the King chose to alter the law. The British had conquered parts of North America, other North American territories had been gained by purchase or session, but the Native Americans retained legal rights including ownership of property.

Borch argues that the view of British jurists by the mid-eighteenth century was that the lands of Indigenous North Americans had been acquired through either conquest or purchase. Blackstone's reference to 'desert and uncultivated' lands was a reference to Barbados,[14] not lands inhabited by hunter-gatherers, so there was no doctrine in British law which supported taking inhabited lands as if they were uninhabited. These were the formative experiences when the British Government decided to establish a colony in New South Wales. It was why in 1768 Cook's instructions had included authorisation to claim lands in the name of the King, but 'with the Consent of the Natives'. Some 17 years later when Sir Joseph Banks was questioned by a House of Commons Committee on Transportation

[10] Frost, 'New South Wales as *Terra Nullius*' (n 8) 513–15.

[11] It was also used in the 20th century in discussions about the ownership of space, see Andrew Fitzmaurice, 'The Genealogy of *Terra Nullius*' (2007) 129 *Australian Historical Studies* 1, 1–15.

[12] Merete Borch, 'Rethinking the Origins of *terra nullius*' (2001) 117 *Australian Historical Studies* 222, 226–27.

[13] *Ibid* 227.

[14] Barbados had been depopulated as a result of slave raids by the Spanish in the 16th century.

about plans to establish Botany Bay, he was asked explicitly whether any district might be 'obtained by cession or purchase'.[15]

Australian legal historians have also been selective in their reading of continental thinkers, such as Christian Wolff and Emer de Vattel, according to Borch. Wolff in his 1749 work, *The Law of Nations Treated According to a Scientific Method*, refuted the notion that the lands of hunter-gatherers could be claimed simply because they were not continuously using those lands: 'Ownership is not lost by non-use.'[16] The Swiss jurist Emmerich de Vattel built on Wolff's ideas and made it clear that, while he believed that cultivation of land was a human duty, agriculturalists could nonetheless only claim parts of hunter-gatherer lands.[17] Consequently by the late-eighteenth century there was no endorsement of the wholesale takeover of Indigenous lands in either English common law or international law. Conquest too had become severely limited as a legal doctrine. How then did the colonies of New South Wales, and later Van Diemen's Land, South Australia and Swan River, proceed without cession of lands or treaties? Were the Australian colonies taken through conquest?

Early Contact: British Sovereignty?

The journals of Cook and Banks clearly established that the eastern coastline of Australia was inhabited. Cook had no opportunity to 'gain the Consent of the Natives' as he had been instructed – a reminder that, despite discussion among jurists, once in colonial spaces explorers, administrators and settlers were entirely pragmatic about the extent of their powers.

As covered in chapter seven, on 26 January 1788, Captain Arthur Phillip hoisted the British flag to take formal possession of the colony of New South Wales. The British landed a significant military force of four companies of marines,[18] as well as their weapons, naval personnel, convicts, tools and invisible baggage such as diseases. The original inhabitants of the Sydney area, the Gadigal people, are one of 29 groups who comprise the Eora nation. The arrival of these strangers on Gadigal country was devastating; especially traumatic was smallpox, which ravaged the local population.

The British Government assumed that their acquisition of New South Wales would proceed on a similar basis to their arrangements with Indigenous people in North America. To that end Governor Phillip's instructions required him to report on the numbers of people who lived around Botany Bay. He was also provided with goods to enable him to barter with the local people so the assumption seems to have been that lands would be purchased although how much land would depend on British and Indigenous peoples' needs.[19] Phillip was soon reporting back that the First Nations were more numerous than expected and uniformly hostile to the British presence. One officer of the First Fleet, Watkin Tench, recorded that 'we had reason to conclude the country more populous than

[15] House of Commons Committee on Transportation cited in Borch (n 12) 230.

[16] Wolff cited in Borch (n 12) 234.

[17] Vattel, *The Law of Nations* cited in Borch (n 12) 234.

[18] Alan Frost, *The First Fleet: The Real Story* (Melbourne, Black Inc, 2012) 65.

[19] Bain Attwood, 'Law, History and Power: The British Treatment of Aboriginal Rights in Land in New South Wales' (2014) 42 *Journal of Imperial and Commonwealth History* 171, 182.

Mr Cook [Captain James Cook] thought it.' Tench further chronicled how Captain Arthur Phillip had landed 'in order to take possession of his new territory and bring about an intercourse between its old and new masters'.[20]

George III's instructions were to make contact but the problem was that the Aboriginal population initially avoided the penal settlement. After several months their aversion to the British presence led to drastic action on the Governor's part; he ordered the capture of an Aboriginal man, Arabanoo, in December 1788. He was initially guarded and fettered and some five months later, in April 1789 after tending stricken members of his community, Arabanoo died of smallpox.[21]

Phillip continued to report on the lack of Aboriginal support for the British presence but in 1793 he returned home to Great Britain. Despite further abductions of Aboriginal people,[22] he had not been able to learn their language or to give an estimate of population across the region,[23] to gain their consent to the British presence, or to organise a treaty. His success was in establishing a beachhead for British colonisation despite the lack of any formal consent from the traditional owners. Undoubtedly the smallpox epidemic had limited the capacity of the Eora Nation to displace the British forces: 'they are sensible of the great superiority of our arms', he had noted in 1789.[24] Such pragmatism was a relief to the Office for War and the Colonies which, by 1793, was pre-occupied with events in revolutionary France and was paying limited attention to events in the tiny convict station at Sydney.

This pragmatism was a common feature of empires. Lauren Benton in her study of the relation of law and geography to imperial powers noted that European sovereignty was usually uneven; its power progressing through enclaves and geographical corridors.[25] Similarly, the colony of New South Wales developed in an ad hoc manner. The matter of British sovereignty over New South Wales was clearly not threatened by rival claims from France or Spain. Nor was the Netherlands prepared to press its claims over Tasmania and in 1803 Governor King was instructed to institute a settlement there. Sovereignty, meaning who has the right of supreme jurisdiction, was not being challenged from Europe and its limit with respect to Aboriginal people could be left to local governors to resolve.

Pause for Thought

Conquest or Cession?

If the presence of British military forces was significant in the decision of governors not to negotiate with First Nations, how might the Australian legal situation have been

[20] Watkin Tench, *A Narrative of the Expedition to Botany Bay* (Electronic text SETIS, London, 1789) Ch 8.

[21] Tench provides a touching account of the smallpox outbreak and Arabanoo's capture and death in Watkin Tench, *A Complete Account of the Settlement at Port Jackson* (Electronic text SETIS, London, 1793) Ch 3.

[22] The kidnapping of Colbee and Bennelong is discussed in detail in Inga Clendinnen, *Dancing with Strangers* (Melbourne, Text, 2003).

[23] The population of Australia, Tasmania and Torres Strait in 1788 is still not known. Anthropologists have estimated 750,000 people.

[24] Phillip cited in Attwood (n 19) 184.

[25] Lauren Benton, *A Search for Sovereignty: Law and Geography in European Empires, 1400–1900* (Cambridge, Cambridge University Press, 2010).

different if it had just been a few private settlers or missionaries, as in New Zealand and Canada?

You need to think about the power imbalance between small numbers of traders and missionaries and large numbers of First Nations on their own country. New South Wales however began with a large military presence. Further advice on answering is online.

Sovereignty was more than an abstract matter to governors trying to deal with convicts, ex-convicts and settlers moving onto new Aboriginal lands. Violence broke out frequently and governors had to deal with the question of whether they were required to provide protection to whites if they were committing offences against Aboriginal people on Aboriginal land. Settlers never or rarely admitted such actions but, when First Nations attacked other Europeans in retaliation and in accordance with their own law even if there were rumours that other whites had provoked the attack, governors invariably responded with the use of force.

There was also the problem of Aboriginal people committing offences against another Aboriginal person within the settlement where white jurisdiction was a fait accompli. Initially, colonial courts did not interfere with crimes between or amongst Aboriginal peoples. *R v Ballard*[26] concerned the killing of an Aboriginal man by another Aboriginal man (referred to in the law report as 'Dirty Dick'). Sydney magistrates committed the man to stand trial on a charge of murder. The central question was whether the Supreme Court had jurisdiction for a criminal offence committed between two Aboriginal people ('*inter se*'). Forbes CJ of the Supreme Court of New South Wales commented that:

> it has been the practice of the Courts of this country, since the Colony was settled, never to interfere with or enter into the quarrels that have taken place between or amongst the natives themselves. ... This has been found expedient for the mutual protection of both sorts of people; but I am not aware that British laws have been applied to the aboriginal natives in transactions solely between themselves, whether of contract, tort, or crime. Indeed it appears to me that *it is a wise principle to abstain in this Colony, as has been done in the North American British Colonies,* with the institutions of the natives which, upon experience will be found to rest upon principles of natural justice.[27]

As recent legal historians have emphasised, Forbes followed North American experience[28] and discharged the male prisoner. The Supreme Court had no jurisdiction.

Within years, however, this position changed. In *R v Murrell*,[29] defence counsel for the Aboriginal Murrell argued that New South Wales was not originally 'desert', that it had not been conquered nor ceded and that the Court therefore did not have jurisdiction. Burton J however saw it differently. With less than four years' experience in the colony, he concluded that Aboriginal people were 'not in such a position regarding strength as to be considered free and independent tribes. They had no sovereignty'. Burton's wording is significant;

[26] (1828) NSW Sel Cas (Dowling) 2.

[27] *Ibid* (emphasis added).

[28] Borch (n 12); Lisa Ford, *Settler Sovereignty: Jurisdiction and Indigenous People in America and Australia, 1788–1836* (Harvard, Harvard University Press, 2010).

[29] [1836] NSWSupC 35.

his emphasis is on the military strength of the First Nations, not unlike Arthur Phillip's comment regarding 'the great superiority of our arms' discussed above. First Nations' sovereignty did not have to be reckoned with because British military force was greater than the fighting power of the local First Nations.

Governors and the Lieutenant-Governor of Van Diemen's Land had had to call upon this military power to quell First Nations' resistance repeatedly over the intervening decades. Martial law was declared, and the military called to arms to deal with violence on the Hawkesbury River in 1798, around Bathurst in 1824 and in Van Diemen's Land in the 1820s. In 1826 George Arthur issued a proclamation declaring that acts of aggression from Tasmanian Aboriginal people would be repelled 'as if they proceeded from an accredited state'. In 1830 when he instituted a military line to displace Aboriginal people from lands now claimed by settlers, he also introduced 'a **levee en masse**'.[30] The Colonial Office used the same language when giving advice about dealing with Aboriginal aggression to Governors Brisbane and Darling on the mainland. There is a very clear problem with this wording and these actions – they recognised that there had been no cession of these territories by their Aboriginal owners; despite Burton's view, these First Nations were being treated as 'an accredited state' and governors were acknowledging a limit to British territorial sovereignty. Declaring martial law to fight Aboriginal people was tantamount to acknowledging that Australia was being acquired through conquest.[31] Military force was required to occupy the country.

Levee en masse (French): civilian conscription to support the military operations

As Evangelical politics began to influence British Parliament, the bloodshed on the Australian frontiers would no longer be tolerated. Conquest had been accepted as a necessary part of acquiring an empire in the eighteenth century, but now Whig idealists opposed it. A new approach was required, and the Colonial Office in London would no longer authorise colonial governors to call out the military against Aboriginal people.[32]

A New Legal Fiction

Henceforth, the Whigs insisted, English law would protect the lives of Aboriginal people just as it protected the lives of British settlers. Aboriginal people were British subjects and entitled to the protection of British law. The Colonial Office recognised that the conflict was being provoked by settlers on Indigenous lands. If violence and bloodshed were the reality on the Australian frontiers, then this was not to be defined as war between sovereign states but criminal acts by British subjects on both sides of the conflict. Despite their humanitarian motives, the Colonial Office did not surrender the claim of British sovereignty; instead, it created a new legal fiction. First Nations were not at war with British settlers and were not accredited states; they were British subjects. Frontier attacks must be

[30] Lyndall Ryan, 'The Black Line in Van Diemen's Land: Success or Failure?' (2013) 37 *Journal of Australian Studies* 7.

[31] Charles D Rowley, *The Destruction of Aboriginal Society* (London, Penguin, 1972) 20.

[32] Henry Reynolds, *The Law of the Land*, 3rd edn (London, Penguin, 2003) 100–02.

Figure 9.3 Governor Davey's (in fact, Lieutenant-Governor Arthur's) Proclamation to the Aborigines, 1816 (c 1828–30)

This is an 1860s reproduction – with racist additions and factual errors – of 500 proclamation boards ordered to be distributed by Governor Arthur in 1828 at the height of interracial conflict. Four scenes painted on huon pine board were intended to explain the idea of 'equality before the law' to Aboriginal peoples in Tasmania but Arthur pressed on with military action to repress the Palawa nations of Tasmania.

Public Domain. National Museum of Australia.

dealt with as criminal acts, not acts of war, whatever the actual on the ground experience of Aborigines and settlers.

This same humanitarian impulse did however recognise Aboriginal rights in land even if it did not recognise First Nations jurisdiction and sovereignty. Governor Gipps' was appointed to carry out the new humanitarian policy in New South Wales which was that the Crown owned all the lands of New South Wales, but Aboriginal people continued to have rights to that same land; that meant that Aboriginal people had the right to continue to hunt, gather and travel on their country if it was Crown land or under pastoral lease. Leaseholders had only limited rights over what remained Crown land.[33]

The claim was that British law applied across the whole of eastern Australia and settlers had no right to go to war against First Nations. All Indigenous peoples as subjects of the Queen were not only amenable to that law but also protected by it. This noble ideal sounded fine at Downing Street. The political reality, however, was that settlers were determined to remove Aboriginal rights in land and protections in law. First Nations had also never ceded their sovereignty or agreed to the application of English law on their country. The discontinuity between the language of governors and the Colonial Office, and the language of settlers, became extreme as the former talked of law and rights while the latter, the settlers, talked of war. This was the context for the only occasion in which settlers were prosecuted for a mass killing of Aboriginal people.

The Myall Creek Massacre and Trials

On 18 December 1838, seven men were publicly hanged at Sydney Gaol for the massacre of approximately 30 Wirrayaraay people of the Gamilaroi nation near Myall Creek, part of the Gwydir River catchment in northern New South Wales. The circumstances of the Myall Creek massacre were and are shocking by any standard but, still, settlers overwhelmingly backed the perpetrators. So strong was public support that pastoralists across New South Wales funded the defence of the accused men. In June 2008, the Heritage Minister Peter Garrett included the massacre site on the National Heritage List. Its National Heritage Listing notes, this 'was the first and the last time the Colonial Administration intervened to ensure the laws of the colony were applied equally to Aboriginal people and settlers involved in frontier killings.'[34]

The Myall Creek massacre was not the first massacre of Aboriginal peoples – nor was it the last. The prevalence of frontier violence by the 1830s normalised it to stockmen, settlers and convicts. The Whigs in office in London were determined to send a message that this violence must end so it fell to their appointee, Governor Sir George Gipps, who had only arrived in the colony in February 1838, to make sure action was taken against the perpetrators. The hostile reaction from settlers and pastoralists contributed to a public backlash against Sir George Gipps and against his Attorney General, John Plunkett. In the end, the

[33] *Ibid* 139–44.

[34] Australian Government, 'National Heritage Places – Myall Creek Massacre and Memorial Site' (Department of Agriculture, Water and the Environment, 2010), available at environment.gov.au/heritage/places/national/myall-creek.

Myall Creek massacre was the only mass killing that was ever prosecuted in the Australian colonies.[35]

On 10 June 1838, a group of 12 stockmen comprising a free settler and assigned convicts had arrived armed at a squatting run located at Myall Creek. The squatting lease was owned by Henry Dangar. The station manager, William Hobbs, had allowed a group of friendly Aboriginal people to camp at the station and local Wirrayaraay men were employed at neighbouring stations. Aboriginal children at the station had English nicknames and could speak some English. Relations were friendly, but it was not to last. While manager Hobbs was away, stockmen sought retaliation for loss of cattle. They knew that the old people, women and children at Dangar's squatting run were not responsible for the loss. Nevertheless, the men surrounded the Aboriginal families, roped them together, dragged them into the bush, and killed them. A convict hut keeper managed to save some Wirrayaraay boys from being killed. Two days later, the men returned to the squatting run, heaped the decapitated bodies together and set them alight. They fled the scene and continued their killing spree.

When the manager, William Hobbs, returned, he saw the charred remains and informed a neighbouring station manager. That station manager informed a **squatter** who travelled 250 miles on horseback to report the crime. The newly appointed governor, Sir George Gipps, assigned a police magistrate, Edward Denny Day, to investigate. Day found bone fragments and took depositions from 19 witnesses. The information in the depositions led to the arrest of 11 of the 12 offenders. Gipps placed the arrested men on trial for wilful murder. The twelfth offender, John Fleming, was a free man, a local pastoralist, whereas the other accused men were all serving or ex-convict workers. Fleming fled and escaped without charge. He allegedly committed further atrocities with his brother in New South Wales and south-west Queensland. Many settlers were outraged that the men were even being prosecuted.[36]

Squatters: in the 1820s settlers began illegally moving their grazing herds onto Crown and Aboriginal land. Governors were forced to introduce a licensing system to legitimise this practice but even after the licences became pastoral or grazing leases, the original term remained in use

The Solicitor-General and Attorney-General of New South Wales, John Plunkett, prosecuted those responsible for the massacre in two trials. Evidence proved difficult because the remains were burnt. None of the witnesses at the first trial could swear that the remains of a large body belonged to Wirrayaraay Elder, 'Daddy', who was known to be very tall. The jury returned a verdict of 'not guilty'. All 11 accused were acquitted. One juror remarked to a Sydney newspaper: 'I knew the men were guilty but I would never see a white man hanged for killing a black'.[37]

After the verdict, Plunkett indicated to Dowling CJ that he would 'present a further indictment against them for murder at the next sittings of this honourable Court'. A second

[35] For information on other massacres, see Centre for 21st Century Humanities, 'Colonial Frontier Massacres in Australia, 1788–1930' (Newcastle, University of Newcastle, 2019), available at c21ch.newcastle.edu.au/colonial-massacres/. See also Lyndall Ryan, 'The Myall Creek Massacre: Was it Typical of the Time?' in Jane Lydon and Lyndall Ryan (eds), *Remembering the Myall Creek Massacre* (Sydney, NewSouth Publishing, 2018) 85, 85–99.

[36] For more details on Fleming, see Patsy Withycombe, 'The Twelfth Man: John Fleming and the Myall Creek Massacre' in Lydon and Ryan (n 35) 38–51.

[37] Letter from 'An English Juryman' *The Australian* (Sydney, 8 December 1838) 2.

trial was ordered. Of the 11 men involved, seven were re-arrested and tried again for the wilful murder of a single Aboriginal boy, a toddler named 'Charley'. Plunkett hoped that one of the excused men would now give evidence but under pressure from the station owner none cooperated. Due to the notoriety of the first trial and harassment of jurymen, assembling an impartial jury for the second trial was so difficult that the Sheriff had to **'pray a tales'**.[38] The seven men were found guilty of wilfully murdering Charley. The Executive Council found that there were no grounds for clemency. The men were hanged.

Pray a tales': an ancient legal rule enabling, if the judge thinks it necessary, qualified bystanders to be removed from the street for jury duty

The success of the second Myall Creek trial was remarkable given logistical problems starting with tracking down witnesses, procuring evidence and securing the arrests of 11 men. Had there not been a diligent police magistrate based near present-day Scone in New South Wales, as opposed to the pastoralists who, as discussed in chapter eight, comprised the bulk of the unpaid rural magistracy, it is doubtful evidence could have been procured. There was still the insurmountable difficulty in the first trial of establishing the identity of Aboriginal victims and protecting prosecution witnesses and jurors. The Crown had intended to pursue a third trial of the remaining four accused, but the disappearance of the Aboriginal witness Davy (Yintayintin) forced Plunkett to drop the case in February 1839.[39]

Pause for Thought

R v Kilmeister

No sworn Aboriginal testimony was able to be given in this trial for the murder of 28 Aboriginal people, but Attorney-General Plunkett did intend to try the four men remaining from the first trial in 1839. In this third case arising from events at Myall Creek the prosecution was going to rely on an Aboriginal witness.

Questions to Consider

1. Why did this third trial not proceed?
2. What do all the Myall Creek cases tell us about the dissonance between the official claim that Aboriginal people were British subjects, and that British sovereignty was beyond question, and the reality on the ground?
3. If the colonial government could not control its frontiers, did it have sovereignty?
4. How does the level of violence affect the assessment as to whether the Australian colonies were acquired through conquest?

Australian settlers had fought for legal rights and championed the law when it worked in their favour but, now, they ranted and raved against its use in the defence of Aboriginal rights. Many historians have argued that, rather than convincing settlers of the rights of

[38] The difficulties that the Attorney-General faced with juries in this case are covered in *The Australian* (Sydney, 27 November 1838, 1 and 2 December 1838) 2.

[39] Ryan (n 35) 36.

Aboriginal people as British subjects, the Myall Creek trials simply forced them to resort to more underhand methods so that if word ever reached Sydney of their murderous activities no reliable evidence could be used against them in a court of law.[40]

Plunkett, as Attorney-General, never gave up on the ideal of the rule of law and of Aboriginal people's equal rights to the protections of that law. Knowing how squatters and workers stuck together when it came to uncovering their misdeeds, Plunkett repeatedly pressed for the right of Aboriginal people to give evidence in courts of law. Aboriginal witnesses were not Christian and so could not swear an oath on the Bible. Aboriginal men accused of assaults on settlers could be condemned on the sworn statement of a settler while at the same time assaults on Aboriginal people were easily blocked by a settler code of silence. On occasions courts allowed Aboriginal witnesses to give unsworn testimony but this could be ignored by juries. Compare these circumstances to the status of defendants in English courts discussed in chapter four. On four occasions between 1839 and 1849 Plunkett drafted legislation to allow Aboriginal evidence in courts but was repeatedly blocked. Aboriginal evidence was not allowed in New South Wales and Queensland courts until 1876.[41] Some colonies did however allow Aboriginal evidence so it is important to explore the extent to which this reform enabled legal equality for Aboriginal subjects of the Crown.

'One Law for All' in Other Australian Colonies

By the early-nineteenth century, aware that the Dutch had no interest in following up seventeenth-century claims over New Holland with settlement, the French and the British commenced exploration and charting of the western coastline. On 2 May 1829, Captain Fremantle landed at Swan River and officially took possession of the western part of the continent in the name of the King.[42] The Swan River Colony operated independently of New South Wales. Its first Governor, Captain Stirling, read the proclamation establishing the colony which asserted that:

> And whereas the Protection of Laws doth of Right belong to all People whatsoever who may come or be found within the Territory aforesaid. I do hereby give Notice that if any Person or Persons shall be convicted of behaving in a fraudulent, cruel or felonious Manner towards the Aborigines of the Country, such Person or Persons will be liable to be prosecuted and tried for the Offence, as if the same had been committed against any other of His Majesty's Subjects.[43]

So one law, English law, was to apply to all without any recognition of Aboriginal law or sovereignty. Yet the very next line of the proclamation established a local militia to guard against Aboriginal attack: 'And whereas the Safety of the Territory from Invasion and from

[40] Amanda Nettelbeck, '"Equals of the White Man": Prosecution of Settlers for Violence against Aboriginal Subjects of the Crown, Colonial Western Australia' (2013) 31 *Law and History Review* 357.

[41] See generally Libby Connors, 'Witness to Frontier Violence: An Aboriginal Boy before the Supreme Court' (2011) 42 *Australian Historical Studies* 230.

[42] *Instructions to Captain Fremantle* at Documenting a Democracy: Western Australia, available at foundingdocs.gov.au/area-aid-9.html.

[43] *Lieutenant-Governor Stirling's Proclamation of the Colony 18 June 1829 (UK)* at Documenting a Democracy: Western Australia, available at foundingdocs.gov.au/area-aid-9.html.

the Attack of hostile Native Tribes may require the Establishment of a Militia Force which on emergency may be depended on to assist His Majesty's Regular Troops.'

It seems that local Whadjuk people were being recognised as an enemy nation. Within three years, killings on both sides had accelerated tensions. Despite Aboriginal attempts at conciliation the Whadjuk elder, Midgegooroo, was said to be among those who retaliated when one of his brothers was killed by the military. On 17 May 1833, Midgegooroo was captured and, without due legal process, killed by firing squad, the 'first and only death by firing squad in Australia', according to historian Anna Haebich.[44] By 1832, Governor Stirling returned to Great Britain to request further support. Despite advice from other officials and some settlers to seek a treaty,[45] Stirling instead advised his successor that the Whadjuk 'must be overawed and convinced of the power of the Whites'.[46]

South Australia was established in the aftermath of the horrific bloodshed of Governor Arthur's Black Line and at the height of the humanitarians' political ascendancy.[47] It was intended to be very different to the other Australian colonies. It was a private venture, not run by the Admiralty but by a company, the South Australian Land Commission, and peopled by free settlers not a small elite with a convict labour force. The Colonial Office was determined that it should not repeat the violence of the other colonies and the plans for colonisation were delayed until provisions for ensuring Indigenous rights were in place. Settlement was only to be allowed where there was no Aboriginal presence, white settlement was to be concentrated and restricted so that settlers did not venture onto Aboriginal lands beyond the reach of authority, land was to be purchased from Aborigines and there was to be one law for all.[48] Until the Kaurna people were converted to Christianity and educated, an Aboriginal Protector was to be appointed to ensure their rights under the law.[49]

Yet in South Australia too, a martial process was approved in August 1840 when a group of European shipwreck survivors were killed by Milmenrura people on the Coorong. This attack was outside the bounds of the new settlement beyond the reach of the Protector and the plans of the Colonial Office. Here on the south coast were Aboriginal people with no contact with English settlers and no knowledge of English law. Outraged settlers called for a response and Governor Gawler approved a military-style expedition by police. It resulted in a summary trial and crude hanging of two Aboriginal men, Mongarawata and Moorcangua, on the Coorong.[50]

While many settlers urged and applauded official aggression towards Aboriginal people there were also voices of dissent in both new colonies. James Stephen Jr, Permanent Under-Secretary of the Colonial Office, was determined to enact the recommendations of the House of Commons' 1837 Select Committee on Aboriginal Tribes[51] which had recommended equal treatment under law. However, when Governors Gipps and Hutt

[44] Anna Haebich, *Dancing in Shadows* (Crawley WA, University of Western Australia Press, 2018) 35.

[45] *Ibid* 30–31.

[46] Stirling cited in *ibid* 29.

[47] Reynolds (n 32) 99–102.

[48] Alan Pope, *One Law for All? Aboriginal People and Criminal Law in Early South Australia* (Canberra, Aboriginal Studies Press, 2011) 2–6.

[49] Reynolds (n 32) 106–07; 111–15; Pope (n 48) 2–6.

[50] Pope (n 48) 17–18.

[51] House of Commons, *Report of the Parliamentary Committee on Aboriginal Tribes (British Settlements)* (Aborigines Protection Society, 1837).

(Western Australia) separately proposed *Aboriginal Evidence Acts* in 1839 and 1841 they were disallowed as a result of legal advice to the Colonial Office. Stephen then had to draft a *Colonial Evidence Act* passed by the British Parliament in 1843 so that the colonies could again draft legislation for royal assent.[52] Western Australia and South Australia both succeeded not least because Hutt argued that it would enable better prosecution of Aboriginal accused not just defence of Aboriginal victims. Although Plunkett had used the same argument in New South Wales, aggressive squatting representatives repeatedly voted against any legislation there.

Were outcomes any better for Aboriginal people in these colonies? Up to the 1880s both colonies sustained more successful prosecutions of Europeans for violence committed against Aboriginal people than the eastern colonies – 29 settlers in Western Australia[53] and 14 in South Australia.[54] However, closer analysis reveals the very unequal punishments meted out to Europeans for violent assault and murder than for Aboriginal defendants; fines were standard punishment for settlers; only one white man, an ex-convict, was ever hanged for killing an Indigenous person.[55] These same studies indicate that Western Australian courts sentenced 25 Aboriginal men to death while South Australia executed 23 including Mongarawata and Moorcangua (the two executed for the shipwreck of the *Maria* atrocity).[56] In similar language to settlers in the east, Western Australian lawyer, Edward Landor, bitterly opposed allowing Aboriginal evidence. He condemned the 'morbid sentimentality' of the Colonial Office for imposing it on his colony, arguing that the British Government had sanctioned conquest. Instead of the hypocrisy of English law, argued Landor, military law should have been introduced owing to the settlers' 'right of power'.[57]

Although prominent men such as Landor thought that applying law to frontier situations was absurd, settlers maintained this language superficially long after Governor Gipps had departed Australian shores and self-government had been won by each colony. In Queensland, frontier killings were officially endorsed through the institution of the Queensland Native Police. The force had been founded by Governor Gipps as part of government infrastructure to support Aboriginal Protectors and to bring Aboriginal people under the law but, by 1856,[58] reports of its wanton violence sparked repeated government inquiries. But, after self-government in 1856, pastoralist language became more overt. Local settlers now controlled their local parliaments, and the Colonial Office had no powers of oversight. In 1858 and again in 1861 pastoralists gave evidence that if the force were to be disbanded that they would take the law into their own hands.[59] Other colonies avoided this

[52] Russell Smandych, 'Contemplating the Testimony of "Others": James Stephen, the Colonial Office, and the Fate of Australian Aboriginal Evidence Acts, circa 1839-1849' (2006) 10 *Legal History* 118.

[53] Eight were acquitted. Nettelbeck (n 40) 356.

[54] Seven were acquitted. South Australian figures are until 1862 only. See Table 2 in Pope (n 48) 178–79.

[55] Pope (n 48) 149–50, 178–79; Nettelbeck (n 40) 389–90.

[56] Nettelbeck (n 40) 364; Table 1 in Pope (n 48) 175–78.

[57] Landor's memoir cited in Nettelbeck (n 40) 363.

[58] Libby Connors, '"Within an Hour's Ride" of the Capital: The Problem of Sovereignty in 1859' (2015) 17 *Journal of Australian Colonial History* 83–100.

[59] Select Committee on the Native Police Force, Queensland Legislative Assembly, 1861, available at aiatsis.gov.au/sites/default/files/catalogue_resources/92123.pdf; evidence of William Archer, Select Committee on Murders by the Aborigines on the Dawson River, Legislative Assembly of New South Wales, 1858, 873, available at aiatsis.gov.au/sites/default/files/catalogue_resources/91884.pdf. See also Jonathon Richards, *The Secret War: A True History of Queensland's Native Police* (St Lucia, Queensland, University of Queensland Press, 2008).

843

1858.

Legislative Assembly.

NEW SOUTH WALES.

MURDERS BY THE ABORIGINES ON THE DAWSON RIVER.

REPORT FROM THE SELECT COMMITTEE

ON

MURDERS BY THE ABORIGINES ON THE DAWSON RIVER;

TOGETHER WITH

THE PROCEEDINGS OF THE COMMITTEE,

MINUTES OF EVIDENCE,

AND APPENDIX.

ORDERED BY THE LEGISLATIVE ASSEMBLY TO BE PRINTED,
3 *August*, 1858.

SYDNEY:

PRINTED BY WILLIAM HANSON, GOVERNMENT PRINTER,
PHILLIP-STREET.

1858.

331—*a*

Figure 9.4 Select Committee on Murders by the Aborigines on the Dawson River, 1858

Criticism of the unlawful actions of the Queensland Native Police were met with defiance by pastoralists living on stations that would soon become part of the new colony of Queensland.

Legislative Assembly of New South Wales, *Report from the Select Committee on Murders by the Aborigines on the Dawson River together with the proceedings of the committee, minutes of evidence and appendix* (1858).

Public Domain. Australian Institute of Aboriginal and Torres Strait Islander Studies

1927.

WESTERN AUSTRALIA.

ROYAL COMMISSION

OF

Inquiry into Alleged Killing and Burning of Bodies of Aborigines in East Kimberley

AND INTO

Police Methods when Effecting Arrests.

COMMISSIONER: G. T. WOOD, ESQ., S.M.

Presented to both Houses of Parliament by His Excellency's Command.

[FIRST SESSION OF THE THIRTEENTH PARLIAMENT.]

PERTH:
BY AUTHORITY: FRED. WM. SIMPSON, GOVERNMENT PRINTER.

1927.

No. 3.

APPROXIMATE COST OF PAPER:
Printing and Lithos. (1,000 copies), £165.

11927/27

Figure 9.5 Western Australia, *Report of Royal Commission of Inquiry into Alleged Killing and Burning of Bodies of Aborigines in East Kimberley and into Police Methods When Effecting Arrests* (1927)
Public Domain. Parliament of Western Australia.

controversy by each maintaining a single colonial police force with Aboriginal trackers to pursue Aboriginal resistance. The most infamous mass killings of Aboriginal people as a result of police operations were the Forrest River Massacre in the Kimberley in Western Australia in 1926[60] and the Coniston Massacre in the Northern Territory in 1928.[61]

Despite the desire to end the killings across the colonies, the attempts to deny conquest in the 1830s and instead impose one law for all on Australian frontiers did not end the violence. Instead, it proved how weak claims of British sovereignty were – the Colonial Office could not impose British law on settlers who flagrantly flouted their own legal system; while Aboriginal people had never ceded their own laws. Inequality across the racial divide was not going to be resolved by Aboriginal access to court rooms alone. Settlers were determined to wrest lands from First Nations. The new legal fiction of 'one law for all' enabled them to conceal the violence of conquest through the rhetoric of policing.

Historical Cameo

Judge John Walpole Willis

John Walpole Willis (1793–1877) was the first resident judge of the Port Phillip district of the Supreme Court of New South Wales (1841–43). During his judicial career, he had the ignominy of being removed from colonial office twice out of four judicial appointments.

Willis' legacy has been overshadowed by unfavourable historical accounts that focus on his irascibility as a judge. He struggled with long-term health issues that may partly account for some of his behaviour. In one case, he reprimanded a barrister, a Mr Edward Sewell, for appearing before him with a 'fiercely voluminous moustache'. The courtroom was not the place for 'A Whiskered Pandour or a fierce Hussar!' Willis' constant interruption of legal counsel resulted in a reproach by the press that he did so 'sometimes sneeringly, sometimes pettishly, and always debatingly'. Despite his faults, Willis had a brilliant legal mind and was a stickler for procedure. *R v Bonjon* will be explored in this cameo as an example of Willis' legal mind.

Born in Wales, Willis completed his education at Rugby and Charterhouse, from which he was expelled in 1809 for participating in a riot. In 1816, he was called to the Bar. His judicial career began in 1827 with his appointment as judge to the Court of Chancery in Upper Canada (now Ontario). There he argued with colonial authorities over the

[60] Kate Auty, 'Patrick Bernard O'Leary and the Forrest River Massacres, Western Australia: Examining "Wodgil" and the Significance of 8 June 1926' (2004) 28 *Aboriginal History* 123; Chris Owen, *Every Mother's Son is Guilty: Policing the Kimberley Frontier of Western Australia 1882–1905* (Crawley WA, UWAP, 2016). *Royal Commission of Inquiry into Alleged Killing and Burning of Bodies of Aborigines in East Kimberley and into Police Methods When Effecting Arrests* (Perth, 1927), available at aiatsis.gov.au/sites/default/files/docs/digitised_collections/remove/93281.pdf.

[61] National Museum of Australia, available at www.nma.gov.au/exhibitions/warlpiri/works/coniston; Monument Australia monumentaustralia.org.au/australian_monument/display/80059.

composition of the court, leading to Willis' amoval as judge by the Upper Canada House of Assembly. The language in the statute creating the Court of Equity supported Willis' view that the Court could not sit in banco without the Chief Justice present. The Privy Council vindicated Willis' conduct. Ultimately, it set aside the House of Assembly's order of amoval. Then, Willis was appointed Vice-President of the Court of Civil and Criminal Justice of British Guiana in South America. In British Guiana, Willis quarrelled once more with government officials as well as with slave-owning sugar planters. Both groups were appointed as court officials. These exclusives had control over the colony's administration. When Chief Justice Wray retired in November 1835, Willis was overlooked for the chief justiceship. As well as public and professional disputes Willis also fell out with his wife. He ended up leaving British Guiana to remarry. He had gained a parliamentary divorce from his first wife in 1833, a sign of his elevated class position in British society. He then petitioned for another judicial appointment.

In April 1837, Willis accepted an appointment as puisne (pronounced 'puny') judge of the Supreme Court of New South Wales. A vacancy had opened with the retirement of Chief Justice Francis Forbes. In November 1837, Willis joined Chief Justice James Dowling and Justice William Burton on the Supreme Court bench. Willis and Dowling were soon at odds with one another. To end the friction, the Governor of New South Wales, Sir George Gipps, sent Willis away to the Port Phillip District (Melbourne) to act as its first resident judge, but the following year Sir George Gipps reported that Willis was 'unfit for the calm and dispassionate administration of justice'. He too moved for Willis's amoval in 1843. This decision too was subsequently overturned by the Privy Council in 1846 but Willis was given no further judicial appointments.

His most famous address from the bench while in Australia was *R v Bonjon*, a case he presided over in September 1841, five years after *R v Murrell*.[62] It involved the question whether an Aboriginal man, Bonjon, was subject to the jurisdiction of the Supreme Court of New South Wales on the charge of murdering another Aboriginal man, Yammowing. Willis ruled that New South Wales was not unoccupied at the time of British settlement nor had Aboriginal people consented to British occupation nor to the loss of their sovereignty. They were therefore not subject to British law but free to continue to exercise their own laws. It was a powerful speech but its claims were subsequently rejected in Sydney and later by the Colonial Office despite Willis's assertion that he was not 'bound by the opinion of either Mr Chief Justice Forbes, Mr Justice Burton, or Mr Chief Justice Dowling' in *R v Murrell*. Historian Janine Rizzetti argues that the case 'was more about Willis than it was about Bonjon'.[63] It was a product, not of concern for the original inhabitants, but 'another manifestation of Willis' rivalry with his brother judges in Sydney'. Respectful application of the law to Aboriginal people and settlers alike was more an illusion than a reality. Nonetheless it is another example of how unclear British sovereignty was from the colonies' foundations.

[62] [1841] NSWSupC 92; *R v Murrell* (n 29).

[63] Janine Rizzetti, 'Judge Willis, Bonjon and the Recognition of Aboriginal Law' (2011) *Australia & New Zealand Law & History E-Journal*.

The Melanesian Labour Trade

Between 1863 and 1904, Pacific Islanders were 'recruited' to work in northern New South Wales and in the colony of Queensland. Melanesian peoples provided indentured labour for budding agricultural industries, notably the late nineteenth century sugar industry in Queensland. More than 62,000 people were recruited largely from the island groups of New Caledonia, Solomon Islands and Vanuatu.

Note: The labourers who came to Queensland were from diverse societies but were predominantly from Melanesian cultures. They were given the polite label of 'Pacific Island labourers' but were also derogatorily referred to as 'Kanakas'. 'Kanak' is the name of the Indigenous people of New Caledonia, but 'Kanaka' is not an acceptable term in English because of its racist history.

In the founding years of the trade, Islanders were recruited by deception, violence and outright kidnapping but, later, once Islanders understood the nature of the three-year labour cycle, some signed on willingly.

Slave ownership was abolished in the British Empire in 1833 (see chapter four), one of the final measures to secure abolition of slavery throughout the empire; this and the cessation of convict transportation discussed in chapter seven set the Melanesian labour trade in broader context. By the 1850s, the search for a cheap and pliable labour force commenced in earnest. As covered in chapter eight, most Australian colonies also achieved self-government during this decade. Regulation would now be the responsibility of colonial parliaments dominated by pastoralists and, in Queensland, sugar planters. With no convicts available, Queensland instead used **indenture** or contracts to bind Pacific Island labourers to come to the colony for a three-year period, at the end of which the recruiters were to return them to their island homes. An indenture bound a servant to his or her master for a defined period of time under strict conditions and at much lower rates of pay than non-indentured staff. These contracts were in use in Queensland until 1906.

Indenture: a work contract which bound an employee to an employer for a set period of time stipulating rate of pay and conditions of work

From its inception in the 1860s, the Melanesian labour trade was compared to slavery. Historians have been slightly more equivocal – historical interpretation has varied depending on whether historians focused on labour exploitation or on the callous decision to deport these workers forcibly after the passing of legislation to enact the White Australia Policy. Whatever the emphasis, historians have agreed that it was a system marked by economic aggression and exploitation of non-white peoples in positions of cultural dislocation where they could not defend their rights and that the ending of the scheme was motivated by white racial ideology.

In the nineteenth century, publicity surrounding abuses in the recruitment process heightened concerns of enslavement. Mortensen describes two prevailing forms of abuse:

> First, the more prevalent abuse was the engagement of islanders who did not appreciate the nature or conditions of indentured service. This was especially so before 1875 when contact between Melanesians and Europeans was only being established, there were few returning labourers to explain the nature of service in Queensland, and interpreters were scarce. There was also blatant misrepresentation, particularly about the period of service. The second abuse was physical

Figure 9.6 *Group of South Sea Islander Women Workers on a Property in Cairns* (ca 1890). White Overseer, Mounted, at the Back of the Group

State Library of Queensland, Image no: APO-025-0001-0013.

abduction, euphemised as 'blackbird-hunting' or 'blackbirding'. This was a more generally held concern about the labour trade, even amongst planters.[64]

Owing to the contentious nature of this labour the colonial Government promised it would regulate the trade. The first attempt at policing the Melanesian labour trade came with the *Polynesian Labourers Act 1868* (Qld). Since Queensland's laws had no extraterritorial effect, it could not be enforced outside Queensland waters and reports of unscrupulous blackbirders continued. New Zealand-based Anglican Bishop John Patteson was appointed Bishop of Melanesia in 1861. He regularly visited the islands of the south-west Pacific and protested the deceitful practices of the recruiters. One audacious ruse was to use the Bishop's name to entice Islanders on board recruiting vessels and then abduct them. In 1871 the Bishop landed alone at Nukapu Island and was clubbed to death by islanders supposedly in retaliation for recent blackbirding.[65]

[64] Reid Mortensen, 'Slaving in the Australian Courts: Blackbirding Cases, 1869–1871' (2000) 4 *Journal of South Pacific Law*, available at paclii.org/journals/fJSPL/vol04/7.shtml.

[65] David Hilliard, 'Patteson, John Coleridge' (1990) *Dictionary of New Zealand Biography*, Te Ara – the Encyclopedia of New Zealand, available at teara.govt.nz/en/biographies/1p10/patteson-john-coleridge.

Figure 9.7 JW Beattie, *Bishop John Coleridge Patteson* (ca 1900)
Auckland War Memorial Museum – Tamaki Paenga Hira. PH-NEG-6526.

The Bishop's death led to an outcry in the colonies and Great Britain. In 1872, the British Parliament passed the *Pacific Islander Protection Act 1872* – also known as the Kidnapping Act. The Kidnapping Act introduced three measures that briefly curbed the trade until demand for labour in Queensland ballooned. The three measures were, first, to place government agents on recruiting vessels; second, licensing measures for the trade were tightened; and, third, British naval patrols of the islands commenced. Imperial and colonial legislation followed: the *Pacific Islanders Protection Act 1875* (UK)and the *Pacific Islanders Labourers Act 1880* (Qld).

Controversy continued for the next 20 years but Queensland insisted on defending its sugar industry. As a result of a promise made to secure Federation, the Commonwealth Government finally banned the trade in 1904. Despite humanitarian concerns about the trade, the Commonwealth did not protect the interests of the South Sea Island labourers when it ended recruitment. Instead, recruitment was phased out to assist the sugar planters and then it intended to deport all Melanesian workers to secure a White Australia. Between 1904 and 1908 – despite South Sea Islanders' protests – the Commonwealth Government deported more than 7,000 former Melanesian labourers under the *Pacific Island Labourers Act 1901* (Cth), one piece of legislation instituting the White Australia Policy, discussed further in chapter 11.

At the time, Queensland's South Sea Islander population was 9,324. Questionable recruitment practices and poor record keeping, including errors in precisely recording Islanders' original island homes, led to some Islanders being deported to the wrong island entirely where they were killed as intruders. It was a heartless process.

Some Melanesians hid to avoid deportations and a small number who had arrived in Queensland before 1879 were exempt from the round-up. This community endured despite being treated as aliens in the newly federated White Australia. That meant that they could not vote or own land, had to fight for the right of their children to public education, and were banned from working in agriculture and the sugar industries, the areas where they had skills and experience. Today they number many thousands and maintain a distinct heritage as Australia's South Sea Island community.[66]

Pause for Thought

Slaves or Contractors?

Most nineteenth-century concern was about the process of South Sea Islander recruitment rather than about work conditions, but did the existence of a work contract guarantee a non-exploitative working relationship?

Questions to Consider

1. What were some of the problems with these indentures or contracts?
2. What were some of the 'unfree' conditions that Melanesian workers had to endure?

There are helpful links here.

Annexation of the Torres Strait Islands to Queensland

The history of the Pacific Islander labour trade provides a fresh perspective on the issue of sovereignty and the burgeoning field of international law in the late-nineteenth century. Australian settlers and British subjects were behaving in ways that would be deemed illegal or, at a minimum, unscrupulous at home, but here they were beyond national boundaries, operating in small scale societies where village chiefs were the only means to challenge them. Even within Australian colonial borders new problems of jurisdiction arose as the marine environments of tropical Australia became new frontiers.

Torres Strait lies at the northern tip of Australia and separates Queensland's Cape York Peninsula from the island of New Guinea. Two of the 274 small islands, Saibai and Boigu,

[66] For a succinct summary of the South Sea Islander community's petitions to stop deportations and of the institutional discrimination the community endured, see Clive Moore, 'Used and Abused: the Melanesian Labour Trade' in V Burgmann and J Lee (eds), *A Most Valuable Acquisition* (Fitzroy Vic, McPhee Gribble/Penguin, 1988) 165–69.

are within kilometres of the Papua New Guinea mainland. The reason for this proximity lies in the annexation of the Torres Strait Islands to Queensland in 1872 and, in particular, 1879.

Between 1859 and 1872, the Colony of Queensland only had control of islands within three miles (or 4.8 kilometres) of the coast, while islands beyond that limit were supposedly the responsibility of New South Wales. In the mid-1860s a pearling rush began in Western Australia and by 1870 international pearlers had arrived in the Torres Strait Islands. In a similar fashion to sugar-planting in Fiji, the industry attracted colonial entrepreneurs keen to make their fortune beyond the bounds of government regulation and humanitarian concern. Questionable white pearlers as well as skilled fishers and pearlers from Japan, China and Southeast Asia converged on northern Australia in these decades, founding multicultural communities, some of which have survived to the present day. These marine frontiers, like Australia's land frontiers, also became sites of racial conflict and exploitation. White pearlers brought indentured Melanesian labourers to the Torres Strait while in Broome Malays and Indonesians were recruited alongside Aboriginal people and both were subjected to similar coercive work practices. There was already growing concern about illegal blackbirding activities in New Guinea which also remained outside the control of any of the western powers including Great Britain.

The colonial Queensland Government, aware of the potential revenue from fishing, pearling and guano mining in the Torres Strait and the Great Barrier Reef, provided the impetus for the annexation of the Torres Strait Islands and the extension of Queensland's maritime boundary during the 1870s. Motivated by commercial interest, colonial authorities nonetheless also claimed to be concerned about protection of Torres Strait Islanders who, like Aborigines on the north coast of Western Australia, were subjected to abuse and coercion from the pearl luggers.

In 1872, Letters Patent were issued granting the Governor of Queensland authority over 'all islands within sixty miles from the coast' of the Colony. Islands within 60 miles (ie 96.6 kilometres) were controlled by Queensland. The 1872 Letters Patent took in most, but not all, Torres Strait Islands. The Colonial Office adopted a recommendation that the maritime boundaries of Queensland be extended to include Murray (including Mer, Dauer and Waier) and Darnley (or Erub) Islands.

The pearl rush and the Pacific Island Labour Trade raised unsettling questions about jurisdictional limits. In 1874, Great Britain annexed Fiji partly owing to concerns about unscrupulous white planters there and their abuse of indentured servants. Then in 1878, Queen Victoria passed further Letters Patent 'for the rectification of the Maritime Boundary of the Colony of Queensland, and for the annexation to that Colony of (certain) Islands lying in Torres Straits, and between Australia and New Guinea'. The revised border of Queensland comprised all the islands of the Great Barrier Reef with the northernmost limit within metres of the New Guinea mainland. The Governor of Queensland was given authorisation by proclamation: 'to declare that, from and after a day to be therein mentioned, the said Islands shall be annexed to and form part of Our said Colony'.

Queensland's legislature had to enact the *Queensland Coast Islands Act 1879*. On 21 July 1879, the Governor of Queensland issued a proclamation that 'the Islands described in the Schedule shall be annexed to and become part of the Colony of Queensland, and shall be and become subject to the laws in force therein'. Issues surrounding the legality of the Islands' annexation by Queensland were resolved by the *Colonial Boundaries Act 1895* (UK). Since the islands were annexed to the colony, they remained part of Queensland at federation.

Questions about Queensland's maritime boundaries persisted into the twentieth century. Following Papua New Guinea's independence in 1975, its government was unsurprisingly indignant about Australia's maritime border coming so close to its southern shores. The Torres Strait Island community had been in political conflict with Queensland Premier, Sir Joh Bjelke-Petersen but, when the Commonwealth Government appeared ready to concede some of their islands to New Guinea, the community voted overwhelmingly to remain part of Australia, forcing the Federal Government to negotiate a new maritime boundary only.[67]

Conclusion

There is a huge gulf between the parliamentary and legal achievements of the early colonists explored in chapter eight and the fate of the First Nation peoples in the nineteenth century. This chapter has unravelled some of the historic causes of the structural inequality experienced by Indigenous peoples under Australian law. This chapter explored how English law came to dominate over lands that had been claimed by Indigenous nations for millennia. The question of jurisdiction was not settled for many decades; the eventual denial of Aboriginal sovereignty helps to explain how the violence of Australia's frontiers remained hidden for so long.

Australian settlers were actively seeking new economic opportunities in this century and in the 1860s began to bring Indigenous peoples from the neighbouring islands of the south-west Pacific to Queensland and northern New South Wales in what is referred to as the Pacific Islands labour trade. Australia today has a South Sea Islander community of several thousand people who are the descendants of these workers. The exploitation of marine environments also threatened the First Nation peoples of the north, especially Torres Strait Islanders; colonists soon discovered that jurisdiction of their territory was also problematic. The last part of the chapter discussed how this last question of territorial claim was resolved.

[67] Treaty between Australia and the Independent State of Papua New Guinea concerning sovereignty and maritime boundaries in the area between the two countries, including the area known as Torres Strait, and related matters, 18 December 1978*, available at un.org/Depts/los/LEGISLATIONANDTREATIES/PDFFILES/TREATIES/AUS-PNG1978TS.PDF.

10

Federation

Introduction

> Whereas the people of New South Wales, Victoria, South Australia, Queensland, and Tasmania, humbly relying on the blessing of Almighty God, have agreed to unite in one indissoluble Federal Commonwealth under the Crown of the United Kingdom of Great Britain and Ireland, and under the Constitution hereby established ...[1]

On 1 January 1901, the six independent, self-governing Australian colonies of New South Wales, Tasmania, Western Australia, South Australia, Victoria and Queensland united to form the Commonwealth of Australia. As this chapter charts, the process by which the Australian Constitution was agreed was 'unprecedentedly democratic by the standards of the time', albeit far from 'inclusive'.[2] Federation was finally assured following referenda held in five Australian colonies between 1898 and 1899, and in Western Australia in 1900. A first round of referenda in 1898 was followed by a second round in 1899 where five of the six British colonies ultimately approved a draft Constitution Bill. With the approval of 'the people', the Constitution Bill was sent to British Parliament for ratification. On 9 July 1900, British Parliament enacted the *Commonwealth of Australia Constitution Act 1900* within which the Australian Constitution is contained. The Preamble to the Constitution mentions five of the six Australian colonies only, because the people of Western Australia had not yet voted to federate based on the draft Constitution Bill.

The people of Western Australia gave their consent on 31 July 1900. Western Australia, the most isolated Australian colony and the newest to be granted responsible government in 1890,[3] had prevaricated on the question of Federation. On this question, the population was sharply divided between the colony's well-established families around Perth and new settlers lured to the goldfields region by the promise of gold.[4] Within a decade of self-government, Western Australia's population had almost quadrupled from 47,000 to 179,000[5] following the discovery of gold at Coolgardie and Kalgoorlie in the early 1890s. The boom placed Western Australia on a stronger financial footing, yet the economy required strengthening in the event gold ran out.[6] Indeed, half of Western Australia's annual revenue derived

[1] Australian Constitution Preamble.

[2] Nicholas Aroney et al, *The Constitution of the Commonwealth of Australia: History, Principle and Interpretation* (Cambridge, Cambridge University Press, 2015) 4.

[3] *Constitution Act 1889* (WA).

[4] Thomas Musgrave, 'The Western Australian Secessionist Movement' (2003) 3 *Macquarie Law Journal* 95, 97.

[5] *Ibid.*

[6] See generally Matthew Tonts, 'State Policy and the Yeoman Ideal: Agricultural Development in Western Australia, 1890–1914' (2002) 27 *Landscape Research* 103.

from inter-colonial tariffs on goods – a lucrative revenue stream that would soon cease if Western Australia agreed to federate.[7] As newcomers arrived from the eastern colonies a critical mass of support for Federation developed. Sir John Forrest's colonial Government repeatedly refused to put the Constitution Bill to the vote of the Western Australian people 'for acceptance or rejection'.[8] The well-established families, contentedly isolated from the eastern colonies,[9] backed the Government. However, threat of separation (or secession) from the goldfields – a population swollen with pro-Federation settlers from the east – forced the colonial Government to pass an enabling bill providing for a referendum on the Constitution Bill.[10]

This triumphant image of the road to Federation is, for the most part, unreal. First, that image sits uncomfortably with the depressing reality that many people were excluded from voting for a federated Australia on no other basis than the colour of their skin, gender or their impecuniosity. Put another way, the pre-Federation franchise in the colonies did not represent the whole of the Australian people. Second, a 'white Australia' was envisioned for the new nation – an 'Anglo-Saxon monoculture' that would mute the voices of Indigenous Australians and relentlessly exclude non-European migrants for much of the twentieth century – and onwards.[11] Third, the pre-Federation years were turbulent times. The decade preceding Federation was punctuated by a severe economic depression followed, and exacerbated, by a sustained drought. The late 1880s had marked the end of a boom period in land and stock market speculation.[12] The largely unregulated Australian banking system consequently suffered, resulting in a large-scale banking crisis in 1893.[13] Maritime workers' and shearers' attempts to improve their working conditions culminated in strike action and the birth of the Australian labour movement.[14] Unemployment and poverty dramatically increased over the 1890s.

This chapter outlines the Federation movement with particular focus on its legal dimensions. It first examines the influence of the *United States Constitution* and Canada's *British North America Act 1867* on the structure and final form of the *Australian Constitution*. Next, the chapter turns to the Federation debates and referenda of the 1890s. The chapter concludes by identifying important elements of the Australian Constitution, notably Australia's distinctive judicial structure and the office of Governor-General.

[7] Alan George Lewers Shaw, *The Story of Australia* (London, Faber & Faber, 1961) 195. The Constitution removed the States' ability to impose inter-colonial tariffs on goods with the exception of Western Australia which retained import duties for five years after Federation: see Australian Constitution s 95.

[8] Wendy Hillman, 'The 1900 Federal Referendum in Western Australia' (Mar 1978) 2 *Studies in Western Australian History* 51, 52.

[9] The overland telegraph connected Western Australia to the rest of the country in 1877. There was no road or rail connection.

[10] Musgrave (n 4) 97–98.

[11] Raymond Evans, Clive Moore and Kay Saunders, *1901–Our Future's Past* (Sydney, Macmillan, 1997) 14–15.

[12] Charles R Hickson and John D Turner, 'Free Banking Gone Awry: The Australian Banking Crisis of 1893' (2002) 9 *Financial History Review* 147, 148.

[13] David Tolmie Merrett, 'The Australian Bank Crashes of the 1890s Revisited' (2013) 87 *Business History Review* 407, 410.

[14] See generally Robert Mason and Rebecca Damjanovic, 'The Start of It All? Heritage, Labour and the Environment in Regional Queensland' (2018) 25(2) *Queensland Review* 208.

Learning Resources

The content in this chapter is supported by:

Glossary	Chapter Overview	Historical Cameos	Constitutional Detours	Pause for Thought
Latin and Other Legal Specific Terms are Defined	The Federation Movement Secession Federation Debates The Commonwealth of Australia Office of Governor-General	Henry Parkes Alfred Deakin Catherine Helen Spence	Secession Women's Suffrage	What if Women Wrote the Australian Constitution?

Chapter Overview

Place	Time Period	Dates	Key Figures	Key Institutions	Key Terms
• The Australian colonies • Commonwealth of Australia	• Late-Victorian and Edwardian eras	• Late 19th and early 20th centuries	• Sir Henry Parkes • Sir Samuel Griffith • Andrew Inglis Clark • Edmund Barton • Vida Goldstein • Enid Lyons	• Colonial and state parliaments • High Court of Australia • Federal and state courts • United States Constitution • British North America Act 1867 • Governor-General • Tenterfield Oration • Australian Natives' Association	• Federation • Autochthonous expedient • Federal Jurisdiction • Original Jurisdiction

Learning Objectives

At the end of this chapter, readers should understand:

- The historical context behind the writing of the *Australian Constitution*.
- The similarities and differences between the federal experiences of the United States and Canada against the Australian experience.
- Why racial exclusion was a 'given' under the new Commonwealth.

The Federation Movement

Influence of the *United States Constitution* and Canada's *British North America Act 1867*

The structure and form of the *Australian Constitution* loomed large throughout the Federation debates of the 1890s. At the Australasian Federation Conference in Melbourne in February 1890, colonial leaders took the opportunity to debate the merits of the Canadian and American federal models of which they were unquestionably well-versed.[15] New South Wales statesman Sir Henry Parkes initially favoured the Canadian model, but his assumption that it would be followed was quickly dispelled following the Melbourne conference in early 1890.[16] Delegates from the 'small' Australian colonies opposed the Canadian model.[17] Tasmania's Andrew Inglis Clark and Queensland's Sir Samuel Griffith considered it to be too centrally driven and imperialist.[18]

In 1867, the three British colonies of Canada (Ontario and Quebec), Nova Scotia and New Brunswick had amalgamated as the Dominion of Canada. The Canadian confederation also *divided* the North West Territory into new Provinces to enlarge the Dominion. Drafted and enacted by British authorities, Canada's *British North America Act 1867* enumerated powers to central government and thus limited the power of the provinces.[19] Any unlisted powers remained central. That was too centralist for the Australians, a view summarised by South Australian John Cockburn at the Sydney Convention in 1891:

> We know the tendency is always towards the central authority, that the central authority constitutes a sort of vortex to which power gradually attaches itself. … Government at a central and distant part is never government by the people, and may be just as crushing a tyranny under republican or commonwealth forms as under the most absolute monarchy.[20]

The Canadian model nevertheless provided a template for a successful Federation under a Westminster system of government, showing how the Australian colonies could bridge the divide between Federation and the loyalties owed to the Crown within the British Empire. In contrast to the Canadian experience, American federalism resulted from 13 British colonies in North America coming together, although in Australia's case it would be without war or revolution.

The *Australian Constitution* borrows heavily, but not exclusively, from the *United States Constitution*. One striking similarity is the adoption of the names of the United States' Houses of Congress as Australia's two Houses of Parliament – the House of Representatives and the Senate, rather than Canada that followed Britain in its lower house's name, the House of Commons. Likewise, the first three chapters of the *Australian Constitution* were structured after the *United States Constitution*, although not with the strict separation of powers that the American Founding

[15] John Andrew La Nauze, *The Making of the Australian Constitution* (Melbourne, Melbourne University Press, 1972) 16–19.

[16] *Ibid* 17.

[17] *Ibid.*

[18] See Helen Irving, 'Making the Federal Commonwealth, 1890–1901' in Alison Bashford and Stuart Macintyre, *The Cambridge History of Australia* (Cambridge, Cambridge University Press, 2013) 242, 253.

[19] La Nauze (n 15) 16–17.

[20] *Debates of the National Australasian Convention*, Sydney, 3 April 1891, 707–08 (John Cockburn).

Fathers foresaw. Further, the existing Australian colonies became States, not Provinces as in the case of Canada, to underline their continued independence under Federation.[21]

Notable features of the *US Constitution* reflected in the *Australian Constitution* include:

- The Preamble's declaration of an 'indissoluble' federal Commonwealth was in response to the recent history of secession and civil war in the United States, and an effort not to have it repeated in Australia.[22]
- The use of the term 'Commonwealth' was adopted from the republican constitutions of Massachusetts, Pennsylvania, Virginia and Kentucky. The title for the new nation, 'Commonwealth of Australia', met some initial resistance after it was chosen at the 1891 National Australasian Convention.[23] For Queen Victoria in particular, the title was 'obnoxious' and the word 'Commonwealth' harked back to 'Cromwell and his republican form of government' (see chapter three).[24]
- Australia's Houses of Parliament, named after the Houses of Congress (the House of Representatives and Senate), combine the democratic and federal elements in the same way as the *United States Constitution* combines them.
- The House of Representatives is to be elected by 'the people of the Commonwealth', in particular those who vote for 'the more numerous House of Parliament of the State'.[25]
- The Senate is to be *elected* as a house in which the Australian States have equal representation, as in the United States.[26] In Canada, members of the Senate are *appointed*. Canada's ten Provinces are divided into four divisions of 24 senators, who are appointed by the Governor-General on the recommendation of the Prime Minister.
- The residual powers not enumerated in section 51 (and elsewhere) are left for the States.
- Judicial review – a minimum standard of which is entrenched in section 75(v) of the *Australian Constitution*[27] – was accepted by the High Court of Australia as early as *D'Emden v Pedder*,[28] and the authority of *McCulloch v Maryland*[29] and US decisions generally were recognised.
- *Marbury v Madison*[30] was cited as authority early in the interpretation of the *Australian Constitution* and by the founding fathers and drafters, for instance Griffith CJ and Barton J in *Ah Yick v Lehmert*.[31]
- Provisions adopted directly from the *United States Constitution* were sections 80 (guarantee of trial by jury),[32] 116 (freedom of religion), 117 (privileges and immunities clause) and 118 (full faith and credit clause).

[21] La Nauze (n 15) 258; Aroney et al (n 2) 234.
[22] See the constitutional detour on secession in this chapter.
[23] Irving (n 18) 243.
[24] Sidney Lee, *Queen Victoria: A Biography* (Smith, Elder & Co, 1904) 548.
[25] *Australian Constitution* s 30.
[26] Aroney et al (n 2) 46.
[27] For a more in-depth discussion of s 75(v), see James Stellios, 'Exploring the Purposes of Section 75(v) of the Constitution' (2011) 34(1) *UNSW Law Journal* 70.
[28] (1904) 1 CLR 91.
[29] 17 US 316 (1819).
[30] 5 US 137 (1803).
[31] (1905) 2 CLR 593.
[32] Section 80 is only a guarantee of trial by jury for an accused tried on indictment for a federal criminal offence.

In any case, the Canadian experience had some impact on the *Australian Constitution*, particularly in the enumeration of legislative powers. Thus, the wording in section 91 of the *British North America Act 1867*[33] inspired the opening words in section 51 of the *Australian Constitution*, namely that: 'Parliament shall, subject to the Constitution, have power to make laws for the peace, order and good government of the Commonwealth with respect to the specified powers.' Some legislative powers included in section 51 of the *Australian Constitution* were borrowed from the *British North America Act*,[34] including bills of exchange and promissory notes;[35] 'lighthouses, lightships, beacons and buoys';[36] legal tender;[37] banking;[38] marriage[39] and divorce.[40]

Constitutional Detour

Secession

The colony of Western Australia was a reluctant participant in the Federation movement. Factors contributing to this reluctance included Western Australia's geographical isolation and its newly acquired status as a self-governing colony.[41] More significantly, though, Western Australia feared losing half of its revenue that it collected through inter-colonial tariffs or customs duties – taxes imposed on goods entering the colony.[42] The *Australian Constitution* would abolish the states' ability to levy intra-Australian tariffs and assured free trade within Australia.[43] The Commonwealth assumed exclusive control over the imposition of customs and excise duties,[44] although the Constitution did not lay down the nature of the federal tariff.[45] The Constitution did however grant a concession to Western Australia: its interstate tariffs would remain intact for the first five years of Federation.[46] Once Western Australia lost its tariff autonomy in 1906, Western Australian Parliament carried a resolution that Federation 'has proved detrimental to the best interests of this State, and that the time has arrived for placing before the people the question of withdrawing from such union.'[47] Nothing came of the motion, however. The Great Depression reignited Western Australia's grievances over the Commonwealth's economic and fiscal policies that favoured the eastern Australian States.

[33] It is also referred to as the *Constitution Act 1867*.

[34] La Nauze (n 15) 51.

[35] *British North America Act 1867* (Can) s 91(18) ('BNA Act'); *Australian Constitution* s 51(xvi).

[36] BNA Act s 91(9) ('Beacons, Buoys, Lighthouses, and Sable Island'); *Australian Constitution* s 51(vii).

[37] BNA Act s 91(20); *Australian Constitution* s 51(xii) ('currency, coinage, and legal tender').

[38] BNA Act s 91(15) ('Banking, Incorporation of Banks, and the Issue of Paper Money'); *Australian Constitution* s 51(xiii).

[39] BNA Act s 91(26) ('Marriage and Divorce'); *Australian Constitution* s 51(xxi).

[40] BNA Act s 91(26); *Australian Constitution* s 51(xxii) ('divorce and matrimonial causes; and in relation thereto, parental rights, and the custody and guardianship of infants').

[41] Musgrave (n 4) 96.

[42] *Ibid* 95, citing Shaw (n 7) 195.

[43] *Australian Constitution* ss 88, 90, 92.

[44] *Ibid* s 90.

[45] La Nauze (n 15) 41.

[46] *Australian Constitution* s 95. At the end of this five-year period, duties would reduce by one-fifth annually.

[47] Western Australia, *Parliamentary Debates*, Legislative Assembly, 26 September 1906, 1871 (Frederick Monger).

On 8 April 1933, Western Australians voted by a two-thirds majority to withdraw from the Commonwealth. The State Government had to determine how to complete the secession of Western Australia from the Federation: would the State unilaterally secede, seek an amendment to the *Australian Constitution* through the referendum procedure of section 128, or proceed by petition to the British Parliament to amend the *Constitution Act*?[48] In 1934, the Western Australian Government petitioned the British Government requesting its withdrawal from the Federation and reinstatement as a self-governing dominion of the British Empire. A Joint Select Committee was appointed to consider the petition, but the Committee determined that it could not receive the petition citing the constitutional practice that the United Kingdom would not interfere with the internal affairs of a dominion without its consent.[49]

Although the point may seem so obvious that it owes no explanation, an Australian State cannot unilaterally withdraw or secede from the Commonwealth without the consent of the Commonwealth and all the States. The constitutional basis for this prohibition is perhaps less clear.[50] Constitutional writers throughout the twentieth century thought the insertion of 'indissoluble' in the Preamble prevented the unilateral secession of a State.[51] As already mentioned in this chapter, the Preamble refers to the agreement of Australian colonies to unite in 'one indissoluble Federal Commonwealth'. Gregory Craven has argued against this proposition, observing that preambles are relevant only as aids in the interpretation of ambiguous statutory provisions.[52] Instead, Craven contends that the unilateral secession of an Australian State is inconsistent with section 3 of the *Constitution Act*.[53] Section 3 imports a 'continuing bond of union'[54] by using words of 'unlimited futurity',[55] providing that 'on and after a day therein appointed' the colonies 'shall be united in a Federal Commonwealth under the name of the Commonwealth of Australia'.[56]

Historical Cameo

Sir Henry Parkes

Knighted in 1877, **Henry Parkes** (1815–96), was a five-time Premier of New South Wales and an ardent supporter of the federal cause. Parkes' 1889 Tenterfield Oration is one of his better-known political feats. At the age of 74, the British-born Parkes became Premier

[48] Musgrave (n 4) 107.
[49] *Ibid* 121.
[50] See generally Gregory Craven, 'The Constitutionality of the Unilateral Secession of an Australian State' (1984) 15(2) *Federal Law Review* 123.
[51] *Ibid* 124 fnn 3–6, 125–26.
[52] *Ibid* 131, 134–35.
[53] *Ibid* 137.
[54] *Ibid* 140.
[55] *Ibid* 137, 138.
[56] *Australian Constitution* s 3.

of New South Wales for a fifth time. By this time, Parkes had served as politician in New South Wales for close to 40 years. He was also the last surviving member of the colony's first Legislative Assembly after responsible government. Shortly thereafter, Parkes was consumed by the federal cause.

Henry was the youngest of seven children born to tenant farmers in Warwickshire. For three generations, the Parkes family had lived and worked on the Stoneleigh estate owned by the Leigh family. Henry was eight when his family were evicted from the estate. Three years later, Henry's father was sent to debtors' prison (see chapter six) where he remained for 18 months. Henry himself had little formal education, having left school aged 10 to provide for his family. When he was 12, Parkes was apprenticed to a bone and ivory turner for eight years. During this time, Parkes became interested in Chartism, a movement advocating economic and political reform including universal manhood suffrage. In 1836, Parkes married his first wife, Clarinda. The following year, he finished serving his articles of apprenticeship and started his own bone and ivory turning business in Birmingham, but the business soon collapsed.

In an 1839 letter to *The Charter*, a London newspaper, Parkes wrote: 'I am one of the many who cannot now obtain the means of living in their native country. In a fortnight's time I shall be gone to seek a better home in the wilderness of Australia.' In July 1839, a penniless Parkes reached Sydney with his wife Clarinda and their newborn daughter. Two years later, Parkes secured a well-paying government job with the Customs House but after a disagreement with his employer he grudgingly returned to his original trade. He opened a shop in Sydney's centre selling his wares and imported fancy goods. While juggling an expanding household and an initially successful business, Parkes found other fulfilling pursuits at odds with his lack of formal education. Parkes was a talented writer. Throughout the 1840s, he wrote articles and contributed poems to colonial newspapers. He continued his interest in Chartism, campaigned for universal male suffrage, and challenged the continuation of convict transportation to New South Wales. Parkes played a prominent role in the Great Protest Meeting of 1849, campaigning against the arrival of the convict ship, the *Hashemy*, and the threatened revival of convict transportation to New South Wales.

Between 1850 and 1858, Parkes was the editor and proprietor of a left-leaning newspaper, *The Empire*. Parkes contested a Legislative Council by-election for Sydney, a seat vacated by William Wentworth, in early 1854. This was Parkes' second campaign for election, and this time Parkes was declared the winner. His campaign was based on the platforms of universal education, free trade, and the extension of the franchise. Parkes bettered his performance in the 1856 election winning a seat in the newly established and wholly elected Legislative Assembly. *The Empire*'s financial difficulties forced Parkes to resign his seat in December 1856. He had borrowed heavily to support his new lifestyle and expand the newspaper's operations. He re-entered parliament in 1858 but when *The Empire* collapsed later that year Parkes once more surrendered his seat. He was bankrupt.

With the help of friends, Parkes weathered bankruptcy proceedings and re-entered politics once more. Between 1861 and 1862, he toured England as a paid government lecturer on emigration. His family scraped by in Sydney. The mission did not secure a single migrant. When Parkes returned to Sydney in early 1863, he set up an import business over his family's objections. In 1866, Parkes secured his first cabinet post as Colonial Secretary. This portfolio provided Parkes with the opportunity to introduce sweeping social reform in areas such as education, hospitals, police and railways. The import business failed in 1870 and, once more, Parkes became bankrupt. Despite all his business failures, Parkes was re-elected to Parliament and became Premier of New South Wales for the first time in 1872. He was knighted in 1877. During Parkes' career in politics, he reformed hospitals and prisons and introduced free, non-secular public education. At the same time, however, Parkes' government introduced anti-Chinese legislation designed to restrict the influx of cheap labour. Parkes faced a third bankruptcy in the late 1880s.

Parkes, during a regular meeting with the New South Wales Governor Lord Carrington in June 1889, confidently claimed that he could federate the colonies 'in twelve months'.[57] Carrington replied: 'Then why don't you do it? It would be a glorious finish to your life.'[58] In October, he sailed for Brisbane to meet with Queensland officials and parliamentarians to suggest a federal convention. On his rail journey back to Sydney, Parkes paid a visit to his one-time constituency, Tenterfield, and delivered a speech at the town's School of Arts. Later referred to as the Tenterfield Oration, the speech called for a Federation of the six Australian colonies. Parkes compared the colonies' population with the American colonies' population at the time the United States was formed. Concluding that the numbers were 'about the same', he said: 'what the Americans had done by war, the Australians could bring about in peace'.[59] The speech was well received by the public. The Federation movement had begun. Parkes presided over the National Australasian Convention in 1891.

Aspects of Parkes' life remain puzzling. Despite decades in business and politics, Parkes was remarkably thin-skinned. Alfred Deakin regarded Parkes as 'jealous of equals, bitter with rivals and remorseless with enemies–vain beyond all measure, without strong attachment to colleagues and with strong animal passion'.[60] Parkes prospered in government while his businesses floundered time and again. He took loans from wealthy friends and overextended himself financially. On the home front, Clarinda had grown estranged from her husband. A year after Clarinda's death in 1888, Parkes married his second wife, Eleanor (Nellie) Dixon, who had been his mistress for some years. Parkes and Nellie had four children together before their marriage. When Nellie died of cancer in 1895, she left five children under the age of 12 motherless. Three months later, an 80-year-old Parkes married for a third time to Nellie's 23-year-old maid, Julia. In April 1896, the Grand Old Man of Australian politics died.

[57] Helen Irving (ed), *The Centenary Companion to Australian Federation* (Cambridge, Cambridge University Press, 1999) 407.

[58] *Ibid.*

[59] 'Sir Henry Parkes at Tenterfield – Banquet to the Premier – A Brilliant Reception' *Sydney Morning Herald* (Sydney, 25 October 1889) 8.

[60] Alfred Deakin, *The Federal Story: The Inner History of the Federal Cause, 1880–1900* (Melbourne, Melbourne University Press, 1963) 27.

Federation Debates

Australasian Federation Conference, 1890

In 1889, Sir Henry Parkes privately communicated with the Victorian Premier, Duncan Gillies, with a proposition to establish a national government.[61] Following an exchange of letters, Parkes went on to deliver the Tenterfield Oration (see cameo above) in which he exhorted the colonies to 'unite and create a great national Government for all Australia'. Parkes' motivations for pursuing the federal cause remain unclear. The speech encouraged the colonies to send delegates to an informal meeting to discuss whether Federation was appropriate.

Between 6 and 14 February 1890, the Australasian Federation Conference was held in the Legislative Council chamber of Victorian Parliament in Melbourne. The proceedings and debates were recorded.[62] Thirteen delegates endorsed by their colonial Parliaments were sent to the Conference chaired by the Victorian Premier Duncan Gillies. New South Wales, Queensland, South Australia, Victoria, Tasmania and New Zealand each sent two delegates.[63] Western Australia sent one,[64] while Fiji sent none. On the first day of the Conference, Parkes opened with a motion:

> That, in the opinion of this Conference, the best interests and the present and future prosperity of the Australasian Colonies will be promoted by an early union under the Crown, and, while fully recognising the valuable services of the Members of the Convention of 1883 in founding the Federal Council, it declares its opinion that the seven years which have since elapsed have developed the national life of Australasia in population, in wealth, in the discovery of resources, and in self-governing capacity, to an extent which justifies the higher act, at all times contemplated, of the union of these Colonies, under one legislative and executive Government on principles just to the several Colonies.[65]

The motion was carried on the final day of the Conference, though 'Australasia' was amended to 'Australia'.[66] Three other resolutions, first proposed by Deakin,[67] were affirmed:

1. New Zealand and Fiji ('the remoter Australasian Colonies'[68]) were given the option to join at some later date.
2. The Conference delegates were 'to induce the Legislatures of the respective Colonies to appoint, during the present year, delegates to a National Australasian Convention, empowered to consider and report upon an adequate scheme for a Federal Constitution'.[69]

[61] Winston Gregory McMinn, *A Constitutional History of Australia* (Oxford, Oxford University Press, 1979) 102–03.

[62] For transcripts of the proceedings, follow this link: http://parlinfo.aph.gov.au/parlInfo/search/summary/summary.w3p;adv=yes;group=;orderBy=customrank;page=0;query=%221890%20Australasian%20federation%20conference%22%20Dataset%3Aconventions;querytype=;resCount=Default.

[63] *Official Record of the Debates of the Australasian Federation Conference*, Melbourne, 6 February 1890, i.

[64] *Ibid.*

[65] *Ibid* x.

[66] *Official Record of the Debates of the Australasian Federation Conference*, Melbourne, 14 February 1890, 111 (Sir John Hall).

[67] *Official Record of the Debates of the Australasian Federation Conference*, Melbourne, 6 February 1890, x.

[68] *Official Record of the Debates of the Australasian Federation Conference*, Melbourne, 14 February 1890, 111 (Sir John Hall).

[69] *Ibid.*

3. The 'National Australasian Convention' would consist of 'not more than seven members from each of the self-governing Colonies' and 'not more than four members from each of the Crown Colonies'.[70]

At the banquet hosted on the first night of the 1890 Conference, the former Premier of Victoria James Service warned delegates of the 'lion in the way'[71] of Federation: the tariff.[72] In his view, either the lion had to be killed *or it would kill Federation.*[73] Tariffs or duties on imports, even on goods from other Australian colonies, were one of the major sources of government revenue in the colonies. Quite understandably, the tariff question featured significantly in the Federation debates of the 1890s. By maintaining inter-colonial tariffs, the concern was that this would inhibit the creation of a common market within a federated Australia. The Protectionists and the Free Traders were divided on this issue. Protectionists wanted to protect local industry by increasing duties on foreign imports. The Free Traders were not in favour of making foreign imports prohibitively expensive. They advocated for a limited tariff scheme on specific items. Government revenue could be generated from other sources. Sir Henry Parkes, the New South Wales Premier, responded to Service by saying the tariff was not a barrier to Federation and that 'the crimson thread of kinship runs through us all'.[74]

National Australasian Convention, 1891

The first Federation Convention was held in the New South Wales Legislative Assembly in Sydney between 2 March and 9 April 1891. Sir Henry Parkes, as Premier of the host colony, was elected as Chairman. Each Australian colony sent seven delegates; New Zealand sent three.[75] All of the delegates were men. The proceedings were open to the public and press.[76] The discussion surrounding Federation had progressed from *whether* the colonies should federate at all – the question dominating the 1890 Conference – to *how* they might do so.

The work of the Convention was divided into a few stages. The first stage involved seven sitting days where the delegates debated a series of resolutions originally proposed by Parkes.[77] The resolutions embodied four objects of Federation: the preservation of 'state rights'; the establishment of intercolonial free trade; the conferral of customs powers on federal government; and federal control over defence.[78] A further resolution resolved that

[70] *Ibid.*
[71] Later becoming the 'lion in the path'.
[72] 'The Banquet', *The Age* (Melbourne, 7 February 1890) 6; 'The Premier's Banquet', *Sydney Morning Herald* (Sydney, 7 February 1890) 8. See also Irving (n 57) 37.
[73] *Official Record of the Debates of the Australasian Federation Conference*, Melbourne, 10 February 1890, 4 (Sir Henry Parkes). See also McMinn (n 61) 98.
[74] 'The Banquet to the Delegates – Speeches by Mr Service and Sir Henry Parkes', *The Daily Telegraph* (Sydney, 7 February 1890) 5; 'The Premier's Banquet' (n 72) 8; 'The Banquet' (n 72) 6.
[75] *Official Record of the Debates of the National Australasian Convention*, Sydney, 2 March 1891, 2–3.
[76] La Nauze (n 15) 38.
[77] *Ibid* 39.
[78] *Ibid* 37.

the Constitution would establish three arms of government: a legislature, a judiciary and an executive.[79] In the next stage, the Convention delegates divided into three committees focusing on constitutional, financial and judicial business. The Drafting Committee of the Constitutional Committee produced a draft Constitution Bill. Tasmanian Andrew Inglis Clark and South Australian Charles Kingston had already circulated draft constitutions among the delegates. During the Easter recess, the drafting sub-committee convened on the Queensland government steamship, the *Lucinda*, revising earlier drafts of the Constitution.[80] On the conclusion of that trip, the sub-committee had a draft Constitution Bill that provided for a federal nation with an executive under responsible government and a judiciary represented in a superior court. Many of the enumerated powers now listed in section 51 of the *Australian Constitution* were in the 1891 Constitution Bill. The terms used by the Convention to refer to the two Houses of Parliament, the House of Representatives and the Senate, became more common.

In the lead up to the 1891 Sydney Convention, Western Australia remained uncommitted. Western Australia's recent move to responsible government accounts for its lukewarm attitude to the Convention. The Forrest Government resolved to send delegates a day before the Conference was due to commence. The Western Australian delegates arrived by steamer a week late, resulting in some annoyance from other delegates.[81]

Corowa Federation Conference, 1893

Australian Natives' Association (ANA): a friendly society established in Victoria in 1871 for white Australian-born men. The ANA was non-partisan and non-sectarian. From 1884, the ANA pushed the cause of Federation. Edmund Barton and Alfred Deakin were members

The Corowa Conference took place on 31 July and 1 August 1893 as an informal gathering of Federationists. The Conference, dominated by members of the **Australian Natives' Association**, convened in the border town of Corowa on the New South Wales side of the Murray River. Following the Federation Convention of 1891, an economic depression intervened and enfeebled the Federation movement. The 1891 draft Constitution was unlikely to be adopted by the colonial legislatures. Seventy-two delegates from Federation Leagues – non-official organisations to campaign for and promote Federation – rallied together at Corowa for two days to discuss what *could* work.

On the second day a resolution was carried: 'That in the opinion of this Conference the best interests and the present and future prosperity of the Australian colonies will be promoted by their early union under the Crown.'[82] After lunch on the second day, a Bendigo

[79] *Ibid* 37–38.

[80] *Ibid* 64–68.

[81] *Official Record of the Debates of the National Australasian Convention*, Sydney, 2 March 1891, 7–8 (James Munro): 'And whilst I am exceedingly anxious that every courtesy should be shown to the representatives of Western Australia, I do not think it wise, after we have deliberated over the matter and come to the conclusion to meet on the 2nd March, to postpone the transaction of business for another week.'

[82] See also Irving (n 18) 257–58.

lawyer, Dr John Quick, proposed a three-step plan towards Federation (the 'Corowa Plan'). The plan was for each colonial legislature to:

(1) 'pass an act providing for the election of representatives
(2) to attend a statutory convention or congress to consider and adopt a bill to establish a federal constitution for Australia, and
(3) upon the adoption of such bill or measure it be submitted by some process of referendum to the verdict of each colony'.[83]

The plan was later adopted at the Hobart Premiers' Conference in 1895 and taken to the Federal Convention of 1897–98, after which referenda of 1899 and 1900 adopted the Convention's 1898 bill.

National Australasian Convention, 1897–98

In three sessions over 1897 and 1898, colonial delegates met to draft a new Constitutional Bill.[84] Before the first session of the National Australasian Convention started, popular elections were held in New South Wales, South Australia, Tasmania, and Victoria to determine which ten delegates would represent their colony. Queensland had not reached this stage because its Parliament was still debating whether to hold an election. New Zealand did not send a delegate. Three weeks later, 50 delegates descended on Adelaide. On 22 March 1897, in the South Australian House of Assembly chamber, the South Australian Premier, Sir Charles Kingston, was chosen as Convention President. In a Convention led by Sir Edmund Barton, certain resolutions were moved and three Committees (Finance, Judiciary and Constitutional) formed. A Drafting Committee prepared a new Constitution Bill based on 1891's draft Constitution Bill.

Convention debates centred on issues of federal finance, power over rivers, and the make-up and powers of Senate. The Convention delegates preferred direct election, rather than appointment, of Senators. The process for constitutional amendment – by referendum – was decided. The Adelaide session concluded with a resolution that the draft Constitution be put before each colonial legislature for consideration.

The second session of 1897 was aborted. It was convened in the Legislative Assembly chamber of New South Wales Parliament in Sydney. It achieved little, lasting for approximately three weeks in September. Though four new delegates from Western Australia were sent, Queensland was not represented for the colony was still debating the merits of an election. About 300 suggested amendments from colonial legislatures were received.

The third session, and first for 1898, was more productive (if the length of records is any measure – a mammoth 2,500 pages). This Convention session was held between 20 January 1898 and 17 March 1898 in the Victorian Legislative Assembly chamber in Melbourne. An entire draft Constitutional Bill was prepared. New and old topics were broached: how Commonwealth powers were to be allocated being one such topic. Additional federal powers were agreed upon: industrial arbitration, and old age and invalid

[83] *Official Report of the Federation Conference*, Corowa, 31 July and 1 August 1893, 37 (John Quick).
[84] Records of the 1897–98 Constitutional Conventions are available online.

pensions. The delegates agreed on a prohibition against establishing religions (see section 116 of the *Australian Constitution*) and a process for breaking parliamentary deadlocks ('double dissolution'). At the conclusion of the third session, the draft Constitution Bill was adopted.

At the Hobart Premiers' Conference of 1895, it was agreed that approval by Australian voters on a draft Constitution Bill was needed before the Constitution would be sent to the Imperial Parliament for enactment. Thus, the draft Constitution Bill was voted on twice in two referenda between 1898 and 1900. After the first Constitution Bill referendum failed in 1898, the colonial Premiers convened a meeting in Melbourne in early 1899 (the Premiers' 'Secret' Conference). Amendments satisfactory to the Premiers were made to the 1897–98 Constitution Bill. The amended Bill went to a second referendum in the colonies during 1899. This second referendum succeeded.

Referenda on the Constitution Bill

By referenda held in 1898, the electors of four colonies – New South Wales, South Australia, Tasmania, and Victoria – were asked the question: 'Are you in favour of the Proposed Federal Constitution Bill?' People were asked to cross out 'Yes' or 'No' next to the question. To facilitate the elections and the referendum, each colony passed an Enabling Act. The *New South Wales Enabling Act* required 80,000 'Yes' votes before the referendum passed.

Due to the fact that New South Wales' statutory minimum was not achieved at the first referendum and, though the three other colonies reached their minimums, the colonies delayed until New South Wales had agreed to federate.

Figure 10.1 Referendum Results, 1898–1900[85]

1898	**Yes**	**No**
New South Wales	71,595	66,228
South Australia	35,800	17,320
Tasmania	11,797	2,716
Victoria	100,520	22,090
1899	**Yes**	**No**
New South Wales	107,420	82,741
Queensland	38,488	30,996
South Australia	65,990	17,053
Tasmania	13,437	791
Victoria	152,653	9,805
1900	**Yes**	**No**
Western Australia	44,800	19,691

[85] Helen Irving (ed), *The Centenary Companion to Australian Federation* (Cambridge, Cambridge University Press, 1999) 416.

Figure 10.2 *Australian Federation Referendum Results* (1899)

Results of the 1899 Federation Referendum written on a blackboard in the foyer of Hotel Australia, Sydney

National Library of Australia, PIC Box P2202 #P2202, nla.obj-136434299.

Second referenda took place in 1899 after the Premiers' 'Secret' Conference. The defeated Constitution Bill was amended. A second referendum was agreed to, except that New South Wales would hold its referendum first. New South Wales amended its Enabling Bill to remove the voting threshold and to make voting simpler. South Australia's referendum was in fact held first. All colonies recorded a successful result in their referenda.

Western Australia left its referendum until 1900. Only then had the colony decided to hold a referendum, which is why the Preamble of the Constitution omits Western Australia. Covering clause 3 made provision for Western Australia to 'be united in a Federal Commonwealth under the name of the Commonwealth of Australia', but only 'if Her Majesty is satisfied that the people of Western Australia have agreed thereto'.

The next step after the Constitution Bill was accepted at the second referendum was to send it to England for ratification. On being invited by Joseph Chamberlain – the British Secretary of State for the Colonies – a delegation of colonial representatives was sent to London (known as the London Delegation, 1900).

Two issues loomed large. First, clause 74 of the proposed Constitution, which restricted appeals to the Judicial Committee of the Privy Council, was opposed by Chamberlain. A major compromise was reached: constitutional matters could only be appealed from the High Court to the Privy Council with the High Court's certification.[86] The second concern related to Western Australia's request for its customs duties to be preserved for five years if it joined the Commonwealth as an 'Original State'.[87] This is reflected in section 95 of the Constitution.

Figure 10.3 *The Crowd Watching the Result Board at the Courier Building on Saturday Night* (1899)

Crowd at the Intersection of Queen and Edward Streets in Brisbane, waiting for the Queensland results of the 1899 Federation Referendum.

John Oxley Library, State Library of Queensland, Negative number: 109593

Federation would proceed. In 1900, the *Commonwealth of Australia Constitution Act 1900* (UK) was enacted in British Parliament. The colonies, including Western Australia, federated as the Commonwealth of Australia on 1 January 1901.

[86] *Australian Constitution* s 74.

[87] *Commonwealth of Australia Constitution Act 1900* (UK) cl 6.

Historical Cameo

Alfred Deakin

Alfred Deakin (1856–1919) was a journalist, lawyer and politician who was Australia's first Attorney-General and served three terms as Prime Minister between 1903 and 1910. He actively participated in the Federation movement.

Deakin was the second and last child born to gold rush immigrants, William and Sarah Deakin, in Melbourne on 3 August 1856. In 1849, Deakin's newlywed parents boarded a ship bound for South Australia. Enticed by the discovery of gold, however, the young couple and their daughter Catherine soon moved to the neighbouring colony of Victoria. By the time of Alfred's birth in 1856, William was running a successful coaching business with his brother-in-law.

In an era of large families, the Deakin household was most unusual. With only two children, William and Sarah could give their children an excellent education. Catherine was sent to a new Ladies' School in Kyneton, 85 kilometres north of Melbourne, where a four-year-old Alfred joined her as the school's only boy.[88] Catherine was devoted to her younger brother Alfred, writing that 'I worshipped the baby as I have the man during all our lives.'[89] Three years later, a seven-year-old Alfred was enrolled at Melbourne Church of England Grammar School. In 1871, Deakin qualified for entry to the University of Melbourne. After a 'rudderless' year undecided on a career,[90] Deakin enrolled as a 'student at law' at the University of Melbourne in 1872. On the completion of his law studies, Deakin would receive a certificate of admission to the Victorian Bar. During his studies, he was active in the University's debating club and became immersed in the Melbourne spiritualist movement. At the spiritualists' Sunday school in 1874, Deakin met his future wife Pattie Browne.

Deakin was admitted to the Bar in 1877. An introduction to the editor-proprietor of Melbourne's *The Age* newspaper, David Syme saved Deakin from a flagging legal career. Deakin wrote regularly for the paper between 1878 and 1883. During this time, Deakin's political beliefs shifted from free trade to protectionism for which Victorian state politics would become associated. In 1884, Deakin joined the Victorian-based Australian Natives' Association. By this point, the Association had adopted the cause of Federation and publicly supported Queensland's annexation of New Guinea.[91]

In 1879, Deakin won the seat of West Bourke. While it was a decisive victory, Deakin resigned soon after. It emerged that a polling booth in the electorate had closed early due to a shortage of ballot papers, denying the vote to 10 men.[92] He was re-elected to West

[88] John Andrew La Nauze, *Alfred Deakin: A Biography* (Sydney, Angus & Robertson Publishers, 1979) 16.
[89] Judith Brett, *The Enigmatic Mr Deakin* (Melbourne, Text Publishing, 2018) 427.
[90] *Ibid* 45.
[91] *Ibid* 138.
[92] *Ibid* 89.

Bourke in 1880. The first piece of legislation he introduced to Parliament reflected his enduring concern for animal welfare.[93] From 1883 to 1890, he was a cabinet minister in coalition governments. From 1886, he was unanimously elected leader of the coalition's Liberal caucus. Deakin's coalition government introduced legislation to regulate working conditions in factories, to establish an irrigation scheme on the Murray, and to control the lives of Aboriginal people.[94] He represented Victoria at London's Colonial Conference in 1888. Following his government's defeat in 1889, Deakin was relegated to the backbench.

Throughout the 1890s, he maintained a steady practice at the Bar and faithfully participated in the Federation movement. Deakin's involvement in the movement started with the 1890 Federation Conference through to the 1900 London Delegation. At the 1891 and 1897–98 Federation Conventions, Deakin was a member of the Constitutional Committees. Together with other leading Federationists, Deakin created a Federation League, and encouraged Edmund Barton to establish a Sydney branch. Deakin joined the Protectionist Association, the National Anti-Sweating League, the Australian Natives' Association, the Imperial Federation League, and the Federal Council of Australasia.

When Barton retired in September 1903, Deakin succeeded him as Prime Minister and Minister of External Affairs. Deakin served three terms: 1903–04, 1905–08, and 1909–10. At the first Federal election in 1902, the Protectionists narrowly defeated the Free Trades and Labour. The first federal Labour ministry formed in 1904. Deakin retired from politics in 1913. He died in 1919, survived by his wife and three daughters.

The Commonwealth of Australia

The *Commonwealth of Australia Constitution Act 1900 (UK)*

The *Australian Constitution* was passed as an Act of the British Parliament in 1900. The *Commonwealth of Australia Constitution Act 1900* (UK) has nine 'covering clauses' or sections. The Federal Council of Australasia, discussed in chapter eight, was abolished in covering clause 7. Covering clause 4 provides that the Constitution would 'come into operation on the day so appointed'. That date was 1 January 1901. On this day, a federal system of government, in which the six existing colonies became the six states of Australia, was established. Under this federal system, power is shared between the central government and state governments.

Covering clause 9 contains the *Australian Constitution*. The Constitution is divided into eight chapters and comprises 128 sections. Chapters I, II and III of the Constitution invest legislative, executive and judicial power in three arms of government, as set out in Figure 10.4.

[93] *Ibid* 119.
[94] *Aboriginal Protection Amendment Act 1886* (Vic), referred to as the *Victorian Half-Caste Act 1886*.

Figure 10.4 The Three Arms of Government

The Legislative

- The legislative power of the Commonwealth is vested in the Federal Parliament comprising the Queen and the two houses of Parliament: *Australian Constitution* s 1

The Executive

- The executive power of the Commonwealth is vested in the Queen and exercised by the Governor-General as the Queen's representative: *Australian Constitution* s 61.

The Judicial

- The judicial power of the Commonwealth is vested in the High Court of Australia; other federal courts as federal Parliament creates; and such other courts that it invests with federal jurisdiction: *Australian Constitution* s 71.

Though copied from the *United States Constitution*, the first three chapters separating the three arms of government do not in reality provide for a strict separation of powers.[95] The Judicature is, however, strictly separate from Parliament and the Executive Government.[96]

High Court of Australia

The design of the federal judicature is laid out in Chapter III (sections 71–80) of the *Australian Constitution*. Section 71 provides for the establishment of the High Court of Australia and 'such other federal courts as the Parliament creates'. It also allows Federal Parliament to invest federal jurisdiction in State courts. First written in the 1891 draft, section 71 had been influenced by the role and powers of the United States Supreme Court. In contrast to the US Supreme Court, the High Court of Australia has appellate jurisdiction from federal and State courts. The US Supreme Court can only hear appeals from federal courts or in cases involving federal matters determined in State courts.

With the Commonwealth's enactment of the *Judiciary Act 1903*, the High Court of Australia was established in 1903. The first three appointments to the High Court bench were made. The first Chief Justice of the High Court was Sir Samuel Griffith. He was joined by Sir Edmund Barton and Sir Richard O'Connor as Justices. The first Justices of the High Court had been closely connected with the drafting of the *Australian Constitution*. This familiarity undoubtedly influenced the first court's intergovernmental immunities doctrine, which will be discussed in chapter 11. The number of justices were increased from three to five in 1906, and five to seven in 1913. Appeals from the High Court to the Judicial Committee of the Privy Council remained possible until 1975.[97]

[95] Aroney et al (n 2) 33–34, 392, 556–57.
[96] *Ibid* 556–57.
[97] *Privy Council (Limitation of Appeals Act 1968* (Cth); *Privy Council (Appeals from the High Court) Act 1975* (Cth).

The Privy Council's Continuing Role

Until 1986, the Judicial Committee of the Privy Council in London was the final avenue of appeal for Australian courts. While Privy Council appeals from the High Court had been abrogated by Commonwealth legislation in 1968 and 1975,[98] appeals remained from State courts exercising State jurisdiction until the passage of the *Australia Acts 1986* (Cth and UK). Many of the political figures in this text have had the title 'Sir' before their name because they were knighted. The same year of the Australia Acts the knighthoods of the Order of Australia were abolished following the abolition of imperial honours in 1975.

The *Judicial Committee Act 1833* (UK) created the Judicial Committee of the Privy Council to hear appeals from the British colonies. It was the ultimate court of appeal within the colonial judicial hierarchy. Because of the Privy Council's apex status, Australian courts were bound by Privy Council decisions. In *Viro v The Queen*,[99] the High Court unanimously held that it was not bound by Privy Council decisions. This decision followed the termination of appeals to the Privy Council *from the High Court* on matters of state, territorial and federal jurisdiction. There were still appeals from the State Supreme Courts to the Privy Council at this point. Before *Viro*, however, the High Court had shown signs of dissent. The High Court had departed from Privy Council (and – at the same hierarchical level – House of Lords) decisions that it felt were wrong.[100]

The precise role to be played by the Privy Council was one of the most contentious issues to emerge at the Conventions and, afterwards, at the 1900 London Delegation.[101] At the Conventions, arguments were led for the preservation of Privy Council appeals, for confining appeals to certain questions, and for the wholesale abolition of appeals.[102] Clause 74, the most contentious clause of the draft Constitution, envisaged that no appeal could be taken to the Privy Council 'in any matter involving the interpretation of this Constitution or of the Constitution of a State, unless the public interests of some part of Her Majesty's Dominions, other than the Commonwealth or a State, are involved.' The Secretary of State for the Colonies, Joseph Chamberlain, opposed this form of clause 74.

When the draft Constitution was brought to London in 1900, a compromise was reached between the colonial delegates and Chamberlain 'over port and cigars', a reminder of the male dominated political world that had endured for centuries.[103] The final form of section 74 would preserve a general right to appeal to the Privy Council for civil and criminal matters. For constitutional matters, appeals from the High Court were designed to be more limited. Where a case involved a constitutional matter between the Commonwealth and a

[98] *Ibid*.

[99] (1978) 141 CLR 88.

[100] See, eg, *Parker v The Queen* (1963) 111 CLR 610, 632 (Dixon CJ): 'Hitherto I have thought that we ought to follow decisions of the House of Lords, at the expense of our own opinions and cases decided here, but having carefully studied *Smith's Case* I think that we cannot adhere to that view or policy. There are propositions laid down in the judgment which I believe to be misconceived and wrong. They are fundamental and they are propositions which I could never bring myself to accept. I shall not discuss the case.' Although Dixon CJ delivered a dissenting judgment, all other members of the High Court agreed with this passage: at 324 (Taylor, Menzies, Windeyer and Owen JJ).

[101] Scott Bennett, *The Making of the Commonwealth* (Melbourne, Cassell, 1971) 168–71; La Nauze (n 15) 248–69.

[102] Bennett, *ibid* 168.

[103] La Nauze (n 15) 263.

State ('*inter se* cases') or between two or more States, the High Court would have to grant a s 74 certificate to enable the litigants' appeal to the Privy Council. The High Court issued its only certificate in 1912.[104] Still, the High Court's position as the ultimate court of appeal in cases of federal jurisdiction was severely compromised. First, appeals could be taken directly to the Privy Council from State courts exercising State *or* federal jurisdiction. Second, even if a State case in matters of federal jurisdiction was heard in the High Court, special leave to appeal to the Privy Council was available.

Investing Federal Jurisdiction in State Supreme Courts: The 'Autochthonous Expedient'

The use of State courts for the exercise of federal jurisdiction was described in the *Boilermakers' Case* as the 'autochthonous expedient'[105] – a convenient solution devised to suit local conditions. Chapter III of the Constitution sets up the conditions for State courts to exercise federal jurisdiction. As has been mentioned, section 71 of the Australian Constitution not only provided for the establishment of the High Court, it gives Federal Parliament the discretionary power to create other federal courts. In sections 75 and 76 of the Constitution, nine areas of original federal jurisdiction are outlined. The High Court has original jurisdiction in the matters outlined in the five paragraphs of section 75. This is supplemented by section 76 which confers additional federal jurisdiction in the matters set out in the section's four paragraphs. The Commonwealth, authorised by section 76, has conferred jurisdiction on the High Court 'in all matters arising under the Constitution or involving its interpretation'[106] and 'in trials of indictable offences against the laws of the Commonwealth'.[107] In addition, section 77(iii) allows the Commonwealth to 'make laws investing any court of a State with federal jurisdiction' in relation to the matters outlined in sections 75 and 76.

Investing federal jurisdiction in State courts was considered less costly and simpler for the Commonwealth than to establish a lower federal court structure. In this respect, the *Australian Constitution* did not follow the *United States Constitution*, where matters of federal law are dealt with entirely within a separate system of federal courts – the United States District Courts, the Circuit Courts of Appeals and the Supreme Court of the United States. Arguments of economy and simplicity are borne out by the lengthy 70-year period between Federation and the establishment of federal courts in the mid-1970s. The Commonwealth had only established specialised industrial relations and bankruptcy courts before then.[108] Federal matters were dealt with almost exclusively within the State and Territory courts – and, for that matter, most federal matters can still be dealt with in the State and Territory courts to this day. The Federal Court of Australia and the Family Court of Australia were created as lower federal courts in the mid-1970s.[109] In addition to the Federal Court

[104] *Colonial Sugar Refining Co Ltd v Attorney-General for the Commonwealth* (1912) 15 CLR 182.

[105] *R v Kirby; Ex parte Boilermakers' Society of Australia* (1956) 94 CLR 254, 268 (*Boilermakers' Case*).

[106] *Judiciary Act 1903* (Cth) s 30(a).

[107] *Ibid* s 30(c).

[108] *Commonwealth Conciliation and Arbitration Act 1904* (Cth); *Conciliation and Arbitration Act 1956* (Cth) s 26; *Bankruptcy Act 1930* (Cth).

[109] See *Federal Court of Australia Act 1976* (Cth); *Family Court of Australia Act 1975* (Cth).

with its broad federal jurisdiction and the Family Court with its specialised family law jurisdiction,[110] the Federal Circuit Court of Australia possesses a narrower federal jurisdiction as vested in it by the Commonwealth.[111]

The Office of Governor-General

The monarch is the head of State in a constitutional monarchy. The functions of Australia's Head of State are regulated by the *Australian Constitution*. In the first place, the Queen or the King of Australia is part of Federal Parliament.[112] The monarch appoints the Governor-General as his or her representative.[113] Under section 61, the executive power of the Commonwealth is vested in the Queen but is exercised by the Governor-General as the Queen's representative. The executive power of the Commonwealth 'extends to the execution and maintenance of this Constitution, and of the laws of the Commonwealth'.[114] The Governor-General is empowered to establish 'such departments of State of the Commonwealth' as he or she thinks fit.[115] The monarch is the Queen (or King) of Australia. Thus, while in England the current Queen is known as Elizabeth II, in Australia she is Queen Elizabeth the Queen of Australia, as the Commonwealth of Australia postdates the sixteenth-century reign of Elizabeth I.

As examined in chapter four, the principle of responsible government means that the Crown acts on the advice of its Ministers. In turn, those Ministers are members of and responsible to Parliament. Thus, the Queen appoints the Governor-General on the Prime Minister's advice. Similarly, the Governor-General acts on the advice of Ministers of the Crown who are responsible to Parliament. Those Ministers must, in accordance with section 64, 'be members of the Federal Executive Council, and shall be the Queen's Ministers of State for the Commonwealth'. In other words, Ministers must be members of Parliament (and answerable in and to Parliament), and this corresponds with the principle of responsible government. Ministers of State for the Commonwealth are appointed and hold office 'during the pleasure' of the Governor-General.[116]

The executive power of the Commonwealth is not limited to 'the execution and maintenance of this Constitution, and of the laws of the Commonwealth'.[117] Indeed, the Governor-General possesses a limited number of 'reserve powers', which may be exercised without ministerial advice. Most exceptionally, as will be explored in the next chapter, this includes the power to appoint and dismiss a Prime Minister depending on whether that person has the support of Parliament. The usual indicators of parliamentary support are

[110] *Australian Constitution* ss 75(iii), (v), 76(i), (ii).
[111] *Ibid* s 76(ii). See also *Federal Circuit Court of Australia Act 1999* (Cth) ss 10, 10AA.
[112] *Ibid* s 1.
[113] *Ibid* s 2.
[114] *Ibid* s 61.
[115] *Ibid.*
[116] *Ibid* s 64.
[117] *Ibid* s 61.

the passage of annual 'supply' bills authorising parliamentary expenditure[118] or a vote of confidence in the House of Representatives. In 1975, the Senate's refusal to pass supply bills resulted in a genuine constitutional crisis, where Governor-General Sir John Kerr used his reserve powers to dismiss the incumbent Prime Minister Gough Whitlam. Much still remains to be learned about this event following the release of major archival papers, discussed in a later chapter. It is, on the other hand, conventional for the Governor-General to appoint as Prime Minister the parliamentary leader of the party or coalition of parties with the majority of seats in the House of Representatives.

The detail provided on the executive power in Chapter II of the Constitution is limited and, by itself, inconclusive. Thus, its scope within a system of responsible government is best understood by reference to the development of British constitutional law over the course of the seventeenth, eighteenth and nineteenth century as considered in chapters three, four and six. For instance, the convention of appointing a Prime Minister with support on the floor of the lower house of parliament is a reflection of the Westminster system of responsible government. These principles developed in the UK without the benefit of a written constitution. In contrast, Australia's written constitution embodies a system of responsible government by implication,[119] and principles not explicitly stated in the text are supported by convention. Section 64 is a good example. It explicitly recognises the convention that cabinet ministers must be members of Parliament, but it does not address the related convention that ministers must maintain the confidence of Parliament to remain in office.[120]

Constitutional Detour

Women's Suffrage

In 1894, South Australia became the first place in the world to grant women, including Aboriginal women, the right to vote and stand for Parliament. A number of Aboriginal women from the Ngarrindjeri mission at Point McLeay, near the mouth of the Murray River in South Australia, enrolled to vote. At a local government level, female ratepayers had been able to vote in South Australia since 1861.

Counting Aboriginal women from the Ngarrindjeri mission, South Australian women voted for the first time at general elections in 1896. In 1899, Western Australia followed South Australia's lead; however, section 12 of the *Constitution Act Amendment Act 1893* (WA) excluded Aboriginal people from enrolling to vote 'except in respect of a freehold qualification'. Only women in South Australia and Western Australia voted in the referenda on Federation. In 1902, the *Commonwealth Franchise Act 1902* (Cth) allowed women to vote and run for Federal Parliament. The 1902 Act excluded Indigenous

[118] *Ibid* ss 81, 83.
[119] *Australian Constitution* ss 44(iv), 53, 57, 62, 63, 64; *Nationwide News Pty Ltd v Wills* (1992) 177 CLR 1, 47 (Brennan J); *Lange v Australian Broadcasting Corporation* (1997) 189 CLR 520, 557, 561.
[120] Aroney et al (n 2) 408.

Australians from the franchise. While all Australian States had enfranchised 'women' by 1908, Aboriginal and Torres Strait Islander men and women could not vote in federal elections until the passage of the *Commonwealth Electoral Act 1962* (Cth).

In the first federal election of 1903, four women nominated and stood for election to Federal Parliament: three for the Senate – the most famous of whom was the Victorian suffragist Vida Goldstein – and one for the House of Representatives. None of the women candidates were successful, and it would be 40 years before this was achieved. In 1943, Enid Lyons was elected to the House of Representatives and Dorothy Tangney to the Senate.

Historical Cameo

Catherine Helen Spence

Catherine Helen Spence (1825–1910) was a writer, social reformer, preacher and Australia's first female political candidate. Spence was depicted on the reverse side of the Australian five-dollar note issued for the centenary of Federation in 2001.

Born in Melrose on the Scottish borders in 1825, Spence was the fifth of eight children of David, a solicitor and banker, and his wife Helen. Spence received a good education and would have continued her education at an advanced school for girls in Edinburgh.[121] Her teenage ambitiousness led a much older Spence to reflect that she 'wanted to be a teacher first, and a great writer afterwards'.[122] Spence's father dashed her plans through a failed speculation in foreign wheat, which caused the family to suffer financial ruin and social disgrace.[123] This episode not only put paid to Catherine's aspirations for higher education but it prompted the family's migration to the fledging colony of South Australia in 1839. Her father secured an 80-acre section of land in the colony and later held down a position as town clerk of Adelaide. David's death in 1846 compelled Spence to find work. For a short time, she worked as a governess and opened a school.

Spence wrote extensively. In the 1840s, she contributed anonymously to her brother-in-law's newspaper, *The South Australian*. Spence later branched out to novels viewing them as 'the line of least resistance'.[124] She anonymously published *Clara Morison* in 1854 and *Tender and True* in 1856. When she published her third novel *Mr Hogarth's Will* in 1865, she used her name and revealed herself to be the author of her first two novels. Other novels followed. Eventually, in the late 1870s, she became a regular paid contributor of *The South Australian Register*.

[121] Susan Magarey et al (eds), *Ever Yours, C H Spence* (Adelaide, Wakefield Press, 2005) 29.
[122] *Ibid.*
[123] Susan Magarey, *Unbridling the Tongues of Women: A Biography of Catherine Helen Spence* (Adelaide, University of Adelaide Press, 2010) 27.
[124] *Ibid* 41.

Her writings promoted the foundation of kindergartens and supported the advanced education of girls.[125] In Australia's first civics textbook, *The Laws We Live Under*, Spence proclaimed that

> [t]he progress of the world … depends on the character and conduct of its women as much as on that of its men; and there can be no greater mistake for girls to make than to suppose they have nothing to do with good citizenship and good government.[126]

In later life, she collaborated with her niece to form the Kindergarten Union and the all-female South Australian Co-operative Clothing Factory.[127] Spence was also an active member of school and welfare boards. She co-founded the Boarding-Out Society in 1872, which superintended the fostering of orphaned and destitute children to South Australian families.[128] Spence was the first woman to serve on a school board in South Australia, and was appointed a member of the State Children's Council and the Destitute Board.

Spence spent 50 years of her life advocating the cause of proportional representation or, as she called it, 'effective voting'.[129] Adequate parliamentary representation of minorities was at the crux of this movement.[130] It involved a system of quota representation. After Spence read a review article by John Stuart Mill in 1859 on Thomas Hare's system of proportional representation, her childhood interest in electoral reform rekindled and took on a life of its own.[131] In late-1861, she published a pamphlet entitled *A Plea for Pure Democracy: Mr Hare's Reform Bill applied to South Australia*. She formed the Effective Voting League of South Australia in 1895 and stood as candidate for election to the 1897 Federal Convention using effective voting as her platform. She was however unsuccessful, coming twenty-second in a field of 33 candidates. Spence was so devoted to the cause of proportional representation that she was slow to throw her support behind the women's suffrage movement. She joined the Women's Suffrage League of South Australia in 1891.

Spence never married. In her autobiography, she claimed that her Calvinist upbringing made her 'shrink from the possibility of bringing children into the world with so little chance of salvation'.[132] Nevertheless, when her sister Mary died in 1870, Spence raised her orphaned niece and nephew. She raised children of other families as well. Spence, 'the "Grand Old Woman" of Australasia',[133] died on 3 April 1910 in Norwood, a suburb of Adelaide.

[125] *Ibid* 102.

[126] *Ibid* 102, quoting Catherine Helen Spence, *The Laws We Live Under* (Adelaide, Government Printing Office, 1880) 8.

[127] *Ibid* 162.

[128] *Ibid* 84.

[129] *Ibid* 132.

[130] *Ibid* 123–39.

[131] *Ibid* 123.

[132] Catherine Helen Spence, *An Autobiography* (Adelaide, WK Thomas & Co, 1910) 19. She converted to Unitarianism in 1856.

[133] See, eg, 'Death of Miss Spence – The "Grand Old Woman" of Australasia – A Picturesque Identity' *The Register* (Adelaide, 4 April 1910) 13.

Pause for Thought

What if Women Wrote the Australian Constitution?

In her 1994 article 'A Gendered Constitution – Women, Federation and Heads of Power', Helen Irving asked whether women would 'have written a different Constitution from the one we inherited in 1901?' It is a thought-provoking question: women played no direct role in drafting the *Australian Constitution*. The Constitution was written by men and, for the most part, approved by male electors. Indeed, by the time Federation was achieved, only the colonies of South Australia and Western Australia allowed women to vote. But, during the last quarter of the nineteenth century, women activists were campaigning not only for suffrage but also moral and social reform such as the control of prostitution, child welfare and sanitation. These 'domestic and familial' matters of such great concern to women activists were left out of the heads of power in section 51 of the Constitution.

Questions to Consider

1. What if, as Irving pondered, Australian women achieved the vote in the early 1890s?
2. Would women have been elected as delegates to the Federation debates?
3. Given their political concerns over domestic and familial matters, what would the Constitution have looked like?

Conclusion

This chapter has provided the historical and legal context behind the writing of the Australian Constitution. It explored the Federation movement, highlighting the Federation debates and the popular vote that enabled the Commonwealth of Australia to form. Background on women's suffrage and Catherine Helen Spence interrupted the chapter to highlight instances where Australian women actively participated in the Federation movement. Early in the chapter parallels were drawn between the *Australian Constitution* and the federal experiences of the United States and Canada. The remainder of this chapter focused on the structure of the *Australian Constitution* and fundamental constitutional principles. The next chapter takes the story of Australia's federation into the twentieth century, focusing on the gradual removal of Australia's constitutional links with the United Kingdom.

11

Australian Constitutional Independence and Legal Developments of the Twentieth Century

Introduction

As late as 1950, when Prime Minister Robert Menzies gave an address to the Australian Institute of International Affairs, he bemoaned the decline of the British Empire, now officially the British Commonwealth. In a de-colonising post-war world, Menzies worried about how the new Commonwealth lacked 'the old high instincts and instantaneous cohesion which sprang from the fact that we were, all over the British world, as indeed we remain in the old Dominions, the King's subjects and the King's men'.[1] The 'old Dominions' here is code for the white-dominated settler dominions of Canada, South Africa, New Zealand and Australia. For Menzies and for many Australians, whiteness, Britishness and loyalty to the Crown were essential to their world view. His values highlight how British imperial sentiment remained strong in Australia half a century after Federation. For most Australians, Federation had been viewed as strengthening the Empire and Australia's role in it, and any weakening of Australia's links to Great Britain was not to be contemplated.

This chapter explores how the political values of whiteness and Britishness came into conflict in the early decades of the twentieth century and how the disconnect between British interests and Australian interests galvanised the parliament during World War II, leading to the first steps towards constitutional independence. The common law tradition remained an important bedrock during the repressive mood of the Cold War when the High Court declared legislation intended to ban communists to be unconstitutional. It was not until 1975 that many Australians discovered how extensive the reserve powers of the Crown were under Australia's Constitution. On 11 November in that year the Governor-General sacked the democratically elected Prime Minister in what many regard as a constitutional crisis. In the aftermath, further steps towards constitutional independence were taken but anomalies at the state level remained. These were finally resolved in the 1980s culminating in an invigorated High Court which made a number of significant constitutional interpretations between 1985 and 1995 under Mason CJ.

[1] Roy Milne Lecture, 1950, 3 cited in Alan Watt, *The Evolution of Australian Foreign Policy: 1938–1965* (London, Cambridge University Press, 1967) 276.

Learning Resources

The content in this chapter is supported by:

Glossary	Chapter Overview	Historical Cameos	Pause for Thought
Latin legal and political terms are defined	The chapter begins with an overview explaining its intentions and focus	Sir Isaac Isaacs Herbert Evatt	Judicial Review During the Cold War The Dismissal

Chapter Overview

Place	Time Period	Key Figures	Key Cases and Institutions	Key Terms
• Australia	• 1901 to 1990s	• Egon Kisch • Isaac Isaacs • Robert Menzies • HV Evatt • Owen Dixon • Gough Whitlam • John Kerr • Bob Hawke • Joh Bjelke-Petersen	• Engineers' Case • Communist Party Case • High Court of Australia • Governor-General	• White Australia Policy • Federal and state rights • Balfour Declaration • Statute of Westminster • Judicial review • The Dismissal • Constitutional independence • High Court activism

Learning Outcomes

At the end of this chapter, readers should understand:

- The broad powers which public support for a White Australia policy gave the Commonwealth Government.
- How the High Court's interpretation of the Constitution responded to changing Australian political circumstances.

- How judicial review preserved the doctrine of separation of powers and the rule of law in the face of parliamentary over-reach in 1951.
- The stages that removed Australia's constitutional links to the United Kingdom, including the effects of the 1975 constitutional crisis.

White Australia Policy

Soon after Federation, the first Commonwealth Parliament enacted the *Immigration Restriction Act 1901* (Cth) and the *Pacific Island Labourers Act 1901* (Cth) to give effect to a centralised immigration policy commonly referred to as the 'White Australia Policy'. As the name suggests, the purpose of the *Immigration Restriction Act 1901* was to restrict immigration from particular countries in order to create a white Australia, which was a central plank of the Federation movement. To achieve this, non-white immigration had to stop. The second piece of legislation, the *Pacific Island Labourers Act 1901*, resulted in the deportation of approximately 9,000 Melanesian labourers between 1908 and 1914.[2] As explored in chapter nine, racism and racial exclusion had started decades before Federation. As well as effectively excluding Indigenous Australians from legal protection, the Australian colonies had introduced legislation targeted at Chinese immigration and this focus broadened to include Japanese, Indians and Melanesians.

The vehemence with which Australia pursued this racial goal caused the first division between Australia and Great Britain which had responsibility for foreign relations and for managing a racially diverse empire. Joseph Chamberlain, Secretary of State for the Colonies (1895–1903) urged the Australians not to cause offence to other British subjects when pursuing their white Australia goals, hence the decision to introduce a dictation test.[3]

Immigration Restriction Act 1901

Between 1901 and 1958, in accordance with the *Immigration Restriction Act 1901* (Cth), Commonwealth officials administered a dictation test to exclude non-white immigrants from Australia. This element of the Act was modelled after 1897 legislation enacted in Natal, a colony in southern Africa, later a province of South Africa.[4] The Natal model was adopted in Australia to neutralise objections from British, Japanese and Indian representatives about legislating explicitly on racial grounds. The 'trick' of the Natal model was to avoid explicit racial exclusion; instead a literacy test was used as an indirect means to exclude 'undesirable immigrants'. Clearly educated and bi-lingual non-whites who were proficient in English might pass a simple dictation test so in the end Parliament decided on a test in any European language and this was later amended to 'any prescribed language'. In this way, migrants and even visitors, were excluded from the country ostensibly on the basis of language proficiency, rather than on any explicit racial ground.

The Australian dictation test required an officer to choose a passage of 50 words and then dictate the passage to the applicant applying for entry into Australia. If an applicant was unable to write out the passage, he or she failed the test. By failing the test, the applicant

[2] Clive Moore, 'The South Sea Islander Community and Deportation' (1999) 4 *The New Federalist* 22.

[3] Stuart Macintyre, *A Concise History of Australia* (Cambridge, Cambridge University Press, 2009) 143; Russel Ward, *A Nation for a Continent* (Richmond Vic, Heinemann, 1977) 32.

[4] The province is now known as KwaZulu-Natal.

was deemed to be a 'prohibited immigrant' and refused entry into Australia. From 1901 to 1958 the test effectively blocked about 2,000 migrants.[5] As covered in chapter nine, Australia already had a racially diverse population in 1901; the Act now forced non-Anglo-Australians to apply for an exemption to the test each time they temporarily left the country.

15/70

Book No. 130

Form No. 21. COMMONWEALTH OF AUSTRALIA. No. 82

DUPLICATE. *Immigration Restriction Acts 1901-1905 and Regulations.*

CERTIFICATE EXEMPTING FROM DICTATION TEST.

I, Percy Whitton the Collector of Customs for the State of Victoria in the said Commonwealth, hereby certify that Florence May Meu Loong hereinafter described, who is leaving the Commonwealth temporarily, will be excepted from the provisions of paragraph (*a*) of Section 3 of the Act if he returns to the Commonwealth within a period of 3 years from this date.

Date 24/2/15

Percy Whitton
Collector of Customs.

DESCRIPTION.

Nationality Chinese — Birthplace Melbourne
Age 3 yrs — Complexion olive
Height not taken (too young) — Hair black
Build slight — Eyes dark brown
Particular marks none

(For impression of hand see back of this document.)

PHOTOGRAPHS.

Full Face:— Florence May Meu Loong

Profile:— Florence May Meu Loong

Melbourne

Date of departure 14/4/16 — Destination China
Ship St Albans

Date of return — Ship
Port

Customs Officer

Figure 11.1 Exemption Certificate for Three-Year-Old Florence Loong Issued in 1915

After the Immigration Restriction Act was passed in 1901, migrants from Asia and their Australian born children had to apply for a Certificate Exempting from the Dictation Test when they left Australia so that they would not be banned from re-entry.

Florence May Meu Loong – application for Certificate of Exemption from Dictation Test (1915).

Permission given by the National Archives of Australia. NAA: B13, 1915/3487, Item ID 777609.

[5] Eric Richards, *Destination Australia* (Sydney, University of New South Wales Press, 2008) 126.

The legislation was so broad that it was open to political misuse. From 1912, the dictation test was employed to exclude any visitors or migrants deemed unwanted by the Government of the day. Many of the exclusions were based on political and even moral objections of government ministers, rather than racial grounds, so not surprisingly publicity surrounded some cases.[6]

The Case of Egon Kisch

One of the most contentious cases was that of Egon Kisch, a multilingual Czech citizen and journalist, of Jewish background and with left-wing sympathies, who was denied entry into Australia in 1934 after refusing a dictation test set in Scottish Gaelic. The previous year, 1933, was a momentous one marked by growing international tensions and disturbing events such as the burning of the Reichstag and the appointment of Adolf Hitler as Chancellor of Germany. Kisch had been imprisoned in Germany for anti-Nazi journalism and then expelled from that country. In Australia the peace movement opposed the rise of Nazism and invited Kisch to Melbourne to address a peace conference – the All Australia Congress Against War and Fascism. Kisch planned to disembark in Perth and travel overland by train.

Three weeks before Kisch was due to arrive in Perth, the Attorney-General Robert Menzies issued a declaration maintaining that Kisch was 'undesirable as an inhabitant of or visitor to the Commonwealth'. Menzies drew this conclusion of undesirability 'from information received from another part of the British Dominions through official channels'. The Captain was informed of the Attorney-General's declaration and consequently when the ship, the *Straithaird*, reached Perth Kisch was held on board. When it reached Port Melbourne, Kisch decided to jump more than five metres to the pier to escape detention but in the process broke his leg and was carried back on board.

The *Straithaird* travelled on to Sydney where Kisch's supporters engaged a Sydney solicitor, Christian Jollie Smith, who briefed Maurice Blackburn and Albert Piddington KC. Smith secured a writ of *habeas corpus* (see chapter three) for Kisch directed at the ship's captain. A single Justice of the High Court, Evatt J, found in Kisch's favour. The Commonwealth Government was unable to produce evidence that it had received information through official channels. Thus, the Minister's declaration did not meet the required statutory form to justify exclusion, ie that Kisch 'from information received from the government of the United Kingdom … through official or diplomatic channels, [was] undesirable as an inhabitant of, or visitor to, the Commonwealth'.[7]

Though Kisch had won the *habeas corpus* proceedings, it was not over. Commonwealth authorities met his ship in order to now exclude him from using the dictation test. The problem was that Kisch was a versatile European linguist, so Constable McKay administered a

[6] *Ibid* 123, 125.
[7] *R v Carter; Ex parte Kisch* (1934) 52 CLR 221, 225.

dictation test in Scottish Gaelic. Kisch, who refused to comply, was promptly arrested and charged under the *Immigration Restriction Act 1901*.

Kisch was granted bail. At trial, Piddington argued that Scottish Gaelic was not a European language as contemplated by the Act. He cross-examined Constable McKay and a retired police inspector, John McCrimmon, about Scottish Gaelic. Piddington pointed out that McCrimmon, after asserting the accuracy of McKay's translation, had completely mistranslated a Scottish Gaelic passage: a passage from the Lord's Prayer, no less. Kisch was however convicted and sentenced to a term of imprisonment. He appealed to the High Court. The majority found that Scottish Gaelic was not a European language within the meaning of the Act.[8]

Figure 11.2 Czech Writer Egon Kisch Addressing a Crowd on the Dangers of Nazism, Sydney Domain, 1935

S Hood, *Huge crowd in the Domain to hear Communist Party speaker Egon Kisch* (1934). *Hood Collection, State Library of New South Wales, Home and Away – 4742, IE1317247.*

As further proof of its political misuse, and of how transparently the dictation was designed to fail, Gerald Griffin, an Irish-born New Zealander who had also been invited to speak at the Melbourne Peace Congress was also subjected to the dictation test, which he failed. The Kisch case was the reason subsequent generations of Australians referred to the language test as 'the Gaelic test'.

[8] For details of the Kisch case, see Heidi Zogbaum, *Kisch in Australia: The Untold Story* (Melbourne, Scribe, 2004). Kisch also published his own account of his time in Australia in *Australian Landfall* (translated by John Fisher & Irene and Kevin Fitzgerald) (Australian Book Society, 1969).

Changing Views of States' Rights

Case Study of *Amalgamated Society of Engineers v Adelaide Steamship Co Ltd*

From 1903 to 1919, the Griffith High Court had protected States' rights, maintaining that the doctrines of implied governmental immunity and reserved state powers were implicit within the *Australian Constitution*. The implied governmental immunity doctrine saw the Constitution interpreted in a way that the Commonwealth and the States were entirely sovereign in their respective spheres. Resting on the federal character of the *Australian Constitution*, the doctrine meant that the Commonwealth was immune from the operation of State legislation and the States were immune from Commonwealth legislation. The doctrine was confirmed, applied and refined in a series of cases from 1904 to 1907. Each of these decisions was overturned by the *Amalgamated Society of Engineers v Adelaide Steamship Co Ltd* ('the *Engineers' Case*').[9] The Griffith Court had also ruled in 1908 and again in 1909 that the Commonwealth could not legislate in a way that would impair a State's exercise of its residual or reserve powers. This position too was overruled by the *Engineers' Case*. By 1920, the three founding judges had left the High Court, O'Connor died in 1912,[10] Griffith retired in 1919[11] and Barton died in 1920.[12] Membership of the Court had also been increased from three to five, and then to seven members in 1913. By 1920 entirely fresh faces on the High Court brought an end to the two doctrines of the Griffith Court.

The *Engineers' Case* had its origins in an industrial dispute. Ironically, the Amalgamated Society of Engineers, the union for the engineers, was represented by Bob Menzies who would later found the Liberal Party of Australia. Victoria and New South Wales were respectively represented by Jack Latham and Bert (HV) Evatt, both of whom were later appointed High Court judges. The High Court had to decide two issues. The first was whether the Commonwealth had the power to make laws binding on the states with respect to conciliation and arbitration of industrial disputes which reached beyond the limits of one state and which bind the states as employers. The other was whether an industrial dispute existed between the Amalgamated Society of Engineers and the Western Australian Minister for Trading Concerns within the meaning of section 51(xxxv) of the Constitution.

A majority of the High Court rejected the doctrines of implied governmental immunity for the States and their reserved powers. Knox CJ and Isaacs, Rich and Starke JJ delivered a joint majority judgment. Higgins J's reasons were similar to the majority judgment. Duffy J was the Court's sole dissentient. The majority held as follows:

> Applying these principles to the present case, the matter stands thus:-Sec 51 (xxxv) is in terms so general that it extends to all industrial disputes in fact extending beyond the limits of any one State, no exception being expressed as to 'industrial disputes' in which States are concerned; but

[9] (1920) 28 CLR 129.

[10] Martha Rutledge, 'O'Connor, Richard Edward (Dick) (1851–1912)' (*Australian Dictionary of Biography*, 1988), available at adb.anu.edu.au/biography/oconnor-richard-edward-dick-1102/text13691.

[11] RB Joyce, 'Griffith, Sir Samuel Walker (1845–1920)' (*Australian Dictionary of Biography*, 1983), available at adb.anu.edu.au/biography/griffith-sir-samuel-walker-445/text11119.

[12] Martha Rutledge, 'Barton, Sir Edmund (Toby) (1849–1920)' (*Australian Dictionary of Biography*, 1979), available at adb.anu.edu.au/biography/barton-sir-edmund-toby-71/text8629.

> subject to any special provision to the contrary elsewhere in the Constitution. ... However valid and binding on the people of the State where no relevant Commonwealth legislation exists, the moment it encounters repugnant Commonwealth legislation operating on the same field the State legislation must give way. This is the true foundation of the doctrine stated in *D'Emden v Pedder* in the so-called rule quoted, which is after all only a paraphrase of sec 109 of the Constitution. ... The principle we apply to the Commonwealth we apply also to the States, leaving their respective acts of legislation full operation within their respective areas and subject matters, but, in case of conflict, giving to valid Commonwealth legislation the supremacy expressly declared by the Constitution, measuring that supremacy according to the wry words of sec 109. That section, which says 'When *a law* of a State is inconsistent with *a law* of the Commonwealth, the latter shall prevail, and the former shall, to the extent of the inconsistency, be invalid,' gives supremacy, not to any particular class of Commonwealth Acts but to *every* Commonwealth Act.[13]

The *Engineers' Case* is also an authority for the literal rule of interpretation – that the words of the Constitution must be read in its natural and ordinary sense: 'if the text is explicit the text is conclusive, alike in what it directs and what it forbids.'[14] Higgins J gave an extended definition of the literal rule in the decision.

This literal interpretation stands in contrast to the experience of the three original High Court Justices. Griffith CJ and O'Connor and Barton JJ were active participants of the Federation movement, ministers in colonial governments, and Barton was the first Prime Minister; they must have known what was intended in the interpretation of the Constitution. However, Windeyer J's statement in *Victoria v Commonwealth* ('the *Payroll Tax Case*') is particularly apt in contextualising the *Engineers' Case* decision against the demand that constitutional interpretation be in touch with national needs:

> in 1920 the *Constitution* was read in a new light, a light reflected from events that had, over twenty years, led to a growing realization that Australians were now one people and Australia one country and that national laws might meet national needs. ... reading the instrument in this light does not to my mind mean that the original judges of the High Court were wrong in their understanding of what at the time of federation was believed to be the effect of the *Constitution* and in reading it accordingly.[15]

Constitutional Independence in Australia

Treaty of Versailles 1919

There had been a growing sense of Australian national identity ahead of state identity as a result of Australian experiences in World War I. The sense of Australian-ness was augmented by the peace conference at Versailles following the War's end in 1919. Australia, New Zealand, Canada and South Africa were each given a seat at the conference table rather than merely being represented by Great Britain and invited to join the League of Nations at its foundation. This was recognition by the rest of the world that these British dominions were self-governing nations and all four became signatories of the resulting treaty. The *Treaty of Peace (Germany) Act 1919* (Cth) carried the Treaty of Versailles into effect.

[13] The *Engineers' Case* (n 9) 154. A longer excerpt from the judgment is given on the website.
[14] *Ibid* 150.
[15] (1971) 122 CLR 353.

Figure 11.3 J Finnemore, *The Signing of the Treaty of Peace at Versailles*, 28 June 1919 (1919)
Public domain. Australian War Memorial Accession no. ART 16770.

Australia's aim for the post-war period was not independence however but to re-build the British Empire. Nonetheless, Australian Prime Minister Billy Hughes embarrassed the British delegation by blocking a Japanese resolution on racial equality in the League of Nations charter. Japan, an ally of Great Britain, was deeply offended but Hughes was determined to defend the White Australia policy from any possible threat.[16] Hughes made his mark on the international stage for defending a racist migration policy rather than independence per se.

Balfour Declaration of 1926

Strong imperial sentiment in Australia was apparent too when Britain resumed the practice of Imperial Conferences after the War. These were a means of consulting members over empire-wide matters. In 1926 the dominions of Canada and South Africa were much more forthright in their demands for greater independence. Arthur Balfour, former Prime Minister of the United Kingdom (1902–05), chaired the 1926 Imperial Conference of British Empire leaders, and under pressure from South Africa and Canada issued the Balfour Declaration.

It proclaimed that Great Britain and its Dominions were 'equal in status' with respect to 'any aspect of their domestic or external affairs'. Great Britain and its Dominions were 'autonomous communities … though united by a common allegiance to the Crown, and freely associated as members of the British Commonwealth of Nations'. Balfour nonetheless

[16] Macintyre (n 3) 166–67.

insisted that Great Britain remain ***primus inter pares*** when it came to foreign policy, promising only greater consultation with the Dominions over international affairs.

The main concession made in the Balfour Declaration was that governors-general would no longer be appointed by the King on the advice of the British Prime Minister, although the process was not clarified until the Imperial Conference of 1930. The governors-general were now to hold the 'same position in relation to public affairs in the Dominion as is held by His Majesty the King in Great Britain, and that he is not the representative or agent of His Majesty's Government in Great Britain'.[17] This meant that the Governor-General of Australia could now be appointed on the recommendation of the Australian Prime Minister, and such an appointee would no longer be answerable to the King of England but was to loyally support the local parliament. This had not been the practice previously when governors-general had made critical reports of Australian governments because their first allegiance was to the Government of Great Britain.[18]

Primus inter pares (Latin): first among equals

Conservative governments disapproved of the change and the constitutional situation was not clear but in 1930, the Scullin Labor Government[19] had an opportunity to appoint an Australian-born Governor-General and chose Sir Isaac Isaacs. Although the change was resisted by King George V,[20] the former Chief Justice of the High Court became Australia's first Australian-born Governor-General in 1931. Another Australian was not appointed until 1947 when the Chifley Labor Government appointed Sir William McKell. A non-Labor Government would not appoint an Australian until 1965 when Lord Richard Casey took the office.[21]

Historical Cameo

Sir Isaac Isaacs

Sir Isaac Alfred Isaacs (1855–1948) was a politician, Justice of the High Court of Australia (1906–30) and the first Australian-born Governor-General (1931–36).

Born in Melbourne, Isaacs was the first of six children of Alfred, a Jewish tailor originally from Russian Poland, and Rebecca Isaacs (née Abrahams). Isaacs' parents were married in London and immigrated to Victoria in 1854. Isaacs spent his childhood in two north-eastern Victorian towns, Yackandandah and nearby Beechworth where he became dux of Beechworth Grammar School. Before finishing school, Isaacs was employed as a pupil teacher. He passed teachers' examinations and, for five years, taught at local state and grammar schools.

After unsuccessfully suing the headmaster of his school for unpaid wages, Isaacs quit teaching to take up law. While working as a law clerk for the Crown Law Department in Melbourne, he enrolled in a law degree at the University of Melbourne in 1876. In 1880,

[17] Balfour Declaration 1926 (Imperial Conference) 3.

[18] Stuart Macintyre, *Oxford History of Australia: Volume 4 1901–1942* (Oxford, Oxford University Press, 1986) 180.

[19] James Scullin was Prime Minister of Australia 22 October 1929–6 January 1932.

[20] John Waugh, 'An Australian in the Palace of the King-Emperor: James Scullin, George V and the Appointment of the First Australian-Born Governor-General' (2011) 35 *Federal Law Review* 236, 237–38.

[21] For critical reception of both decisions, see Ward (n 3) 279, 351–52. Links to biographical details of the governors-general are available here.

he graduated with a Bachelor of Laws with first class honours, followed by a Master of Laws in 1883. In 1882, Isaacs left the Crown Law Department for the Victorian Bar where he gradually built up a substantial practice mostly centred on commercial law matters. He was noted by his colleagues for his breadth of knowledge and his attention to detail. Isaacs was appointed QC in 1899. By 1886, Isaacs was doing well enough to move his parents from Beechworth to a capacious two-storey house in Auburn, Melbourne. In 1888, Isaacs married Deborah (Daisy) Jacobs with whom he had two daughters, Marjorie and Nancy.

In 1892, while still at the Victorian Bar, Isaacs was elected to a seat in the Legislative Assembly as Member for Bogong. His political policies mirrored his commercial interests at the Bar. During the conservative Patterson Ministry, he acted as Solicitor-General, a position he resigned from after a dispute with the Attorney-General. Isaacs wanted to prosecute members of a bank board for their failings during the economic collapse of the 1890s and his stance won him support from the press and the public. In 1894, he was re-elected and the new government offered Isaacs the office of Attorney-General (1894–99), which he accepted.

Isaacs was elected as the fifth of 10 Victorian delegates to the 1897–98 Constitutional Conventions. Though a leader at the Victorian Bar and a popular public figure, Isaacs was unpopular with his parliamentary peers and fellow delegates. He was denied a role on the constitutional drafting committee. Isaacs' participation in the Federation Movement revealed the strength of his nationalism. He favoured the restriction of appeals to the Privy Council, the establishment of a High Court with membership independent of the State Supreme Courts, and strong federal powers. Isaacs' commitment to the Constitution Bill, though he had doubts about some elements of it, grew during the Federation campaign. He publicly claimed that: 'Every vote for the Bill is a brick that will help to raise the edifice of the Nation.'

Isaacs left State politics when he won the seat of Indi in the first federal elections. Throughout his time in politics right up to his appointment to the High Court in 1906, Isaacs continued to practice as a barrister at the Victorian Bar. On 12 October 1906, the second Deakin Government appointed Isaacs as the fourth and HB Higgins as the fifth Justice of an expanded High Court. The views of the foundation High Court Justices were directly opposed to the views of the new appointees. The first three Justices were protective of States' rights whereas Isaacs favoured a constitutional interpretation gravitating towards the Commonwealth. In time, Isaacs' views prevailed. In the *Engineers' Case*, the High Court's literal reading of the Constitution expanded federal constitutional power. Isaacs J read the majority judgment with the concurrence of Knox CJ, and Starke and Rich J.

Isaacs' personality was polarising, but he was also subject to anti-Semitism. Erstwhile judicial colleagues, Griffith and Barton, were cautious. In private correspondence with Griffith, Barton described Isaacs as an insincere 'Jew boy'.[22] Isaacs was criticised by his contemporaries for vanity and dogmatic certainty; on the other hand, Isaacs' knowledge, industry and memory were admired.

[22] Griffith-Barton correspondence cited in Michael Kirby, 'Sir Isaac Isaacs: A Sesquicentenary Reflection' (2005) 29 *Melbourne University Law Review* 880, 895.

In 1921, Isaacs was created a Privy Councillor and, in 1928, was knighted for meritorious services to the nation. On 2 April 1930, Isaacs succeeded Adrian Knox as Chief Justice of the High Court. Isaacs held the office of Chief Justice for less than a year before taking office as Governor-General on 22 January 1931. Isaacs was the first Australian to hold the office of Governor-General as earlier governors-general had tended to be English aristocrats. For the first time the appointment of the Governor-General followed a recommendation to the monarch from the Australian Prime Minister, James Scullin (and not the British Prime Minister). King George V disliked the change made by the Balfour Declaration and confirmed at the Imperial conference in 1930 but Isaacs carried out his functions as Governor-General, especially on constitutional questions, with considerable aplomb. His appointment was also popular with the Australian people. Isaacs retired from public office in 1936. In retirement, Isaacs publicly opposed **Zionism** and the establishment of a Jewish State in Palestine in a series of letters to the *Hebrew Standard*. He was of the opinion that a national or ethnic identity did not represent the Jewish identity; it was a religious identity. His opinions on Zionism and Israel caused disruption within the Jewish community.

Zionism: Jewish nationalist movement mobilised in the late nineteenth century to advocate for a national Jewish State in Palestine which the UN created as the State of Israel in 1948

Figure 11.4 Governor-General Sir Isaac Isaacs at an Official Event
Photographs of Sir Isaac Isaacs, mainly showing him at various official ceremonies (1933–1947). *Mitchell Library, State Library of New South Wales, PXA 894, IE3141660.*

Isaacs died at his Melbourne home on 11 February 1948, survived by his wife Deborah (Daisy) and two daughters. He was given a state funeral.[23]

[23] Zelman Cowen, 'Isaacs, Sir Isaac Alfred (1855–1948)' (*Australian Dictionary of Biography*, 1983), available at adb.anu.edu.au/biography/isaacs-sir-isaac-alfred-6805/text11773.

Statute of Westminster 1931

Canada and South Africa continued to press for greater autonomy so following the Imperial Conference of 1930, the British Government enacted the Statute of Westminster 1931 'to give effect to certain resolutions passed by Imperial Conferences held in the years 1926 and 1930.' The Statute of Westminster applied only to the Dominions that had participated in the 1926 and 1930 Imperial Conferences, namely Canada, Australia, New Zealand, South Africa, the Irish Free State and Newfoundland (which has since become part of Canada).

The Statute of Westminster extended the autonomy of these named British Dominions in a number of ways. It finally removed the power of the British Parliament to veto laws passed by the Dominions on the grounds of repugnancy and the British Parliament could no longer make laws that bound the Dominions. Most importantly it allowed the Dominions to pass laws covering extra-territorial operations – this was essential under international law to allow the Dominions to develop their own diplomatic service and establish separate foreign policy.

However, the Statute of Westminster also had to be ratified by the Australian Parliament before it could come into effect.[24] Conservatives were in office in Australia from January 1932 to October 1941 and refused to ratify the substantive clauses. Some like Attorney-General Robert Menzies expressly opposed it.[25]

Australia in World War II: *The Statute of Westminster Adoption Act 1942* (Cth)

Australia had still not ratified the statute when Britain declared war against Nazi Germany on 3 September 1939. Robert Menzies, now Prime Minister, solemnly informed the Australian people via radio broadcast, 'Britain has declared war … as a result, Australia is also at war.' When Japan rapidly moved into south east Asia in the early months of 1942, Australia's unpreparedness for military aggression in its own sphere became a national crisis.

The Australian Government had failed to independently assess the situation in Asia, instead relying on British advice and focusing support behind the British war effort. Australia had developed its own navy in 1910–11 but in November 1939 the Royal Australian Navy was placed under the control of the British Admiralty. This meant that Australia's naval forces were now serving under the *Naval Discipline Act 1866*. The crucial difference between this Act and Australia's own *Defence Act 1903* (Cth) was the British reliance on use of the death penalty – in 1903 Australian parliamentarians

[24] *Statute of Westminster* s 10.

[25] Commonwealth, *Parliamentary Debates*, House of Representatives, 25 August 1937 (Robert Menzies, Attorney-General).

had insisted in the face of British opposition that it apply only in cases of mutiny, treason and desertion to the enemy and any such decision had to be confirmed by the Governor-General. At the height of the military crisis in the Pacific, in April 1942, two crew members of *HMAS Australia* were found guilty by court martial of murder and the Australian Government discovered it had no means of intervening to prevent their official execution.[26]

This was the catalyst finally for the Australian Parliament to agree to the ratification of the Statute of Westminster. Despite anxieties about weakening the 'silken threads that have bound us to the mother country',[27] enabling legislation was passed and came into operation on 9 October 1942 but with retrospective provisions to cover the start of the War. Attorney-General HV Evatt then commuted the sentences of the two Australians.

The Australian Parliament now had full independence although none of the provisions of the Statute of Westminster applied to the States.[28] Thus, the British Parliament could still override state legislation and the monarch still appointed State governors. Acts of the British Parliament enacted before the commencement of the Statute of Westminster also continued to apply by paramount force until amended by an Act of Dominion Parliament. The incongruous position of the States would emerge as a problem during a later constitutional crisis but the pressing issue of the 1950s was the role of the High Court in defending the rule of law during the Cold War.

Judicial Review During the Cold War

In *Australian Communist Party v Commonwealth* ('*Communist Party Case*')[29] the High Court struck down the *Communist Party Dissolution Act 1950* (Cth) as constitutionally invalid. The legacy of the Communist Party case is two-fold: first, it affirmed the rule of law and, second, it confirmed the power of judicial review (explored in chapter five).

In December 1949, Robert Menzies again became Prime Minister when a Liberal-Country Party coalition won the Federal election. International tensions were rising as the Cold War commenced. One of the Coalition's election platforms was to ban the Communist Party. The Coalition had secured 61 per cent of seats in the House of Representatives, though Labor had the majority in the Senate.

[26] Chris Clark, 'The Statute of Westminster and the Murder in *HMAS Australia*, 1942' (2009) 179 *Australian Defence Force Journal* 18, 18–20.

[27] Commonwealth Parliamentary Debates cited in Clark, *ibid* 23.

[28] *Statute of Westminster Adoption Act 1942* (Cth) s 9(1).

[29] (1951) 83 CLR 1.

Figure 11.5 Queen Elizabeth II and Robert Menzies at a State Banquet in Canberra, 1954

Royalty – Queen and royal family – Queen Elizabeth and Prime Minister Robert Menzies, Parliament House Australia (1954).

Permission given by National Archives of Australia. NAA: A1773, RV490, Item ID 11497709.

On 27 April 1950, the Communist Party Dissolution Bill was introduced into the House of Representatives. The Bill relied on the defence power,[30] the incidental power[31] and the executive power[32] of the Constitution to justify its attempts to dissolve the Australian Communist Party ('CPA').

During World War II, the Menzies and Curtin Governments had used the Commonwealth's defence power to ban the CPA using the *National Security (Subversive Associations) Regulations 1940* (Cth). Leading members were interned as were those of the pacifist church, Jehovah's Witnesses. These earlier provisions were found unconstitutional in the *Jehovah's Witnesses Case*.[33] Now with popular opinion behind him, Menzies again sought to ban the Communist Party.

The *Communist Party Dissolution Act 1950* received Royal Assent on 20 October 1950. The Act's lengthy Preamble asserted that measures in the Act were 'necessary' to ensure the security and defence of Australia as well as the maintenance of the Australian Constitution

[30] *Australian Constitution* s 51(vi).
[31] *Ibid* s 51(xxxix).
[32] *Ibid* s 61.
[33] (1943) 67 CLR 116.

and the law. The CPA was to be declared an unlawful association and dissolved,[34] while its property confiscated without compensation.[35] The measures did not stop there; affiliated organisations could also be dissolved by declaration of the Governor-General.[36] The Act had broadly defined 'affiliated' as any organisation that had members of the CPA on its governing body, or individuals who were deemed by the Government to be advocating or supporting communism.[37] Furthermore, individuals could be declared communist without being a member of the Communist Party, for simply being 'alleged' to be a communist or 'likely to engage in prejudicial activities'.[38] An Australian would not need to be a member of the CPA to be an unlawful person under the Act.

The Menzies Government was not only targeting the CPA but also many leading trade unions whose executive included CPA members, as well as numerous civil society organisations. Communist Party members were involved in many community associations such as peace movement groups and even the Australian Housewives Association. All were now at risk of being declared unlawful.

The Australian Communist Party, unions, and union officials challenged the constitutional validity of the legislation on the day of its enactment. The plaintiffs sought from the High Court a declaration that the *Communist Party Dissolution Act 1950* was void and an injunction to restrain the Government from enforcing the Act's provisions. Instead of issuing an injunction, Dixon J stated a case and reserved two questions of law for the Full High Court:

1. Did the validity of the Act depend on proof in court of the facts recited in its Preamble, and were the plaintiffs entitled to adduce evidence to support their denial of those facts?
2. If not, was the Communist Party Dissolution Act 1950 (Cth) invalid in whole or in part?

Dixon was pointing to one of the fundamental tenets of English law:[39] that accused Australians must be deemed innocent until the Government had provided proof in a court of law that they were in fact a communist.

On 9 March 1951 the High Court handed down its decision. Five of the seven Justices answered the questions with a 'No' and a 'Yes' respectively. A six to one majority struck down the *Communist Party Dissolution Act 1950* as constitutionally invalid. The Act did not leave the question of whether an association or individual was guilty of subversion for judicial determination; the Act already declared that the Australian Communist Party was guilty in its recitals. The Governor-General was then given the machinery to declare associations and individuals. Put another way, the Act applied to specific persons or associations, rather than to specific conduct. It did not 'define the conduct alleged

[34] *Communist Party Dissolution Act 1950* (Cth) s 4(1).
[35] *Ibid* s 4(2).
[36] *Ibid* s 5.
[37] *Ibid* s 5(3).
[38] *Ibid* s 9.
[39] See chapter four of this volume.

to be prejudicial to the execution or maintenance of the Constitution or the laws of the Commonwealth or the means of combating it'.[40] The connection between the conduct and the legislative powers engaged was tenuous at best. The Act simply allowed Parliament and the Governor-General to declare bodies or persons as illegal on being themselves satisfied. This is a function of the judiciary, not the legislature or the executive. Here the High Court re-asserted principles discussed in chapter five regarding judicial review and the separation of powers.

Figure 11.6 Sir Owen and Lady Dixon
Herald & Weekly Times, *Sir Owen Dixon [picture]* (1950).
Herald & Weekly Times Limited Portrait Collection, State Library of Victoria, Accession no: H38849/1127.

Prime Minister Menzies was very unhappy with the High Court decision and immediately called a referendum to change the Constitution to give the Commonwealth power to make laws with respect to Communists and Communism. It was great political timing as the High Court challenge had sown deep division inside the Labor Opposition.

Vehement anti-communists inside the Labor Party attacked those whom they assumed were communist sympathisers. The Labor Deputy Leader was Bert Evatt. Although he was the Labor Deputy Leader, Evatt – then still a barrister – had represented the Communist-affiliated Waterside Workers Federation in the High Court challenge. Many in the Labor Party thought this a politically disastrous move on Evatt's part as it gave the impression that Evatt had Communist sympathies. As a barrister, Evatt considered that professional ethics demanded that he represent anyone who briefed him. Furthermore, he was committed to the rule of law and deeply concerned about the implications for Australian

[40] *Communist Party Case* (n 29) 231 (Williams J).

civil liberties posed by the legislation, principles which the anti-communists refused to acknowledge in the midst of Cold War fears. Although Evatt's argument before the High Court was successful, internal party tensions increased when Ben Chifley died in June 1951 and Evatt became Leader of the Opposition.

Internal politics grew even worse when Doc Evatt on principle campaigned against the referendum. Menzies painted him and his party as soft on communism, but Evatt led a remarkable campaign in convincing Australians to vote 'No' on 22 September 1951. The referendum failed narrowly: 50.56 per cent against 49.44 per cent for 'Yes'.[41] Anti-communist agitators inside the federal Labor Party soon walked out to form the Democratic Labour Party (DLP), weakening the Australian Labor Party and leaving it out of office for another two decades.[42] By the time Gough Whitlam's ALP formed government in 1972, a generation of Australians was hungry for change.

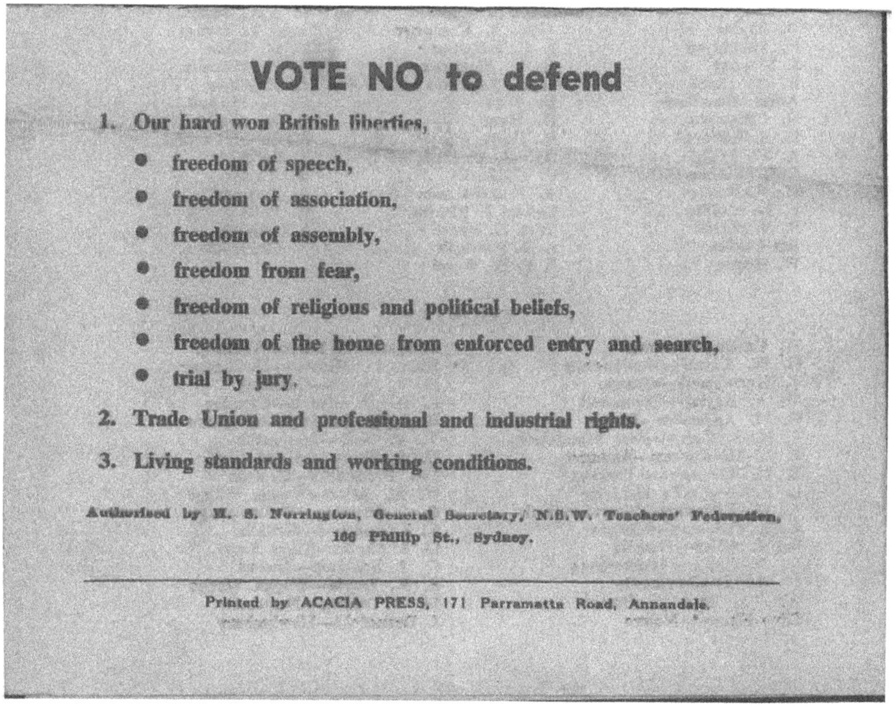

Figure 11.7 The NSW Teachers Federation Advocates a No Vote in the 1951 Referendum
'No' Campaign, 1951 Referendum (1951) 4.
National Archives of Australia. NAA: B2836, GROUP 5, Item ID 412656.

[41] Australian Electoral Commission, 'Referendum Dates and Results' (24 October 2012), available at aec.gov.au/Elections/referendums/Referendum_Dates_and_Results.htm.

[42] For details of these tumultuous events from Evatt's perspective, see John Murphy, *Evatt: A Life* (Sydney, New South, 2016) 268–360. For a general overview of the period, see Macintyre (n 18) 215–31.

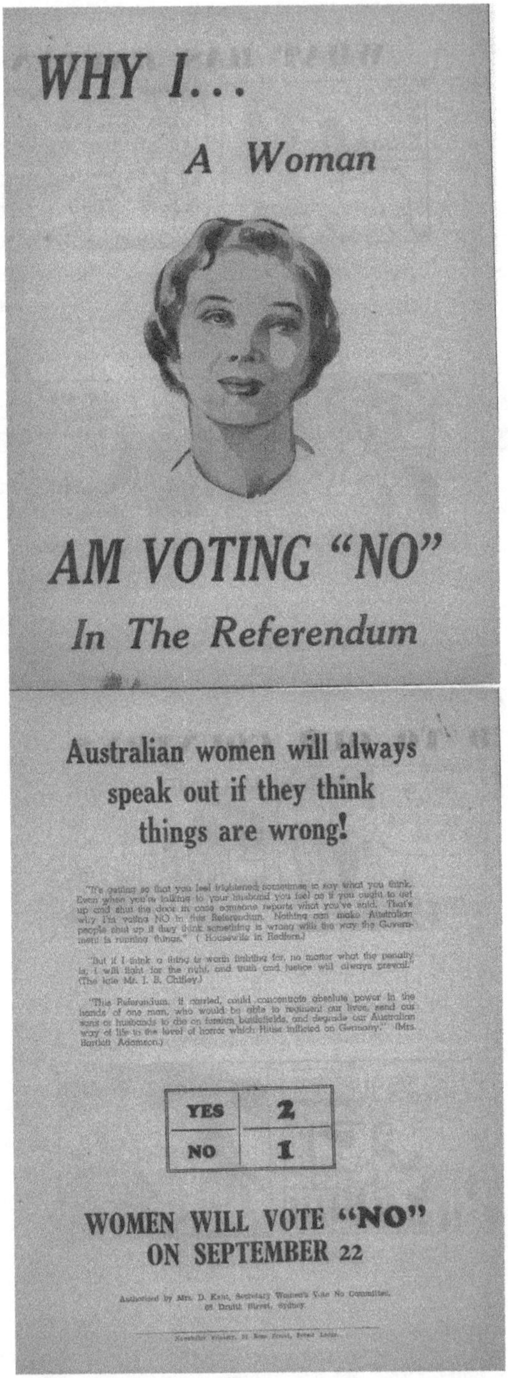

Figure 11.8 1951 Referendum Campaign Material

'No' Campaign, 1951 Referendum (1951) 4.

National Archives of Australia. NAA: B2836, GROUP 5, Item ID 412656.

Historical Cameo

Herbert Evatt

Herbert Vere (Doc) Evatt was a State and Federal Labor politician, the youngest ever Justice of the High Court of Australia (1930–40), Leader of the Opposition (1951–60), and Chief Justice of New South Wales (1960–62). Evatt was President of the General Assembly of the United Nations (1948–49) when the Assembly adopted the Universal Declaration of Human Rights on 10 December 1948.

Born on 30 April 1894 at East Maitland in New South Wales, Bert Evatt was the fifth of eight sons to John Ashmore Hamilton Evatt and Jane Sophia (Jeanie) (née Gray). Jeanie raised her six surviving sons on her own after her husband's death in 1901. Around 1904, Jeanie sold the Evatt hotel in East Maitland and moved the family to Sydney. After leaving Fort Street High School in 1911, Bert studied Arts and Law at the University of Sydney. He graduated with two university medals and first-class honours in his Bachelor of Arts (1915), Master of Arts (1917) and Bachelor of Laws (1918). Two of his younger brothers, Ray and Frank, were killed in World War I. Due to an eye condition, he was rejected three times for active service.

In 1918, Bert was admitted to the New South Wales Bar. In 1920, he married the American-born Mary Alice Sheffer. They had met as undergraduates at the University of Sydney. The couple later adopted two children, Peter and Rosalind. Evatt earned a Doctor of Laws (LLD) from the University of Sydney in 1924. The nickname 'Doc Evatt' stuck. During the 1920s, Evatt's legal career flourished. As a junior barrister, he appeared for the State of New South Wales – against the unions – in the *Engineers' Case*. In 1926, he was elected to the Legislative Assembly as Labor Member for Balmain. He took silk as a King's Counsel in 1929. In October 1930, he quit State politics to focus his energies on his Bar practice.

On 19 December 1930, at the age of 36, Evatt became the youngest ever appointee as a Justice of the High Court (1930–40). Personal relations between members of the High Court were fractured. Latham CJ – who had been Federal Attorney-General as a member of the Nationalist Party (ie, equivalent to the modern Liberals) – staunchly opposed Evatt. The two exchanged barbs in letters and telegrams during the course of the 1930s, including this note from 1935: 'Dear Evatt, I acknowledge receipt of your letter of Thursday last – much of it is meaningless to me. Yours sincerely, John Latham'.[43] Evatt also refused to attend judicial conferences with Starke J. Relations were increasingly unpleasant. During his decade on the High Court Evatt published four scholarly works on Australian history.[44] In August 1940, Evatt reversed the career path of many High

[43] Murphy *ibid* 161.

[44] HV Evatt, *The King and His Dominion Governors* (Oxford, Oxford University Press, 1936); HV Evatt, *Injustice within the Law: A Study of the Case of the Dorsetshire Labourers* (Sydney, Law Book, 1937); HV Evatt, *Rum Rebellion: A Study of the Overthrow of Governor Bligh by John Macarthur and the New South Wales Corps* (Sydney, Angus & Robertson, 1938); HV Evatt, *Australian Labour Leader: The Story of WA Holman and the Labour Movement* (Sydney, Angus & Robertson, 1940).

Court Justices and announced that he would resign from the High Court bench to enter federal politics. The next month, Evatt won the seat of Barton, which he held until 1958.

During the wartime Curtin Government, Evatt served as Attorney-General and Minister for External Affairs (1941–49). In 1950 the Labor Party opposed Menzies' Communist Party Dissolution Bill but owing to internal dissension allowed it through Parliament. Evatt's advice was that the Act would be constitutionally challenged: 'it filled [Evatt] with an unholy joy to think what the High Court would do to it once it became law'.[45]

While still Deputy Leader of the Opposition, Evatt represented the Communist-led Waterside Workers' Federation and its General Secretary, James Healy, in the *Communist Party Case* which the Menzies Government then used to attack Evatt claiming that he had communist sympathies. Evatt was criticised for accepting the brief – the Menzies Government ignored the cab-rank rule which determined that it was a barrister's duty to accept a brief – whether he agreed with their cause or not. Evatt was vindicated by the High Court's decision which found in the plaintiffs' favour. Ben Chifley died in June 1951 and Evatt was appointed Leader of the Opposition (1951–60); he then led the 'No' campaign for Menzies' 1951 Communist Party Dissolution Referendum. He successfully turned popular support in favour of banning the Communist Party around with the 'No' vote narrowly winning, defeating Menzies' plan to ban a political party.

In early September 1951, Evatt was in Moree speaking to a crowd from the back of a Holden ute. He urged the crowd to 'Vote No' in Menzies' upcoming 1951 Referendum. Eight-year-old Mary Gaudron, curious about the references to the Constitution, raised her hand and asked Evatt, 'Please sir, what's a Constitution?' After Evatt explained what it was, Gaudron asked, 'Is it like the Ten Commandments?' to which Evatt replied: 'You could call it the Ten Commandments of government.' She asked where she might get a copy. Evatt gave Gaudron his postal address at Parliament House so that she could write to him for a copy.[46] Inspired by this encounter, Gaudron studied Arts-Law at the University of Sydney and went on to become Australia's first female and, at the time, third youngest Justice of the High Court of Australia.

During the 1950s, Evatt's mental health deteriorated, and his behaviour became increasingly erratic. He was eventually removed from the Labor leadership and appointed Chief Justice of the Supreme Court of New South Wales (1960–62). In 1962, Evatt suffered a severe stroke and was forced to retire. Evatt died on 2 November 1965 at Canberra survived by his wife, Mary Alice, and their two children. He was given a state funeral. Evatt's niece, Elizabeth Evatt, also had a distinguished career in law. She was the first Chief Justice of the Family Court of Australia (1976–88).[47]

[45] Kylie Tennant, *Evatt: Politics and Justice* (Sydney, Angus & Robertson, 1970) 260.

[46] Mary Gaudron, 'Speech' (UNIFEM International Womens' Day Breakfast, Adelaide, 20 September 2005), available at web.archive.org/web/20070929022937/http://www.womenlawyerssa.org.au/publicationsandspeeches/hon-mary-gaudron-qc-at-the-unifem-international-womens-day-breakfast.

[47] GC Bolton, 'Evatt, Herbert Vere (Bert) (1894–1965)' (*Australian Dictionary of Biography*, 1996), available at adb.anu.edu.au/biography/evatt-herbert-vere-bert-10131/text17885. There are many other biographies of Evatt. For his role in international relations, see WJ Hudson, *Australia and the New World Order* (Australian Foreign Policy Publications Program ANU, 1993).

Pause for Thought

Judicial Review during the Cold War

Whenever governments pass sweeping new powers of surveillance, a common response is 'If you have nothing to hide, you have nothing to fear.' Was this the case with the Menzies Government's *Communist Party Dissolution Act*? Who might have unexpectedly fallen under this Act and how would it have affected their personal circumstances? If you are not sure, you might like to investigate Australians who were named in Parliament by Prime Minister Menzies when debating the Bill and read some general histories about Australia during the Cold War.

International tensions have increased and abated a number of times since the ending of the Cold War and governments everywhere have used heightened tensions to introduce contentious anti-terror legislation.

Questions to Consider

1. Authoritarian political and religious ideologies including some forms of Marxism in the 1950s oppose the rule of law, so how far should societies which cherish this political value tolerate them?
2. How would you defend the rule of law but maximise freedom of speech?
3. Are there principles that should guide governments that seek to defend freedom of speech from ideologues that do not respect it?

Further advice is available here.

The Dismissal of Gough Whitlam

Menzies and his successors in Coalition Governments were in office continuously for 23 years. When Gough Whitlam and the Labor Party won the election on 2 December 1972, there was considerable shock and indignation among the now Opposition members. In this period elections for the House of Representatives and the Senate were held separately and Whitlam had won control of the Lower House but was in the minority in the Senate. Despite a mood for change across the country, the Coalition refused to cooperate with Whitlam's agenda and used the Senate to block his reforms. More Government Bills were rejected by the Senate in 1973 than in the previous 72 years of Federation.[48]

Repeated blocking of his Bills enabled Whitlam to call a double dissolution election in May 1974 under section 57 of the Constitution. Whitlam again won the election. His mandate was still not recognised by the Opposition parties, however, and an historic joint sitting of both Houses was required to pass the Bills that had triggered the election in the first place. The Whitlam Government had won three more Senate seats but so had the Coalition, with one seat going to a small party based in South Australia, the Liberal Movement, and one to an Independent who later joined the Liberal Party.[49] The Senate was thus finely balanced until two deaths saw parliamentary traditions broken in audacious political acts aimed at destroying the Whitlam Government.

[48] Graham Freudenberg, *A Certain Grandeur: Gough Whitlam in Politics* (Ringwood Vic, Penguin, 1987) 295–96.
[49] *Ibid* 303, 373.

The first was the death of Douglas Menzies of the High Court,[50] enabling a Labor Government to make only its second appointment to the High Court since 1946. Whitlam chose his Attorney-General, Senator Lionel Murphy, to fill the vacancy thereby in turn creating a **casual vacancy** in the Senate. Under section 15 of the Constitution, it fell to State parliaments to nominate a suitable replacement. Since 1949 the practice had been to replace an outgoing senator with someone from the same party, but in 1975 the Premier of New South Wales, Tom Lewis, refused to do so. Then in June, Labor Senator Bert Milliner died and the Premier of Queensland, Joh Bjelke-Petersen, similarly refused to appoint a Labor member as a replacement. Both premiers were bitter political opponents of Whitlam whose government had now lost two senators. Despite winning a general election in May 1974, Whitlam again had to face a hostile senate.

> Casual vacancy: arises when any member resigns, dies or leaves between elections. It must therefore be filled by a by-election in the House of Representatives but in the Senate, with its more complex voting system, by an appointment process

In the lead up to the double dissolution election in May 1974, the Government had been beset by controversy over what became known as the Gair Affair. As 1975 progressed an atmosphere of scandal engulfed the Government. There was the Morosi Affair and the Loans Affair with the latter causing significant damage to the Whitlam Government's reputation.

The Coalition, now with a one seat majority in the Senate, renewed its campaign of blocking **Appropriation** bills to force another early general election of the House of Representatives to be held at the same time as the half-Senate election. Even if the Senate balance had been even, a constitutional provision (section 23) requires equal votes in the Senate to 'pass in the negative' so a second reading of the supply bills could have been obstructed.

> Appropriation: essential elements of a government's annual Budget. They contain detailed estimates of the expenditure for government agencies and services

As required following the presentation of the Budget, the House of Representatives passed two money bills: Appropriation Bills (No 1) and (No 2). These are bills which authorise government expenditure including public servants' salaries and social welfare payments. They had passed the lower house three times, but the Senate deferred them twice in October and once in early November. This was high stakes destined to cause anxiety for many Australians across the country but especially in Canberra since government funds were due to run out on 30 November 1975. Whitlam's position was that the Australian people had given him a three-year mandate to govern only 18 months previously and that the Opposition should, respecting that result, not force another early election. For three years there was an atmosphere of conflict and strife. Now the Opposition raised the stakes even higher. Gough Whitlam had publicly stated that the half-Senate election could be brought forward in order to resolve the impasse but, on 16 October, Bob Ellicott, Liberal Member for Wentworth and a former Solicitor-General in the McMahon Liberal Government, issued a media release urging instead that the Governor-General dismiss the Government.[51]

[50] Sir Douglas Menzies was a first cousin of Robert Menzies and appointed by a Menzies Government to the High Court in 1958. John M Williams, 'Menzies, Sir Douglas Ian (1907–1974)' (*Australian Dictionary of Biography*, 2000), available at adb.anu.edu.au/biography/menzies-sir-douglas-ian-11109/text19779.

[51] 'Justified in Acting' *Canberra Times* (Canberra, 17 October 1975) 11.

The essence of a *constitutional* monarchy like Australia is that the monarch (or her representative) always acts on the advice of her responsible ministers. In the British system of government, 'reserve powers' are those that the monarch or her representative can exercise without the advice of ministers. Some of these are commonplace. Deciding which party leader can form a government is an exercise of 'reserve powers' because there are not yet ministers to advise the monarch or her representative. In practice there is no point in appointing a prime minister who cannot win a vote of confidence in the House of Representatives. Ellicott wanted the Governor-General Sir John Kerr to use his reserve powers to sack a prime minister even though he had the confidence of the House of Representatives.

Figure 11.9 M Brown, *Sir John Kerr* (1965)

Permission given by Australian News and Information Bureau, National Archives of Australia. NAA: A1200, L55967, Item ID 30921692.

Whitlam's Solicitor-General, Maurice Byers, wrote a reply refuting Ellicott's position which was provided to Sir John Kerr on 6 November. Whitlam assumed that the matter was settled since the Governor-General did not counsel him otherwise, as is the responsibility of the Crown.[52] Sir John Kerr, however, failed to inform his Prime Minister that he had already

[52] Freudenberg (n 48) 376–77.

canvassed use of the reserve powers with the Queen's private secretary and with Anthony Mason of the High Court. The Attorney-General's Department was advising Whitlam that the fundamental issue was the Senate's breach of convention by refusing Supply to a prime minister with the support of the House of Representatives, and the Governor-General failed to provide him with any other view.

There had been many occasions when governors-general had sought the advice of the Chief Justice of the High Court but in 1975 the Chief Justice was Sir Garfield Barwick, former Attorney-General and Minister of External Affairs in Menzies Liberal Governments. He and Bob Ellicott, the member of the Opposition who had urged the use of the reserve powers, were cousins.[53] In October when Kerr had asked Whitlam if he should consult with the Chief Justice about the Senate impasse, Whitlam's advice was that it would be inappropriate and that the *Australian Constitution* did not define the chief justice as an adviser; rather, the Law Officers provided constitutional advice. He reminded Kerr that the Statute of Westminster had changed the relationship of governor-general and prime minister.[54] Kerr had already sought the advice of another High Court judge, Sir Anthony Mason, who was also later Chief Justice of Australia (1987–95). Mason advised Kerr to warn the Prime Minister that his commission would be terminated if he refused to call a general election.[55]

On 10 November 1975, Sir Garfield Barwick provided Kerr with written advice regarding the constitutional situation. Barwick's opinion was that:

> the Senate has constitutional power to refuse to pass a money Bill; it has power to refuse supply to the Government of the day. … a Prime Minister who cannot ensure supply to the Crown, including funds for carrying on the ordinary services of Government, must either advise a general election (of a kind which the constitutional situation may then allow) or resign. If, being unable to secure supply, he refuses to take either course, Your Excellency has constitutional authority to withdraw his Commission as Prime Minister.[56]

On the morning of 11 November Kerr rang Malcolm Fraser the Leader of the Opposition to be sure that if he was made prime minister he would pass supply and call an election. Kerr wanted assurances that there would be no charges laid in relation to the Loans Affair and no royal commission into it.[57] Whitlam arrived at Yarralumla, the Governor-General's official residence, to request a half-Senate election; instead, the Governor-General handed him a letter dismissing him. Kerr acted as Barwick had advised but without the warning to Whitlam that Mason had recommended. In accordance with section 64 of the Constitution, Whitlam was dismissed at 1 pm on 11 November 1975. Fraser was installed as caretaker Prime Minister until a general election on 13 December 1975. Labor senators were unaware that their Prime Minister had been sacked when the Senate passed supply bills that afternoon. When Fraser announced his caretaker status to the House of Representatives, the

[53] Jenny Hocking, *Gough Whitlam: His Time: The Biography*, vol 2 (Carlton Vic, Miegunyah, 2012); Paul Kelly and Troy Bramston, *The Dismissal: In the Queen's Name* (Melbourne, Penguin, 2015) 142.

[54] Freudenberg (n 48) 389. For more sources on this section see the website.

[55] In 2012 Mason gave a statement of his advice to Kerr in response to the publication of volume 2 of Jenny Hocking's biography of Gough Whitlam. It is available here: whitlamdismissal.com/2012/08/27/mason-largely-confirms-kerrs-account-of-discussions.html.

[56] Cited in Kelly and Bramston (n53) 201.

[57] *Ibid* 23. For further reading, links to Whitlam's speech and advice about the Pause for Thought, see the website.

House voted to reappoint Whitlam as Prime Minister. Kerr then declined to meet with the Speaker of the House or to comply with the House of Representatives' resolution.

Protests broke out across the country. Most Australians were unaware that the Governor-General possessed such powers. Nonetheless, the Coalition convincingly won the election that followed. The Liberal Party of Australia and the National Country Party secured 91 seats in the House of Representatives, an increase of 30 seats compared to Labor's 36 seats.[58]

Figure 11.10 Sydney Protest over the Dismissal 24 November 1975

The Sydney Domain on 24 November 1975, at the ALP policy launch for the election precipitated by the 1975 Australian Constitutional Crisis (1975).

Photo by Takver, GNU Free Documentation Licence, Tirin at the English-language Wikipedia, CC BY-SA 3.0, https://creativecommons.org/licenses/by-sa/3.0.

Whether the dismissal was correct in principle has been questioned over and over again. In accordance with the principle of responsible government, only a government which loses the confidence of the lower house of Parliament (the House of Representatives in Australia) must ask the Governor-General to dissolve Parliament or resign. On this view, the Whitlam Government was not bound to be dismissed. It could not secure supply from the Senate – the upper house – but it retained the confidence of the House of Representatives.

[58] Stephen Barber and Sue Johnson, 'Federal Election Results 1901–2014', Parliamentary Library (17 July 2014), available at parlinfo.aph.gov.au/parlInfo/download/library/prspub/3283353/upload_binary/3283353.pdf;fileType=application/pdf.

A government cannot govern without money, however, and the *whole* Parliament (House of Representatives and Senate) must approve the supply of money. That was something that the Whitlam Government could not secure, largely because of the way the New South Wales and Queensland Governments ignored the 1974 election result when they filled Senate vacancies. The Governor-General does have an obligation to maintain the running of the Government, so Kerr's dilemma was a real one.

Pause for Thought

The Dismissal

The Governor-General who preceded Sir John Kerr was Sir Paul Hasluck. Hasluck was elected to the Federal Parliament as a Liberal in 1949. In successive Menzies Governments he was Minister for Territories, Minister for Defence and Minister for External Affairs. In 1969 after he contested a leadership ballot which Sir John Gorton won, Hasluck was appointed Governor-General. His term expired on 30 April 1974, but he remained in office to swear in the second Whitlam Labor Government in July 1974.

Hasluck was meticulous in observing the duties of the Governor-General. In retirement he published *The Office of the Governor General*[59] in which he succinctly defined the 'role of the Crown to discuss, counsel and warn'.[60] Whitlam wanted Hasluck to serve a second term, but his wife's health made this impossible. Instead, he provided Whitlam with a list of possible replacements among whom was John Kerr, then Chief Justice of the New South Wales Supreme Court. In 1977, in the aftermath of the dismissal, Hasluck visited Buckingham Palace where he discussed Kerr's actions with Sir Martin Charteris, the Queen's Private Secretary. According to Kelly and Bramston, Sir Martin asked Hasluck whether, when Kerr sacked Whitlam, he acted as a politician or a judge. Charteris was inclined to the view that Kerr 'had acted judicially on the facts' but Hasluck felt Kerr's thinking had been 'more political than judicial'.[61]

Questions to Consider

1. What aspects of this conflict were political and what aspects were constitutional?
2. How else might Sir John Kerr have responded to the problem of the pending lack of supply for the Government?
3. How did he fail the obligation to 'counsel' his Prime Minister?

Further advice is available here.

Despite all the parties' political differences, in the aftermath of the Dismissal, there was agreement that some constitutional flaws quickly needed addressing. Four referendum questions were put to voters on 21 May 1977. Though a proposal for simultaneous House of Representatives and Senate elections failed, a proposed amendment concerning the filling

[59] Paul Hasluck, *The Office of Governor-General* (Melbourne, Melbourne University Press, 1979).

[60] Cited in Malcolm Allbrook, 'Hasluck, Sir Paul Meernaa (1905–1993)' (*Australian Dictionary of Biography*, 2017), available at adb.anu.edu.au/biography/hasluck-sir-paul-meernaa-18555/text34447.

[61] Kelly and Bramston (n 53) 14.

of Senate casual vacancies was approved.[62] The Menzies-McLarty Agreement of replacing a senator with a member of the same political party was adopted as law. That new senator's term would expire at the end of the original senator's term. Section 15 of the Constitution was amended to incorporate this change. The constitutional anomalies between the states and the Commonwealth took further debate.

Commonwealth and State Alignment: Australia Acts 1986

One of the legacies of the Whitlam Government was the growth of Australian nationalism and impatience with anachronistic imperial trappings. In the aftermath of so much political rancour it became apparent that there was bipartisan support for Australian engagement with its own region of the Asia-Pacific, for example, for the system of Australian honours which replaced imperial knighthoods and for modernising the Queen's titles in Australia. It fell to state premiers to oppose many of these Whitlam initiatives. The role of two state premiers in the dismissal has already been discussed. Although the 1977 referendum had corrected one glaring misuse of state power, concerns remained regarding the anomalous relationships between the states and the monarch and between the states and British Parliament. The Fraser Government in 1982 and the Hawke Government which succeeded it in 1984 began talks to end these inconsistencies which had come to the fore as a result of the Dismissal and were the unfinished business of the Statute of Westminster.

The consent of the Queensland Premier is a remarkable part of this story. Sir Joh Bjelke-Petersen had opposed Whitlam's nationalism and in response emphasised a Queensland identity. He had also opposed Whitlam's democratic initiatives instead asserting royalism; yet this Premier eventually also agreed to aligning the State's Constitution with the Statute of Westminster's provisions thereby diminishing the Queen's constitutional power. In 1985 the Australia Acts resolved the difference in constitutional positions between the States and the Federal Government, and the relationship of the States with the United Kingdom. The Prime Minister of Australia, Bob Hawke, and the Premiers of the six Australian States agreed to pass individual Acts to bring the constitutional status of the Commonwealth and the States into line. This would reflect 'the status of the Commonwealth of Australia as a sovereign, independent and federal nation'.

The *Australia (Request and Consent) Act 1985* (Cth) was enacted by the Commonwealth Parliament in December 1985 in response to uniform legislation passed by each Australian State between September and October 1985. To ensure the process was completed without blemish, the Commonwealth and the States applied section 51(xxxviii) of the Constitution and the 'request and consent' provisions of the Statute of Westminster to invite the UK Parliament to pass the Australia Act and thus cut its constitutional ties with Australia. Each State Act requested that the Commonwealth Parliament enact draft legislation set out in Schedule 1 of their legislation. The same was requested of the UK Parliament with its draft legislation set out in Schedule 2.

[62] The four issues and their results are available on the Australian Electoral Commission website aec.gov.au/Elections/referendums/Referendum_Dates_and_Results.htm.

As a result, UK Parliament can no longer legislate for a state or territory,[63] nor does it have responsibility for state government matters.[64] The *Colonial Laws Validity Act 1865* no longer applies.[65] Importantly, a Governor as the Queen's representative in a State is now appointed by the Queen on the advice of the State Premier (and not the British Government).[66]

Termination of Privy Council Appeals

The final severing of colonial ties was the States' relations with the Privy Council. The Australia Acts also ended appeals to the Judicial Committee of the Privy Council from any Australian court.[67] From the late 1960s, the Australian Parliament incrementally legislated to end appeals in civil and criminal cases to the Privy Council in London. The *Privy Council (Limitation of Appeals) Act 1968* (Cth) abolished appeals in future cases involving the application of Commonwealth law. In other words, appeals in all matters of federal and territorial jurisdiction were abolished. This is known as a 'grandfather clause': the new rule restricting appeals applied to future cases; the old rule to pending appeals. Next, the *Privy Council (Appeals from the High Court) Act 1975* (Cth) barred appeals from the High Court relating to all matters of state jurisdiction. Direct appeals from a State Supreme Court to the Privy Council were still possible until they were abolished by the *Australia Acts 1986* (UK and Cth). The last Australian case was determined by the Privy Council in 1987. Section 74 of the Constitution is the only remaining avenue of appeal to the Privy Council; however, the High Court considers this jurisdiction 'obsolete'.[68] In any event, the High Court is the final appeal court in Australia. The legal effects of this would be felt in the decade following the passage of the Australia Acts.

The Mason Court

Between 1987 and 1995, Sir Anthony Mason presided over the High Court as Chief Justice. Former Attorney-General Michael Lavarch cited the Mason Court as 'among the most exciting and important in the Court's history'.[69] The Mason Court was a remarkably stable period for the High Court. The composition of the High Court was almost unchanged over the eight years that Mason was its leader. Only one Justice was replaced: McHugh J took the place of Wilson J, who resigned in 1989. Apart from this replacement, membership of the other six justices – Mason CJ and Brennan, Deane, Dawson, Toohey, and Gaudron JJ – was a constant.

The Court in this period made significant constitutional interpretations on matters guaranteeing freedom of interstate trade; prohibiting discrimination on the basis of interstate

[63] *Australia Act 1986* ss 1–3.
[64] *Ibid* s 10.
[65] *Ibid* s 3.
[66] *Ibid* s 7.
[67] *Ibid* s 11.
[68] *Kirmani v Captain Cook Cruises Pty Ltd (No 2)* (1985) 159 CLR 461, 465.
[69] Lavarch cited in Andisheh Partovi et al, 'Addressing "Loss of Identity" in the Joint Judgment: Searching for "The Individual Judge" in the Joint Judgments of the Mason Court' (2017) 40 *University of New South Wales Law Journal* 670, 671.

residence; recognising freedom of political communication; and procedural fairness in administrative law among others. These decisions reinforce why the Mason Court has been regarded as the most 'activist' High Court in Australian legal history – in terms of being the most willing to make radical changes to the law and in the interpretation of the *Australian Constitution*. In part, it is thought that, after the Australia Acts, the High Court no longer competed with the Privy Council as the final court of appeal on questions of Australian law and was completely free to craft the law in the direction that it wished. Mason himself did not necessarily lead these developments although he consistently supported them. Sir William Deane, who later became Governor-General (1995–2001), is often regarded as the intellectual leader of the Mason Court. The Mason Court also included the first woman to be appointed to the High Court: Mary Gaudron. Deane and Gaudron often wrote joint judgments together.

Figure 11.11 Governor-General Sir William Deane Opening the Paralympic Games Sydney 2000

Australian Governor-General Sir William Deane makes the official opening speech at the 2000 Sydney Paralympic Games Opening Ceremony (2000).

One of the most momentous decisions of the Mason Court was the Mabo decision of 1992, a moment in Australian legal history first discussed in chapter one in the context of medieval land tenure. While much of the twentieth-century legal experience was remarkable for the way in which colonial limitations were challenged, for Indigenous Australians its fetters are still not effectively removed. This unfinished business is the subject of chapter 12.

Conclusion

This chapter charted developments which contributed to constitutional independence in twentieth century Australia. The importance of two landmark constitutional cases of the High Court, the *Engineers' Case* and the *Communist Party Case*, were outlined. The first case saw federal power triumph over the powers of States, while the second case reaffirmed the principle of judicial review and the importance of the rule of law. The White Australia Policy, the constitutional issues surrounding the Whitlam Government's dismissal, termination of Privy Council appeals, and the Mason Court revolution were explored.

The chapter included historical cameos of two former Justices of the High Court of Australia: Sir Isaac Isaacs and HV Evatt. Another two cameos of influential judges of the twentieth century, Sir Owen Dixon and Michael Kirby are available on the website. Each made lasting contributions to Australian law, politics or both. Isaacs and Dixon served as Chief Justices of Australia and Isaacs as the first Australian-born Governor-General.

12

The Painful Legacy of Colonialism: Aboriginal and Torres Strait Islander People and the Law in Modern Australia

Introduction

In 1963, the year before The Beatles toured Australia, a mining company asked the Queensland Government to evict the residents of a Presbyterian mission at Mapoon in North Queensland. The mission, founded in 1891, had enabled Aboriginal people to remain on their ancestral lands. In 1959 however the Queensland Government excised hundreds of square miles of land from the mission for a bauxite mining lease for Comalco. Aboriginal people objected to this high-handed treatment and decided to defend their mission and their lands until 1963 when Queensland Police removed people at gunpoint, held them under police guard, shot their dogs and then burnt their church and homes. Mrs Jean Jimmy said that the police 'gave us an hour to pack some belongings … We were forced to leave old Mapoon and everybody had tears'.[1] These were remarkable years in Aboriginal politics and when young Aboriginal activists formed the National Tribal Council in 1970 their policy manifesto asserted that 'Aborigines and Islanders in Australia need more lawyers than welfare officers'; it also included a call for federal laws to prohibit 'all forms of racial discrimination'.[2]

This chapter focuses on changes to Australian law in the late twentieth century that were the result of hard-fought campaigns by Indigenous Australians to remove discriminatory legislation denying them fundamental human rights. While Australian historians refer to the period before Federation as the colonial period, Aboriginal and Islander Australians had to wrestle with the legacy of a Federal Constitution which expressly excluded them, confining them to the powers of the states which continued colonial policies of political and legal exclusion. Consequently, the chapter begins with the 1967 campaign to amend the *Australian Constitution*.

[1] *Tribune*, 8 April 1964 cited in Bain Attwood and Andrew Markus, *The Struggle for Aboriginal Rights: A Documentary History* (Crows Nest NSW, Allen & Unwin, 1999) 208. Final removals at gunpoint took place in November 1963. See also Marcia Langton, 'Koowarta: A Warrior for Justice: A Brief History of Queensland's Racially Discriminatory Legislation and the Aboriginal Litigants Who Fought it' (2014) 23 1 *Griffith Law Review* 24.

[2] National Tribal Council, Policy Manifesto, adopted 13 September 1970 cited in Attwood and Markus (n 1) 249.

The 1967 Referendum to change the Constitution was the most successful referendum in Australian history but racial discrimination remained entrenched. The denial of access to land was particularly bitter for First Nations who found themselves thwarted in efforts both to buy land and to have the courts recognise their right to homelands held from 'time immemorial'. The Federal Government's passing of the *Racial Discrimination Act 1975* (Cth) ('RDA') enabled Aboriginal peoples to challenge intransigent state governments. This is important context for understanding the High Court's recognition of native title at common law.[3]

Lack of access to land was only one of many grievances that Australia's First Nations wrestled with. The chapter looks briefly at attempts to address the Stolen Generations and the Stolen Wages that were a product of state Aboriginal Protection Acts. Despite several successes, Indigenous Australians fear that colonial conditions could be reimposed on them with each change of government and so have repeatedly called for constitutional recognition so that their human and civil rights will no longer be a casualty of white indifference. In 2017 First Nations asked for 'Voice Treaty Truth' but this straightforward request has been met with a slow and passive response worthy of Australia's colonial past.

Learning Resources

The content in this chapter is supported by:

Glossary	Chapter Overview	Historical Cameos	Pause for Thought
Latin legal and political terms are defined	The chapter begins with an overview explaining its intentions and focus	Faith Bandler	How Colonial History is a Major Obstacle to the Native Title Process
		Eddie Mabo	Understanding of the Three Pillars of the Uluru Statement from the Heart

[3] *Mabo v Queensland (No 2)* (1992) 175 CLR 1 ('*Mabo (No 2)*').

Chapter Overview

Place	Time Period	Key Dates
• Australia	• Second half of the 20th century	• 1967, 1971, 1975, 1992, 2017

Key Figures	Key Cases and Institutions	Key Terms
• Faith Bandler • Pearl Gibbs • Jessie Street • Milirrpum • Munffaraway • Daymbalipu • Richard Blackburn • John Koowarta • Joh Bjelke-Petersen • Gough Whitlam • Eddie Koiki Mabo, James Rice, David Passi, Sam Passi, Celuia Mapo Sale • Kevin Rudd	• 1967 Referendum • Gove Land Rights Case • Deaths in custody • Stolen generations • Stolen wages • National Apology • Aboriginal courts • Mabo 1 and 2 • Northern Territory Intervention • Uluru Statement from the Heart	• Colonialism • Colonial legacies • Land rights • International treaty obligations

Learning Outcomes

At the end of this chapter, readers should understand:

- The importance of the 1967 Referendum in ending the constitutional exclusion of Indigenous people.
- The overturning of the concept of *terra nullius* in Australian law and persistence of Aboriginal title under the Crown.
- The importance of the *Racial Discrimination Act 1975* (Cth) in challenging racially discriminatory actions by the states.
- The colonial legacy that led to campaigns for reconciliation and constitutional recognition culminating in the Uluru Statement.

1967 Australian Referendum

Indigenous Australians and the Right to Vote

Myths have circulated about what the 1967 Referendum did. The 1967 Referendum was only partially relevant to voting rights in Australia. As discussed in chapter ten at Federation the Commonwealth Parliament initially decided to leave determinations as to who could vote in the hands of the states but when it legislated for white women's right to vote in 1902 it simultaneously excluded Aboriginal and Torres Strait Islanders from participation in Commonwealth elections. The problem then arose in World War I that Aboriginal servicemen could serve overseas and die for their country but were not able to vote in Australia's elections. By World War II, the *Commonwealth Electoral (War-time) Act 1940* gave serving personnel voting rights for the war's duration. The Chifley Government then made this permanent for Indigenous ex-servicemen in 1949. Finally, in 1962, the Menzies Government gave Indigenous Australians the right to vote in Commonwealth elections[4] and Commonwealth electoral officers began enrolling Aboriginal people on electoral rolls.[5]

Amending the Constitution

Aboriginal people began agitating for constitutional change in the late 1950s. Their campaign was led by Pastor (later Sir) Doug Nicholls, Faith Bandler, Kath Walker (Oodgeroo Noonuccal), Charlie Perkins and Pearl Gibbs, among others.

Figure 12.1 *Miss Teresa French (sic) Calls for a Yes Vote, in Sydney's Wynyard Park*, 18 May 1967

Mitchell Library, State Library of New South Wales, ON 161/208, IE16760962. Courtesy SEARCH Foundation (CC BY 4.0), https://creativecommons.org/licenses/by/4.0/.

[4] Richard Broome, *Aboriginal Australians: A History Since 1788*, 5th edn (Crows Nest, NSW, Allen & Unwin, 2019) 208, 219–20.

[5] Links to relevant legislation and more information about Indigenous people's enfranchisement are available on the website.

Aboriginal people were fed up with the retrograde and repressive administration of Aboriginal affairs by the states which continued to control Indigenous people's lives through colonial era legislation. They wanted the Commonwealth to intervene but that was impossible under the *Australian Constitution* which contained three clauses – sections 25, 51(xxvi) and 127 – specifically directed at Aboriginal and Torres Strait Islander people.

Section 51(xxvi), as originally enacted, empowered the Commonwealth to make laws in relation to 'the people of any race, *other than the aboriginal race in any State*, for whom it is deemed necessary to make special laws'.[6] As discussed in earlier chapters, the Federation debates took place in an intellectual context of deep racism. Section 51(xxvi) provided a federal power to introduce the white Australia policy and specific controls on migrants, including Chinese, Indian and Melanesian people.

At the same time, this clause specifically excluded Aboriginal and Torres Strait Islander people because the states did not want the Commonwealth to have control over 'their natives'. Because cheap Aboriginal and Torres Strait Islander labour underpinned the pastoral, pearling and fishing industries, the States had no intention of relinquishing their authority over Indigenous peoples in their jurisdiction. There was also the widespread belief in 'doomed race' theory – that Aboriginal people were 'dying out' so that this was not a power the Commonwealth needed to be too concerned about. Section 51(xxvi) was an indomitable barrier to a nationwide response to Aboriginal affairs.

Figure 12.2 Yorta Yorta Man, Sir Douglas Nicholls, Sworn in as Governor of South Australia, Government House, Adelaide, 1 December 1976

Personalities – Aboriginal and Torres Strait Islander – Sir Douglas Nicholls, Inauguration as Governor of South Australia (1977) National Archives of Australia. NAA: A6180, 5/1/77/5, Item ID 11345723.

[6] Emphasis added.

The other section, section 127, prohibited the counting of 'Aboriginal natives' when 'reckoning the numbers of the people of the Commonwealth, or of a State or other part of the Commonwealth'. It was included because of the tussle between the big and small colonies over how many electorates each state would have and how they would be determined. Victoria and New South Wales had no intention of allowing Queensland and Western Australia to use large populations of Indigenous Australians in their northern regions to earn additional seats in the Federal Parliament. Its purpose was to prevent Aboriginal and Torres Strait Islander people from being included in tabulations of population that were used to decide seats in the House of Representatives.

In the end it did not prevent Aboriginal and Torres Strait Islander people from being counted in the census. In some early censuses only those who lived close to European settlements were recorded, but Aboriginal and Torres Strait Islander peoples have been included in all Australian censuses since 1911. However, from 1911 to 1966, 'full blood' Aboriginal and Torres Strait Islander Australians were not 'enumerated' for the purposes of deciding how many seats a State would have in the House of Representatives, even if they had been counted in the census. Here again is 1901 racial ideology in play – the statistician distinguishing between 'full bloods' and 'half-castes' – language which is deeply offensive today. The Commonwealth Statistician consistently took the view that Aboriginal and Islander people who were not 'full blood' – that is to say, Aboriginal people with some white heritage – should be 'enumerated' for the purposes of allocating federal seats. Until this section was removed it was clear that the Commonwealth Parliament was not representing Indigenous Australians. They could not form electorates and there was no power to legislate on their behalf. The repeal of section 127 was necessary to ensure that all Australians, including *all* Aboriginal and Islander people, were enumerated when deciding how many seats a State should get in the House, and that their representation was proportional to all other Australians.

Of the three constitutional clauses mentioned, only section 25 remains in its original form, which provides:

> For the purposes of the last section, if by a law of any State all persons of any race are disqualified from voting at elections for the more numerous House of Parliament of the State, then, in reckoning the number of the people of the State or of the Commonwealth, persons of that race resident in that State shall not be counted.

Once all states had enfranchised Indigenous people this section was of no effect.

The Referendum to change sections 51(xxvi) and 127 was put to the people in May 1967 and was the most successful referendum in Australia's history. There was a 94 per cent voter turnout, although residents of the Northern Territory and the Australian Capital Territory were not entitled to vote owing to their status as territories. A record 90.77 per cent of Australian electors voted 'yes' to change two of these three constitutional clauses. The subsequent *Constitution Alteration (Aboriginals) Act 1967* (Cth) amended s 51(xxvi) and repealed s 127 of the Constitution, meaning that:

1. Aboriginal people were included in future national censuses; thus, s 127 of the Constitution was repealed.
2. The Federal Government had the power to make laws for Aboriginal people (s 51(xxvi).

It was a great victory. Later, however, the High Court decided that the amended race power, allowing the Federal Government to make 'special laws' for Aboriginal and

Torres Strait Islander people, does not necessarily mean that the power must be exercised beneficially.[7]

The great disappointment for Indigenous Australians was the failure of the Holt and successive Gorton and McMahon governments to act on the Referendum. Some young Aboriginal people concluded that there was little point in playing the white man's political game politely and instigated a more radical Aboriginal movement. Equality was not going to be enough – they took up a demand of Aboriginal people from the earliest days of white settlement – they wanted rights to their land.

Historical Cameo

Faith Bandler AO[8]

Faith Bandler was born Ida Lessing Faith Mussing in 1918 at Tumbulgum, New South Wales. She was one of the initiators and leading campaigners for the successful 1967 Referendum to change the *Australian Constitution*. She later became a writer and an advocate for Australia's South Sea Islander community.

Figure 12.3 Faith Bandler Speaking at Sydney Town Hall, 1970
Faith Bandler, Vice President, FCAATSI, Sydney Town Hall (1970).
Mitchell Library, State Library of New South Wales, ON 161/534, IE4565816. Courtesy SEARCH Foundation (CC BY 4.0), https://creativecommons.org/licenses/by/4.0/.

[7] See *Kartinyeri v Commonwealth* (1998) 195 CLR 337 ('the *Hindmarsh Island Case*').
[8] Officer of the Order of Australia.

Faith was one of eight children born to Peter Mussing and Ida Venno. Her mother was of Indian and Scottish descent. Her father was from the island of Ambrym in Vanuatu; he had been kidnapped as a 13-year-old in 1883 and forced to work on sugar cane plantations near Mackay in Queensland. After Federation when the deportations designed to create a White Australia commenced, Peter crossed into New South Wales and married Ida Venno who was Australian born. Being married to an Australian spared him from further threat of deportation.

Faith attended high school in Murwillumbah where she was protected from racial abuse by kind teachers but had already learnt fierce independence and anti-racism from her father. She moved to Sydney where she was a dressmaker's apprentice. When war in the Pacific began, she and her sister joined the Australian Women's Land Army. One of her brothers had joined the Australian Imperial Force and died in 1943 as a prisoner-of-war on the Thai-Burma Railway.

Returning to Sydney at the end of World War II she became involved in the peace movement and moved into left-wing progressive circles. In 1952 she married Hans Bandler, an engineer and Jewish refugee who had survived both Dachau and Buchenwald concentration camps and made his way to Australia. In 1954 their daughter Lilon was born.

Through the Australian Peace Council, Faith met Pearl Gibbs.[9] Gibbs was an Aboriginal rights activist and feminist who worked in several organisations with Lady Jessie Street, Australia's leading feminist and peace activist, whose husband Sir Kenneth Street became Chief Justice of New South Wales in 1950. Pearl Gibbs and Faith set up the Aboriginal-Australian Fellowship (AAF) in 1956 and Jessie Street urged them to campaign on amending the discriminatory provisions of the *Australian Constitution*.[10] The AAF played a leading role in the ten-year campaign that culminated in the Referendum.

When the AAF joined the Federal Council for Aboriginal Advancement (FCAA), Faith also became involved in that organisation becoming the NSW secretary in 1963 and NSW Campaign Director in 1967. She was a charismatic speaker and broadcaster and tireless in her efforts to win over diverse Australians to the cause.

In 1968 in recognition of the distinctive identity of Australia's Torres Strait Island communities, FCAA changed its name to the Federal Council for the Advancement of Aboriginal and Torres Strait Islanders (FCAATSI). From 1970 to 1972 Faith was national secretary but disappointment over the lack of meaningful action stemming from the constitutional change, radicalisation of the Aboriginal movement, and Faith's disillusion over the continued marginalisation of Australia's South Sea Island community saw a change in her priorities.

[9] Heather Goodall, 'Gibbs, Pearl Mary (Gambanyi) (1901–1983)' (*Australian Dictionary of Biography*, 2007), available at adb.anu.edu.au/biography/gibbs-pearl-mary-gambanyi-12533/text22555.

[10] Heather Radi, 'Street, Lady Jessie Mary (1889–1970)' (*Australian Dictionary of Biography*, 2002), available at adb.anu.edu.au/biography/street-lady-jessie-mary-11789/text21089.

She had hoped that removing the discriminatory clauses in the Constitution would see an end to racism generally and improvements for all non-white Australians; now she began to research her father's experience and to fight for recognition of her own people. In 1977 after travelling to Ambrym to meet her father's family she published *Wacvie*, a novel about her father's kidnapping. She also co-authored with Len Fox, a history of the AAF in 1983 and wrote her account of FCAATSI, *Turning the Tide* in 1989.

By the 1990s she was increasingly recognised for the vital role she had played in fighting for justice and human rights for Indigenous peoples. In 1997 Nelson Mandela bestowed on her the Meritorious Award of the Sydney Peace Foundation. She had already been awarded an honorary doctorate by Macquarie University in 1994 and the Human Rights Medal by the Human Rights and Equal Opportunity Commission. In 2009 she was made a Companion of the Order of Australia.[11]

Faith Bandler died on 13 February 2015. Prime Minister Tony Abbott offered the family a state funeral.

The rise of Aboriginal activism was fortuitous because the international mining industry began to discover the mineral wealth of northern Australia in the 1960s heralding several famous clashes between Aboriginal communities and mining corporations. As the residents of Mapoon were being evicted from their mission in 1963, Aboriginal people at a Methodist Mission at Yirrkala on Gove Peninsula in Arnhem Land in the Northern Territory were shocked to discover that 390 square kilometres of their lands were also excised for bauxite mining. Because the Northern Territory did not yet have self-government, the Commonwealth had issued the lease to Nabalco (now Alcan Gove Pty Ltd) without consulting the Yolngu traditional owners.

The *Gove Land Rights Case*

Milirrpum v Nabalco Pty Ltd[12] or the *Gove Land Rights Case* has the distinction of being the first reported decision addressing Aboriginal land rights or native title in Australia. The action was initiated by the Rirratjingu, Gumatj, Djapu and ten other clans while comparable native title litigation was being heard in Canada. The Yolngu people's traditional homelands include the Gove Peninsula (Arnhem Land) in the Northern Territory. The Yolngu did not want mining operations on their country. On behalf of 13 clan groups, three of the Yolngu's leading men, Milirrpum, Munggurrawuy and Daymbalipu had writs issued out of the Northern Territory Supreme Court claiming damages, an injunction, and **declarations** against Nabalco.

Declaration: a formal statement presenting the plaintiff's claim

[11] Marilyn Lake, 'Faith Bandler' (*The Encyclopaedia of Women and Leadership in Twentieth Century Australia*), available at womenaustralia.info/leaders/biogs/WLE0231b.htm.

[12] (1971) 17 FLR 141 ('*Gove Land Rights Case*').

Since the Yolngu had held and exercised rights over the Gove Peninsula 'from time immemorial', their legal counsel argued that those rights – 'communal native title' – were legally enforceable.[13] In consequence of this communal native title, the plaintiffs contended that the Yolngu people 'had remained in quiet and undisturbed possession' of the land until Nabalco

> entered the said land with bulldozers, excavators, trucks and other machinery … and [had] broken down the native bush, erected structures, taken valuable bauxite ores, destroyed or damaged plant life and destroyed or driven away animal life and violated sacred areas and objects of the Rirratjingu and Gumatj clans.[14]

Milirrpum, Munggurrawuy and Daymbalipu provided evidence of their continued occupation, hunting, gathering and exclusion of all others from their lands and of their own laws governing it. It was detailed legal argument disproving *terra nullius*.

In a lengthy decision, Blackburn J of the Northern Territory Supreme Court held that the assertion of British sovereignty extinguished the traditional land rights of the Yolngu people of the Gove Peninsula. Their evidence establishing native law and custom was held not to form part of the common law of Australia. While the Yolngu people had a system of law, 'a subtle and elaborate system of social rules and customs',[15] Blackburn J considered that this system 'did not provide for any proprietary interest' over the claimed lands.[16] Furthermore, Blackburn J concluded that '[i]n a settled colony there is no principle of communal native title except such as can be shown by prerogative or legislative act, or a course of dealing'.[17] Some 82 years after *Cooper v Stuart*,[18] the Northern Territory Supreme Court had re-affirmed the concept of *terra nullius*.

Land Rights Movement

Disappointment over the decision in the *Gove Land Rights Case* reached beyond the Aboriginal community and prompted calls for the statutory recognition of Aboriginal land rights. Among them was Gough Whitlam, then leader of the Opposition at the federal level. On being elected Prime Minister in 1972, Whitlam declared his intention to 'legislate to give Aboriginal Land Rights – because all of us as Australians are diminished while the Aborigines are denied their rightful place in this nation'.[19] After Whitlam's dismissal in 1975, the Fraser Government sponsored the passage of the *Aboriginal Land Rights (Northern Territory) Act 1976* (Cth), under which large tracts of Northern Territory land were vested in Aboriginal Land Councils.

[13] *Ibid* 150.
[14] Amended statement of claim cited in Attwood and Markus (n 1).
[15] *Gove Land Rights Case* (n 11) 267.
[16] *Ibid* 274.
[17] *Ibid* 223.
[18] (1889) 14 App Cas 286.
[19] Gough Whitlam, 'Election Speech' (Museum of Australian Democracy, 13 November 1972), available at electionspeeches.moadoph.gov.au/speeches/1972-gough-whitlam.

Figure 12.4 Vincent Lingiari of the Gurindji with PM Gough Whitlam at Wattie Creek, 1975
Penny Tweedie, Australian Information Service.

Some of the States also began to move on the issue. In 1981, the South Australian Parliament passed the *Pitjantjatjara Land Rights Act 1981* (SA). It granted rights to and freehold title over 103,000 square kilometres of land to the Pitjantjatjara people. Following the Northern Territory model, the New South Wales Government also enacted the *Aboriginal Land Rights Act 1983* (NSW). The Act transferred title to certain tracts of land to Land Councils and, in addition, established a scheme to compensate local Aboriginal people for loss of traditional lands. By the early 1990s, however, the mechanisms established by the New South Wales Act were proving to be ineffective with hundreds of outstanding claims.

The *Commonwealth Racial Discrimination Act 1975*

In September 1975, the Whitlam Government ratified the international treaty, the *International Convention on the Elimination of All Forms of Racial Discrimination*, which had been adopted by the United Nations in 1966. To implement the treaty domestically, the Whitlam Government passed the *Racial Discrimination Act 1975* ('RDA') which abolished the right or freedom to discriminate on racial grounds. The text of the Convention is found in the RDA's Schedule. The Convention recites that the parties to the Convention:

> Resolved to adopt all necessary measures for speedily eliminating racial discrimination in all its forms and manifestations, and to prevent and combat racist doctrines and practices in order to promote understanding between races and to build an international community free from all forms of racial segregation and racial discrimination.

The Preamble of the Act outlines that it was enacted:

> in pursuance of all relevant powers of the Parliament, including, but not limited to, its power to make laws with respect to external affairs, with respect to the people of any race for whom it is deemed necessary to make special laws and with respect to immigration.

The three key provisions of the RDA are sections 8, 9 and 10. Section 9(1) makes it unlawful to

> do any act … which has the purpose or effect of nullifying or impairing the recognition, enjoyment or exercise, on an equal footing, of any *human right or fundamental freedom* in the political, economic, social, cultural or any other field of public life.

Section 10(1) expressly prohibits the states and territories from denying rights because of race. These provisions are important because they have been used in litigation by Indigenous Australians and this chapter discusses two of the most important.

Though the RDA may be repealed or amended by an ordinary Commonwealth Act of Parliament, the Act has been used as a constitutional check on unequal or discriminatory State or Territory law. The standards of equality and non-discrimination enshrined in the RDA have seen litigants invoke section 109 of the Australian Constitution to invalidate State law for inconsistency, or Territory law for repugnancy, with Commonwealth law. This function took form in cases involving racial discrimination against Aboriginal and Torres Strait Islander people, out of which cases native title developed. Two of these cases, *Koowarta v Bjelke-Petersen*[20] and *Mabo v Queensland (No 1)*,[21] are now discussed.

Koowarta v Bjelke-Petersen

Between 1974 and 1976, Johnny Koowarta and other Aboriginal stockmen applied to the Aboriginal Land Fund Commission for funds to purchase the Archer River Pastoral Holding's property and its stock located on their traditional lands. They were members of the Winychanam community, a group of the Wik nation of the Cape York Peninsula. Agreeing to the request, the Commission entered a written contract with the lessees to purchase the lease and stock on behalf of Johnny Koowarta and his Winychanam people.

To transfer the lease, the Commission required consent from Kenneth Tomkins, the Queensland Minister for Lands, under the *Land Act 1962* (Qld). The Minister refused to grant consent or permission to transfer the lease in June 1976. In December that year, the Minister outlined his reasons for refusing that permission, which included the following:

> The question of the proposed acquisition of Archer River Pastoral Holding comes within the ambit of declared Government policy expressed in Cabinet decision of September 1972, which stated: The Queensland Government does not view favourably proposals to acquire large areas of additional freehold or leasehold land for development by Aborigines or Aboriginal groups in isolation.[22]

[20] (1982) 153 CLR 168.
[21] (1988) 166 CLR 186 ('*Mabo (No 1)*').
[22] *Koowarta v Bjelke-Petersen* (n 20) 176 (Gibbs CJ).

Koowarta brought an action against the State of Queensland and the Minister for Lands alleging breaches of sections 9 and 12 of the RDA. The defendants **demurred** to the plaintiff's statement of claim alleging that the RDA was beyond the powers of the Commonwealth and that Koowarta, not being a person aggrieved, had no 'standing' to bring the action. Those questions of law were referred to the High Court. Koowarta and the Commonwealth argued that the RDA was supported by two heads of power in section 51 of the Constitution: the race[23] and external affairs powers.[24]

> Demur: to raise objections to a pleading on grounds of law or constitutionality

Queensland brought a second action in the High Court. It sought a declaration that the RDA was **ultra vires** and invalid. The High Court determined with a majority of six to one that sections 9 and 12 were not validly made under the race power. A four to three majority, however, held that the sections were valid in accordance with the external affairs power and Koowarta was indeed an 'aggrieved person' under the RDA. Being 'a matter of international concern', the RDA was covered by the external affairs power.

> *Ultra vires* (Latin): 'beyond the powers'

The matter was remitted to the Supreme Court of Queensland which in 1988 decided in John Koowarta's favour. It was a pyrrhic victory for Koowarta: to thwart his people's ownership, the Queensland Government gazetted the Archer River lease as a national park. In 2012, however, Premier Campbell Newman transferred the re-named park to Aboriginal ownership. The area is now jointly managed as Oyala Thumotang National Park. The one section not transferred became Aboriginal freehold land. Sadly, John Koowarta did not live to see it; he died in 1991.[25]

Mabo v Queensland (No 1)[26]

In 1982, the same year that John Koowarta commenced legal action to sue the State of Queensland, another group of Indigenous people in north Queensland also went to court over their land. Four Torres Strait Island men, Eddie Koiki Mabo, Reverend David Passi, Sam Passi, James Rice, and one woman, Celuia Mapo Sale, sought declarations that the Meriam people were the customary owners of the Murray Islands (or Mer) in the Torres Strait and possessed native title rights to the land, seas, seabeds and reefs. Their argument visited many of the same points raised by Milpirrum in 1971 but also, considering decisions in Canadian courts, enlarged it; the Crown's sovereignty was subject to their rights from time immemorial, they argued, and their rights as Mer people continued to exist after annexation by the Crown.[27]

[23] *Australian Constitution* s 51(xxvi).
[24] *Ibid* s 51(xxix).
[25] Langton (n 1) 16–17.
[26] *Mabo (No 1)* (n 21).
[27] Garth Nettheim, 'The Influence of Canadian and International Law on the Evolution of Australian Aboriginal Title' in Hamar Foster, Heather Raven and Jeremy Webber (eds), *Let Right be Done: Aboriginal Title, the Calder Case, and the Future of Indigenous Rights* (Vancouver, University of British Columbia Press, 2007) 177–97.

Figure 12.5 Joh Bjelke-Petersen, Premier of Queensland 1968–1987
Portrait of Sir Johannes Bjelke-Petersen (1980).
Courtesy of Queensland State Archives, Item ID ITM1432108.

The Queensland Government agreed that Meriam people had owned their land from time immemorial but denied that any native title 'right' remained, emphasising its 1879 legislation annexing all the islands.[28] At the same time, however, the Murray Islands had been reserved by proclamation for the Meriam people in 1882. In 1912, the Governor-in-Council reaffirmed the reservation by ordering that the Murray Islands be permanently reserved, apart from two areas of leased land, for use by the Meriam people under Queensland's *Land Act 1910*. The High Court remitted the matter to the Supreme Court of Queensland so that issues of fact raised in the plaintiffs' statement of claim could be heard and determined.

To block the Islanders' claim, the Bjelke-Petersen Government had in the meantime passed the *Queensland Coast Islands Declaratory Act 1985* (Qld). The legislation, applying to the Murray Islands, made certain declarations concerning the Crown's late nineteenth

[28] Discussed in chapter nine of this volume.

century annexation of the Torres Strait Islands to Queensland. Sections 3, 4 and 5 of this Act are significant. By section 3, it was:

> declared that upon the lands [this included the Torres Strait Islands] being annexed to and becoming part of Queensland and subject to the laws in force in Queensland – (a) the islands were vested in the Crown in right of Queensland *freed from all other rights, interests and claims of any kind whatsoever and became waste lands of the Crown in Queensland* for the purposes of sections 30 and 40 of the Constitution Act; (b) the laws to which the islands became subject included the Crown lands legislation then and from time to time in force; (c) the islands could thereafter be dealt with as Crown lands for the purposes of Crown lands legislation then and from time to time in force in Queensland.[29]

In addition, section 4 stated: 'Every disposal of the islands or part thereof purporting to be in pursuance of Crown lands legislation after the islands were annexed to and became part of Queensland shall be taken to have been validly made and to have had effect in law according to its tenor.' Section 5 provided that no compensation was payable to any person for 'any right, interest or claim alleged to have existed prior to annexation.'

In short, the Government's plan was to use statute to deny any residual rights in the land and to refuse compensation for any rights it had extinguished. This was the basis of the Queensland Government's defence. The plaintiffs raised objections to several paragraphs in Queensland's amended defence. The Supreme Court hearing was adjourned so that the High Court could consider the plaintiffs' demurrer.

Figure 12.6 Morning Recess Murray Island, May 1989

Left to right: Jack Wailu [witness for plaintiffs] Greg McIntyre [plaintiffs' solicitor] Rev Dave Passi [plaintiff] Eddie Mabo [plaintiff] Bryan Keon-Cohen [plaintiffs' jnr counsel] Meriam Islander, Sam Passi [witness for plaintiffs].

© Bryan Keon-Cohen.

[29] Emphasis added.

Before the High Court, counsel for *Mabo* argued that the amended defence was bad at law. The Queensland legislation was 'wholly inconsistent' with sections 9 and 10 of the RDA because it infringed the human right or fundamental right to 'own property alone as well as in association with others'.[30] In consequence, the Queensland statute was inoperative because it was inconsistent with the RDA and, moreover, section 109 of the *Australian Constitution*. Section 109 provides that, in the event of inconsistency between State law and Commonwealth law, 'the latter shall prevail, and the former shall, to the extent of the inconsistency, be invalid'.

The majority of the Court held that the *Queensland Coast Islands Declaratory Act 1985* was inconsistent with section 10 of the RDA. The Act treated the customary property rights of the Meriam people differently to the rights resulting from a Crown grant. The *Queensland Coast Islands Declaratory Act 1985* was constitutionally invalid. Brennan, Toohey and Gaudron JJ concluded:

> If we accord to the traditional rights of the Miriam people the status of recognized legal rights under Queensland law … the 1985 Act has the effect of precluding the Miriam people from enjoying some, if not all, of their legal rights in and over the Murray Islands while leaving all other persons unaffected in the enjoyment of their legal rights in and over the Murray Islands. Accordingly, the Miriam people enjoy their human right of the ownership and inheritance of property to a "more limited" extent than others who enjoy the same human right.
>
> … s 10(1) of the Racial Discrimination Act clothes the holders of traditional native title who are of the native ethnic group with the same immunity from legislative interference with their enjoyment of their human right to own and inherit property as it clothes other persons in the community. A State law which, by purporting to extinguish native title, would limit that immunity in the case of the native group cannot prevail over s 10(1) of the Racial Discrimination Act which restores the immunity to the extent enjoyed by the general community. The attempt by the 1985 Act to extinguish the traditional legal rights of the Miriam people therefore fails.[31]

After six years Eddie Mabo and the Meriam team had won the first part of their case. The case was returned to the Supreme Court of Queensland to determine **issues of fact**. The Supreme Court's determination was delivered in November 1990. The High Court then heard arguments over four days in May 1991.

Issues of fact: when a fact is in question not a law

Mabo v Queensland (No 2)

By May 1991, however, Eddie Mabo was gravely ill. He died of cancer in January 1992. Celuia Mapo Sale also did not live to hear the judgment delivered five months later. On 3 June 1992, the High Court handed down its landmark decision of *Mabo v Queensland (No 2)* recognising native title in Australia and overruling the *Gove Land Rights Case*. In a six to one decision, the High Court found in favour of the plaintiffs, declaring that the Meriam people were entitled 'as against the whole world to possession, occupation, use and enjoyment of the lands of the Murray Islands'.[32]

[30] *International Convention on the Elimination of All Forms of Racial Discrimination* Art 5(d)(v).
[31] *Mabo (No 1)* (n 21) 218–19. A longer excerpt from the judgment is here.
[32] *Mabo (No 2)* (n 3) 75 (Brennan J).

The High Court could no longer embrace the nineteenth century claim that Australia had been *terra nullius*. It did accept Crown sovereignty, but that sovereignty no longer provided absolute beneficial title but rather 'radical title'. This radical title to land was acquired along with sovereignty but was burdened by 'Aboriginal title' meaning First Nation owners retained traditional rights over their country. The Crown had power to extinguish Aboriginal title if it was done constitutionally. This meant that Aboriginal people could not make claims over lands where native title had already been extinguished by either legislative or executive actions.

This decision hit many Australians like a bombshell. There was exhilaration on the part of Aboriginal Australians who had been arguing for their rights to their lands for more than 200 years. Many Australians in the pastoral and mining industries were outraged and extreme in their denunciations and alarmist predictions.[33] The reality was that the High Court was following common law developments in Canada and New Zealand and the Mabo judgment was a decision that has since been followed in other common law jurisdictions. When Ron Castan, lead counsel for the plaintiff in *Mabo (No 2)*, was asked by a Canadian academic about his argument, Castan claimed he drew on *Calder v Attorney-General of British Columbia*, a famous 1973 land rights case decided by the Supreme Court of Canada.[34] Where Canadians refer to 'aboriginal title', Australians use the term 'native title' and New Zealand courts 'customary law', but it is the same legal concept.

The view that Australia was *terra nullius* upon the arrival of the First Fleet was thoroughly rejected by the High Court. Brennan J remarked that '[t]he fiction by which the rights and interests of indigenous inhabitants in land were treated as non-existent was justified by a policy which has no place in the contemporary law of this country'.[35] Later in his judgment, Brennan J continued:

> [t]he common law of this country would perpetuate injustice if it were to continue to embrace the enlarged notion of *terra nullius* and to persist in characterizing the indigenous inhabitants of the Australian colonies as people too low in the scale of social organization to be acknowledged as possessing rights and interests in land.[36]

The Crown could only take absolute beneficial title when land is *terra nullius* – desert and uninhabited. If territory is occupied, as Australia was in 1788, the Crown acquires what is known as radical title to land. It follows that the Crown cannot acquire absolute beneficial ownership of occupied territory 'to the exclusion of the indigenous inhabitants'.[37] The majority of judges found that native title to land survived the Crown's acquisition of sovereignty and radical title. Brennan J observed:

> Native title has its origins in and is given its content by the traditional customs observed by the Indigenous inhabitants of a territory. The nature and incidents of native title must be ascertained as a matter of fact by reference to those laws and customs.[38]

[33] See Richard Broome's discussion of the response in *Aboriginal Australians* (n 4) 284–86.

[34] Christina Godlewska and Jeremy Webber, 'The *Calder* Decision, Aboriginal Title, Treaties, and the Nisga'a' in Foster, Raven and Webber (eds) (n 27) 7. See also Nettheim (n 27) 177–97.

[35] *Mabo (No 2)* (n 3) 42 (Brennan J).

[36] *Ibid* 58.

[37] *Ibid* 48.

[38] *Ibid* 58.

However, the Crown might have extinguished native title since acquiring sovereignty by 'a valid exercise of sovereign power inconsistent with the continued right to enjoy native title'.[39] For example, freehold grants extinguish native title.

For native title to have survived then, an Aboriginal or Islander group needs to:

- Have maintained connection with their lands and to occupy it according to their customs.
- Identify and be acknowledged as a member of a recognised Aboriginal community.
- Have continued spiritual and cultural connection with their country.

Traditional laws and customs of the relevant Aboriginal or Torres Strait Islander people determine continuous native title at common law. Moreover, the native title rights cannot have been extinguished by legislative or executive action since Crown sovereignty.

Historical Cameo

Eddie Mabo

Edward Koiki Mabo was born on 29 June 1936 in the village of Las on the island of Mer (Murray) in the Torres Strait. He was the leading plaintiff in the High Court case that first recognised native title.

Eddie was the fourth child of Robert Zesou Sambo and Annie Poipe who died shortly after his birth. In accordance with island custom, he was then adopted by his Uncle Benny and Auntie Maigo Mabo. Their language was Meriam and Eddie also spoke Torres Strait creole. At the age of ten his grandfather spent several weeks teaching him about Malo whose spirit determined the laws of the land and the laws of the stars of Taigai which underpin Meriam law and culture. His grandfather also instructed him on his land and sea boundaries including fish traps and his ancestors going back several generations which in local law were the basis of his inheritance.

At high school Eddie's teacher stressed to him the importance of learning English if he wanted to travel to the mainland and his proficiency earned him appointment as interpreter for a medical research team visiting the Torres Strait in the 1950s. In 1959 he moved to Townsville and married Bonita Nehow, an Australian-born South Sea Islander, in the Methodist Church at Ingham. In these years Eddie took work pearling, cane cutting and labouring on the railways, hard labouring work that brought him into contact with the trade union movement. He proved himself adept at public speaking, became used to working with white Australians, and soon represented Aboriginal and Torres Strait Islander workers in trade union bodies. From 1962 to 1969 he was secretary to the Aborigines Advancement League (Queensland), playing a leading role in the Queensland campaign for the 1967 Referendum.

Eddie and Bonita had seven children and adopted another three. On top of his advocacy for ATSI people he became involved in education, co-founding with Burnum Burnum

[39] *Ibid* 69.

the Black Community School in Townsville (1973–85). Hostility to the school from the local newspaper and the Queensland Education Department was one of many racist barriers he confronted. In 1972 Eddie like many other Indigenous people was still under the powers of the Director of Aboriginal and Island Affairs. When he learned that his father was dying of tuberculosis, he travelled with his family from Townsville to Thursday Island only to be denied permission to return to Mer to see him.

If the Director's actions were intended to deter his activism, it had the opposite effect. Eddie organised a conference to discuss the outcome of the 1967 Referendum and there met Henry and Margaret Reynolds. Eddie became a gardener at James Cook University and would sometimes sit in on lectures. He was shocked to discover, after a chance conversation with historians Noel Loos and Henry Reynolds, that he was not the legal owner of his family's land on Mer. Legally the island was Crown land.

Eddie was co-chair of the Townsville chapter of the Aboriginal Treaty Committee and in 1981 it worked with the James Cook University Student Union to host a conference on land rights. Leading figures from government, legal and history circles as well as Eddie and other Murray Islanders spoke. The decision was made to launch a legal case on land rights.

In 1990 Eddie was diagnosed with cancer. He had already given detailed evidence regarding his grandfather's instruction in cultural knowledge to the Court. He died in January 1992 before the High Court handed down its famous judgment. An elaborate headstone erected in his honour at Belgian Gardens Cemetery in Townsville was immediately desecrated. The Federal Government provided financial assistance to the family so that his remains could be returned to the Torres Strait. On 18 September he was reburied at the village of Las. In 1992, he was posthumously awarded the Human Rights Medal.

Native Title at Last!

Once the High Court acknowledged native title, Federal Parliament had to establish a process to manage Aboriginal claims and to re-assert the validity of all past extinguishment. A tense 15 months followed the High Court decision as Aboriginal people lobbied the Government for legislation that would facilitate their rights while the resources sector lobbied to minimise Indigenous rights. In December 1992, Prime Minister Paul Keating launched the International Year of Indigenous People with his now famous Redfern Speech. The idealism of this speech did not match the hard-headed negotiations still taking place over native title legislation. After an exhausting six days of parliamentary debate, the *Native Title Act 1993* (Cth) ('NTA') finally passed the Senate at 11.58 pm on 21 December 1993.[40] The States and Territories also enacted native title legislation in response to the *Mabo (No 2)* decision.

[40] Broome (n 4) 289.

Commencing on 1 January 1994, the NTA was intended as a special measure for the advancement and protection of Aboriginal and Torres Strait Islander people and to be read and construed according to the RDA. Political discord was by no means over – in 1994 the Government of Western Australia challenged the NTA in the High Court. The High Court not only upheld it but ruled that the Western Australian Government's own legislative response to the legislation was inoperative in *Western Australia v Commonwealth*.[41]

The major objects of the NTA, outlined in section 3, are:

1. To provide for the recognition and protection of native title.
2. To establish ways in which future dealings affecting native title may proceed and to set standards for those dealings.
3. To establish a mechanism for determining claims to native title.
4. To provide for, or permit, the validation of past acts, and intermediate period acts, invalidated because of the existence of native title.

Perhaps not surprisingly given the level of discord which preceded it, the legislation makes it exceedingly difficult for Aboriginal people to prove a claim. Three essential attributes must be proved to the satisfaction of the Federal Court:

1. Claimants must provide proof of continuous use of the land according to Aboriginal custom.
2. They must prove their membership of a specific First Nation or clan group.
3. This Indigenous community must also prove that they have maintained continuous cultural traditions and connection with their lands.

Indigenous history discussed in earlier chapters points to some of the problems these criteria raise. More obstacles are considered in the following sections of the chapter.

Pause for Thought

How Colonial History is a Major Obstacle to Native Title Process

Before commencing this reflection, please re-read chapter nine on the position of Indigenous peoples before the law in the nineteenth century and into the twentieth. How would extensive frontier violence have affected Indigenous families and communities? How in turn would it have impacted their personal identity and sense of belonging? How did police and settler massacres affect an individual's ability to maintain connections to land and connections to family?

In the late nineteenth and first half of the twentieth centuries, colonial government policies explicitly aimed to destroy Aboriginal identity to turn 'half-caste' children into white Australians. Aboriginal families, First Nation identities and Aboriginal languages were

[41] (1995) 183 CLR 373. For Western Australia and hostility from other political actors, see Broome (n 4) 289–90.

intentionally destroyed in the process. If you do not know about this history, you might like to check the website and read ahead then come back to this activity.

Questions to Consider

1. What problems would indentured Aboriginal workers have in proving their continuous connection to their lands?
2. How did poor wages and related poverty affect ability to maintain family and maintain connection to country?
3. How difficult would it be for members of the Stolen Generations to prove their membership of a family or community?

Under the NTA the onus of proof rests with the Aboriginal community who must present genealogical details and knowledge of country as well as proof of physical connection over many decades. Aboriginal representatives have argued that this onus of proof should be reversed. Native title should be a given and state governments should have to prove to the court when and how they extinguished Aboriginal rights over different lands.

Questions to Consider

1. What evidence would state governments have to present to prove this?
2. What would be the effect of proving to the court that all Aboriginal people were 'moved' from particular parcels of land?
3. What evidence would the State have to present to prove that there could be no living descendants of particular family groups?[42]

Despite the difficult negotiations of 1993, the Indigenous community reached another land rights milestone in 1996. At the start of the year, Drummond J had ruled that the Wik people had lost their native title rights when a pastoral licence was granted over their lands near the Gulf of Carpentaria. They appealed the decision. Just before Christmas 1996, the High Court handed down its decision in their favour in *Wik Peoples v Queensland* (the '*Wik Case*').[43] Nineteenth century grazing legislation had acknowledged Aboriginal rights. Pastoral leases and native title co-exist.[44]

Again, there was an outcry from primary producers. John Howard won the Federal election in March 1996 and promised he would pass legislation to further extinguish native title so that daily operations of farmers and graziers continued 'without fear of interference or hindrance'.[45] After further political negotiations which excluded Indigenous Australians the Howard Government passed the *Native Title Amendment Act 1998*. By statute, native title was extinguished over seven per cent of Australia and 22 per cent of Queensland.[46]

[42] You can read other suggestions for reform of native title from stakeholders in the 2013 House of Representatives Committee Report via **this link**.

[43] (1996) 187 CLR 1.

[44] Broome (n 4) 296–302.

[45] Prime Minister Media Statement, 1 May 1997, available at australianpolitics.com/1997/05/08/howard-amended-wik-10-point-plan.html.

[46] Broome (n 4) 302.

The Legal Foundations of the Stolen Generations and Stolen Wages

Native title was great news for Aboriginal people still living on their traditional lands but for many Indigenous Australians the achievement was bittersweet. Proof of continuous connection to country was an elusive dream for thousands of Indigenous Australians whose daily lives had been controlled by restrictive colonial 'protection' legislation over many decades.

Figure 12.7 'Protection' Legislation by State and Territory[47]

Victoria	*Aboriginal Protection Act 1869* (Vic)
New South Wales	*Aborigines Protection Board 1883* (NSW) *Aborigines Protection Act 1909* (NSW) *Aborigines Protection Amending Act 1915* (NSW)
Queensland	*Aboriginal Protection and Restriction of the Sale of Opium Act 1897* (Qld)
Western Australia	*Aborigines Act 1905* (WA)
South Australia	*Aboriginal Act 1910* (SA)
Northern Territory	*Aboriginals Ordinance 1911* (Cth)

This was vastly different 'protection' to that proposed in Governor Gipps' day. Reserves and missions were created with white officials in charge and Aboriginal people forcibly removed onto them. Although the word 'protection' appears in the title of colonial legislation, none of these laws protected: all of them enabled state governments to control Aboriginal people. The denial of fundamental human rights within these statutes is shocking to modern eyes as Indigenous Australians suffered a loss of civil liberties which white Australians took for granted.

One purpose of these statutes was to define an Aboriginal person based on their parentage. Using the offensive language of nineteenth century racial ideology, officials defined and categorised Aboriginal subjects as 'full bloods', 'half-castes', 'quarter-castes' and so on. Percentage of Aboriginal blood was used by officials to decide the level of control to be imposed over individuals. Being defined by the Government as 'under the Act' gave officials the power to control the work an Aboriginal person could undertake, who they could marry, where they could live, their right to free speech, whether they could form or join a union and their freedom of movement, among others. The painful issue that drove Aboriginal campaigners in the 1990s was the removal of children from their families.

Stolen Generations

Coined in 1981, the phrase 'Stolen Generations' refers to the generations of Aboriginal and Torres Strait Islander children who were forcibly removed from their families and

[47] This is not a complete list. The accompanying website has a link to numerous other statutes which gave State and Territory governments' power to direct Indigenous people's work and family life.

communities pursuant to Commonwealth and State government policies of protection and later assimilation. Grounds for removal of children were broad; indeed, under the New South Wales' *Aborigines Protection Amending Act 1915*, officials did not have to give a cause to remove Aboriginal children from their parents. Though these laws differed between states, commonalities emerge. In general, each State had a dedicated board or office led by a Chief Protector with control and custody of Aboriginal children. Following removal, Aboriginal children were fostered, adopted, or placed in government or church-run institutions. In 1997, the publication of the *Bringing Them Home: Report of the National Inquiry into the Separation of Aboriginal and Torres Strait Islander Children from their Families* brought wider public attention to the Stolen Generations. The Report concluded:

> that between one in three and one in ten Indigenous children were forcibly removed from their families and communities in the period from approximately 1910 until 1970. In certain regions and in certain periods the figure was undoubtedly much greater than one in ten. In that time not one Indigenous family has escaped the effects of forcible removal (confirmed by representatives of the Queensland and WA Governments in evidence to the Inquiry). Most families have been affected, in one or more generations, by the forcible removal of one or more children.[48]

Figure 12.8 Prime Minister Kevin Rudd

J Donegan, *The Australian Minister of Foreign Affairs The Honourable Kevin Rudd during a bilateral meeting at the Pan Pacific Hotel* (2011).

[48] *Bringing Them Home: Report of the National Inquiry into the Separation of Aboriginal and Torres Strait Islander Children from their Families* (Sydney, Human Rights and Equal Opportunity Commission, 1997).

On 13 February 2008, attention was again directed at the issue when former Australian Prime Minister, Kevin Rudd, formally apologised to the Stolen Generations on behalf of successive parliaments and governments.

Stolen Wages

As well as control of children, the various Aboriginal Acts also gave State Governments power over Aboriginal employment and their wages and conditions. White employers could hire Aboriginal workers only under contracts and permits issued by Protection Boards and Protectors.

From 1901, a Queensland amendment legislated for a minimum wage for Aboriginal Queenslanders working under permit; it was only a fraction of the non-Aboriginal wage so demand for Aboriginal workers in the pastoral industry and in domestic service was high. In 1918, Queensland Aboriginal workers in the cattle industry were awarded two-thirds of the pay of white station hands but this scale was suspended on account of the Great Depression.[49] Amendments in 1901, 1904 and 1919 also required Aboriginal and Torres Strait Islander wages to be paid directly to the State Protector. Money was deposited in the workers' name in a Government bank account. Part of the rationale was that Aboriginal people did not know how to handle money, so the Government was enforcing a system of savings. Only a small percentage of an Aboriginal and Torres Strait Islander worker's overall wage was returned as 'pocket money'. When, after a lifetime of arduous labour, retired Aboriginal workers applied to the Government to have their savings returned, it was denied to them. Officials said that much of it had gone into general revenue and could no longer be traced. This refusal to return wages legitimately earned is referred to as 'stolen wages'.

As shocking as this is, the Queensland situation for Aboriginal workers was 'generous' compared with Western Australia and the Northern Territory which did not stipulate any minimum wage for Aboriginal workers. Their legislation forced Aboriginal people to work for rations as late as the 1950s, although cattle stations near the Queensland border had to introduce a wage to keep Aboriginal workers who naturally preferred pocket money in Queensland to no money at all. Nonetheless, once Western Australia and the Northern Territory did finally legislate a minimum wage rate, they too compulsorily deducted enforced savings.

The Indigenous campaign to recover these stolen wages was not the first Aboriginal campaign around underpayment for their labour. In 1965 Aboriginal stockmen worked with trade unions to challenge racially discriminatory clauses in the Pastoral Industry Award and won. However, the Conciliation and Arbitration Court allowed employers three years to phase in the new award payments, depriving Aboriginal workers of $4 million in wages.[50] The campaign to recover lost wages was similarly difficult. The Queensland Government was the first to offer compensation in 2002[51] but the sums were tokenistic, and the Aboriginal campaign continued across the country.

[49] Broome (n 4) 130.
[50] *Ibid* 145.
[51] On the inadequacies of the Queensland scheme, see the 'Submission to the Senate Legal and Constitutional References Committee Inquiry into Stolen Wages' (Australian Human Rights Commission, 1 August 2006), available at humanrights.gov.au/our-work/legal/inquiry-stolen-wages.

In December 2006, the Senate Legal and Constitutional References Committee concluded its Inquiry into Aboriginal and Torres Strait Islander stolen wages. The Inquiry terms of reference included the number of Aboriginal and Torres Strait Islander workers affected by so-called 'protection' legislation in each State and Territory, financial arrangements to withhold or preclude access to wages, and the extent of mismanagement of wages owed to Aboriginal people and Torres Strait Islanders. The Senate Committee's recommendations included a national compensation scheme, unfettered access to State and Territory archives on stolen wages, and community education programmes. The Commonwealth failed to enact these recommendations.

Campaigners again turned attention to state governments whose responses continued to be inadequate. In 2016 Hans Pearson led a class action against the State of Queensland which the Queensland Government finally settled out of court in 2019 for $190 million.[52] A class action to recover stolen wages and payments is underway in Western Australia[53] and discussions about similar legal action continue in South Australia and the Northern Territory.

Deaths in Custody

Between 1980 and 1989, 99 Aboriginal and Torres Strait Islander people died while held in police custody or other forms of detention. As the deaths increased, the United Nations added its concern to the voices of Aboriginal families. The year before Australia's official celebrations of the bicentenary of British settlement, the Commonwealth was forced to act based on 'growing public concern that deaths in custody of Aboriginal people were too common and public explanations were too evasive to discount the possibility that foul play was a factor in many of them'.[54]

The Royal Commission into Aboriginal Deaths in Custody (1987–91) individually investigated the deaths in custody of 88 Indigenous men and 11 Indigenous women between 1980 and 1989. Aiding investigation into these deaths were files maintained by State agents recording 'each life to a degree that few non-Aboriginal peoples [sic] lives would be recorded'.[55] In addition to these records, stories from family and friends about each person gave the Royal Commission a better understanding of the person's life. Social, cultural, and legal factors connected with each death were considered.

The Royal Commission's Final Report, which gave 339 recommendations, underlined that authorities' lack of insight into their duty of care as well as want of proper care was, in many (but not all) cases, causally related to the death in custody. Early and repeated contact with the criminal justice system was an 'almost universal' feature of each death in custody. The Final Report also associated the overrepresentation of Aboriginal people in custody with social, economic and cultural marginalisation. Unequal laws and pervasive racism – whether overt, hidden or institutional – were given as factors underlining 'how the assaults that have been made on Aboriginal society have affected particularly

[52] Documents relevant to the case and the resulting redress scheme are available at www.stolenwages.com.au/.

[53] See 'Western Australia Stolen Wages Class Action' (Shine Lawyers), available at www.shine.com.au/service/class-actions/stolen-wages-class-action?gclid=Cj0KCQiA5bz-BRD-ARIsABjT4nhUy0-6R0FfeK_EQAOGl0rdm-FHU2KZl6A_IkDsFuhBdWfssQ0SkrZoaAp7cEALw_wcB.

[54] Commonwealth, Royal Commission into Aboriginal Deaths in Custody, *National Report* (1991) vol 1, 1.1.

[55] *Ibid* vol 1, 1.2.11.

young Aboriginal men in a way which tends to bring them into contact with the criminal justice system'.[56] The answer to these disadvantages was empowerment: the will to renewal and to self-determination, the support of broader society, and maintenance of a policy of self-determination.[57]

Indigenous Sentencing Courts

The Royal Commission highlighted the extent to which Aboriginal people and Torres Strait Islanders are overrepresented in Australia's courts and prisons. One response to this problem has been the introduction of Aboriginal sentencing courts in every State and Territory except Tasmania.

These courts allow Elders, respected persons from the offender's community or a 'community justice group' to be involved in deliberations leading to a magistrate's sentencing of Indigenous offenders. Their roles vary across states and territories but, in all jurisdictions, Elders interact directly with Aboriginal defendants to understand their circumstances and then liaise on their behalf with the magistrate. Thus, as well as the aim of diverting Indigenous defendants from imprisonment options, these courts have goals of increasing First Nations participation in the judicial process and making the justice system more culturally inclusive.

Figure 12.9 Aboriginal Sentencing Courts by State or Territory

Jurisdiction	Name of Court	Year Established	Relevant Legislation
Australian Capital Territory	Galambany Circle Sentencing Court[58]	2004	*Magistrates Court Act 1930* (ACT)
New South Wales	Circle Sentencing Court	2002	*Criminal Procedure Act 1986* (NSW) *Criminal Procedure Regulation 2010* (NSW)
Northern Territory	Community Courts	2005[59]	Darwin Community Court Guidelines
Queensland	Murri Court	2002[60]	*Community Services (Aborigines) Act 1984* (Qld) *Community Services (Aborigines) Regulation* 1998 (Qld)
South Australia	Nunga Court	1999	*Criminal Law Sentencing Act 1998* (SA)

(continued)

[56] *Ibid* vol 1, 1.7.3.

[57] *Ibid* vol 1, 1.7.

[58] Previously named the Ngambra Circle Sentencing Court.

[59] Suspended 2011 for adults and 2012 for youths. In 2019 the draft Northern Territory Aboriginal Justice Agreement called for the reintroduction of the courts which the newly elected Attorney-General promised in August 2020. See Sarah Smit, 'Territory's Indigenous Attorney-General Plans to 'make a big difference' in Top End' *National Indigenous Times* (Mosman Park, 25 September 2020), available at nit.com.au/territorys-indigenous-attorney-general-plans-to-make-a-big-difference-in-top-end/.

[60] Abolished 2012; reinstated 2016.

Figure 12.9 ***(Continued)***

Jurisdiction	Name of Court	Year Established	Relevant Legislation
Victoria	Koori Court	2002	*Magistrates' Court Act 1989* (Vic) *Magistrates Court (Koori Court) Act 2002* (Vic) *Children & Young Persons (Koori Court) Act 2004* (Vic)
Western Australia	Community Courts	2006[61]	*Sentencing Act 1995* (WA)

The contribution of Elders is significant for many Aboriginal offenders who respect the views of their Elders more highly than that of the magistrate. It also has positive effects on Indigenous pride in a process which otherwise is highly demoralising.

There are some shortcomings to these courts, however. In Queensland for example, Aboriginal people must first plead guilty before they can become eligible for the Murri Court, thus contributing to high conviction rates. In all jurisdictions there are restrictions on the types of offences which can be heard. Victoria, New South Wales and the Northern Territory exclude sexual offences from Aboriginal sentencing courts while Victoria and the Northern Territory do not cover family violence. Queensland does not allow any offences for which the penalty is more than six months' imprisonment. New South Wales and the Australian Capital Territory omit drug offences and those suffering from drug addiction who must continue in the mainstream court system. Furthermore, alternative sentences are by no means 'soft', usually requiring close supervision of offenders and referral to treatment services. While Elders can help to limit cultural misunderstandings, the system still requires cross-cultural training for all court personnel. Nonetheless these Aboriginal courts are now accepted as 'a permanent feature of the Australian criminal court system'.[62]

The Northern Territory Intervention

On 21 June 2007, the Australian Government announced a national emergency to address concerns about the welfare of Aboriginal children in communities across the Northern Territory. A week before the **Northern Territory Intervention** was announced, the Northern Territory Board of Inquiry into the Protection of Aboriginal Children from Sexual Abuse released a report based on eight months of investigations and consultation entitled 'Little Children are Sacred'. Less than two months later, in August 2007, the Federal Parliament ignored the Report and instead enacted a range of legislative measures to 'stabilise and protect communities in the crisis area'.[63]

> Northern Territory Intervention: the colloquial term used for Commonwealth Government's Northern Territory Emergency Response which commenced in 2007

[61] Discontinued 2015.

[62] Elena Marchetti, 'Indigenous Sentencing Courts: Brief 5' (Indigenous Justice Clearinghouse, 2010) 4, available at .indigenousjustice.gov.au/wp-content/uploads/mp/files/publications/files/brief005.v1.pdf.

[63] Mal Brough, Minister for Families, Community Services and Indigenous Affairs, 'Media Release' (*Parliament of Australia*, 21 June 2007), available at parlinfo.aph.gov.au/parlInfo/search/display/display.w3p;query=Id%3A%22media%2Fpressrel%2F8ZFN6%22;src1=sm1.

The measures under the *Northern Territory National Emergency Response Act 2007* (Cth) included:

- The seizure of administrative control over Aboriginal settlements, and the compulsory acquisition of leases for those settlements, for a minimum five-year period.
- The clean-up and repair of Aboriginal communities through the work-for-the-dole programme.
- Imposing alcohol restrictions on Northern Territory Aboriginal land.
- Controlling how and for what purpose welfare payments were used through a new basics card.
- Requiring compulsory health checks of Aboriginal children.
- Making income support and family assistance payments dependent on school attendance.

The Commonwealth ignored the advice from affected Aboriginal communities in the 'Little Children are Sacred' Report and instead imposed a top-down response using police and the military to implement some of these measures. There was no consultation with Aboriginal communities. Criticism of the Intervention from Aboriginal organisations was widespread. The following year the Rudd Government and the successive Stronger Futures policy of the Gillard Government maintained the legislative measures introduced because of the 2007 Northern Territory Emergency Response.[64]

The Uluru Statement from the Heart

The idea of constitutional recognition for Australia's First Nations has its origins in debates about reconciliation in the early 2000s. The process towards reconciliation travelled a bumpy path. Since 1967, Aboriginal peoples' fight for legal rights had been slow, challenging work and just as gains were achieved governments would create new obstacles. So too with the national campaign for reconciliation, but in 2007 there was a breakthrough, when Prime Minister Howard promised he would support constitutional recognition of Aboriginal and Torres Strait Islander people. To progress the idea in 2015 a Referendum Council was appointed with **bipartisan** support. The Referendum Council was given the formidable task of finding a proposal that met the will of diverse Aboriginal and Torres Strait Islander peoples and could be put to the Australian people in a referendum. The Council commenced consultations with all Australians including organising 12 regional dialogues with First Nation people across the country.[65] These dialogues culminated in a four-day 2017 National

Bipartisan: when both major parties capable of forming a government [ie, Lib-NP and ALP] agree on a policy or action

[64] For more detail on the legislative changes required for the Northern Territory Emergency Response, including suspension of the *Racial Discrimination Act 1975*, and on the modifications to the Intervention under the Rudd and Gillard governments, see 'What is the Northern Territory Intervention?' (Castan Centre for Human Rights, Monash University), available at monash.edu/law/research/centres/castancentre/our-areas-of-work/indigenous/the-northern-territory-intervention/the-northern-territory-intervention-an-evaluation/what-is-the-northern-territory-intervention.

[65] 'Dialogues' (*Referendum Council*, 2 January 2019), available at www.referendumcouncil.org.au/dialogues.html.

Constitutional Convention for Aboriginal and Torres Strait Islanders held at Uluru which produced the Uluru Statement from the Heart.

Figure 12.10 Sovereignty Sign at the Aboriginal Tent Embassy, Canberra (2015)
Dhx1 – Own work (CC0 1.0), https://creativecommons.org/publicdomain/zero/1.0/.

The Statement affirmed that Aboriginal and Torres Strait Islander peoples' sovereignty over the 'Australian continent and its adjacent islands' 'has never been ceded or extinguished'. In succinct sentences it explains the long legacy of Australian colonialism in three straightforward ideas – the need for an Indigenous Voice, for a Treaty and for Truth. It calls for substantive constitutional change and associated reform. It is fine rhetoric, viewed by many as poetic in its simplicity:

We, gathered at the 2017 National Constitutional Convention, coming from all points of the southern sky, make this statement from the heart:

Our Aboriginal and Torres Strait Islander tribes were the first sovereign Nations of the Australian continent and its adjacent islands, and possessed it under our own laws and customs. This our ancestors did, according to the reckoning of our culture, from the Creation, according to the common law from 'time immemorial', and according to science more than 60,000 years ago.

This sovereignty is *a spiritual notion: the ancestral tie between the land, or 'mother nature', and the Aboriginal and Torres Strait Islander peoples who were born therefrom, remain attached thereto, and must one day return thither to be united with our ancestors. This link*

> *is the basis of the ownership of the soil, or better, of sovereignty.* It has never been ceded or extinguished, and co-exists with the sovereignty of the Crown.
>
> How could it be otherwise? That peoples possessed a land for sixty millennia and this sacred link disappears from world history in merely the last two hundred years?
>
> With substantive constitutional change and structural reform, we believe this ancient sovereignty can shine through as a fuller expression of Australia's nationhood.
>
> Proportionally, we are the most incarcerated people on the planet. We are not an innately criminal people. Our children are aliened from their families at unprecedented rates. This cannot be because we have no love for them. And our youth languish in detention in obscene numbers. They should be our hope for the future.
>
> These dimensions of our crisis tell plainly the structural nature of our problem. This is *the torment of our powerlessness.*
>
> We seek constitutional reforms to empower our people and take *a rightful place* in our own country. When we have power over our destiny our children will flourish. They will walk in two worlds and their culture will be a gift to their country.
>
> We call for the establishment of a First Nations Voice enshrined in the Constitution.
>
> Makarrata is the culmination of our agenda: *the coming together after a struggle.* It captures our aspirations for a fair and truthful relationship with the people of Australia and a better future for our children based on justice and self-determination.
>
> We seek a Makarrata Commission to supervise a process of agreement-making between governments and First Nations and truth-telling about our history.
>
> In 1967 we were counted, in 2017 we seek to be heard. We leave base camp and start our trek across this vast country. We invite you to walk with us in a movement of the Australian people for a better future.[66]

The Final Report of the Referendum Council was delivered on 30 June 2017. It includes the Uluru Statement and two recommendations arising from the Statement. The first is that a referendum be held to include in 'the Australian Constitution … a representative body that gives Aboriginal and Torres Strait Islander First Nations a Voice to the Commonwealth Parliament'. The Constitution should recognise First Nations and their right to a voice, but the parliament should define the structure and functions of such a representative body.

The second recommendation is for 'a Declaration of Recognition … passed by all Australian Parliaments … ideally on the same day … to unify all Australians'. Thus, the Report met the demands of those Australians who wanted a symbolic statement and those who demanded more than token acknowledgement. The Report notes that the Uluru Statement also calls for a Makarrata Commission 'to supervise a process of agreement-making between governments and First Nations and truth-telling about our history' but

[66] The Uluru Statement forms part of the Referendum Council's final report, available at www.referendumcouncil.org.au/final-report.html.

concludes that this could be enacted through legislation rather than constitutional amendment and was therefore outside the Council's terms of reference.

The Turnbull Government did not respond to the Final Report until 26 October when the Prime Minister, Attorney-General and Minister for Indigenous Affairs held a joint press conference at which they rejected its recommendations as neither 'desirable [nor] capable of winning acceptance in a referendum'. You can read their accompanying media release here.

Pause for Thought

Understanding of the Three Pillars of the Uluru Statement from the Heart

Read both the Uluru Statement from the Heart and the Ministers' response.

Questions to Consider

1. Did the Uluru Statement or the Referendum Council Report ask for seats in Parliament? Did they ask for a separate constituent assembly, as claimed in the Ministers' statement?
2. What existing bodies provide advice to government without representatives in either the House of Representatives or the Senate? If you need to research this you might like to check which bodies are required to report to Parliament; consider, for example, statutory bodies and agencies such as ASIO and the Auditor-General.
3. There have been representative elected bodies representing Indigenous Australians in the past. Can you name any? Why do they no longer exist?
4. If First Nations people do not want specified seats in parliament, why do they want their Voice enshrined in the Constitution?

Conclusion

This chapter began with the 1967 Referendum and the successful Aboriginal campaign to amend the Constitution. It then discussed Aboriginal attempts in the 1970s to have the courts recognise their rights to their homelands, such as the *Gove Land Rights Case* and John Koowarta's dispute with the Queensland Government which even refused to allow him to *purchase* his land. These actions were part of a broader Aboriginal rights campaign and famously culminated in the High Court's *Mabo* decision in 1992.

Aboriginal campaigners then had a busy decade as governments passed legislation covering native title, contention over the personal harm caused by the Stolen Generations and over decades of Stolen Wages under the various state Protection Acts. The international Black Lives Matter movement had its precursor in Australia in the 1980s when disturbing numbers of Aboriginal men died in official custody, which led to a Royal Commission into Aboriginal Deaths in Custody. Other attempts at reversing the negative relationship between Aboriginal people and the criminal justice system included Aboriginal sentencing courts introduced in several states. These efforts by government and the courts to listen to the pain of Aboriginal exclusion came to a sudden halt in 2007 with the Northern Territory Intervention and its non-consultative approach including overriding of the RDA. Despite this reversal the Referendum Council persisted with a proposal for constitutional recognition of Australia's Indigenous peoples and in 2017 produced its final Report which included the Uluru Statement.

A few weeks later, the Turnbull Government announced that 'the Government does not believe such a radical change … has any realistic prospect of being supported by a majority of Australians in a majority of States'. This does not sound hugely different to Judge Burton's claim in 1836 that Aboriginal people were 'not in such a position with regard to strength as to be considered free and independent tribes'.[67] Non-Indigenous Australia remains numerically bigger and more powerful than the 250 plus First Nations – it is still asserting its might just as governors ignored questions of sovereignty and jurisdiction in the colonies' early decades.

Figure 12.11 Hon Michael Kirby and Professor Paul Brand at USQ Legal History Colloquium 2019
Courtesy of David Martinelli © University of Southern Queensland.

This history has covered many millennia from the ancient law of the First Nations of Australia through to the folkright of the Anglo-Saxons and the common law of the Norman kings. Law of the High Middle Ages included notable innovations in actions. The struggle between King and Parliament rocked England in the seventeenth century, leading the United States to introduce the radical idea of a written constitution to guarantee rule of

[67] *R v Murrell* [1836] NSWSupC 35; see chapter nine of this volume.

law and checks on arbitrary power. Even as these principles were being enshrined, in Great Britain the common law facilitated new levels of exploitation of colonial peoples and the poor through slavery and the public brutality of the Bloody Code. It was the latter which led to the colonisation of Australia where ex-convicts and their allies had to fight for these legal principles again in a new setting. The great tragedy was that they used this same law to disregard the ancient laws of this continent and its peoples.

This history has highlighted that the law is not fixed. Each generation has used the courts to defend or assert rights; in so doing they re-shaped the law for new circumstances. Australia's new Constitution in 1901 was amended several times in the twentieth century, as it undoubtedly will be again in the twenty-first. First Nations have offered Australians a constitutional way to overcome the dilemmas of its colonial past – how will a new generation of Australians respond?

INDEX

Introductory Note

References such as '178–79' indicate (not necessarily continuous) discussion of a topic across a range of pages. Wherever possible in the case of topics with many references, these have either been divided into sub-topics or only the most significant discussions of the topic are listed. Because the entire work is about 'Australia' and 'legal history', the use of these terms (and certain others which occur constantly throughout the book) as entry points has been minimized. Information will be found under the corresponding detailed topics.